News Clippings from Harrisburg Mining District, Silver Reef & Leeds, Utah

1869 - 1924

Compiled from the Deseret News, Iron County Record, Salt Lake Tribune, The Union, Washington County News & with contributions from other regional papers.

Often while working on family history (genealogy) I wonder about more than is listed on the pedigree sheets and am so grateful for their sacrifices and love for the generations to follow.

Some of the names include: Adams, Angell, Barbee, Baxter, Beans, Blackner, Burgess, Colbath, Creedius, Crosby, Dalton, Dille, Ferris, Fields, Foster, Ford, Fuller, Granger, Gregerson, Grundy, Hamilton, Hanson, Harris, Hartley, Hartman, Hogan, Jarvis, Jessup, Jolley, Judd, Kuhn, Leany, Leatham, Lightner, Louder, May, McArthur, McDonald, McMullen, McQuaid, McQuarrie, Miller, Milne, Moody, Newton, Nichollo, Nichols, Olsen, Paddock, Parie, Paris, Parker, Parry, Pierce, Potter, Richards, Savage, Schlappy, Scott, Sterling, Sullivan, Talbot, Tullis, Vincent, Welte, Westover, Wicks, Wilder, Wilkinson

Some of the articles are easier to read than others, please consider that they are nearly 100 years old.

ISBN-13: 978- 1505865318

ISBN-10: 150586531X

Correspondence.

We are indebted to the courtesy of President George A. Smith for the following:

HARRISBURG, WASHINGTON CO.,
June 4th, 1869.

Prest. Geo. A. Smith.—Dear Brother:—It is a general time of health. Bread is very scarce. Our cotton looked well till yesterday, when the "hoppers" paid us a flying visit and eat it up; some pieces of corn were also destroyed. The "hoppers" have been flying north and south as the wind carried them for some time. On Saturday, the 12th instant. Middleton was visited by large swarms, and much damage was done. At this place, last spring, we lost all our wheat, fruit, young trees and vines. No grapes this year, and we did hope they would let us alone. Our only hope now is to raise a crop of corn; we shall plant as late as August 1st if we can get the seed. Corn is very scarce for seed, being now three dollars per bushel. The bread question is quite an important one at present. What is ahead we know not. Our only trust is in Him who rules all things. Our orchards and vineyards are sadly injured, and we shall hardly get a taste of fruit this year. Washington loses one-third of its Wheat crop; St. George one-half. The crops being destroyed in the northern settlements, will make it hard for us if we raise no corn.

William Laney, of Harrisburg, was cut off from the church of Jesus Christ of Latter-day Saints, June 12th 1869, by the High Council at St. George.

The town of Leeds was visited on the 12th instant by the "hoppers" and the fields stripped of cotton and corn. Bennington has changed its name, it is now called Leeds.

With assurances of respect I remain your brother.

JAS. LEWIS.

LEEDS, Jan. 30, 1876.

Editor Deseret News:

This town, or village, is likely, on account of the recent discovery of silver mines near by, to become of more importance than heretofore. We are located on or near the line which divides Washington and Kane counties. This being the case it is almost an open question to which county we belong, although I believe it is generally conceded that we belong to Washington county. The distance by wagon road from here to St. George is 18 miles. The soil in this vicinity, although not so fertile as in some other parts, yet, by proper cultivation, yields a fair and in some cases abundant remuneration to the farmer for his labor. One of the best features of this locality is the climate, which, although not so warm as at St. George, is sufficiently warm for the production of crops of a similar character to those produced there, prominent among which is the grape.

Our school affairs are not in so prosperous a condition as is desirable, although there is a prospect of improvement as soon as our school and meeting-house is completed. Nevertheless a visit to this part of the Territory by that energetic and untiring advocate of education, Territorial Superintendent O. H. Riggs, would be attended by beneficial results.

We have not yet been subjected to certain "civilizing" influences, although we may have them before long, judging by the way in which miners are arriving and mines being discovered in this vicinity. The number of mines reported to have been discovered hereabouts I am unable to state, but there are quite a number.

While upon this subject I should like to correct a statement which I saw in the NEWS a short time since, in regard to the locality from which Mr. Barbee is said to have obtained his ore. The statement referred to is to the effect that Mr. Barbee obtained his ore from close by where the rock for the Temple was quarried. Now to my certain knowledge the ore referred to was obtained within one and a half miles of this place. You will perceive that your informant was in error.

Respectfully,

A SUBSCRIBER.

Deseret News
July 19, 1876

A Brutal Assault.—A correspondent sends the following from Leeds—

"A man known as Jack Kirby, last Monday afternoon, July 3rd, went to Barbee's store, in Leeds, and finding Mr. Y. S. Ferris there, approached him and plucked him by the arm, telling him he wanted to see him a few minutes. Taking him out behind the store, in the lot, as Mr. Ferris supposed, to have some conversation, he drew a pistol and struck Mr. Ferris over the left ear, stunning him, and continued to strike him until Mr. Benjamin Paddock went to his relief."

The sole cause of the grudge appears to be that Kirby was refused admittance to a dance, at Washington, about two years ago, and he had the impression that Mr. Ferris was the cause.

LEEDS, Washington Co.,
Utah, Feb. 1, 1877.

Editor Deseret News:

I left St. George this morning to attend to tithing business in this ward. The mining fever seems to subside a little, although to many persons engaged their prospects are quite flattering. Some of the men who just located mines in this county are moving south to Arizona and Mexico.

To-day the weather is warm and pleasant, and some have commenced gardening.

President Young's health is much improved. The Temple work is nearly completed, and several of the mechanics have returned to their homes. Preliminary surveys have been made with a view to getting out the waters of the Virgin River for irrigation purposes, and reclaiming some five thousand acres of good land for cultivation, where our young men and many families from the north can make pleasant homes, within a few miles of St. George and its beautiful Temple.

Your brother in the gospel,
A. F. MACDONALD.

Salt Lake Tribune
February 16, 1877

THE *Silver Age* is the title of a new weekly paper to be started at Silver Reef City, Leeds Mining District, by Joseph Field, of Beaver. The first number will appear on March 1st.

Deseret News
March 15, 1877

Beaver *Enterprise*, March 15—
Charley Lee, who escaped from the sheriff, has not yet been captured.

The Leeds Mill Company is shipping from four to six bars of fine bullion every other day.

Salt Lake Tribune
March 1, 1877

SILVER REEF ITEMS.

[Pomologist, Feb. 20th.]

There is an extensive quarry of marble within a few miles of the city, already opened.

We are told it is about ten miles from this camp to the coal mines on the head of Ash creek.

At the Butler and Loughroy mines deposits large and rich have just been struck, which is causing considerable excitement.

The demand for mechanics is more than supplied. When a few more stamp mills get in motion, their help will be in demand.

The mill of the Leeds Mining Company, with ten stamps, are turning out now about $4,000 a day, and are employ about fifty hands.

Our markets are well supplied with almost every desirable article of country produce, with prices very reasonable, if not really low.

The Leeds Mining Company are about to add to their mill ten more stamps, when they will be able to "pan out" from $6,000 to $8,000 per day.

Mrs. Gramb, late of Pioche, is negotiating for the erection of a large stone building, on the corner east of our office, for a hotel and boarding house.

The amount necessary to pay for the construction of the telegraph line to Silver Reef has been subscribed, and it is hoped that an office will be opened in a few days.

There are abundant quarries of nice sandstone for buildings, very near Silver Reef, easily quarried, looks well and is the cheapest building material in the long run.

A post office has been established at Silver Reef and R. H. Paddock, Esq. appointed postmaster. The office will be opened for the accommodation of our citizens with the least possible delay.

We have just learned that the celebrated Grand Gulch mine has been leased for five years, to a company of practical smelters, who are to proceed immediately to erect furnaces at the mine. This looks like business.

SILVER REEF,

August 26th, 1877.

Editors Deseret News:

Noticing a paragraph in the NEWS of the 21st inst. in regard to the fire at Shauntie, which says, "a mining camp *near Leeds* was almost entirely destroyed by fire," I take the liberty of informing you and the public generally that *the* mining camp near Leeds is called *Silver Reef*, Shauntie being not nearer than from 90 to 100 miles. Silver Reef is so called from the ridge of white sandstone showing itself among the granite and red sandstone surrounding it, where the principal mines are found.

It is about two miles north of Leeds, its altitude being much greater, on the mountain side. It contains about fifty large and substantial frame houses, a dozen stores, several saloons, assay offices, printing office, justice's office, post and express offices, restaurants, shops, wash houses etc., one large lodging house, owned by P. Harrison, having cost $9,000, with its elegant furniture, carpets, etc.

There are in the vicinity three mills for working silver ore, and ere six months there will be as many more. The Leeds Company, with their mill of ten stamps, are taking out $1,000 worth of silver every twenty-four hours. Judge Barbee just shipped a small dab of ore to Hunter & Goss' mill, on the river, which will turn out $200,000 worth of silver.

Weather moderate. Tons of fruit in market, of all kinds. Prices very low. WEAD.

SILVER REEF, Oct. 9th, 1877.

Editors Deseret News:

Yesterday W. F. & Co's express shipped nine bars of bullion, weighing from 75 to 100 lbs. each, the whole being valued at about ten thousand dollars. This is the result of only a few days work of the mills owned by the Leeds Co., and Hunter & Goss.

The Pioneer mill, which has for some time been lying idle from lack of power, is now being cleaned up and will soon be at work. Having obtained a large new boiler it is thought the engine will be large enough to run all the machinery. During the absence of the proprietor it is under the superintendence of Capt. F. M. Bishop, formerly of Salt Lake City.

A rich mine has recently been discovered, containing horn silver in great amount, by Mr. Al. Grant, who has for some time had charge of the Duffin Mine. Judge Barbee is working his mine constantly and shipping nearly 20 tons of rich paying ore every 24 hours.

A curious case of taking the law in one's own hands occurred yesterday. A man named Boyd seeing a team in the street, the owner of which, he alleged, was indebted to him, unhitched and drove off the animals, with the apparent intention of keeping them until the debt was liquidated. Public indignation was high, and Boyd was promptly arrested, and will be tried in Justice Paddock's court soon.

Strangers are arriving every day. Buildings are going up, and everything looks encouraging.

Weather, for the past month, has been very pleasant. Plenty of clouds but no rain. Fruit about gone.

WEAD.

Correspondence.

St. George, Sep. 29, 1878.

Editors Deseret News:

Of late there has been some little excitement over the capture of several horse thieves, who have stolen quite a number of animals from the neighborhood of Pioche, and had come through this way, and rendevouzed for the night in a house at Middletown, some three miles east of here. The sheriff, A. P. Hardy, having heard of their whereabouts, took a posse and surrounded the house, guarded the corral where the horses were, and waited for the appearance of the thieves, or daylight to procure their arrest. About four o'clock in the morning they made a break to escape, when the posse found it necessary to fire upon them, wounding one and capturing two. One slightly wounded, made his escape, and is reported to have made his way to Silver Reef, where he stole a horse and departed for parts unknown.

A few days ago a deputy sheriff from Pioche, Nevada, with a guard came and demanded the two prisoners, gave a bond for their safe delivery in Pioche, and departed. When near Damoron Valley, they state that a party of masked men, four in number, presented their rifles at the deputy and party, took the prisoners, shot them to death, and told the deputy to "make tracks" or they would serve him the same. This is as stated by those who saw the deputy after the murder of the men. One of the men killed is one of the party who murdered a man on the Muddy a short time ago.

Deseret News
March 26, 1879

At Leeds, Washington County, February 8th, 1879, after a lingering illness of ten years, EUNICE C. YOUNG ANGELL, wife of Solomon Angell.

Deceased was born November 22nd, 1789; baptized into the Church of Jesus Christ of Latter-day Saints in December, 1833, passed through the persecutions, and died in full faith of a glorious resurrection, leaving her husband, 5 children, 34 grand-children, 5 great-grand-children and a numerous circle of friends.—[COM

Deseret News
April 27, 1881

At the residence of Nathaniel Ashby, St. George, April 13th, 1881, JOSEPH MARK, son of Richard H. and Esther Ann Busby Ashby, of Leeds; born December 21st, 1879.

Deseret News
June 15, 1881

Fire at the Reef.—A special from Silver Reef, received on Saturday evening, states that at daybreak that morning a fire broke out in the rear of a lodging house kept by Mrs. Bush, and before it could be extinguished, had spread to several adjoining frame buildings which were soon enveloped in flames and burned to the ground. A light breeze from the north excited the apprehension that the whole town was doomed to destruction, but the flames were finally subdued, after five dwelling houses had been consumed. The house of Mrs. Bush was insured for $1,500. The entire loss will aggregate $5,000. Cause of fire not stated.

Deseret News
September 20, 1881

At Leeds, Sept. 20th, 1881, SoLOMON AN-
GELL.

Father Angell was born in the town of
Florence, Oneida County, New York, on the
21st of April, 1806, was baptized into the
Church of Jesus Christ of Latter-day Saints
in 1834, by Leonard C. Rich. He was a member of Zion's Camp, assisted to build the
Kirtland Temple and received his blessings
in that House of God. He passed through the
persecutions with the Saints and arrived in
Salt Lake Valley in 1848, was called to fill a
mission in Southern Utah in 1865, and remained faithful to the call till death called him to
another sphere. He died as he had lived, in
full hope of a glorious resurrection.

Deseret News
February 1, 1882

From Milford to Silver Reef passengers are conveyed by Gilmer &
Saulsbury's stage line and from
Silver Reef to St. George by Lund
and Judd's coaches.

The Union
May 1, 1882

Mr. B. F. Johnson, of Spring Lake Villa, who is on his way to Arizona, has arrived at Silver Reef, with a portion of his family. His brother Joseph E. and family are to accompany them south.

The Union
December 12, 1882

The Silver Reef *Miner* of the 2nd. inst asser s that he Barbee and Walker Mill will soon be in operation, as their business is about settled.

Deseret News
June 16, 1883

LETTER FROM LEEDS.

FATAL ACCIDENT—CROPS IN DIXIE —MILLS AT THE REEF, ETC.

Our esteemed correspondent Geo H. Crosby, wrote from Leeds on June 7th:

On Saturday last, 2nd inst., as Hyrum Stirling, son of Wm. Stirling, was returning from delivering a load of hay to the Stormont mill, and as near as can be ascertained he stopped and picked up a horseshoe, and was probably getting on the wagon or putting the shoe on when the team started. Other teams were in front and behind, but owing to the dust could not see the team, but ran to the spot as soon as possible and found the young man was dead, having been instantly killed. He was 13 years old last November, and a quiet, good boy. He took dinner with his father and Mother, brothers and sisters at about 12, and about 6 o'clock was brought home a corpse. The family have the general sympathy of the community in this their deep distress. The funeral took place on Sunday, being the largest I ever saw in this place.

Crop prospects in Dixie are not very good as a large share of the peaches, apples, apricots, etc., were killed with frost, and we had a very dry winter, and consequently water is getting scarce at several places Mining at Silver Reef is not very lively, but the Christy and Stormon Mills keep running steadily, and the old Leeds Mill has been running for the last two months and will probably run till the end of June, and the Barbee Mill will probably start up in July. This camp is about the only market for the hay, etc. of St. George, Washington, Santa Clara, Leeds and in fact all the Dixie settlements, consequently when business is dull at the Reef cash is scarce.

Deseret News
April 14, 1884

SILVER REEF, April 14, 1884.
Thomas Bess, a workman in the
Buckeye mine, was killed last night by
a rock from a blast prepared by himself. He was fearfully mangled.

Deseret News
June 11, 1887

BROWN.—At Leeds, June 11, 1887, of in-
flammation of the kidneys, John Brown.
He was born August 24, 1810, in the State of
New York, was a member of the "Mormon
Battalion," during the conflict with Mexico,
and was a faithful Latter-day Saint until
the day of his death. He leaves a wife and
numerous friends to mourn his loss.

Deseret News
September 28, 1887

Leeds Items.

"Thistle" sends us from Leeds an
account of a surprise party, which, as
it relates to an affair of only local interest, is not reproduced.

Quite a number of people in Leeds
are sick with malarial fever, but, as
October usually brings convalescence
to this class of sufferers, it is hoped
that all will soon recover.

A few days ago Jos. T. Wilkinson's
son Joseph had his foot crushed in
the cog wheels of a molasses mill,
while he and his brother were playing
with the machine. One toe had to be
amputated. The lad is progressing
favorably.

Election Judges.

The Utah Commission have made the following additional appointments of judges of election for the places named:

MILLARD COUNTY.

Fillmore—Edwin Bartholomew, A L Robinson, J A Melville.

Kanosh—Charles Crane, G B Chesley, Geo Crane.

Meadow—Joseph Adams, John Stredder, A Greenhalgh.

Holden—Nicholas Paul, Enoch Dodge, J S Gyles.

Scipio—George Monroe, P O Nielsen, Orville Thompson.

Deseret—W A Ray, G H Cropper, Edward Webb.

Oak City—George Finlinson, Edward Lyman, Henry Roper.

Lemmington—Christian Oversen, L W Stout, Robert Crosby.

Snake Valley—W C Barry, David Simonsen, Brigham Young.

IRON COUNTY.

Paragoonah—J S Barton, D A Lamoreaux, J B Davenport.

Parowan—G S Halterman, P D Stoops, H L Adams.

Cedar Precinct—Evans Williams, James Corlett, John Middleton.

Summit—John White, J A Dalley, Moroni Dalley.

Kannarra—J S Pollock, George Williams, Samuel Pollock.

WASHINGTON COUNTY.

Silver Reef—S W West, J H Gardiner, L Cushing.

Leeds—R H Ashby, M E Paris, C A Connelly.

Washington—J P Chidester, S A Dunn, M M Harmon.

St. George—F L Daggett, Richard Bentley, A P Hardy.

Bloomington—J W Carpenter, William Atkin, Sr, Archibald Sullivan.

Santa Clara—Rudolph Free, John Stahly, Jacob Free.

Pine Valley—J M Thomas, J B Bracken, Jr, R B Gardner.

Gunlock—Jeremiah Leavitt, G S Coleman, W O Holt.

New Harmony—Francis Prince, Orin Kelsey, J F Pace.

Pinto—J H Harrison, N D Forsyth, O E Knell.

Hamblin—G O Holt, James Canfield, W Mathie.

Hebron—D M Tyler, G W Laub, C H Bahum.

Toquerville—J T Willis, Wm Bayer, Matthew Batty.

Duncan's Retreat—D B Ott, R W Reeve, N B Badger.

Grafton—J H Ballard, G H Wood, Jr, Daniel Morris.

Virgin City—Henry Cornelius, Jos Hilton, Leroy W Beebe.

Rockville—H T Stout, Frank Slaughter, V A Smith.

Shonesburg—C S Stevens, Jos Millett, Jr, E W Stevens.

Springdale—S K Gifford, Christian Larsen, Jas Mullett.

Deseret News
July 11, 1888

A Silver Reef Fire.

On Saturday night several buildings on Main Street, Siver Reef, Utah, were destroyed by fire. The blaze started in an unoccupied store belonging to a Mrs. Hays, and spread north and south along the street. On the south side the flames stopped wιen they reached the cross street and had nothing more in that direction to burn. To the north, the blaze reached the fireproof store of Jas. M. Louder, where it was checked. Most of the buildings were unoccupied. The losses are, Mr. Louder, $500; Mr. Jordan, $150; Mr. Quirk, $6,000; Mr. Sinclair $100; besides other smaller amounts.

Deseret News
July 30, 1888

DEATH OF CHARLES HUBER.

Particulars About His being Drowned in a Fish Pond.

LEEDS, Utah, July 30, 1888.

Editor Deseret News:

The following is an account of a man by the name of Huber, a native of Germany, sometimes known by the name of Dutch Charley, who, on the evening of July 25, was found dead in a small fish pond, near the little town of Leeds.

B. Y. McMullin, the owner of the pond, on his return from Silver Reef (which is situated about one and a half miles from Leeds) on the evening of July 25th, as it was growing dusk, came by his fish pond, a few steps from the road on the way from the Reef. On his leaving the pond he discovered, on the bank, the clothes of some person who evidently had stripped for the purpose of bathing. There being no one in sight from the spot where the clothes were found, though the whole pond was within view, it was feared that something was wrong.

Upon walking around the pond to the opposite side from where the clothes lay, at a distance of about fifteen feet from the bank, the body of some (at that time) unknown man was discovered. A small portion of the back of the head and shoulders appeared above the surface of the water, the body otherwise sinking out of sight. The depth of water where the body lay was supposed by those who took it out, to be about four feet. A very short distance from where the body lay the water was about seven feet deep.

Upon this discovery the officers were immediately notified. A jury was summoned and an inquest held over what proved to be as above stated, the remains of Charles Huber. The verdict of the jury was to the effect that the deceased came to his death by drowning, with no evidence that it was done with suicidal intent.

Deceased was evidently a man who had reached the age of about forty-five years, of a light complexion and was short and heavy set. It is not known that he has any relatives in this country.

B. Y. McMULLIN.

ESTRAY NOTICE.

I HAVE IN MY POSSESSION:

One dark red BULL, 4 years old, branded W on right ribs, vented on right hip; also

on right hip and Sd on right thigh.

One light red COW and Calf, 3 years old,

branded on left ribs, white under belly, white spot in forehead, square crop and swallow-fork in left ear, under slope in right

One light red COW and Calf, 3 years old,

branded on left ribs, square crop off each ear.

If not claimed on or before September 13, at 5 o'clock p. m., will be sold to the highest responsible bidder.

WILLIAM STIRLING,
Poundkeeper.

Leeds, Washington Co.

From the Southern Counties.

A gentleman of this city who has just returned, after a trip of several weeks in the southern counties of the Territory, gives the following information: Millard County has experienced a great scarcity of water, except at Kanosh. At Scipio not more than a fourth of the usual crop of grain will be raised. Many plowed their land up because the seed did not sprout for lack of moisture. Through Beaver and Iron counties, the latter especially, the chinch bug has done much damage to crops. In Washington County, even as far up as Silver Reef, chills and fever have been very prevalent, but there have been no fatal cases.

It is expected that a Stake Academy will be established in St. George this fall. The grape crop in St. George, Washington, Leeds, Santa Clara and Bloomington has been good, but in the settlements up the Rio Virgin the vines were killed by frost last winter, and no grapes at all have been raised there this year. Toquerville produces about a fourth of a crop.

The road leading from Virgin City to Kanab is one on which strangers are often lost. The authorities of Kane County purpose putting up guide boards on that portion of it lying in that county, which should be done its entire length.

In Kane County the deputies have lately been raiding, a prominent object of their efforts being Brother Chamberlain.

The apple crop in Kane County is splendid, and the fruit is entirely free from worms.

In Panguitch the crops have been uninjured by frosts this year, an unusual thing. In this place resides a girl aged 14 years last May, who weighs 241½ pounds. She is a native of the place.

On Monday last the Stake Academy at Richfield, Sevier County, was opened with excellent prospects. Elder Isaac J. Hayes is principal. Crops in this county are generally good.

BROWN.—In Leeds, Washington Co., Utah, Nov. 13, 1888, of pneumonia, Mary Jane, beloved daughter of Ellen Brown, born Feb. 5, 1867, at Bristol, England.

DEATH OF MOSES HARRIS.

Moses Harris, the subject of this sketch, was born July 20th, 1798, in Somerset County, Pennsylvania. He was the son of Silas and Annaretta Wright Harris. His ancestor was among the first settlers of New England. In an early day his father moved into Indiana and settled in Cork County. There Moses became acquainted with Fanny Smith, whom he married Jan. 1st, 1824, and who still survives him, aged 86 years. Both were baptized into the Church of Jesus Christ of Latter-day Saints on Feb. 23rd, 1833. He, in company with his brother-in-law, Wm. Hawks, gathered with the Saints in Missouri in the summer of 1836, and stopped through the winter of 1836 and '37 at Chariton, Missouri, and in the following spring located on Crooked River, Caldwell County. He suffered with the Saints in the persecution of 1838, and in the inclement month of March, 1839, with a one-horse wagon, in which had to be stowed the most necessary household goods, with several children,

he set out for Illinois, leaving all the balance of their property a prey to the mobbers.

He finally settled about five miles west of Montrose, Iowa, in a very destitute condition. He was ordained a High Priest under the direction of the Prophet Joseph Smith in Nauvoo.

The season before the exodus of the Saints from Illinois he moved on a farm nearer Montrose which he had rented. About the first of May, 1846, he took up the line of march with the Saints for the West, and arrived at Council Bluffs about the time that Colonel Allen called on the Twelve for 500 volunteers to go to California. He gave up his eldest son, Silas, who was the main support of the family, in response to the call of the Twelve, to enlist in the Battalion. At the Bluffs he located on Little Pidgeon Creek. In October, 1848, his son arrived from California and, with his assistance, the family were prepared to cross the plains in R. N. Allred's company, in 1849. After they had crossed the Loup Fork, his sister, the wife of William

Hawk, was killed in a stampede. He arrived in Salt Lake valley on the 16th of October and settled in Bountiful, ten miles north of Salt Lake City, where he remained until the spring of 1851, when he joined the company of Charles C. Rich and Amaza Lyman to go to San Bernardino to form a settlement. At that place he purchased forty acres of land at $10 per acre, but not having it quite paid for when the settlement was broken up, he got no title for it, and so lost it with the improvements he had made. He started on his return to Utah in the fall of 1857 in Jefferson Hunt's company, and settled in Washington, Washington County, Utah, in February, 1858. In the spring of 1859 he moved to Harrisburg, which place was named after him by President Brigham Young, he being the only settler there at that time.

In March 1864 he moved with his son John to Berry Valley (now Long Valley), Kane County, Utah, and located at what is now the town of Glendale, where he remained until driven out by the Indians in June 1867. He returned to Harrisburg where he remained about three years, and then assisted in building up the town of Leeds, three miles east of Harrisburg. From this place he moved back to Glendale, Long Valley, and settled near his son Silas, at which place he departed this life March 15th, 1890, after an illness of thirty days, caused by an attack of influenza, which settled in his stomach, causing severe pain. He finally passed peacefully away a few minutes before midnight, aged 91 years, 7 months and 25 days.

He leaves a posterity now living, of five children, 55 grand children and 83 great grand children. Father Harris' long and eventful life, after gathering with the Saints in Missouri, was mostly spent in opening up new settlements. He was very unassuming, and was honest and upright in his dealings with his fellow man, always quietly performing all duties required of him. He was very temperate in his habits. He never faltered nor murmured under all the trying scenes he was called to pass through, and was ever ready to bear a strong testimony to the truth of this Latter-day work. It can truly be said of him, "He has fought the good fight, he has kept the faith," and will come forth in the morning of the first resurrection and inherit all the blessings sealed upon his head in the Temple of the Lord, wherein he passed through all the ordinances given in those sacred places.   WARREN FOOTE.

ST. GEORGE STAKE.

PRESIDENT.—Daniel D. McArthur
St. George.

COUNSELORS.—Anthony W. Ivins,
Erastus B. Snow, St. George.

Washington County, Utah

WARDS.	BISHOPS.
Beelerue	Andrew Gregerson, P. E.
Duncan	David B. Ott, P. E.
Fosters	Wm. Chadburn, P. E.
Glen Edwin	Edwin Hamblin, P. E.
Grafton	James M. Ballard
Gunlock	Franklin O. Holt
Hamblin	George A. Holt, P.E.
Harmony	Wilson D. Pace
Harrisburg	Orson B. Adams, P. E.
Hebron	Thomas S. Terry
Leeds	Brigham Y. McMullin
Middleton	Richard Prince
Mountain Dell	Wm. Isom P. E.
Pine Valley	Wm. Gardner
Pinto	Robert Knell
Price	N. R. Fawcett
Rockville	C. N. Smith
Santa Clara	J. G. Hafen
Shonesburg	Oliver De Mill P.E.
Springdale	Wm. R. Crawford
St. George, 1st Ward	Thomas Judd
St. George, 2nd Ward	Walter Granger
St. George, 3rd Ward	C. A. Terry
St. George, 4th Ward	Thos. P. Cottam
Toquerville	Wm. A. Bringhurst
Virgen	Leroy W. Beebe
Washington	Andrew Sprout
Westover	Charles Westover, P.E.

Iron County Record
January 3, 1891

IRON CITY NOTES.

The boom will be here just as soon as the holidays are over.

Pinto Iron Mining District will come to the front. We have got good property here and the promise of money to develope this winter.

Big Strike!

Pyro Iron Mining District

May and Pottar of Silver Reef have just opened r fine vein of lead ore here which promises to be the biggist thing yet. Further particulars soon.

Don C. Robbins of Salt Lake who has boded several pieces o property here, is expected daily with supplies to begin work which is to last all winter.

Iron County Record
February 14, 1891

SILVER REEF.

Knowing that Mr. Judd was interested in mining in Silver Reef the reporter, asked regarding that old silver-sandstone district. He says the prospects are brighter at Silver Reef than they have been for many years. In the old Stormy King mine, belonging to the Christy Company, the developments have been extending northward from the new shaft into new country, and it now shows up as well as it ever did in that property. Wooly, Lund & Judd have been running the Barbee & Walker, mill in which they worked 1000 tons of ore averaging about 18 ounces silver to the ton.

They have also been running the Christy mill part of the time. The ores crushed were raised by "chloriders," who have been doing well in fact as well as miners did in that camp. About forty miners are working in the district. Mr. Judd is of the opinion if the mines there, now belonging to three companies were thrown into a corporation, that mining could be carried on to large extent, good profit, and that Silver Reef would become a better district than it ever has been.

Tribune.

Deseret News
February 27, 1892

DEATH OF SUSANN SMITH ADAMS.

Editor Deseret News:

It seems as though it would be doing an injustice to many friends (who reside in Utah, adjoining Territories and Mexico) of the worthy dead, not to give notice, through the columns of your paper, of the demise of Susann Smith Adams. She was born May 30th, 1819, in Grason county, Ky. In the fall of 1854 she moved to Morgan

County, Illinois, where she became acquainted with Orson B. Adams, to whom she was married on the 20th of March, 1836. In the fall of the same year she settled in Brown County, Illinois, where she, in connection with her husband, embraced the Gospel in March, 1840. In 1842 she went to Nauvoo, where she lived until 1846. Then she started west with her husband, crossed the Mississippi River on the 10th of June, and arrived at Council Bluffs on the 16th of July. There her husband volunteered in the United States service to go to Mexico in defense of his country. Her wish was to go also, that she might share his burdens in that memorable campaign; consent was obtained, and she packed what little wearing apparel she had in a pillow-slip, and started on that toilsome journey through a wilderness country, with but two quilts for bedding. Without a murmur she waited daily on the sick, administering comfort and cheer to all around her. On the 12th of October she arrived at Santa Fe, rested a few days, and, being left by the main body of the Battalion with those who were considered unable to pursue the journey to California, took up the line of march northward to Pueblo, where she remained during the winter. In the spring of 1847 she arrived at Fort John, now Laramie. There it was learned that the Pioneers were a few days ahead.

Following their trail for 510 miles, her company reached the valley. Just in sight and within three miles of the Pioneers' camp they had quite a time of rejoicing. Traveling down to City Creek, a short distance below the Pioneers' camp, she pitched her tent on the 28th of July, 1847, thanking God for the oasis of the desert, and acknowledging His goodness for the good health and protecting care she had enjoyed, during her weary travels with the batallion and into the valley.

She was now prepared to continue her labors in connection with her husband, as the servants of God might direct. In 1848 Brother Adams raised twenty bushels of wheat, which was much appreciated by her, having lived the first winter and spring on roots and greens.

They now made a home on Mill Creek, where they lived quite comfortably until December 1851. Then they were called to Iron county, where they arrived on the 14th of February, 1852. Here, for the third time, she had her name enrolled as a member of the Relief society, having been a member of that organization in Nauvoo and also in Great Salt Lake.

In 1854 she was set apart by Apostle Geo. A. Smith to wait upon her sex in sickness. For 38 years she humbly pursued her calling with great success, putting her trust in God, she stimulated the faith of those with whom she labored, bringing peace, joy and good cheer to all among whom she administered.

In the fall of 1865 she moved to Harrisburg, Washington County. In 1866 the relief society was organized in that place, and she was chosen president and acted in that capacity till 1877, when she resigned on account of ill-health, and the frequent calls from the sick. In 1883 her health was somewhat improved, and in March of that year she was chosen by Sister E.

Laney as her first Counselor. She held that position up to the time of her death, which occurred at 10 p.m. on the 23rd day of January, 1892, at her residence in Harrisburgh, Washington county, after a protracted illness. With but little pain or suffering she passed away without a struggle.

She leaves a husband, one daughter and mother and an adopted son, twenty-three grandchildren, five great-grandchildren besides three orphan children that she reared and a host of friends to mourn her departure.

Just previous to her departure from this life, she called her son-in-law by name, and impressed upon him the necessity of directing the energies and strength of her grandchildren in those channels that would best promote the interests of the work of God, in which cause she had labored, nothing doubting, for nearly fifty years.

Funeral services were conducted at the Leeds meeting house, where the largest gathering that has met there for years, assembled to pay their last respects to the one they loved so well. Consoling remarks were made by Counselor Leatham and Elders Steele, Doge and Spilsbury.

All spoke in the highest terms of her many virtues and unswerving integrity for the cause of truth. L. W.

OBITUARY NOTES

ANOTHER PIONEER PASSED AWAY.

LEEDS, Wash., Co., Utah, March 22, 1894.—Died in St. George, March 21, 1894, Daniel M. Thomas, born in Richmond county, N. C., 25th Dec., 1809, aged 84 years, 2 months and 24 days.

Bro. Thomas had been a member of the Church of Jesus Christ of Latter-day Saints near fifty years, and was known to have been faithful to the end. He received the Gospel in February, 1844, and was ordained an Elder during the same year, being called to preach the Gospel in his native land soon after. During the first year of his ministry 150 of his own converts were baptized by him. He gathered with the Saints at Winter Quarters in the spring of 1847. At Laramie he joined President John Taylor's company of incoming Saints and was appointed captain of ten in said company. Soon after reaching the valley he was ordained a Seventy and belonged to the Eighth quorum. In 1851 he was called on a mission to San Bernardino under Charles C. Rich and Amasa Lyman. While in California, he was highly respected by the people, both ecclesiastically and politically; and while there was ordained a High Priest, and acted as first Counselor to the President of the Stake. He was elected to the office of justice, and served about seven years; was also postmaster under the government of the United States.

About the year 1857 the Saints on that mission were called to return to Utah and he came with them. He was next called on a mission to assist the Saints in settling Beaver county, U. T., and made his home at Beaver City. He there served as probate judge and postmaster. From there he was called to assist the Saints in making settlements on the Muddy, state of Nevada, and after the settlements there were broken up, he moved to St. George, U. T., the place of his death. While living in St. George he was known to be a faithful Latter-day Saint, and has done a great work in the Temple, officiating for relatives and friends to the number of 400.

ELIJAH THOMAS.

WOOLSEY. — At Silver Reef, Washington county, Utah, March 22, 1895, of cancer in right side and breast, Clarissa Woolsey, aged 81 years, 10 months and 17 days.

Sister Woolsey's home is at New Harmony, Utah, but she was at Silver Reef staying with her daughter when she was called away. She was buried at home, and died as she lived, in full faith of the Gospel.

MINES AND MINING.

A number of people from Harrisburgh, Leeds and Silver Reef have been making new discoveries above Silver Reef, at the foot of Pine Valley mountain. There has been seventeen locations already made and some twenty assays, which run from two to fourteen dollars each in gold, a portion of the rock containing the same being soft. Truly the saying of Isaiah seems to be coming to pass, where he says "For brass I will bring gold, and for iron I will bring silver, and for wood brass, and for stones iron."

Frank Burgess has gone to the new gold strike, above Silver Reef, to examine the new discoveries and probably make a few locations.

We understand that H. Blackner who has leased the Kemple mine, in Silver Reef District, Utah, lately struck a four foot vein of rock that is quite rich in silver.

Mr. Wilson, at De LaMar, is preparing to put in a mill for working gold bearing rock, he being the owner of the April Fool mine.

We are informed that Mr. De LaMar, at De LaMar, Nevada, is putting in an addition to his mill and works in order to increase the working capacity. Everything in that vicinity is in a prosperous condition.

The Dodge Bros have just returned from Bull Valley and report propects in that vicinity in a flourishing condition. They have sunk 65 feet on the Vanderbilt mine and then drifted about 13 feet and have struck the gold spar and expect to find a large ledge as they go on in.

They have also commenced work on the Black Prince mine and have cut in about 20 feet prepartory to commencing a tunnel in order to run into the main ledge. Parties desiring to see specimens from these mines can see them at Walter E. Dodges, in this city

Frank Burgess returned from the new gold fields, above Silver Reef, just as we are going to press and reports the prospects in that vicinity very discouraging. There is gold there but it has not yet been found in quantities that will pay to work it.

DEATH OF JUDGE BARBEE.

He Dies Suddenly in the Blue Bell Mining District, in Tooele County.

Special Correspondence to the NEWS.

VERNON, Tooele County, March 25, —Last night, at 9 o'clock, Mr. Best drove down here from the Blue Bell mining district, distant ten miles from here, informing us that a man had died in camp and inquired for the justice of the peace. He was absent on his ranch about six miles away. David Sharp left on horseback to get the justice, Owen Bennion. This morning we had a coffin made and drove up to camp.

We found Judge Barbee lying on his bunk in his tent just as he died. Mr. Marchant informed us that Judge Barbee had been prospecting all day and came to camp and cooked supper. While Mr. Marchant was looking to see if the coffee was boiled he glanced round and found the Judge lying on the bed dying; he promptly called the other miners just in time to see him die. He apparently experienced no pain and is supposed to have died of heart failure.

Judge Barbee is well known in mining circles. He was sixty-four years of age, and as far as we know had no relatives in Utah. The body was washed and new clothes put on and we drove down here where he was buried. Justice Bennion took charge of his papers. Mr. Marchant informed me that he and Barbee discovered the mines in Leeds, Washington county, and at one time sold out for $100,000 cash; we were told today that he did not have a cent when he died. He had a number of locations in the district and some say they carry assays of gold.　JOHN C. SHARP.

A new tannery is being established at Leeds, Utah.

June, 14, 1896.

Quarterly Conference convened in the Tabernacle at 10 a. m., Prest. D. D. McArthur presiding.

After the preliminary excercises, Prest. McArthur made a few opening remarks bidding all welcome to the conference and asked all to join in seeking for the spirit of God, that we may have a time of rejoicing during this conference.

During Conference the following Bishops reported their wards favorably. Bishop Snow, Pine Valley; Bishop Knell, Pinto; Bishop James Andrus, St. George; Bishop Bunker, Bunkerville; Bishop M c M u l l e n, Leeds.

Married. In St. George, June 23rd, 1896, Donald Fuller and Lavinia Angel, both of Leeds, Washington Co., Utah. May their wedded life be full of bliss.

AN ORDINANCE.

AN ORDINANCE. Creating and defining boundaries of Election Precincts, in Washington County, State of Utah.

The Board of County Commissioners of the County of Washington, do ordain as follows:—

That for Election purposes the County of Washington, State of Utah, shall be divided into precincts with boundaries fixed, as follows:—

Precinct No. One—All of Shonesburg Precinct.

Precinct No. Two—All of Springdale Precinct.

Precinct No. Three—All of Rockville Precinct.

Precinct, No. Four—All of Grafton Precinct.

Precinct No. Five—All of Virgen Oity Precinct.

Precinct No. Six—All of Toqnerville Precinct.

Precinst No. Seven—All of Leeds, Harrisburg and Silver Reef Precincts.

Precinct No. Eight—All of Washington Precinct.

Precinct No. Nine—All of St. George Precinct, lying EAST of the centre line of LOCUST STREET in said City.

Precinct No. Ten—All of St. Georg Precinct, lying WEST of the centre line of LOCUST STREET in said City.

Precinct No. Eleven—All of Bloomington Precinct.

Precinct No. Twelve—All of Santa Clara Precinct.

Precinct No. Thirteen—All of Gunlock Precinct.

Precinct No. Fourteen—All of Pine Valley Precinct.

Precinct No. Fifteen—All of Hebron Precinct.

Precinct No. Sixteen—All of Hamblin precinct.

Precinct No. Seventeen—All of Pinto Precinct.

Precinct No. Eighteen—All of Harmony Precinct.

All of said Precincts, being more particularly described and recorded on pages 3 to 10 inclusive, in a record entitled "Precinct and School District Boundaries," as adopted by the County Court, of Washington County, Territory of Utah, March 6th, 1893.

Passed this 29th day of June, A. D., 1896.

Robert C. Lund,
Chairman.

Attest,
Seth A. Pymm,
County Clerk.

(SEAL.)

State of Utah, } ss
County of Washington. }

I Seth A. Pymm, Clerk of the County Court in and for the County of Washington, State of Utah, do hereby certify that the foregoing is a full, true and correct copy of the Original Ordinance passed by the County Court, of said County, and State, on the 29th day of June, 1896, as the same appears on file and of record in my office.

WITNESS my hand and Official Seal this 30th day of June, one thousand eight hundred and ninety six.

Seth A. Pymm,
County Clerk

The Union
October 3, 1896

Mr. F. S. Dille, of Silver Reef, Utah, came to St. George, on September 30, as a Ward of the county, being on the paupers list. He was ailing when he came, and the jailor succeeded in getting Dr. Afflect to attend him on the 1st inst., but his ailment, heart disease, had advanced too far to be cured and he died on the 2nd of October, being just 73 years of age.

Hon. R. C. Lund, of St, George, who is in the city on business, reports that the Barbee mill at Silver Reef turned out over 5000 ounces of silver during the past month. Mr. Lund also reports that there is great activity at Temple bar on the Colorado river, just over the Nevada line, where the Temple Bar company has 150 men at work on their placer claims.—Tribune.

The Jury List.

The following is the list of jurors of Washington County, drawn by the County Clerk and Assessor, Jan. 13th, 1897, to serve during the year of 1867:

Springdale—Freeborn D. Gifford.

Rockville—Alfred L. Hall, John Dennett.

Grafton—Edw. H. Bullard.

Virgin City—Ira Bradshaw, Frank H. Isom.

Toquerville—Geo. M. Spilsbury, Heber L. Naegle, Hamilton M. Wallace, Lorenzo Stack, Jr.

Leeds—B. Y. McMullin, Erastus C. Olson, Hyrum Leary.

Washington—Neils Nisson, Andrew Sproul, Chas. Westover, Jas. O. Wilkins.

St. George—Wm. Atkin, Samuel L. Adams, Wm. O. Bentley, Haden W. Church, Geo. T. Cottam, Wm. J. B. Carter, Chas. W. Dodge, Heber T. Empey, John Eardley, Jed M. Gates, Sherman C. Hardy, Geo. T. Jarvis, Samuel Miles, Jr., James McArthur, Hector A. McQuarrie, Alex Y. Milne, Joseph Orton, John E. Pace, Richard Prince, David Rogers, Heber C. Smith, Erastus B. Snow, Nils Sandberg, Wm. A. Terry, Wm. H. Thompson, Geo. T. Whitehead.

Bloomington—Lars J. Larsen.

Santa Clara—Wm. Tobler.

Gunlock—John T. Laub.

Pine Valley — Wm. Gardner, Orlando H. Bracken, Benj. H. Burgess.

Hebron—Wm. J. Truman.

Pinto—Walker J. Knell.

Harmony—Wm. A. Ridd.

FRANCIS L. DAGGETT,
County Clerk.

THOS. P. COTTAM,
Assessor.

Deseret News
May 22, 1897

Demise of a Noble Woman.

At 6 a. m. today, May 22, 1897; Sister Margaret Buchanan Leatham, wife of William Leatham, died at the family residence, 852 w South Temple street. The immediate cause of death was childbirth. Deceased was born April 13th, 1853, in Glasgow, Scotland, where she embraced the Gospel in 1868. She emigrated to Utah in 1841 and was married to her husband soon after her arrival. They resided in Leeds, Washington county, until about three years ago, when they came to this city. The husband and family are plunged into the deepest grief by her unexpected decease. She was indeed a noble woman, being all that could be desired as a wife and mother, and true Latter-day Saint, her faith in God being ever unwavering. Besides her sorrowing husband she leaves ten children, two others, including the one to whom she so recently gave birth, being with her in the paradise of God.

The funeral services will be held at the Sixteenth ward meeting house at 4 p. m. tomorrow, (Sunday). Friends of the family are invited to attend.

The Union
June 12, 1897

Leeds, Utah, June 10, 1897.

In Jubilee notes of your paper of June 5 you state that Mrs Mary Meeks lives at Toquerville &c. You are mistaken in her name and residence. Her name is Sarah Meeks she was born December 12, 1802, and lives at Leeds, Washington County, Utah .

A publication of the correction will oblige, Respectfully.

Mrs. Peggy J. M. Hamilton,
her daughter.

The Union
October 30, 1897

This week we had a pleasant call from Art Louder, son of James N. Louder who formerly lived at Silver Reef, Utah.

The Union
January 31, 1898

MOONSHINER CAUGHT.

On Monday, January 31, 1898, J. B. McCoy, U. S. Revenue Agent and Assistant Towne, got track of a place on the Rio Virgen, 5 or 6 miles south of Leeds, Washington County, Utah, where liquor was being distilled contrary to law, and they accompanied U. S. Deputy Marshal Joseph T. Atkin, to the place where they found Henry Stocks the man who ran the still and the marshel arrested him, and the still and paraphernalia were demolished. Mr. Stocks was then taken to St. George and brought before Justice F. L. Daggett, where he plead guilty of illicit distilling of liquor. His bonds were placed at $500.00, which he failed to procure, and he was placed in the county jail to await the order of the U. S. officers at Salt Lake City.

Deseret News
March 5, 1898

FULLER—Elijah R. Fuller, was born June 13, 1811, in Windham, Green county, New York, and died at Leeds, Utah, on Dec. 28, 1897, aged 86 years, six months and 15 days.

Brother Fuller died in full faith of the Gospel and with the hope of a glorious resurrection. He had been a sufferer for many years, and bore his afflictions patiently. He leaves a numerous posterity to mourn his loss, being the father of thirty-two children and leaves a host of grandchildren.—[Cem.]

Deseret News
March 17, 1898

GOUDY HOGAN.

Goudy Hogan was born Sept. 16, 1829, in Telemarken, Tens Prestejeld, Overy, Norway. His parents, Erick G. M. and Helga Hogan, were naturally very religious, and belonged to the Lutheran church. In 1837, when the deceased was eight years of age, Hogan and family left Norway for America. This was for the purpose of bettering his financial condition. He sold his small farm for $500, and in the face of bitter opposition from relatives and friends, left his native land and settled in Illinois, not far from Nauvoo. Goudy was the oldest of five children, two of whom died during the journey. Hogan and family embraced the Gospel in 1843. The deceased was then 14 years of age, and had worked for strangers a considerable part of the six years the family had been in America. During the winter of '46 Goudy volunteered to join the Mormon battalion; he was, however, rejected on account of his extreme youth. He endured many hardships during this and the following year before starting on the journey westward. Goudy was 19 years of age when, on the 22nd of Sept., 1848, he, together with his father and family, arrived in Salt Lake valley. They were among the first to settle at Bountiful, and here for the fifth time in life, young Hogan helped to build a home for his father. In 1853, he built a home for himself, and on the 24th of December of that year was married to Christina and Bergethe Nelson. In 1860 he moved to Richmond, Cache county. Here he was engaged in nearly every enterprise, and was an active member in the Church. In 1874 he was called to move to the southern part of Utah to help settle the country. Taking part of his family, he left Richmond the same fall and settled at Leeds, where he was appointed Bishop. He was called upon and filled an honorable mission in Norway in 1877, returning to his home at Leeds in 1879. He moved back to Richmond in 1887, where he resided at the time of his death, Jan. 30, 1898. He has had twenty-five children, ten of whom are living, and forty-eight grandchildren.

The deceased has been failing in health for many years, with rheumatism, adn was confined to his bed for two months prior to his death. He was a consistent and devoted Latter-day Saint, exact and punctual in the performance of all his duties. He always paid a full and honest tithing, and contributed thousands of dollars to charitable purposes. He was honest and upright in his dealings, and passed away owing no man a dollar. The funeral was held in the meeting house in Richmond, on Thursday, Feb. 3, 1898, when appropriate remarks were made by a number of the brethren, some of whom had been acquainted with Brother Hogan over fifty years. All of his children that were in reach were present, one son, Heber D. Hogan, being on a mission in the United States.—[Com.

Scandinavian Star please copy.

SILVER REEF

The mining expert, Wm. Huntley, is still here, doing good work.

The Barker quartz mill has just closed down, having completed a successful run of 200 tons of ore.

This camp is still among the producers and the outlook is good. Some new ground is being opened up in which good bodies of silver ore have been uncovered. There is fifteen men at work extracting ore at the present time.

R. S. M.

Silver Reef, Utah, June 15, 1898.

A marriage license was obtained here on the 9th inst. by James Mc Knight, of Minersville, and Mrs Elizabeth Wilkinson, of Leeds. They were united in the Temple.

George A. Kuhn and Miss Leone Harris, both of Leeds, took out a marriage license on the 7th inst. and were married in the Temple.

LEEDS.

We are all enjoying good health here. This is hardly worthy of note as this is probably the most healthy place in the country and perhaps in the state.

Crop prospects are good, our water holding out far beyond our expectations. Our fruit was hurt considerably by the late frost, plums and apricots being all destroyed, Peaches are not more than one-fifth of an average crop. Apples, pears and grapes are good. Harvesting wheat is in progress. The second crop of lucern will be tackled next week.

Our mining interests are about as usual. Chloriders are busy extracting ore and some claim the prospects are good for the future. While our mining interests are on a small scale, owing to the low price of silver, it is of much benefit to the county, as from eighteen to twenty thousand dollars worth of bullion is shipped annually from here.

Our worst drawback here is lack of sufficient population to give material aid in erecting schools and in works of a public nature. We are in hopes this will be overcome in the future. Owing to its healthy location and central situation, on the main thorofare of our county and with good water-power facilities, it should be a splendid place for manufacturing enterprises as our state grows in population and wealth.

B. M.

R. G. McQuarrie was in from Silver Reef this week.

Smith Harris and wife were in from Silver Reef on Thursday and returned on Friday.

HARRISBURG

Editor, THE NEWS:—I have to painfully inform you of the death of my little ten-year-old son. He was the only boy in the family and his services as helper were hopefully anticipated as his male parent is well advanced in years and the remaining members of the family of very poor health and weakly constitution, yet all depending upon their labor for support. The inhabitants of the entire village kindly contributed to his comfort during the brief period of his dangerous illness, and to a respectable preparation and enterment in the grave. The Bishop and choir of Leeds were in attendance and everything that a kind consideration for the afflicted parents could suggest was done. His obituary in the abstract would read:

Died, at Harrisburg, Washington Co., Utah, July 6, 1898, of hemorrhage of the lungs, Willard R. Smith, son of Job and Sarah P, Smith, aged ten years and nine months.

Our second haying is on and but few hands to attend to it. Our population is chiefly of the feminine gender and of the few males several work out of town.

JOB T. SMITH.

Washington County News
July 16, 1898

Thomas Sterling of Leeds, one of Dixie's wealthiest cattle men, was in Cedar last week Friday enroute home from Salt Lake City. Tom seems to be taking life easy and is growing fleshy.

Washington County News
July 23, 1898

Another of our esteemed citizens,
Mrs. Elizabeth Wilkinson, was united
in the bonds of matrimony, in the St.
George Temple, with the well-known
and worthy James McKnight, last Saturday. The happy couple left here on
Monday for Minersville, the home of
the bridegroom.

Washington County News
August 6, 1898

Marian E. Paris and wife of Leeds
were in St. George Thursday, guests
of the Hardy house. Marian is looking hale and hearty and seems to enjoy
life.

LEEDS.

Water here is very scarce. If there is any fourth crop of hay it will be very light. We have had but one shower of rain this summer, and that barely enough to lay the dust.

Erastus C. Olsen and family, who have been for the last few weeks at Panguitch lake for their health and to get a little rest, returned home last Wednesday, looking and feeling well. During their absence they also visited relatives and friends in the north.

Your correspondent, in company with Wm. Sterling, visited Cedar City on Monday and returned the following Wednesday. The object of their visit was to secure rooms and make other arrangements to send their children to the Branch Normal school the coming school year. During our visit we went to see the newly-erected Normal building, which is now nearing completion, although much is yet to be done in the short space of time to have it ready for the beginning of school in September. We were much surprised and highly pleased with what had been done. Very much credit is due the Cedar people. Were it not done, and a monument there that can not be disputed, we would say it was impossible for such a work to be accomplished in so short a time. The building is a good one, and its site could not be better. Elevated as it is on a high piece of ground that appears to have been put there on purpose, with fine surroundings, we do not hesitate to predict that it will yet be near the center of the city. From its upper windows one has a good view of the entire valley while gazing on the newly harvested and growing crops which entirely surround the school grounds. The scenery is most beautiful. We will here note that it is claimed that the crops of Cedar City are as good this year if not the best that the place has had since it was first settled. A just remuneration for their energy and enterprise. Our fellow townsman, Wm. Sterling, expects to leave Leeds on Friday, the 2nd prox., for the European mission. Their will be a farewell party on the preceding Wednesday, to which all are invited.

B. M.

Leeds, Utah, August 26, 1898.

LEEDS.

We have quite a representation of children this year at the Branch Normal school at Cedar City. Eight registered at the commencement of the term, and three more intend going shortly.

Fruit drying about finished; the crop is light owing to late frost and scarcity of water. The yield of wheat between fourteen and fifteen hundred bushels, more than ever harvested before at this place. This, if properly distributed, would very nearly supply the people with bread.

It is rumored on the streets that our old time friend, Robort G. McQuarrie, is intending to leave Silver Reef, and that another man is coming to take his place as Superintendant of the business there. We will here note that as a straightforward, honorable business man R. G. McQuarrie will be hard to beat, and he will leave with the good wishes of the entire people in his favor.

Our townspeople will be quite few at home this winter, owing to those being away at school and many others who have gone or are going to find labor for the winter. It is going to be hard to keep some of our organizations, more especially the Mutual. We also have a couple of missionaries in the field and possibly more will have to go. There is some feeling of uneasiness among the people owing to the hard times; several families would sell out if they could and move to other parts.

LEEDS.

Wine making now on, but owing to the dry season the yield will be light.

Our old-time friend, Mrs. Elizabeth McKnight is in town, and will remain here a couple of weeks.

Water very scarce, the streams have to be united to irrigate the land before plowing for wheat, and it is very tedious work.

Our children who are students at the Normal school are, according to their reports, well pleased with the school and speak very highly of their teachers.

Mrs. Jane Chidester, of this place expects to start for Arizona in a few days to visit her children who are living there. She may spend the winter with them.

Our school is expected to begin on the 17th inst. We are in need of a Primary teacher to teach the Primary department. Our schools will both be small this season owing to so many attending the branch Normal at Cedar City; all the most advanced pupils will be there.

Unless there is a change our town will have rather a slim appearance this winter. Eleven from Leeds and several from Harrisburg will be away at school. Six have now gone and more going to Arizona to work this winter. It looks to us here that unless a railroad makes its way in this direction, Dixie will be smaller, or the people less in the future than they now are, or have been in the past [Bide a wee; we will have the railroad in time. Ed.]

We are greatly in need of a shoemaker here, one who is capable of both making and mending. A man of this kind could find plenty of work with good pay as there is no one here that pretends to do this kind of labor. There is some property situated on Main street particularly adapted to a business of this kind. It is for sale and can be bought at a very low figure The property consists of a house with four rooms; small lot, fenced, with orchard and outbuildings. Further information can be obtained from Bishop McMullin.

B. M.

DIED—At St. George, on Friday morning, October 21, at 3:40 o'clock, Cora Keate, the beloved wife of Albert Hartman of Silver Reef, in the 40th year of her age. An operation for the removal of a fibroid cystic tumor of the uterus had been performed by Dr. J. T. Affleck, assisted by Dr. Higgins of this place and Dr. Middleton of Cedar City, the day previous and the deceased was apparently recovering nicely, but had a relapse early the next morning which resulted in heart failure. The removed tumor weighed between 25 and 30 lbs. Funeral services were held Friday afternoon. The husband and family have the sympathy of the community in their bereavement.

The following were appointed judges of election for 1898:

Shonesburg—Ira D. Mill, John A. Beal and Benjamin D. Mill.

Springdale—Moses Gifford, Mary J. Cox, Rebecca A. Alred.

Rockville—John R. Terry, John Dennet, Joseph H. Petty.

Grafton—David Ballard, Charles H. Jones, James M. Ballard.

Virgin City—Leroy W. Beebe, John H. Helton, Ira E. Bradshaw.

Toquerville—W. W. Hammond, Susan Bringhurst, Walter H. Slack.

Leeds—W. O. Harris. James G. Wilder, E. C. Olsen.

Washington—Arthur A. Paxman, Andrew H. Larson, Cornelius McReavy.

St. George, East—Seth A. Pymm, Joseph S. Snow, Samuel Miles, Jr.

St. George, West—Robert G. McQuarrie, John E. Pace, Andrew N. Winsor.

Bloomington—L. James Larson, Ruth O. Faucett, William Atkin, Jr.

Santa Clara—Rudolph Frei, John Graf, John Hafen.

Gunlock—John H. Bowler, Jere Leavitt, E. S. Jones.

Pine Valley—Peter Snow, M. E. Bracken, George M. Burgess.

Hebron—William F. Truman, Elias Hunt, Thomas N. Terry.

Hamblin—James Canfield, Mrs. E. S. Canfield, George R. Sinfield.

Pinto—Amos G. Thornton, M. W. Harrison, Joseph Eldridge.

Harmony—L. A. Pace, Gottlieb Schmutz, Albert E. Taylor.

Washington County News
January 11, 1899

LEEDS.

Four and a-half inches of snow here this morning,

M, M, H,

Leeds, Utah, January 11, 1899,

Washington County News
January 21, 1899

An Enthusiastic Prospector.

Mr. John T. Ferris, who claims to have first discovered silver at Silver Reef in 1874, is back in his old haunts, and gave this office a pleasant call on Thursday. Mr. Ferris is enthusiastic over some claims he has just secured, situated on the Duffin reef about two miles southeast of Leeds, and which he has been trying to get for twenty-two years.

He and Andrew F. Gregorson of Leeds, who is backing him, recorded five claims Tuesday, to be known as the Stevenite and the New Era near Leeds; and the Dewey, Little Giant, and Bellevue in the Bellevue hills. The two former are rich in silver in veins running from six inches to two feet. The Dewey, Little Giant, and Bellevue show a vein of cobalt bloom, or cobalt oxide, which is thirteen feet wide in places, and which, Mr. Ferris informs us, will average from 15 to 20 per cent pure cobalt.

Mr. Ferris recently returned from an inspection of the Apex copper mine, which is situated about 18 miles west of this city. He believes this to be a wonderful property. The amalgamite ore in this mine contains 82 per cent copper and some gold.

LEEDS.

All who have stock are feeding them.

We are having a heavy wind from the south today, the 1st. It is to be hoped it will be followed by wet weather.

The buds on our trees are dangerously swelling. Unless cold weather takes the place of the warm weather we are likely to lose our fruit by the spring frosts.

While it's possible for us to get plenty of rain in the valleys, and snow in the mountains between now and April, nevertheless, it is a fact that at present prospects are rather gloomy to us here.

The epidemic that has been prevailing over the principal part of this state has measurably left us. However, there are still some ailing. Sister William Harris is still confined to her bed, and while she is somewhat better we do not think her entirely out of danger. Her speedy recover is hoped for by all who know her.

Deseret News
March 18, 1899

LEEDS.

Heavy Frost—Drouth Affecting the Cattle Interest.

Special Correspondence.

Leeds, Washington Co., March 14.— There was a very heavy frost here last night; water froze in the ditches. The fruit no doubt was injured last night. It is dry and cold, stock suffering. The almonds, apricots and peaches in bloom and lucerne bright and green.

Mrs. Sarah Meeks, the oldest Pioneer, still lives here under the care of her daughter, Peggy Jane Meeks Hamilton. Sister Sarah Meeks was born Dec. 12, 1802, came into Utah in 1847, in Jedediah M. Grant's company, Jos. B. Noble's 50 and Jos. Miller's 10. The old lady has now passed her 96th mile post, and still retains a vivid memory of her early experience.

Washington County News
March 25, 1899

HARRISBURG.

We have had a light fall of rain.

The late frost has spared some of the early fruit.

Frank Hartley started this morning for Cedar City to bring Mrs. Deady home.

Our school will close on April 13th. We will all miss the teacher as she is a great favorite here.

Two wagonloads of children came down from Leeds on Sunday and made things lively for awhile.

Nathaniel Workman is preparing the place he recently bought, opposite the postoffice, for his family.

Willie Matheson and others of Parowan passed through here bound for St. George, where Mr. Matheson and Miss Mamie Conel will be married.

The amount appropriated by the Legislature for roads in Washington County is as follows: For repairing roads in Washington county, between St. George and Rockville, $300; between Leeds and top of Bellevue Blackridge, $300; between St. George and Holt's Ranch, $500.

Marion E. Parie of Leeds was handshaking and smiling upon old friends here Thursday.

Washington County News
April 1, 1899

Robert G. McQuarrie left here Wednesday for Silver Reef, where he will work the mill which is expected to start running this week.

Washington County News
April 8, 1899

LEEDS CORRESPONDENCE.

We are still in need of a shoemaker here.

We had a little rain today and are thankful for it.

We find on examination that all apricots are not killed, to date, by frost.

William Harris has gone to Kingman, Arizona, on some kind of legal business, it is supposed.

The large district school here closes this week. The Primary department will be in session a few weeks longer.

We were honored with the presence of Apostle Woodruff and Elder McMurrin on the 23rd ult., they met with us at meeting where we had a very good representation, and received some valuable instructions. President Seegmiller of the Kanab stake, was also with us.

S. Earl, an old resident of Silver Reef, has returned from Colorado.

R. G. McQuarrie, of McQuarrie & Sons who has been running the Barbee Mill, came in from Silver Reef Wednesday. He reports about twenty men working on the reef, getting out a good quality of silver ore. The mill has closed down for two weeks after running through 100 tons of ore averaging 35 to 40 ounces of silver to the ton. About the same amount of ore of similar quality is on hand which will be run through when the mill resumes running.

W. Harris of Silver Reef passed through here Sunday on a prospecting trip in the Grand Gulch district. He was one of the hands employed to clean out the Jennings property, and thinks that section is going to come to the front.

M. E. Paris of Leeds and a party passed through here Thursday enroute to Parashaunt on a cattle hunt.

James Wilder, Roy Harris and August Kuhn passed through here Thursday from Leeds enroute to Bull Valley on a prospecting trip.

Washington County News
June 24, 1899

Judge Daggett performed the ceremony on Tuesday that bound together for life Thomas Sterling and Miss Harriet S. McMullin of Leeds. Mr. Sterling is one of the most energetic citizens of Leeds, and a real good fellow. THE NEWS joins their many friends in wishing them much happiness

Washington County News
July 8, 1899

M. E. Paris of Leeds, and James G. Wilder of Silver Reef were here on business Monday, and paid this office a very pleasant call.

Washington County News
July 15, 1899

Bert McQuarrie spent the Fourth at Leeds. Leeds has a great attraction for Bert.

Washington County News
July 29, 1899

Albert Hartman and William H. Angell of Leeds left here for the south on a prospecting trip Tuesday. They expect to be gone for a few weeks.

OBITUARY.

WILLARD UTTLEY CARTER, son of William and Harriet Carter, was born at Salt Lake City August 19, 1859, and died in this city on the 16th inst. Deceased came to St. George in 1862, and has resided here since that date. He was married on December 22, 1883, in the Temple at this place to Jane Thomas, by whom he had six children, his wife and five children being left to mourn his loss. Bro. Carter was sunstruck in June last year, and has never been quite well since; he had a stroke of paralysis in July last year. Since June 1898 he had three sunstrokes, the last one occurring last month at Leeds while he was enroute home from Milford. Since July 1898 he had three strokes of paralysis, the last of which caused his death.

Funeral services were held in the Tabernacle on Monday, the speakers being Elders John S. Woodbury, D. D. McArthur, David H. Cannon, John E. Pace and Thomas P. Cottam. Deceased did much work in the Temple, and died a faithful Latter-day Saint.

M. E. Paris of Leeds came in Wednesday evening on business, bringing Roy Grundy with him.

Charles H. Nichols and Miss Chresta L. Hartley, both of Leeds, were married by Judge Daggett Monday

Bert McQuarrie, Will Macfarlane and Louis Chidester attended a wedding dance at Leeds Tuesday night.

John S. Adams, a former resident of Leeds, returned from Chloride where he has been working Thursday. He left for the Sevier the same day to locate a site for a sawmill.

The Drouth Broken.

A thunderstorm that started about 5 o'clock Wednesday morning ended in a heavy downpour of rain, the first rain to amount to anything for nearly two years. Soon every wash carried a raging torrent of water that washed out roads, endangered bridges and did considerable damage, but it is welcome nevertheless. This end of the Modena road near Charles Dodge's farm was washed out to a depth of twelve feet. The wash this side of Middleton where it crosses the road is badly cut up, large rocks weighing many tons being washed down. The roads all the way to Leeds are badly damaged, and this is likely to be the case in other parts of the county that have not yet been heard from. The rain will be of immense benefit to the thirsty cattle ranges.

Washington County News
August 26, 1899

Pine Valley's Bear.

George Burgess, one of the earliest settlers of Pine Valley was in St. George yesterday, and reports great destruction caused by a very large grizzly bear among stock. Thirty-seven cattle, valued at over $1,000, have been killed by this bear near Pine and Grass valleys. Hunting parties have been out frequently for the past three weeks and have often been quite near it, but owing to the thick timber and undergrowth in which bruin has his retreat, it is very difficult to get a shot at him. He has been seen frequently, and Mr. Burgess describes him as being fully 1500 lbs weight, his tracks have been measured and are 11 x 7 inches, showing him to be a big fellow. When closely pressed by the hunters he has torn out some of his hairs in crossing fallen logs, these hairs measure five inches long and are unmistakably those of a grizzly. The last party of hunters got close upon him before they were aware of the fact, a dog belonging to Burgess going into the brush and receiving a clout on the side of the head that bared the bones. A reward of $50 is offered by Pine Valley people for its death. Lyman Andrus and others of Leeds have gone on its trail. The Indians that went up to kill it have "chucked" the job, admitting that they are afraid of it. Its range covers six or eight miles between Pine and Grass Valley.

Isaac Jennings and party left for the Grand Gulch Tuesday. The men of this county that accompanied him to work on the mining property were Joseph Empy, Urie Macfarlane, Ephriam McNeil, Samuel Sullivan, Minor Laub and George Webb of this city, and Oscar McMullin of Leeds.

LEEDS.

Mrs. M. Stocks and family of Silver Reef have gone to Arizona.

The infant daughter of William Sullivan and wife died on the 28th ult.

Charles Worthen and wife, and Mrs. Isaiah Cox, of St. George, are visiting here.

Our schools have commenced with Walter Slack of Toquerville as principal, and Miss Lizzie McMullin as primary teacher.

Elders George E. Miles and A. R. Whitehead of St. George were home missionaries here last Sunday, and gave the people some much needed instructions.

The Barbee Mill at Silver Reef which has been running for some time, has shut down for a few days. I think the ore has turned out well, judging from the smiles worn by the chloriders.

LEEDS.

Bishop McMullin has gone to Cedar City.

The Barbee Mill at Silver Reef is now running again.

Peter Anderson is busy hauling hay from Washington field to his ranch.

Messrs Brassacher and Jasperson of Salt Lake City are down developing the formers mining property on the Virgin river.

LEEDS.

M. E. Paris has just returned from Salt Lake City.

Bert McQuarrie spent Monday here visiting old friends.

Bishop McMullin has gone to St. George with a load of tithing.

Mrs. Deady and family of Harrisburg have moved here for the winter.

W. H. Thompson of St. George passed thru Leeds on the stage Monday enroute to Belview station.

Mrs. William Harris has gone to Cedar City, where she will be under Dr. Middleton's care for several months.

Frank Hamilton has gone to St. George, taking with him Mrs. Oscar McMullin, who is taking her sick babe to Dr. Affleck for treatment.

LEEDS.

M. E. Paris is busy hauling hay from Washington Field.

Thomas Sterling has returned home from Salt Lake City.

Mrs. Forsha, of Silver Reef, has moved to St. George.

N. J. Bowler is here representing the San Francisco Examiner.

Born—A daughter to the wife of George E. Angell. All concerned doing well.

Oscar McMullin has returned from the Grand Gulch, where he has been working for the past three months.

LEEDS.

The weather is cold and windy.

Gottlieb Schmutz of Harmony was in Leeds today selling vegetables.

William Sterling, William Sullivan, and Lon Fuller have gone north for potatoes.

C. O. Connolly of Chloride, Arizona, has been here for the past week visiting relatives and friends.

Frank Hamilton has just returned from Lund, where he has been for freight for Adams' store.

Lon Harris, Clarence McMullin, and Jed Woodard, who are attending the branch Normal at Cedar City, came home for Thanksgiving.

Elder Maxwell, who is traveling in the interests of the Y. M. M., held meeting here Tuesday evening. He was accompanied by Bro. Jackson of Toquerville. They gave us some very good instructions.

On Monday night as the mail stage was coming off the Cottonwood bench, the horses became frightened and ran away, upsetting the buckboard and throwing the driver and his companion out. The team broke loose and ran away The driver and his companion, after pulling each other from beneath the ruins, walked to Harrisburg in search of assistance, but failing trudged on to Leeds, where they procured horses and returned and got the mail, which was taken on to Bellevue horseback. The night being cloudy and very dark made it disagreeable for them.

Washington County News
December 23, 1899

LEEDS.

It is reported that many horses are located on the Bench Lake range

Mrs. William Harris and family have returned home from Cedar to spend the holidays.

David McMullin, who has been at Stateline the past summer, has returned home.

Messrs. Kuhn, Wilder, and Harris have returned from Bull Valley, where they have been for some considerable time doing development work on their mining property.

LEEDS.

Miss Mame Olsen is visiting in St. George.

Mr. and Mrs. Clark, of Canaan ranch, spent Christmas in Leeds.

Miss Minnie Chatterly, of Cedar City, is the guest of Miss Maud Harris.

Mrs. William Beames presented her husband with a baby-girl some time last week.

All those from here who have been attending school at Cedar City are now home for the holidays.

Roy Grundy and Bert McQuarrie were here from St. George to attend the wedding reception of William Stirling and Miss Susie Harris.

Mrs. Ada McMullin and Mrs. Caroline McMullin were summoned to the bedside of their mother, Mrs. Parker of Washington, who is very ill, on the 25th inst.

Christmas passed off very quietly here, nothing going on during the day. In the evening the young folks had a sociable at Mrs. M. J. Hamilton's at which everybody seemed to enjoy themselves.

P. S.—An error was made in last issue. It stated, "The horses were located on Bench Lake range." It should have read, "Locoed on Bench Lake range."

Benjamin Harris of Leeds, and Miss Minnie Chatterly of Cedar City, are visiting here.

LEEDS.

Weather cold and windy.

Mrs. M. J. Hamilton has removed to Silver Reef.

Job T. Smith of Harrisburg has moved to Leeds.

Henry Peterson of Salt Lake City is spending a few days here.

Bishop B. Y. McMullin has returned from a visit to Cedar City.

Thomas Maloney and family have returned to their home at Virgin.

Mrs. Elizabeth Wilkinson, an old resident, has again taken up her abode here, having purchased the Miller residence.

Thos. Sterling of Leeds was in St. George Monday.

Marion E. Paris came in from Leeds Monday on a visit. He has beem sick with the grip, but it was feared for awhile that he had pneumonia. He is walking with the aid of a stick as his ankle was sprained during holidays while playing circus.

LEEDS.

E. C. Olsen and wife were visiting in St. George the fore part of this week.

Mrs. M. J. Hamilton and Mrs. Arthur Nichols, of Silver Reef, are both very sick.

A. F. Gregorson and wife passed thru Leeds Monday enroute to their home at Bellevue from St. George.

SILVER REEF.

Mrs. Charles Nichols of Leeds has been visiting friends in Silver Reef.

James Yorgenson has thirty tons of 50-oz ore out at the Free Coinage mine.

Albert Hartman has a fine body of high grade ore in the south drift of the Thompson.

Silver Reef has enjoyed a coal-oil famine for the past four weeks. Coal-oil will be appreciated when it makes its appearance.

The eight-hour law is being more generally observed here. Hitherto it has been more honored in the breach than in the observance.

We understand that it is the intention of the management here to put in a new Leffel Wheel in the mill. It is an improvement badly needed.

Mrs. Arthur Nichols and Mrs. Margaret Hamilton, both of whom have been quite sick, are improving. Dr. Affleck of St. George has both cases in charge.

One of the best bodies of ore struck by leasers was encountered by James Cobb in the Newton mine. Seven feet of 75-oz ore. Already fifty tons of ore have been mined without any perceptable effect on the ore body.

LEEDS.

Mrs. Hyrum Leany of Harrisburg is very sick.

James G. Wilder of Silver Reef was in Leeds on business today, the 14th.

B. Y. McMullin and daughter, Mattie, were in St. George on business last Saturday.

Elders F. D. Gifford of Springdale, and J. L. Workman of Virgin were here in behalf of the Seventies and attended meeting Sunday.

Mrs. Mary J. Meeks and son of Glendale, Kane Co., arrived here on the 13th and departed on the 14th, taking with them Utah's oldest pioneer, Mrs. Sally Meeks, aged 97 years.

Mrs. William Harris, who has been in Cedar City under Dr. Middleton's care the past winter, came home last week on a short visit, and was ready to return when she was taken suddenly ill. She is now somewhat better.

LEEDS.

Bp. B. Y. McMullin has gone to Milford on business.

The dance given on Washington's birthday was a success.

Chas. A. Workman, Co. Supt. of Schools, was visiting the schools here Tuesday.

The weather continues very dry and windy, so far we have had no rain or snow to amount to anything.

Daniel D. McArthur and David H. Cannon, of the Stake Presidency, held meeting here Friday evening, the 23rd.

Leeds was visited by the Toquerville Dramatic Co. last Saturday night. They presented "The Serf," which was rendered creditably.

The Misses Minnie Hanson and Maud Harris, also Messrs. Lue and Coleman Harris, who are attending school at Cedar City, were home to celebrate Washington's birthday.

LEEDS.

Mrs. Elizabeth Wilkinson and son Harry are visiting in St. George.

On the night of the 3rd inst. the people here were happily surprised by a rain storm.

Mrs. Charles Nichols presented her husband with a bouncing baby-boy on the 2nd inst.

Mrs. Sarah Forsha of St. George, a former resident of Silver Reef, is now visiting her daughter, Mrs. Harris, at that place.

Incorrectly Quoted.

Our last week's clipping from the WASHINGTON COUNTY NEWS with reference to Sally Meeks, aged 97, being "Utah's oldest living person," has elicited the information that Gunnison has a citizen older still than Mrs. Meeks.—Gunnison Gazette.

[No such claim was made by The WASHINGTON COUNTY NEWS. The article referred to spoke of Mrs. Sally Meeks as "Utah's oldest Pioneer," and was evidently misquoted by the Gunnison Gazette. We republish the item, which is from our Leeds correspondence of the 16th ult. Editor, NEWS.]

"Mrs. Mary J. Meeks and son of Glendale, Kane Co., arrived here on the 13th and departed on the 14th, taking with them Utah's oldest pioneer, Mrs. Sally Meeks, aged 97 years."

Young Hartley of Leeds passed thru Santa Clara Monday enroute home from the Muddy valley, where he has been working for some time.

Washington County News
March 24, 1900

LEEDS.

Mrs. William Harris has returned from Cedar City.

Miss Mary Leany of Harrisburg was a visitor here Thursday.

Oscar McMullin, who has been working at the Grand Gulch, is home again.

Cards are out announcing the wedding of Miss Sadie Wilkinson of this place and Isaac Willis of Toquerville.

Miss Vina Chidester, formerly of this place, who has been visiting her mother here, Mrs. Jane Chidester, has returned to Salt Lake City.

Washington County News
March 31, 1900

LEEDS.

Don Fuller is very ill.

The District schools closed on the 23rd inst.

Oscar McMullin and wife are visiting in St. George.

Mrs. B. Y. McMullin is visiting her parents at Washington, Robert Parker and wife.

Orson Harris, William Nicholls, and William Beams have gone to Grand Gulch to work.

Mrs. William Beams has gone to Virgin, where she will reside until her husband returns from Grand Gulch.

Democrats are holding a rally tonight, the 28th inst. The speakers are David H. Morris, James Andrus, and Thomas P. Cottam, all of St. George.

A marriage license was issued on Tuesday by County Clerk Miles to Isaac Willis of Toquerville and Miss Sadie E. Wilkinson of Leeds. They were married by Pres. David H. Cannon.

Washington County News
April 7, 1900

LEEDS.

E. C. Olsen and wife have gone to St. George on business.

Weather quite chilly, light rain this afternoon, the 4th inst.

Election passed off quietly, the results being, King 49, Hammond 8.

Mrs. Hannah Deady and family have moved to Cedar City on account of the drouth.

Coleman and Maud Harris and Miss Julia Ford have returned home from Cedar City.

Job Smith and wife have gone to Panguitch to meet their daughter, Mrs. Milton Stout.

Bert McQuarrie, a popular merchant of St. George, was seen admiring the eagle over the door of the Eagle store the fore part of the week.

ELECTION RETURNS.

PRECINCT.	KING.	HAMMOND.
Shonesburg	10	0
Springdale	16	15
Rockville	19	11
Grafton	27	2
Virgin	40	14
Toquerville	45	32
Leeds	49	8
Washington	65	40
St. George	351	75
Bloomington	15	8
Santa Clara	54	10
Gunlock	22	5
Pine Valley	50	3
Hebron	22	0
Enterprise	9	2
Pinto	21	8
Harmony	12	23

Washington County News
April 28, 1900

LEEDS.

Job T. Smith and family have returned from a visit to Tropic, Garfield county.

Mrs. E. Leany and daughter of Harrisburg were visiting relatives here Wednesday.

Weather cold and cloudy, rain the fore part of the week. Farmers and stockmen alike are rejoicing over the prospects for feed and crops.

LEEDS.

Mrs. Oscar McMullin's baby is quite sick.

Miss Chloe Fuller is quite sick with the grippe.

Isaac Macfarlane passed thru here on the 17th inst.

Isaac Willis and wife have returned from Deer Lodge.

Charles Nichols and family have moved to Silver Reef,

Master Charles Hanson has gone to Cedar City, where he expects to study music under Prof. Anderson.

James Andrus and Samuel Adams were at Silver Reef Tuesday, making some repairs at the Barbee mill. It is expected that the mill will start up about the 23rd inst.

Washington County News
May 5, 1900

SILVER REEF.

The Barbee Mill is running steadily.

Richard Whitehouse has a fine body of high-grade ore in the Thompson mine.

Miss Julia Ford has returned from Cedar City and is visiting friends in this place.

Dr. J. T. Affleck and wife of St. George was visiting friends at the Reef on the 27th ult.

Kuhn and Olsen shipped twenty-one tons of ore from the Newton mine which netted them $1000.

A continuous storm of ten days duration has settled the water question, and this year the farmers of Leeds will be sellers of hay instead of buyers.

LEEDS.

Mrs. H. A. Fuller has gone to St. George.

Mrs. Mary Olsen is visiting relatives in St. George.

Walter H. Slack of Toquerville was in town Monday on business.

Mrs. August Kuhn of Silver Reef was here today visiting her mother, Mrs. Harris.

Bp. B. Y. McMullin and George Angell were in St. George on business the fore part of the week.

Roy Grundy and Bert McQuarrie, former residents of Silver Reef, were shaking hands with old friends here on the 6th.

Bert Harris returned from Cedar City this morning, the 10th, bringing with him his brothers Bennett and Lue, who have been attending school there.

SILVER REEF.

Charles Bastian and wife of Washington were visiting friends in the Reef on the 13th inst.

The Free Coinage mine has been closed down for a few days, awaiting the arrival of supplies.

Richard Higbee of Stateline has joined the chloriders here and is busy taking ore out of the Newton mine.

The Mill shut down on the 18th inst. to make repairs on the engine and wait the arrival of the new turbine wheel.

Four bars of silver bullion, carrying a total of 5532 ounces of fine silver, have just been shipped from the Barbee Mill.

LEEDS.

Cherries are ripe. Weather dry and windy.

The Barbee mill at Silver Reef has shut down until new machinery arrives.

Mrs. Thomas Sterling presented her husband with a ten-pound boy on the 12th inst.

Mrs. Charles Bastian of Washington is visiting her mother, Mrs. Hartley of this town.

Miss Maud Harris returned from St. George, where she had been visiting friends, Tuesday evening.

Mrs. Schlappy and daughter, Mrs. Andrus, both of Middleton, are visiting Mrs. E. C. Olsen here.

LEEDS.

The Barbee mill at Silver Reef has resumed work.

Weather extremely hot and dry; water getting very low.

Joseph Orton and wife of St. George were visiting relatives here Sunday.

W. H. Nichols, who has been working at Grand Gulch for some time, has returned home.

Mrs. John Wilkinson and son Harry have gone to Salt Lake City on business; Mrs. Isaac Willis is keeping house in her absence.

Elder William Stirling, who has been laboring in the Scottish mission for the past twenty-one months, has returned home on account of the illness of his wife.

Job T. Smith and wife entertained a number of their most intimate friends Monday evening, the occasion being their daughter Adelaide's twentieth birthday. The time was spent in music and games.

Prosecuting Attorney D. H. Morris was here on the 30th ult. to prosecute Mrs. M. E. Cobb for appropriating water out of the Harrisburg ditch to water the trees on the Stormont property. He failed to convict defendant.

LEEDS.

Irrigating Problems—Utility of Winter Irrigation Proved.

Special Correspondence.

Leeds, Washington Co., June 12.—Notwithstanding occasional copious rains have seemingly "broken" the drouth, we are still very short of water. As the two last winters have been exceptionally dry, subsoil evaporation is all exhausted, both irrigation and rain has but a very brief and limited effect. Those who have persistently irrigated during the winter receive now returns from their labor in the more durable effect of their present irrigation. But where water runs a long distance in a small ditch as is the case at Harrisburg the evaporation and seepage drinks it all up; exhibiting a practical object lesson on the necessity of using a small stream as near as possible to its source. This is the second summer of a suspension of irrigation water at that place, and hopes are entertained that the owners of the stream may see it to their advantage to place their water where they will not lose it all in a dry time, when most needed. The same measurement of water which runs towards Harrisburg, when used at Leeds with moderate care covers the acreage for which it is measured, while of course the stream is much below the average.

Silver Reef Looking Good.

S. A. Higbee, M. E. Paris and W D. Newton were in this city from Silver Reef Wednesday. Mr. Higbee is the manager of the Barbee mill at the Reef, and from him our reporter learned that everything is looking very prosperous at the old silver camp, but that the mill has shut down for the present awaiting the arrival of a new turbine wheel from the East that has been sidetracked on the railroad somewhere for nearly two months. Mr. Higbee also informed us that W. D. Newton had sold his mine, the Newton, for a large sum of money. This mine has made nearly $4000 for Mr. Newton during the last year, and is one of the new Reef properties.

LOCAL CHRONOLOGY

of the Most Important Events Recorded in the Home Paper for the Newspaper Year Ending June 16, 1900.

JUNE.

20. Home of Daniel Matthews, Sr., of Virgin destroyed by fire.

23. Orin N. Woodbury died.

27. Sterling Russsl of Grafton breaks his left arm by falling from an apple tree.

30. Hottest day of the year, 109 in the shade.

JULY.

3. Kenneth Snow severly burned by the explosion of a toy cannon.

16. Willard Uttley Carter died.

25. Twin girls born to the wife of Francis Hartly at Harrisburg.

29. John Mathis died.

AUGUST.

1. Mary A. B. Larson died.

4. Joseph Hammond died.

5. John W. Isom died at Virgin.

SEPTEMBER.

2. Fourth crop of lucern being harvested.

9. Samuel Brocklebank Hardy died, aged 95 years, leaving 198 decendants.

18. Opening day of the initial Washington County Fair.

20. Closing day of the Washington County Fair, which proved an immense success.

21. The Grand Gulch Mining company started work on their mining property.

23. Twins born to the wife of Emil Barlocker at Pinto.

OCTOBER.

23. Jerusha Cecelia Gray died.

28. Orin Leavitt of Bunkerville died.

NOVEMBER.

1. Ivins Cottam died.

20. Work commenced on the Savanac mine.

DECEMBER.

4. Forwarding business established at Modena.

14. Coldest day of the year; lowest temperature at night 5 degrees above zero.

16. The Dixie copper smelter blew in at its new location in this city.

19. Elizabeth Moore Bleak died.

20. Joseph Prince of Washington had a leg broken by a horse falling on it.

21. Joseph Crawford of Washington has one wrist broken and the other dislocated by a load of wood capsizing with him.

23. Berto Coates breaks his left arm by falling off a horse.

30. Ann Neaderer Sturzenegger died.

JANUARY.

3. Twin girls born to the wife of Lyman Dodge of Toquerville.

4. Edwin Canfield of Gunlock died.

17. Julia Anna Ivins Pace died.

18. Mary Jane Oliver Barlow drowned in an irrigating ditch.

24. Bishop Gottlieb Hirschi of Rockville died.

25. Fire does damage to the extent of $500 at the home of John Eardley, Jr.

FEBRUARY.

10. Fire destroys the cabin and other property at the Copper Mountain mine.

Charles Barnum of Bunkerville has an arm broken by being run over by a wagon.

11. Lamar Gray has his right arm broken by a fall.

14. Mrs. Sally Meĕks, aged 97 years and Utah's oldest pioneer, leaves her home at Leeds to stay with relatives at Glendale.

Berto Coates has his left arm broken.

22. Two mountain lions killed at Grafton.

MARCH.

1. Work resumed on the Copper Mountain mine.
2. Work commenced on the State Southern Experiment Farm.
23. Twin boys born to the wife of Joseph S. Snow.
27. Mary, the eight-year-old daughter of Bishop Jeter and Mary Alice Snow died.

APRIL.

2. Mrs. Neilson of Rockville died.
Twin boys born to the wige of Thomas Adams of Bunkerville.
11. Mrs. Flora C. Dunlap died.
25. St. George Cattle Co. incorporated.
28. Laura Ann Liston Lang died.

MAY.

10. Fire destroyed the home of John Morse.
15. Don Smith Carter accidently shot in right leg
22. William Atkin died.
25. Twin boys born to the wife of Wallace B Mathis.
First early apples on the market.

JUNE.

1. Savanac Copper Mining Co. incorporated.
2. First apricots and pears on the market.
An Indian meets death by accidental shooting at the Indian farm.
4. Peaches ripe.
5. Second crop of lucern being cut.
6. Wheat being harvested.
First crop of figs ripe.

LEEDS.

W. H. Angell has returned home from Silver city.

Early apples, pears. peaches, apricots and currants are ripe.

M. E. Paris, S. A. Higbee and W. D. Newton were in St. George the fore part of the week on business.

Mrs. Sarah Forsha and daughter, June, former residents of Silver Reef, are visiting Mrs. R. S. Harris of that place.

The Misses Julia Ford and Lizzie McMullin have gone to Cedar city, the former for her health and the latter to attend the Summer school.

Elders Richard Morris and A. R. Whitehead of St. George, and George Spilsbury of Toquerville, were here last Sunday in the interest of the Sunday school. William Stirling, Jr., was made Supt. of our Sunday school.

Bishop McMullin returned from Cedar city Monday, bringing with him his daughter, Ada, Miss Minnie Hanson, Clare McMullin and Charles Hanson. All with the exception of Bp. McMullin and Charles Hanson have been attending the branch Normal school.

Washington County News
June 23, 1900

William Stirling of Leeds paid our sanctum a pleasant call Monday. Bro. Stirling has recently returned from the Scottish mission, and reports having enjoyed his labors very much. His wife is seriously ill.

Washington County News
June 30, 1900

are visiting friends and relatives in Leeds.

Born—A daughter to the wife of August Kuhn on the 15th inst.; all concerned doing well.

Housewives are busy bottling and drying fruit; the men are taking care of the hay crop. Weather very hot.

Citizens of Leeds are preparing to celebrate the 4th of July in grand style. The supposed reason of this move is to keep the people from attending the Paris Exposition.

M. E. Paris of Leeds was in St. George on business Wednesday.

Mrs. Walter Dodge arrived on the stage from Leeds Thursday morning

Washington County News
July 7, 1900

The Barbee mill at Silver Reef resumed running last week, and some nice looking silver bullion came in to Andrus & Son's store this week. The mill is now fitted up with a new Leifelle wheel, and is working splendidly.

LEEDS.

Leeds, Utah, July 5, 1900.

Mrs. Julia Beames of Virgin is visiting relatives here.

The weather has somewhat moderated, at present the evenings are really chilly.

The Misses Minnie Hanson and Sarah Chidester are visiting relatives in St. George.

Miss Mattie McArthur of St. George is visiting her cousin here, Miss Maud McMullin.

Mrs. Jane Chidester has gone to Parowan to spend the remainder of the summer with her daughter, Mrs. Lue Meeks.

The Misses Lizzie and Ann McMullin have returned home from Cedar city, where they have been attending the Summer School and Teachers Institute.

The Fourth of July celebration held here was counted by all a success. The program of the day's amusements was a parade and meeting in the forenoon sports and children's dance in the afternoon, and a dance for the adults at night at which a number of young folks from Toquerville were present.

LEEDS.

Leeds, Utah, July 19, 1900.

Miss Sarah Chidester has gone to Parowan to spend a few weeks.

A number of the young people have gone to Panguitch lake for the 24th.

Mrs. S A. Higbee of Silver Reef has returned from Cedar city, where she has been visiting relatives.

Elders Ira McMullin and William Stirling went to Harmony on the 15th inst. to fill a missionary appointment.

W. H. Thompson, of Henriville, Garfield Co, came here on the 14th and returned on the 19th, taking with him Miss Adelaide Smith as his bride.

The date following your name on this

ASSAYER AND CHEMIST—W. E Terhune, with the St. George Copper Mining & Smelting Co. Ores assayed and returns made the same day. Rates reasonable.

Washington County News
July 21, 1900

W. D. Newton of Silver Reef was in this city Wednesday. Mr. Newton says that the mines of Silver Reef are looking better than at any time during the past nine years, and that the Barbee mill is running nicely, the new Liefelle wheel working to perfection.

Another bar of silver bullion was brought down from Silver Reef by Bp. James Andrus yesterday.

M. E. Paris, of Leeds, assessor of Mohave county, Arizona, passed thru here Friday.

Washington County News
July 28, 1900

Over 5000 ounces of bar silver was received by Bishop Andrus from the Barbee mill at Silver Reef, Wednesday.

Deseret News
October 22, 1900

NEW POSTMASTER FOR LEEDS.

[SPECIAL TO THE "NEWS."]

Washington, D. C., Oct. 22.—Helen E. McMullen was appointed postmaster of Leeds, Washington county, Utah, vice Ira S. McMullen, removed.

Deseret News
November 28, 1900

LEEDS.

ONE WEEK OF RAIN.

A Seven Years' Phenomena — Death of Mrs. Sarah A. Stirling.

Special Correspondence.

Leeds, Washington county, Nov. 24.— A solid week's rain in most parts of Utah is nothing of which to make a news item, but in this place where such a thing happens only once in seven or more years, it is, after the protracted drouth, something of a sensation, of which we take much pleasure in making the world duly acquainted.

DEATH OF SARAH ANN STIRLING.

Mrs. Sarah A. Stirling, the president of the Relief Society of this ward, died October 24th, and at the funeral on the following day, Bishop Murdock of Beaver and Elder Spilsbury of Toquer, and other speakers, dilated upon the faithful and useful character of the deceased.

Deseret News
December 8, 1900

MRS. ELIZABETH PIXTON.

Mrs. Elizabeth Pixton, the subject of this sketch, is one of the many women who, coming to Utah in the days of the great exodus from Nauvoo, have taken zealous part in the progressive and philanthropic enterprises which have helped in the upbuilding of the State. Mrs. Pixton was born in England and with her family, who had embraced the principles of the "Mormon" faith, came to America in the "fortys," settling with the rest of her family in Nauvoo.

Shortly after coming to America she was married to Robert Pixton, who at the time of the Mexican war was one of the "Mormon" Battalion whose members served in that conflict. The time of the forming of the battalion was during the troublous period of the exodus from Nauvoo, and Mrs. Pixton with two helpless children was forced to drive her own team across the plains—a task whose difficult nature can be imagined from the hardship and suffering incident to the rigors of the long journey. Arriving in Salt Lake in 1848, Mrs. Pixton was here joined later by her husband, and after a time spent in the capital city—went with him to Taylorsville, which place has, with the exception of a few years spent in southern Utah, been her home. Mrs. Pixton served as president of the first Relief Society organized in Taylorsville, and in Leeds, where she later resided, was appointed to the same position. Upon her return to Taylorsville she was again made president of the Relief Society there, a position which she still holds. She has been an ardent advocate and worker in the suffrage cause and has taken prominent part in the politics of her locality her principles having a pronounced Republican bias. In February last she celebrated her 80th birthday anniversary, the occasion being made memorable by a notable gathering of friends in her honor. Notwithstanding her advanced age she retains her faculties to a remarkable degree of perfection, and still continues to take an active interest in the practical concerns in which she has long taken part.

LEEDS.

Demise of Orson B. Adams, Pioneer Battalion Survivor.

Special Correspondence.

Leeds, Washington Co., Feb. 8.—Orson B. Adams, a pioneer and one of the survivors of the Mormon Battalion, died here Feb. 4, 1901. He came to Utah the year following the pioneer company. In 1850 he started out again in the pioneering expedition which reached Parowan, or rather the place where Parowan now stands, on Jan. 13, 1851, and assisted in the same labor of making it possible to live where savages and wild beasts only had ever maintained an existence. Parowan proved to be one of the hardest places in the Rocky Mountain region in which to maintain civilized existence, but he, unlike many others, stuck faithfully to it, until some further pioneering labor was solicited by the leaders, when ten years after arriving at Parowan he volunteered to help break the way into the present county of Washington, where, at the little town of Harrisburg, he settled and lived until about five years before his death. He was born in the State of New York March 9th, 1815, and was within 33 days of being 86 years of age. At the funeral which was held in the Latter-day Saints' meeting house in Leeds, Feb. 5th, his battalion associate, John Steele of Toquerville, testified to his faithfulness, endurance, patience and courage on the trying journey across the deserts and his steady and consistent conduct during sixty years of his acquaintance, commencing with the time of his baptism into the Mormon Church until his death. Other speakers bore testimony to his virtues as a Latter-day Saint, and as an honest man.

He left but one living child and 12 grandchildren and 9 great grandchildren.

Six grandsons bore his remains to the grave, where the sweet music of the Toquerville choir consigned his spirit to the angels, while his body was laid in the earth.

Nine inches of snow and considerable rain has cheered the hearts of the stock men and farmers during the past week.

Leeds Tailings Dump Bonded.

Encouraging developments continue to come to light concerning the projects being furthered for the handling of the old Silver Reef tailings, says the Dixie Advocate. A. E. Vandercook of San Francisco and Benjamin Hastings of Arizona, were here the fore part of the week, presumably in the interests of J. R. Hull. While Messrs. Vandercook and Hastings were here a bond was secured on the tailings from the old Leeds mill, on a royalty basis of 50 cents per ton, and the bonders agree to handle not less than 60 tons per month and to have their plant ready to commence operations within 90 days. John Kempe, a mining man from California, who had a foresight to locate the tailings as placer ground, was the vendor.

It is learned that the same syndicate that has bonded the Barbee & Walker and Leeds mill tailings have also secured an option on the Christy tailings through the local representative of the Christy Co., R. C. Lund. It is estimated that this mill alone has 218,000 tons. If the option is taken up by the company, there will be in all four plants erected with a total capacity of 100 tons per day.

HARMONY.

Earthquake Shock More or Less Severe Throughout Dixie.

Special Correspondence.

Harmony, Washington Co., Nov. 14.—The harmony of this little hamlet was disturbed last night by a severe shock of earthquake which occurred about 9:30 o'clock. The shock was so severe that it spread fear throughout every home—one described it "as though the bedstead upon which he slept was in the hands of a giant being pushed violently back and forth from south to north." The shock lasted for a full minute, and disturbed the peace of those awake and the slumbers of those asleep.

The same shock was felt at Duffin ranch by the inmates of the house, but was not noticed by a number of cattle men camped in the yard. At Bellevue the shock was also felt. At Leeds the shock was very severe.

Harmony is a quiet little hamlet, presided over by Bishop Wm. Redd; some of the trees have a very old appearance—some apricot trees in the orchard of Mrs. Margaret E. Pace are veritable giants.

The Deseret News is the paper of the little hamlet—being about the only paper taken here.

Deseret News
December 17, 1901

LEEDS.

SHOCKING FATALITY.

Little Child of Bishop McMullin's Burned to Death.

Special Correspondence.

Leeds, Washington Co., Dec. 13.—Alice Laverne, daughter of Bishop McMullin, died on November 27,, of accidental burning, aged five years and twenty-seven days.

The particulars of the above unfortunate accident are in brief as follows: A younger brother and she having obtained matches, kindled a small fire some distance from the house, from which her clothes caught fire and before help could be obtained was fatally burned. She lingered in suffering some fifty hours, and then expired. It was a very severe shock to the whole community, as well as to the grief-stricken parents.

We have recently had the visitation of a Josephite missionary, who was listened to with respectful attention in the delivery of three discourses.

Deseret News
March 6, 1902

Remains of Miss Sterling Will be Forwarded Home Tonight.

Doctors Mayo and Ellerbeck made a careful exterior examination of the remains of the late Jessie Sterling and were convinced that an autopsy was unnecessary in that everything indicated the deceased had died from natural causes. So Undertaker Joseph William Taylor embalmed the body this morning, and will ship it this evening south to Leeds, Washintgon county, as he has been notified by the girl's family to do so. Two lady acquaintances of Miss Sterling called at the undertaker's this morning, to state that they were well acquainted with her in Washington county before coming to Salt Lake, as well as after her arrival here, and spoke in the highest terms of her. Mrs. White, aunt of the deceased, and Miss Annie Malin, the nurse, called at the undertaker's and selected a casket. Mrs. White was indignant at the neighborhood gossip about her niece, as there was not the slightest warrant for it, and moreover she stated that the girl had worked in a restaurant but one day.

Iron County Record
January 21, 1903

Jan, 21st, 1903.

Mr Jessup and family of Harrisburg, are moving to Leeds to-day for the rest of the winter, so as to send their children to school.

Miss Julia Ford left by stage last night for Salt Lake City, where she expects to stay for about three months studying obstetrics.

A howling success struck the home of Mr B. Paris last week in the shape of a son and heir, Mr Paris' boys have heretofore been all girls, hence the success in the present instance.

Mrs Wilder of Silver Reef, took one of her little boys to the doctor at St. George last Sunday. The Child has been ill for some time, and it is reported that he has heart desease.

Last Friday afternoon was spent by the local sports and a delegation from Washington, in horse racing. In the evening there was a show, and to complete the entertainment they had a dance.

Iron County Record
April 10, 1903

Miss Minnie Hanson who has been teaching school at Enterprise, was a visitor at school last Friday. After spending a week at her home in Leeds she expects to return and attend school the rest of the term

We extend congratulations to Miss Minnie Chatterley of this city who we are informed has found a suitable marriage partner in the person of Mr. Ben Harris of Leeds. We wish the young people happiness.

June 24, 1903.

Apricots are ripe.

M. R. Paris has gone to Lund for merchandise.

Preparations are in progress for the celebration of the 4th of July.

Clarence McMullin went to Stateline last week where he expects to remain during the summer.

Miss Minnie Hanson has been taking care of Mrs. Hamilton at Silver Reef, who is sick, this week.

A lad with his arm in a sling, and carrying a printed plea for alms was visiting the houses of the Leeds folks the other day. His traveling companions appeared to be two able bodied men in a fine buggie drawn by a pair of fat horses. Needless to say the contributions under such circumstances were not large.

Iron County Record
July 1, 1903

Leeds July 1st, 1903.

David McMullin who has been working at Milford the past winter returned home last Friday.

Ira S. MdMullin went to Kanarra Saturday. He will lay the foundation of the new District School house.

S. Leroy Harris and family of Silver Reef have been visiting at St. George this week.

Our "Stirling" citizens will have the repairs that they are making on their amusement hall, completed by the 4th. The building has recieved a new coat of paint on the inside.

Iron County Record
July 8, 1903

July 8, 1903.

Bro. and sister Schlappy of Middletown are here visiting with their daughter Mrs. Mary Olsen.

Mr. August Kuhn came home last week from the Dixie mine, where he is employed, to spend the Fourth with us.

Mr. John Tullis of Pinto spent the Fourth in Leeds, putting in most of his time at Stirling's, where Miss Ida seemed to be the principal attraction.

We have had quite a variety of diversion here lately, commencing with the celebration of the Fourth, and embracing dances, theatres, storms, ice cream, etc.

Iron County Record
July 15, 1903

July 15, 1903.

[Received too late for last issue]

Mrs Susan Harris is sick with the chills and fever.

Word was recieved the other day to the effect that our bishop is now a grandfather.

Isaac Willis and family have moved to big Horn, where they expect to make their home.

Neil Forsyth while passing through town the other day took occasion to call upon some of the Normal students.

Miss Bessie Workman of Panguitch is in town for the purpose of bottling fruit, and expects to remain about a month.

Iron County Record
July 29, 1903

July 29, 1903.

Miss Alice Stirling started to States line last Sunday.

Mrs. Elizabeth Wilkinson has been quite sick with the chills and fever, but is some better now.

Will Reams and family have moved in from the Dixie mine and were here for the Twenty-fourth.

The Twenty-fourth passed off quite pleasantly. We had as visitors some of the Virgin City people.

Bp. McMullin started to Milford Monday to meet his wife, who has been in Salt Lake with her daughter, Mrs. Lew Harris, for some time.

I. S. McMullin, who is working on the Kanarra school house, came home Sunday for a short visit, returning to his work by last nights stage.

Frank Anderson and Richard Forsyth were here for the Twenty-fourth, the latter paying most of his attentions to Miss Mame Olsen.

Mr. and Mrs Charles Bastian of St. George came over today on a short visit to relatives. They expect to take a trip on the mountains in the interest of Mrs. Bastian's health.

Iron County Record
September 23, 1903

Sept. 23rd 1903.

Mr. E. Paris brought goods for Hanson's store Monday.

Johny Tullis was again a visitor in the lower part of town last week.

The weather is a few degrees warmer, and a scarciety of rain drops is felt.

Mrs. Susanna Harris who has been sick with chills and fever is much better.

The Young Ladies will begin the work of the season this evening with a feast for the body as well as the spirit.

Miss. Anna Adams of Parowan was here Saturday. Her friends among the Normal students were glad to see her.

Iron County Record
September 29, 1903

Sept. 29th, 1903.

Mrs. Lizzie Mcfarlane of Cedar is visiting her mother Mrs. Brown.

Roy Harris of Long Valley is here visiting his brother William Harris.

Yesterday and to-day it has rained.

Mrs. Hattie Stirling has been sick this week.

Miss Mamie Olson is home again from St. George, where she has been working for some time.

Misses Ann and Etta McMullin and Miss Lylie Olsen will leave this week for school at Cedar City.

By this time the Bell Telephone Co. has its line through Bellevue. It is reported that they intend running a spur over to Toquerville before building to Leeds and on to St. George.

Iron County Record
October 23, 1903

RECENT COPPER DISCOVERY.

Vein of Malachite Ore That Is Forty Feet Wide.

J. S. FERRIS' GRAND DUMP CLAIM.

The Red Metal Discovered in Great Quantities in the Iron Belt of Iron County.

J. S. Ferris, well known in Washington county as an old timer in connection with the famous sandstone formation in the Silver Reef mining district, and who is the finder of the diamonds that have attracted the attention of the people in this part of the state recently, came into town Sunday evening from some copper claims that he has recently found, which he says are likely to rival the big mine near St. George. The vein on the Grand Dump claim is over 40 feet wide on the surface carrying malachite ore and red oxide that looks fine for the width of the vein. These prospects are in close proximity to the Bullion Canyon claims in which a number of our well known citizens are interested, and Mr. Ferris informs us that it is the intention of some of the owners of the Bullion Canyon mine to go out to the new prospects to examine them some time this week.

One claim which Mr. Ferris calls the Red Bird is 12 feet between walls, located on a high volcanic porphry reef. When asked as to the status of the diamond mines or claims, the veteran smilingly assured us that the story is no myth. He discovered the diamond gulch over two years ago and got encouraging returns from specimens that he sent east for inspection at that time, but for reasons which he did not explain he kept quiet. He is now in communication with a prominent jewelry house in Chicago in relation to the matter. Stones as large as partridge eggs he claimed are only a common pick-up in Diamond Gulch. There is something in Utah that people don't know yet, said the old man as he hurried off with the manner of a man that had not a moment to lose.

Nov. 2, 1903.

Miss Minnie Hanson began teaching school at Harrisburg this morning.

Mrs. Lena Kuhn, who has been living with her husband at the Apex mine, is here visiting relatives for a few days.

Last Saturday evening the young ladies gave a Halloween party at the Stirling residence. We hear that they had "Just a lovely time."

Frank Sullivan, while running a horse—race last night, was thrown from his horse and had his arm quite badly hurt. He is unable to use it.

Last Friday afternoon, while playing ball with the children during recess, Mr. Lewis Bastian sprained his ankle quite badly, but is able to continue school this morning.

Mrs. Wardle of Oregon, who has been visiting with her mother, Mrs. Hanson, for some time, was made happy last Wednesday night by the arrival of a pair of twin babies—a boy and a girl—each weighing eight and a half pounds. They are claimed to be the first twins ever born in Leeds.

Miss Julia Ford of Leeds is in Cedar visiting relatives and attending to business. Miss Ford has spent considerable time in Salt Lake City of late years studying obstetrics.

Feb. 1. 1904.

Wm. Sullivan and wife went to St. George Friday to visit relatives.

Our principal, Lewis Bastian, on account of feeling severely sick was obliged to dismiss school before recess for the day. He is somewhat better tonight.

Ice cream, like many other things, has its day. Our young folks have had quite a number of ice cream suppers this winter. Very nice for those who like them.

There were three missionaries here yesterday who held a meeting last night. We hear they are going to set our church right, although they do not belong to any church.

There is quite a bit of sickness at present, bad colds and fevers. Mrs. Ann Thomas is said to be very sick. Mrs. Mary Olson was very sick last week, but is around again at this writing.

Iron County Record
March 26, 1904

By this time the Bell Telephone Co. has its line through Bellevue. It is reported that they intend running a spur over to Toquerville before building to Leeds and on to St. George.

Find Coal at Silver Reef Ledge.

A. B. Harris, who is spending a visit in St. George, accompanied by George Brooks and Sherm Hardy, made a trip to Silver Reef last Sunday. While in that vicinity they discovered what appeared to be an outcropping of coal. The material was tested by burning and was found to ignite readily. Only one outcropping was found, but at this point the vein was about eighteen inches through. Mr. Harris, who is a miner of considerable experience, spoke positively as to the substance being coal, and stated that he believed the find would at least bear investigation.

LEEDS

Leeds, Utah, Nov. 27th, 1904.

Henry Peterson and family have moved to their home at Grapevine.

John Tullis came down from Pinto last Friday and paid an affectionate visit to the Stirling residence.

Mr. Shepperd of Ohio is in the Reef and it is said that he will spend the winter with his daughter, Mrs. Crecelius.

Mrs. Druie Jolly of Big Horn is here visiting her mother, Mrs. Hartley, and it is said she intends to spend the winter here.

Mls Jenine Angell of Leeds, who has been in the hospital in this city for several weeks, was sufficiently recovered to be able to go to Enoch with her sister last Saturday, but was taken worse last Monday and Doctor Middleton was sent for Monday evening. Since then the patient has been very ill, and Thursday her parents came up from Leeds. Today she is reported as not being quite so well as she was yesterday, and the doctor say her condition is extremely critical.

John Tullis returned last evening having went to Shem on a flying trip, and of course the roads were so bad he deemed it advisable to return by way of Leeds. When he reached there he had to wait for his wings to get stronger before pursuing his journey. Never mind, John, there are some "Stirling" young girls in Leeds.

Special Correspondence.

St. George, Washington Co., March 11.— Yesterday County Sheriff Frank R. Bentley and U. S. Internal Revenue Collector Archibald Stewart made a flying trip to Leeds, and were successful in locating two illicit white eye stills, which were seized and brought to St. George today. The government will re-

voke the title to all real estate on which these stills are found. The officers are determined to stop the nefarious business in the county, and this makes the fourth captured within a year.

Iron County Record
March 17, 1905

CALLED AWAY IN BLOOM OF YOUTH.

Miss Jennie Angell of Leeds has Joined the Great Majority.

The death of Miss Jennie Angell of Leeds which occurred at Eno h last Sunday morning, has been antici- pated by her friends and relatives for some time , as the attending physician notified them that her case was incur- able; yet it was hoped that she would rally sucffiiently to enable her to be taken home. The young lady was sixteen years old and was a great favorite among her friends, industri- ous, intelligent and amiable.

She was living in Enoch and attend- ing the school there that her older sister was conducting. She was taken ill about the middle of January and subsequently brought to Cedar for treatment in the hosiptal, where she remained for three or four weeks, and was so much better that she was, at her earnest desire, allowed to re- turn to Enoch, but she had not been there more than two or three days before she was taken down again, and her parents were sent for. Her mother was at her side from then till she passed away. The people of Enoch were unremitting in their kind- ness to the afflicted family and did everything they could to help them in their distress, and Jennie's parents and sister say that they think there is hardly another such kind hearted little community in existence. The remains were taken to Leeds for burial Monday, Sunady having been spent in the preparation of the body for transportation. The funreal took palce at Leeds Tuesday. We extend depest sympathy to the bereaved parents and relatives.

Mr. Lafayette McConnell went down to Leeds the first of the week to attend the funreal of his cous- in, Miss Jennie Angell, who died at Enoch, this county, at 2 o'clock Sunday morning.

.... LEEDS ....

Leeds Utah, April 18,, 190.

The prospects seem quite favorable for another storm.

The health of some of our people is not as good as might be desired.

Alex Y. Milne of St. George has been here the past week painting for different ones in town.

Rumor says that Miss Julia Ford will soon open a hotel here, in fact that Mr. Milne has painted the sign.

About two weeks ago a sweet little baby girl was made welcome at the home of Mr. and Mrs. Wm. Sullivan.

Mr. and Mrs. Dan Parker are the proud parents of a baby boy, which was born last Sunday night. All well.

INFORMATION WANTED.

Mrs. Norman D. Simmons, R. F. D. No. 7, Oswego, N. Y., desires to learn the whereabouts of anyone connected with Catherine Magilvaria Ellsworth, who lived at Payson, Utah, between 1850 and 1860, and moved to southern Utah about 1862 or 1863, living in Leeds and then moving to Kanab, Kane county, where she and her husband, David Ellsworth, passed away. Mrs. Magilvaria had two sons and one daughter before she married Ellsworth, and it is these or their children who are now inquired after.

Leeds, Utah, May 23, 1905.

Oscar S. McMullin and Wm. Beams returned home from the Grand Gulch last week.

We enjoyed the visit of Elders Jarvis and Webb of St. George last Sunday.

Miss Bess Angell has been home for something more than a week, she having finished her school teaching on the 13th inst.

On account of the cave-in at the Dixie mine, David McMullin, Wm. Stirling and Lester Harris came home yesterday.

Mrs. Susie Stirling came home from St. George Friday night, as her sister, Mrs. Maud McQuarrie, is on the improve.

About thirty mining men from California have been in our vicinity during the last two weeks, hunting for almost everything, including wives, coal oil, copper, silver, sand-rock, coal, salt, etc.

........,LEEDS............

Leeds, Utah, May 30, 1905.

A celebration will be held here on Brigham Young's birthday.

Mrs. Eliabeth Wilkinson is on the sick-list.

Wm. Stirling, Sr., is back from St. George again and is able to get around wih the aid of crutches.

Mrs. Ada McMullin was pleasantly surprised last Friday afternoon, when a number of ladies came and sewed a basket of carpet rags for her.

A man known as Dan McMann, who loafed around here after the cave-in at tne Dixie, is said to be Butch Cassady.

A surprise was given to Charles Hanson and Willard McMullin Sunday evening by way of saying good-bye to them for a while, as they went to Newhouse to work the following morning.

.........LEEDS...........

Leeds, Utah, June 5, 1905.

People are hauling their first cutting of hay.

The mill in Silver Reef started to run again Saturday.

Miss Minnie Hanosn will take the state examination in Parowan.

The Leeds people are going to celebrate the Fourth of July.

The Misses Hannah and Florence Deady of Harrisburg have come home from Cedar, having attended the Branch Normal the past winter.

The Misses Lizzie McMullin and Bess Angel will start for Salt Lake Tuesday to attend the summer school.

..........LEEDS...........

Leeds, Utah, June 27, 1905.

A Mr. Stuart is in town and is paynig very marked attentions to one of our fair damsels.

Mrs. Hamilton of Silver Reef started to Montana last week to visit her chilrden who reside there.

On Thursday the Misses Alice and Ruth Stirling and Maude McArthur expect to start to Newhouse.

Quite a number of our people are doctoring for malarial fever, trying to ward it off, while some are already afflicted with it.

Mrs. Arthur Nichols of Silver Reef returned from St. George Sunday night where she has been under the doctor's care for some time. She has been quite sick, but is now some better.

Mr. John Tullis and Miss Ida Stirling of this place started to St. George today and will be married tomorrow. The reception will be held tomorrow evening at the home of the bride. Ida is one of our very nicest and best young ladies.

DR. M. H. HARDY IS CALLED HOME.

Late Superintendent of State Mental Hospital Succumbs to Heart Failure.

DEATH SUDDEN, UNEXPECTED.

Had Been Ailing for Some Time, but Was Thought to be on the High Road to Recovery.

(Special to the "News.")

Provo, Aug. ―. Dr. Milton H. Hardy, one of the best educated men in the state and until quite recently medical superintendent of the state Mental hospital, died last night at his residence in this city, a victim of heart failure. Dr. Hardy had a severe attack of leakage of the heart early in the spring and was confined to his bed for several week. He recovered sufficiently to be out and was thought to be on the high road to complete convalescence, when early this week he suffered an attack of bowel complaint from which he was believed to be recovering. Last night about 11 o'clock Mrs. Hardy prepared

DR. MILTON H. HARDY.

and applied bandages and retired to an adjoining room. Shortly after she returned and found the doctor asleep, and about half an hour later she again went to his bedroom and was shocked to discover that he had closed his eyes in the sleep of death. His little son, who was sleeping with him, had his arms around his neck, showing that the doctor's passing must have been calm and peaceful. The immediate cause of his demise was heart weakness resulting from the disease which attacked him early in the spring.

BIOGRAPHICAL.

Dr. Milton H. Hardy was born in Groveland, Mass., Sept. 26, 1844, and was the son of Josiah G. and Sarah C. Parker Hardy. His parents became converted to the teachings of "Mormonism" and came to Utah in 1857, bringing the members of their family with them and locating in the Twelfth ward, Salt Lake City. Milton entered the Deseret university and in a short time took charge of one of the departments, at the same time pursuing his studies. In 1871, while Dr. Park was absent in Europe, he was acting principal of the University. Dr. Hardy filled a mission to Europe early in the seventies, and for 14 months of his absence was president of the Leeds conference in England. While abroad he pursued his educational studies, visiting the leading cities of Great Britain and the continent in pursuit of knowledge. In 1875, having resigned home, he became principal of the Twelfth district school, and in 1876 was appointed by President Brigham Young to assist in organizing the Young Men's Mutual Improvement associations throughout the state.

When the B. Y. academy, now university, was organized, Dr. Hardy was selected as first assistant to Dr. Karl G. Maeser, remaining till 1883 and also filling the office of county superintendent of the schools of Utah county, superintendent of the Provo city schools and in 1883 was elected territorial superintendent of schools. In 1883 he went to New York to study medicine, entering the medical department of the University of New York, from which he graduated with honors in 1885. After his return he practiced medicine and served as instructor in the University of Utah. In 1896 he was appointed medical superintendent of the insane asylum, which position he held till June of this year. Dr. Hardy made an enviable record in this institution, his great desire for order and cleanliness attracting attention and eliciting highly favorable comment from all visitors. He was instrumental in having the name changed from the Insane asylum to the State Mental hospital. The doctor was also active in church work and has filled many positions of importance and responsibility. He was a member of the general board of the Y. M. M. I. A., and at the time of his demise was first counselor to President Booth of the High Priests' quorum.

Dr. Hardy was married to Miss Libbie Smoot, daughter of the late President A. O. Smoot, in 1876. She, with five children, survive him. The funeral will likely be held on Sunday.

LEEDS

Leeds, Utah, Nov. 22, 1905.

Don. Fuller is sick with quinsey.

SILVER BEARING SANDSTONE

Of Silver Reef.

By James G. Wilder.

SILVER BEARING SANDSTONE.

Silver occurs in rocks of all ages, but in some of them very sparingly; and it is but seldom it occurs in paying quantities in sandstone. The most conspicuous place in which argentiferous sandstone occurs in paying quantities is at Silver Reef, in Washington County, Utah, which place has produced over $8,000,000 in silver up to the year 1900. It was in this locality of Utah that John Barbee, in the year 1873, discovered silver in sandstone reef, near the town of Leeds about 15 miles northeast of St. George, the county seat of Washington County. John Barbee was an old time prospector of California, Idaho, Montana, Nevada and Utah. He had taken part in every great mining excitement for the previous 25 years. In 1872 he had discovered the silver lead mines of Deep Creek, in Western Utah, only to make a failure of smelting the ores of that region at Clifton. His next move was to Southern Utah, and one morning, while he was preparing his breakfast at a campfire near Leeds, he observed a metallic substance on the surface of one of the sandstone masses against which his fire had been built, which he found to be silver, and investigation proved to him that the region round about for a distance of five miles in length and three miles in width, was made up of successive sandstone reefs, each of which carried more or less silver, some of them being too low in value to pay, while others ran as high as 1,000 ounces per ton.

Mr Barbee located a large area of land near the scene of his first discovery at Leeds and farther west on what are know as the Buckeye and White Reefs. He was without money at the time, but it was but a short time before he found the man with the money and as a result a small mill was constructed and set to work and in a very short time was producing silver bullion. At the end of the year 1874 excitement ran high; the fame of silver Reef extended over Nevada Utah and Montana; great numbers of miners flocked in from those territories and in the year 1875 the town of Silver Reef on upper Leeds creek was a thrifty camp. Five mills were employed in treating the ores and about 1,000 men found employment in mining and milling the ore of the district. The principal mines of those halcyon days were the California, Maggie, Buckeye, Tecumseh, Barbee and Walker, Stormont, Thompson, Last Chance, and the Leeds mine. The silver occured as black sulphurets, chlorides, horn silver and native silver in thin sheets, the best values occuring near the surface, but the largest bodies in the deeper workings. As to the source of origin, we know little about the silver of the reef. The problem is difficult of solution, and only the student who is able to patiently work his way through nature's laboratory, will be able to give us the true solution.

The history of Silver Reef as a mining camp, is a strange one. It arose to prosperity rapidly and for eight years continued to produce large volumes of silver. In the year 1883 it had grown to be a handsome little mining city of about 2,500 people. In that year a strike called by the Miner's Union, shut down most of the principal mines, and the decline in the price of silver occuring soon after, completed the work. Now only a few leasers are at work and the output in the year 1904 had declined to 15,000 fine ounces of silver. The Brundage Mining and Reduction Co., composed of Cleveland, Ohio, business men, came into the histoy of Silver Reef a few years since. It purchased water rights, the Barbee and Walker, Leeds, Jumbo and Free Coinage mines and the Barbee mill, which it refitted with new machinery, and now works the leaser's ores. As to what it will do in the future, it maintains a discreet silence, but the mines which are now almost abandoned, will in time become again the scene of activity and life. Millions of dollars have been taken from the old camp, but tens of millions of dollars still remain there.

There exists about ten square miles of mineral land there and only the surface of about one-tenth has been prospected. At present silver mining is not in favor as in years past, but it will always remain a precious and valuable metal. The spots now neglected will again become scenes

of labor and profit, and of these none promise wealth more easily to be obtained than Silver Reef, Utah.

Iron County Record
February 9, 1906

Joseph T. Wilkinson started to Leeds this morning for the purpose of paying a visit to his mother, Mrs. Anna Wilkinson, who has been in very poor health for some time past.

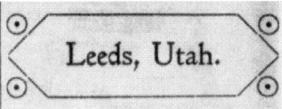

Leeds, Utah.

Leeds, Utah, May 5.

The first cutting of hay is being hauled.

Donald Fuller came back last week on account of illness.

Mrs. Bess Angell Reese came from Salt Lake City Monday to spend the summer at home.

Miss Ruth Stirling will leave Wednesday for Salt Lake City to attend the University summer school.

Mrs. Martha Fleming of De Lamar is spending a few weeks with her parents, Mr. and Mrs. Ira S. McMullin.

Wallace McMullin of this place has completed the three years course at the Beaver Academy and expects to teach next year.

Clair McMullin has gone north to work. He was not sure whether he would go to Salt Lake City, or stop off at Newhouse.

Mr. and Mrs. John Tullis came down from Pinto a few days ago. Mr. Tullis has returned, but Mrs. Tullis will spend the summer at her former home.

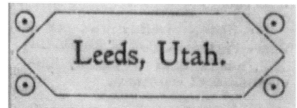

Leeds, Utah.

Leeds, Utah, June 18.

The cutting of wheat has commenced.

Currants, apricots, and early peaches are ripening.

Bishop B. Y. McMullin attended Conference in St. George.

Mr. Hansen is having a lumber addition added to the rear of his house.

Several young people from here went over to Toquerville one day this week to feast on strawberries.

Robert McMullin is home from the Apex for a short time on account of having split a finger while at work.

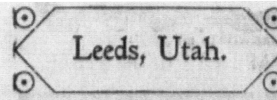

Leeds, Utah.

Leeds, Utah, Sept. 3.

Henry Peterson brought goods to-day for Hanson's store.

Mr. and Mrs. J. C. Crecelius of Silver Reef have returned from Salt Lake City.

Mrs. Miranda McMullin has been very sick the last few days.

Wallace McMullin, who graduated last year from the Beaver school, has engaged to teach in a small town in Beaver County.

E. C. Olsen went to Lund Friday to meet his daughter Mamie, who has been in Salt Lake about a year nursing. She is coming home on a visit.

Leeds, Utah, Sept. 10, 1906.

S. LeRoy Harris of Silver Reef has gone to Pioche to work.

Mr. and Mrs. John Adams of Panguitch are here putting up fruit.

Two wagons carrying fruit left here for Pioche the latter part of the week.

Miss Julia Ford, who has spent the summer in Idaho, has returned home.

Miss Ann McMullin took the stage for Minersville last Friday where she will teach school this year.

George and Nelson Blake of Salt Lake City, nephews of E. C. Olsen are visiting with Olsens.

Mr. Hunt and his wife of Bunkerville, recently married in St. George are visiting Mrs. Hanson, Mrs. Hunt's grandmother.

T. M. Reese of Salt Lake City came to Leeds yesterday. After spending a few days here, he will go to Panguitch to teach school, accompanied by his wife.

Miss Maude McMullin is home from the Apex, spending a week with her mother Mrs. Miranda McMullin, who is much better since last writing.

DOWN IN DIXIE.

Washington County Went Democratic By One Hundred.

(Special to the "News.")

St. George, Utah, Nov. 8.—Touquerville, Leeds, Washington, St. George, Santa Clara, Pineville, Enterprise, Pinto, Dixie, and Shem gives Morris, state senator, Eleventh district, a majority of 185; Powers, Whitecotton and Cottam, Democratic representative, about the same. The St. George vote was: Powers, 327; Howell, 182; Whitecotton, 332; Frick, 174; Morris, 243; Miller, 163; Cottam, 342; Hurschi, 166. Washington county is Democratic by one hundred.

Jos. L. Farnsworth, the veteran hack-line man of St. George, who operates a hack service between St. George and Modena, was in Cedar last Wednesday. Asked in relation to the new mail service between St. George and Modena, Mr. Farnsworth stated that so far as he could see, the change was no advantage to St. George. That even in good weather the patrons of the St. George office did not receive their mail any earlier, and that the new departure was a positive disadvantage to all settlements northeast of St. George. In figuring up the increased expense to the government of giving St. George its mail from Modena, it was estimated at over three thousand dollars. This amount of money is considerable to pay out, if nobody receives any benefit from it. But this is a matter that concerns Uncle Sam only. All that the people of Iron and eastern Washington counties care for is to have connection re-established between Kanarraville and Leeds, and this, we believe, we are entitled to. Mr. Farnsworth said that he understood that the present contractor on the new line is running at a loss, and he expects to see the government change back to the old route via Cedar City, Kanarra and Leeds in the near future.

The Record is in receipt of a de-layed correspondence from Lovell, Bighorn Co., Wyo., telling of the death of William Orson Harris, who died May 15th. Deceased was born in Parowan, Iron county, Sept. 23, 1871, and for a number of years resided at Leeds, marrying Miss Ann Connelley of that place. "Art" was industrious and well respected. He moved from Leeds to Wyoming some four years ago, and has been sick with a complication of diseases for more than a year.

He leaves a wife and six small children, with whom we sincerely sympathize.

LEEDS

Leeds, Feb 6 —Mark Miller, who has been working at Pioche, Nevada, for some time, is here visi-ting with his wife, formerly Miss Maude McMullin

After being closed for three weeks on account of measles, our primary school has begun again.

Plowing and putting in seed grain will commence as soon as the weather will permit

Leeds, Feb 12 —Talk about winter, Dixie is having it now it seems There was quite a little snow fell here the forepart of the week and today there is a cold north wind.

Miss Brenda Angell who has been at La Verkin for the past three or four weeks is home again

Leeds, Feb 25,—An old folks party was given in the Leeds hall Feb 21, and a jolly good time was had Dancing was indulged in until twelve o'clock, then lunch was served Program, songs, recitations, and a violin solo by Jim Nielson Dancing was then resumed until six in the morning Hurrah for the old folks!

Bro David H Morris, Frank Bentley, Miss Maude Snow and Lena Nelson were over to hold mutual and we are sorry to say that there was not a very good turn out

Supervisor Hamilton is making a vigorous attack on our mud hole at the bottom of town with a large force of men and teams Hurrah for Hamilton!

On the twenty second of Feb. born to Mr, and Mrs Mark Miller a bouncing baby boy. Father and son doing well

Dr. J. T, Affleck and wife of St. George passed through Leeds on their way home from Virgin City.

Mrs. Thomas Stirling from Virgin City is down visiting relatives and friends

Leeds, March 18 —A farewell party was given in honor of Mrs Brown, who has been here visiting the past few months with her mother, Mrs Hamilton Mrs Brown expects to leave for her home in Jamestown, North Dakota, tomorrow.

Synn McMullin and Will Sullivan arrived home Sunday from St. George, where they had been visiting relatives and friends

J. M. Wicks returned on the 10th inst. from the Colorado Canyon, where he has been prospecting for some time.

Charles Angell and family have gone to Hurricane, where they will make their home.

Fruit trees are in full bloom and everything indicates a prosperous fruit year

Mark Miller left for Pioche, Nevada, on the 13th inst. on business

Leeds, March 31.—William Angell returned last week from California, where he has been for some time taking in different parts of that state and taking up what work he could find

David Stirling arrived in town yesterday with freight for Stirling's store

The district school of the higher grades will close today.

Farmers are busy tending to their crops nowadays

Washington County News
April 14, 1908

Leeds, April 14 —Miss Mamie Olsen left for Salt Lake city Thursday, where she will get employment in the hospital for some time Her parents returned home from Lund last night where they have been to see her off.

Mrs James McQuaide returned home Thursday She will spend a few months with her parents, Mr. and Mrs Ira S. McMullin

Bert Harris has returned home from Pioche where he has been working for some time

We are having fine weather.

Washington County News
April 28, 1908

Leeds, April 28 —Miss Stella Sullivan returned home Thursday from Virgin, where she had been visiting Mrs Thomas Stirling

Miss Lyle Olson returned home Thursday from Springdale, where she has been teaching school

Ben Bradshaw came down from Virgin Sunday to visit a particular friend

Willie Hartman left Saturday for Goldsprings to find employment

"Grandma" Leany has been very ill for the past few days

The men have been busy cleaning out the water ditches

Oscar McMullin returned from St. George last Friday

Our jail is now finished ready for use

Leeds, May 12 —We had a pleasant rain last night which was greatly appreciated by the farmers

Miss Druie Hartley went down
to St George yesterday to get married to Mr Ben Bradshaw of Virgin

Miss Nellie Andrus is here visiting her aunt, Mrs Mary Olsen

Washington County News
May 19, 1908

Leeds, May 19 —Frank Sullivan
has returned home from Beaver
where he has attended school the
past winter.

Ben Bradshaw and Druie Hartley
were married on the 12th of May by
Bp B Y McMullin They give a
dance at night which was very much
enjoyed

Robert McMullin and Joseph
Stirling have gone to Milford Robert went to bring his sister Edith
home and Joseph has gone for freight

George Olsen who has been on the
sick list is on the improve

Farmers are cutting their first
crop of hay.

Leo Higgins was seen in Leeds
Sunday.

Leeds, May 26 —The boys have gone out to the ranges to gather in the cattle for the June sale

A party in honor of Mrs Olive Mortenson was given at the home of Mrs Annie Hanson

George Olsen has recovered from his illness and is about again.

Miss Edith McMullin returned today from Milford.

Washington County News
June 9, 1908

Leeds, June 9 —Hyrum Leany returned home last night from Beaver with his daughter Libbie who has been very sick.

Mr and Mrs Oscar McMullin returned home last Saturday from St George where they had been to attend the funeral of Mrs McMullin's father, Bro McArthur

Grandma Leany is very, very low.

Washington County News
June 16, 1908

Leeds, June 16 — Mrs Elizabeth Lancy, a pioneer of 1847, passed away at her home in Harrisburg on the 9th inst, at the age of eighty-six. She died as she had lived, faithful to the cause which she had espoused in her youth

Mr and Mrs Charles Angell were over from Hurricane visiting friends and relatives.

Clarence McMullin is here visiting his parents, Mr and Mrs B Y McMullin.

Roy Grundy of St. George was seen in town last week

A number of Leeds people turned out for conference

Washington County News
June 23, 1908

Leeds, June 23 — Early fruit is being bottled We are having very nice weather now, something like fall the last few days

Miss Ellen McArthur of St, George is visiting her sister here, Mrs Isaac McMullin, and friends

Dr J T Affleck and wife of St George passed through here on their way to the Virgin oil field

Bert Harris and William Sullivan, Jr, went to Lund with the cattle that have been sold

Miss Maggie Olsen left for Salt Lake city last Friday to spend the summer there

Washington County News
July 7, 1908

Leeds, July 7 —The Fourth passed off very quietly with a meeting in the forenoon and a children's dance and ice cream in the afternoon

Ed Foster and Frank Whitehead of St. George passed through town today on their way home from Cedar

Miss Ruth Paris has gone to Alamo, Nevada, to spend the summer with her sister, Mrs Stewart

A crowd of young folks went to Hurricane for a dance and a very enjoyable time is reported.

Miss Bess Higgins of St. George was here visiting friends the latter part of last week

Bert Harris returned today from Colorado where he has been helping with the cattle.

A dance was given the night of the second and we had a very enjoyable time

Oscar McMullin has returned from Milford with freight for Hanson's and Stirling

Dr Affleck and wife of St. George passed through town on their way to Virgin

Miss Roxie Cottis of St. George is visiting friends and relatives

People are putting up their second crop of alfalfa

Clarence McMullin left for Pioche last night

Washington County News
July 21, 1908

Leeds, July 21—Mrs Nannie Parker left Monday night to join her husband in Parowan She has been spending the past winter with her parents, Mr. and Mrs David McMullin.

Ira McMullin has gone to Washington to do mason work on the school building

Charlie Hanson has gone to Cedar city to spend the 24th with his best girl

Grain harvest is now in full swing

LEEDS

Archie McMullin, aged 22 years, son of David and Caroline McMullin, was accidentally killed Saturday afternoon, July 25th. As he was returning from Bellevue the horses got frightened and started to run, throwing him out of the wagon which passed over him breaking his neck. Mr. and Mrs Charlie Westover of Washington and Mrs Alice Woodbury of St. George were over to attend the funeral Sunday.

Mr. and Mrs Wallace McMullin are down from Parowan spending a few weeks with the former's parents, Mr and Mrs. David McMullin.

The 24th passed off very quietly with a children's dance, ice cream and a good big rain in the afternoon.

Mr. and Mrs Thomas Stirling of Virgin were here to spend the 24th.

Leeds, August 4 —On July 31st we were visited by a big thunderstorm, during which lightning struck Henry Peterson's barn and the poplar trees in front of Tom Stirling's place.

Dr. J. T. Affleck of St. George passed through this place Sunday morning on his way home from Virgin city, where he had been on business

Mrs John Tullis is down from Pinto visiting her father, William Stirling.

Mrs. Oscar has been ill for about a week, she is improving slowly.

Leeds, August 11 —A crowd of boys came over from Washington yesterday and it looked as though they were having a good time

Willard McMullin returned Saturday from Panguitch, where he has been working the past few months

A few of the Leeds boys who had been having an outing on Pine Valley mountain returned Sunday

County Attorney Horatio Pickett was over from St George yesterday on business

Mrs Dallas Hartman is on the sick list

We had a big rain Sunday night

Leeds, August 17.—The stork paid a visit to the home of Mr. and Mrs J. M McQuaid and left a nice baby boy on the 9th inst.

Frank McMullin returned yesterday from Parowan, where he had been to take his brother Wallace and wife.

J. T Affleck of St. George was called to Leeds last night on business and returned home this morning.

Mrs Charles Angell is over from Hurricane visiting her mother, Mrs. Hartley.

Geo R Lund of St George was in town yesterday on business,

Notice of Cattle Sales

Members of the Cattlemen's Union that sold steers for fall delivery are hereby notified that said steers will be received at Modena Oct 10, and the dates and places for passing on same are as follows Trumbull cattle at Trumbull, Sept. 28; Canaan cattle at Canaan, Sept 30, Virgin cattle at Virgin, Oct 1; Hurricane, La Verkin, Leeds and Toquerville cattle at Toquerville, Oct 2, Springdale, Grafton and Rockville cattle at Ford's pasture, on Kolob mountain, Oct 5; Southern cattle at Pockum, Oct 2, Diamond Valley cattle at Diamond Valley, Oct 5; Pine Valley cattle at Pine Valley, Oct 6, Enterprise and Pinto cattle at Holt's ranch, Oct 7

Efforts will be made to have Santa Clara cattle passed on at Hebron, Oct 8, otherwise they will be passed on at Modena.

D. H. MORRIS

Washington County News
September 3, 1908

Leeds, Sept. 1 —Mrs Alice Fuller who has been very sick for some time is improving slowly.

Willie Hartman returned on Sunday from Pioche, Nevada, where he had been working.

Mrs Lizzie Macfarlane is down from Cedar City visiting her sister, Mrs Julia Ford

Arthur Westover came in Monday with a load of freight for Hanson's store.

Mrs Alpheus Hartley is down from Panguitch visiting relatives.

Washington County News
September 15, 1908

Leeds, Sept 15 —Quite a number of Leeds people went to St. George to attend the Washington County Fair.

Charles Bastian of St. George came here Monday to take his wife home. She had been visiting here

Ira McMullin left Sunday to continue work on the new school building at Washington

J. M. McQuaid left last Friday for Smelter, Nevada, to look after his mining claims

Leeds, Sept 22 —The boys are now gathering their cattle from the range for the cattle sale on the 28th inst

Misses Ethel and Verda Sullivan, Ethel McMullin and Belle Stirling left Wednesday for Beaver to attend the Murdock academy.

Frank McMullin left Wednesday for Provo to attend the B Y U.

Mrs. Alpheus Hartley left Saturday for her home at Panguitch

Mr. Newton of Harrisburg is very sick.

Leeds, Oct. 13 —Stanley, the seven year old boy of Don Fuller, had the misfortune to have his foot partly cut off while playing in the yard yesterday, by his little sister, Verna, who was chopping wood.

Albert Hartman who has been ailing for some time with miners consumption, died Sunday the 11th inst He has long been a resident of Silver Reef, having located there in the early days of the camp.

Baby girls have arrived at the homes of the following, Mrs. Don Fuller, Sept. 30, Mrs. Frank Batty October 12th.

Mrs. Walter Randal is visiting her mother, Mrs. Alice Fuller. Mrs. Fuller still continues quite sick.

Miss Edith McMullin left here the 10th inst for Caliente, Nevada, where she will teach school

Mr. and Mrs Abram Woodbury left here on the 11th inst for their home at Mesquite, Nevada.

Matt Wicks arrived here yesterday to look after his property. He has been at Stateline.

Dr. J. T. Affleck and wife passed through here on Sunday enroute for Virgin.

Some of our boys are on Pine Valley mountain hunting deer.

Mr. and Mrs Oscar McMullin have returned from Newhouse

Bp B Y. McMullin has gone to Beaver.

Washington County News
October 22 1908

FROM OUR FILES OF TEN YEARS AGO

Died, at St. George, on Friday, October 21, Cora Keate, the beloved wife of Albert Hartman of Silver Reef, in the 40th year of her age

Washington County News
October 28, 1908

Leeds, Oct. 26 —Our school begun last Monday with Mr Brigham Jarvis as principal and Miss Louie Foster as primary teacher.

The men are busy putting up their last cutting of hay and making wine We are having fine spring like weather the last few days

A Republican rally was held here on the 27th inst Senator Albert Miller and George F Land were the speakers

Washington County News
November 3, 1908

Leeds, Nov. 8 —Julia Ford, Mrs M E Paris and Mr and Mrs Sullivan went to Virgin Friday to attend William Beams funeral

Miss Ellen McArthur and cousin, Laura Calloway of St George are over visiting Mrs Oscar McMullin.

Ira S McMullin who has been working on the new school building at Washington has returned home

Leeds, Nov. 7 —Miss Louie Foster went to St. George to visit her folks Saturday and returned Monday.

Miss Ruth Stirling left last Thursday for Washington to teach the primary school there

Mrs Martha Randall left for her home at Pima, Arizona, last Thursday.

Miss Alice Stirling has gone to Pinto to visit relatives and friends.

Mrs Pat Holohan of Virgin is spending a few days here.

Mrs J. T. Affleck of St. George is visiting friends here

Leeds, December 1.—Thanksgiving passed off very quietly. The primary children gathered at the school house with their picnic and then had a little dance in the afternoon. They had a jolly good time.

Miss Luie Foster went to St. George Wednesday to spend a few days with her folks and returned Saturday.

Miss Minnie Thanson spent Thanksgiving home with her parents, Mr. and Mrs Peter Thanson

A good many of our Leeds boys went to St George to spend Thanksgiving and returned Friday.

Willard McMullin and Frank Sullivan left Monday for Pioche to work.

Mat Wicks is in town looking after his property.

Sam Pollack is spending a few days in Leeds

Leeds, December 15 —Franklin McMullin, Henry Peterson, William Sullivan, Sr , and Arthur Westover returned on the 14th from a trip to Panguitch where they had been for lumber for the Washington school house They reported the roads good

Ira McMullin returned Saturday from Washington where he has completed the mason work on the Washington school house

Miss Lowe Foster who went to St George to spend conference and visit her folks and friends reported having a very fine time

Mrs Ruth Stirling was home spending Saturday and returned to her post as school marm at Washington Sunday.

The primary school is anticipating a fine time this coming Friday as it is the last day befor their holidays

Ira McMullin left this morning for Harmony to lay a foundation for Davis's dwelling house

Roy Harris has returned from Pioche where he has been working for the past four months

Oscar McMullin left this morning for freight for Peter Hansen's store

Bishop B Y McMullin went to St. George to attend conference

Edward McMullin has gone to Washington for his father

William Stirling was in St George on business last Friday

Mr. and Mrs. Crecelius of Silver Reef have gone to St George to spend holidays

Leeds, Dec. 28 — Mr. and Mrs. Cris. Olsen have gone to St George to spend the holidays with relatives

Mrs M E Paris ruffled a cow off on Christmas day for one dollar a chance. She got twenty dollars for the cow. Lee Scott was the lucky man.

On Christmas day there were a few horse races and a little dance for the children, quite a good time was enjoyed

Mr. and Mrs. Crecelius of Silver Reef have gone to St George to spend holidays

William Stirling, Jr, left for Bull valley Monday to do some work there

Thomas Stirling of Virgin City is in town.

We are having lovely weather again.

Leeds, Jan. 5 —Mrs Brigham Jarvis, Jr , and baby boy are enjoying good health, while papa has a grin on his face that won't come off even in the school room However, we hope that grin isn't everlasting.

On the 31st ult the Relief society give a leap year ball and supper The old year was danced out and the new year danced in. All report a jolly time

An old folks party was given in the Leeds hall on the 30th ult Lunch was served and the evening passed very pleasantly.

A crowd of young people went to Hurricane the night of the 29th ult. to attend a dance, and report having had a nice time

Roy Harris, William Sullivan, Jr., and Frank McMullin left Tuesday for the Fort Pearce country to round up cattle.

Miss Louie Foster has returned from St George to continue her school work after two weeks' holidays

Miss Ruth Stirling left Sunday for Washington, where she is teaching school.

Leeds, Jan 12 — Frank Hamilton was in St. George Saturday to attend district court and returned home Sunday a wiser man than he was when he left.

Mrs Naomi Hartley and daughter, Mrs Drewy Bradshaw left Saturday for Hurricane, where they will spend the rest of the winter

Wilford Laney of Harrisburg is up and around again after a severe sick spell and we hope he can soon get back to his school work.

Mrs Nettie Micleson and Mrs Ida McDonald were here for a few days visiting with friends and relatives

Miss Alice Stirling and Ida Tullis of Pinto are here visiting their folks

AN EVENTFUL LIFE IS ENDED

Captain H. S. Lubbock is Called by Death—Was Noted Figure at Silver Reef in 70s

Alameda, Dec 8 —Captain Henry S. Lubbock, father of City Treasurer Oswald Lubbock, a pioneer of California, and brigadier general in the confederate army, died this morning at the home of his daughter, Mrs Adele Arnold, 2141 San Antonio avenue, aged 87 years. He was ill two months

Lubbock was born in Charleston, S C. He came to California in 1850 by way of the Isthmus of Panama After arriving in San Francisco he went to the Fraser river country in British Columbia, where he mined for a few years, and then returned to San Francisco and engaged in steamboating. He was one of the first men to operate a steamer on the Sacremento river, He also ran the steamer Sophia McLean to Alviso. At the commencement of the civil war Lubbock returned to the south and enlisted in the confederate army. He served on the staff of General Magruder and was in command of the confederate gunboat Bayou City, which attacked and captured the union gunboat Harriet Lane in Galveston harbor Frank R. Lubbock, a brother of Henry S. Lubbock, was the confederate war governor of Texas and was an aid to Jefferson Davis He was captured with the president of the confederacy and was for a time in Fortress Monroe under sentence of death. Another brother, Thomas

Lubbock, was the head of the Texas rangers and was killed in a battle with the union forces, in Tennessee.

Henry L Lubbock was a personal friend of General Grant, and when his brother, the governor of Texas, was a prisoner in Fortress Monroe he besought the head of the union armies to assist him in obtaining a pardon for his relative.

Captain Lubbock lived in Alameda for 29 years For five years he served as an inspector of hulls and boilers in San Francisco, receiving his appointment from President Cleveland He was a member of the Masonic fraternity, and his funeral will be conducted under the auspices of that order in Masonic temple Thursday afternoon

[The foregoing article was handed to the editor by Mr A T. Gregerson of this city, who was well acquainted with Captain Lubbock and informs us that he (Capt Lubbock) installed the water system at Pioche in the early seventies, came to Silver Reef, this county, in 1877 and formed the Christy Mining company, being manager of that company for about seven years, distributing considerable money in this county and doing a deal of good —Editor News]

Leeds, Jan. 17.—Bishop B. Y. McMullin's little boy, Clyde, fell from a wagon loaded with sand and was very badly bruised. It is supposed that the wagon ran over his leg but no bones were crushed. He is improving very nicely.

The cold north wind is blowing and makes it very disagreeable although the health of the people is good.

A son was born to Mr. and Mrs. John Tullis on the 3rd inst; all concerned doing well.

Stockmen from some of the surrounding settlements are gathering cattle near here

Mrs. Eleanor S. Scott and Mrs. Ida Tullis are in town visiting relatives.

Leeds, Jan. 19 —A crowd of our young folks went to Virgin last Wednesday to visit friends and relatives and returned Friday.

Roy Harris and Will Nicles intends leaving on the mail today for Pioche to find employment.

Mrs Sade Paris went to St. George Friday on business and returned Saturday.

Rob McMullin went to Hurricane Saturday on business.

B Y. McMullin has gone to St George on business

We are having spring like weather again.

Leeds, Jan. 26.—A dance was held in the Leeds hall last Wednesday night. Some of the Hurricane young folks came over. It was reported they had a jolly good time Shall be pleased to have them come again

George Lund and his brother Lou were here on the 20th inst. attending business and returned to their home at St. George the next day.

Mrs Ida Tullis left for her home at Pinto Saturday. She has been here visiting her father, William Stirling

William Sullivan, Jr , went to St. George Sunday and returned Monday

Tom Stirling of Virgin was seen on the streets yesterday.

We are having clear weather after one week of storm

Leeds, February 2—Last Friday, George Lund and Sam Fullerton of St George while on their way to La Verkin, met with an accident. The team ran away, throwing both the men out and came back to Leeds, breaking the buggy. The men came back to Leeds to stay that night

Miss Lulo Foster went to St George Friday and returned Sunday. Her brother Charley and Mrs Julia Foster, Pearl Andrus, Nellie Stephens and Clara Church accompanied her, returning to their home the same night.

Mr. and Mrs Oscar McMullin went to St George last week on business They brought Miss Ellen McArthur back with them to spend a week with relatives

Last Sunday Willie Duffin and Hans Anderson from Toquerville came to Leeds to see their best girls

Henry Peterson returned to Leeds last Saturday with a load of shingles for the new school building

Leeds, February, 8—William Sullivan, Sr, Robert McMullin, Tom Sullivan and William Stirling, Jr, left for Lund Friday where they have gone for casing for the Virgin oil fields

Misses Louie Foster and Marie McMullin went to St George on horseback, reported having a jolly time They returned Sunday

Miss Mabel Jarvis has returned to her home at St. George She has been staying with her brother here.

* Mrs J. T. Affleck of St George passed through Leeds Sunday on her way to Toquerville and Virgin.

Oscar McMullin left for Modena Friday where he expects to meet his daughter, Mrs. Mark Miller.

There is a big show for Leeds school building, the foundation being laid.

Arthur Westover went to Lund to take his sister-in-law, Mrs Vilate Batty.

Peter Anderson and son Frank were seen in Leeds Sunday.

Mat Hartley arrived here last Thursday.

Two of Chester Kemp's children ate some arsenic Sunday, not knowing its deadly nature. Prompt work on the part of Dr Woodbury soon put them alright

Resources of Leeds

Editor WASHINGTON COUNTY NEWS: In looking over the natural resources of Dixie, I find that Leeds has its share. It has the greatest number of undeveloped resources of any town in Washington county, among them sites for reservoirs, and water to fill them running to waste from October 1st to April 1st. The best site is at the Grapevine wash, about one mile and a half north of where the county road crosses the wash. The wash passes through some narrows not more than twelve feet wide. Above these cliffs it opens out into quite a wide valley that would make a good reservoir with very little expense if a dam were put in at the narrows.

The land laying between Leeds and the Grapevine wash could all be irrigated in this way. The water could also be brought in to Leeds and water every foot of land that is being cultivated.

On the east side of Grapevine wash there is a strip of land extending from the Red mountain to within one mile of the Virgin river. This could also be irrigated by said reservoir.

The ditch to convey the water from the Leeds creek in the canyon would not have to be over one and one-half miles long.

There is another stream known as Three Pine creek that runs through the Heath wash and in to Cottonwood canyon. Here it sinks and dries away. This with very little expense could be turned into the Leeds creek. The canal needed would be only a short one and this water could also be used to fill reservoir.

Between where the canal would have to be taken out and Pin Valley mountain there is sufficient fall to support a large electric plant.

We invite people to come and investigate these resources   M I

Leeds, February 23—The boys who went to Lund for freight returned Friday. They were fourteen days making the round trip, and report the roads very, very muddy

Miss Ruth Stirling came home from Washington Saturday to spend Washington's birthday with her folks She left this morning to resume teaching in the Washington school

Miss Louie Foster has been visiting friends and relatives in St George She returned Tuesday and reports having had a nice time on Washington's birthday

There has been a number of children sick with bad colds and sore throats, but they are all improving

Oscar McMullin left for Parowan this morning to bring in a load of flour.

Leeds, March 2—Misses Mary Mendenhall and Zilhe Lund accompanied Louie Foster to Leeds Sunday and returned to St George Monday On their way they took in all the beautiful scenery which Miss Mendenhall says surpasses any in the northern part of Utah or Canada

Oscar McMullin returned home from Parowan Sunday, reporting roads fairly good and weather excellent for this time of the year

If the weather man will insure us the same kind of weather as we have had the last two weeks we will soon have our gardens up

Henry Peterson left Monday to bring in freight for Hansen's store

L C. Olsen has been very sick but is slowly improving

Leeds, March 16—The new school house here is going up very rapidly and is expected to be completed soon.

Edward and Lynn McMullin and George Olsen has been down spending a few days in St. George. They enjoyed themselves fine while there

Frank Sullivan who has been out in Pioche working for the last few months arrived home Wednesday.

Miss Lylie Olsen has just returned home from St George where she has been visiting relatives

Watt Wicks arrived in Leeds Thursday with the intention of staying here a month or so

*E. C. Olsen, who has been real sick for the last month, is out around again

Leeds, March 30 —Both schools of Leeds came to a close last Friday, ending with an entertainment for the children, a little dance in the afternoon and a big one at night All the young folks seemed to enjoy themselves fine A crowd from St George and Washington were over to the dance. They all had such a good time that they are coming again

Last Wednesday night a surprise party was given Miss Lula Foster at the home of Mr. and Mrs Oscar McMullen. They spent the evening by having games, recitations, songs and music, then at eleven o'clock lunch was served. The party ended by each and everyone having pleasant smiles upon their faces

I. S. McMullin and wife left last Tuesday for Overton, Nevada to meet their daughter Etta, who has been teaching school in Nevada,

We are having very disagreeable weather, has been storming for three days and still raining

Mrs Lizzie McQuaid has gone to join her husband in some part of Arizona

Bert McQuarrie from St George, is seen around town today.

Roy Harris arrived home Friday, from Piocho.

Leeds, April 6 — Mrs Alice Fuller died this morning at eight o'clock after suffering for several months Her daughter, Mrs. Frank Ballie is at her bedside

Truman Angell and Frank Sullivan and Misses Ellen McMullin and Stella Sullivan went to Virgin to spend Sunday with Mrs Tom Starling

Mr and Mrs Brig Jarvis, Jr. have gone to St George to visit.

There was a light frost last night which nipped the potatoes

Mrs Mark Miller has left to join her husband at Modena

Miss Ella McMullin returned home Sunday. _____

Leeds, April 13 — The funeral services were held over Mrs Alice Fuller last Thursday. Her daughters, Mrs Susie Johnson and Mrs Nellie Bleak came from Hinckley to attend the funeral

Mrs Mary Lund and Mrs. Ella McQuarrie were here Saturday to visit our primary. They gave us some good talk and we would be pleased to have them often

There was a party given on Mr. and Mrs Arthur Westover last night They will leave Thursday to make their home in Hinckley

Leeds, April 27 — A crowd of young people came over from St. George last Saturday and spent Sunday with Mr. and Mrs Chris Olsen

Mr. and Mrs Will Sullivan and Mr. and Mrs. Chris Olsen returned from St George on the 21st inst with the newly wedded couple, Will Sullivan, Jr , and Miss Lyle Olsen

A number of our men folks are out gathering cattle

Leeds, May 4 —William Stirling was taking his young mule to water when some other animal going by started it to run   Mr Stirling had the rope holding the mule wound round his hand, and was dragged about half a block before he could get loose   He escaped with some bruises on his head and hand

On May day the Primary Assn. took picnic and went to the Conly field, where a very enjoyable time was had

Miss Ann McMullin left Sunday for Minersville, where she intends spending the summer with Mrs Woods.

Charlie Angell and Frank Sullivan spent May day at Hurricane and say they had a lovely time.

Misses Myrtle and Leona McMullin spent May day at Washington with relatives.

The men have all turned out today to give our water ditch a good cleaning.

George Olsen and Lynn McMullin went to St. George to spend May day.

Miss Julia Ford is having the outside of her house painted.

Mrs Anna McMullin is on the sick list.

Leeds, May 11—Born, a son to Mr and Mrs Frank McMullin on the 7th inst.

Mr and Mrs Henry Peterson went to St George Monday on business.

Dave Grantham and Matt Wicks left Sunday for Cedar City to visit

Mrs Anna Wilkinson is on the sick

Leeds, June 18—Willard and Miss Edith McMullin returned home last week. Edith has been teaching school at Caliente, Nevada, and Willard has been working at Pioche.

The literary society will give a dance tonight in Leeds hall for to try and get some money to help to fix our meeting house.

Charles Hanson returned home Saturday from Taylor, Arizona, where he has been the past winter teaching school

Truman Angell left last Wednesday for Salt Lake to visit his sister. Mrs Bess Reese

Ira McMullin left yesterday for Lund, will bring freight for Harmony.

William Sullivan, Sr , has gone to Milford for Hanson's freight

James Booth and company of St. George are here

Leeds, June 1—Mrs Ada McMullin went to St George last week to visit her sister, Mrs. John S. Woodbury

Miss Belle Stirling returned home Sunday from Beaver, where she has been going to school this winter

Charles Hansen left for Cedar City last week to take part in commencement week at the Normal.

Washington County News
June 8, 1909

Leeds, June 8 —Misses Ethel Mc-
Mullin and Verda and Ethel Sullivan returned home from Beaver
last week They have been attending school there.

Mrs Joe McDonald of Middleton is staying with Mrs Peggy
Hameton who is quite sick.

E C. Olsen is*having a new
picket fence put up in front of his
home

Our men have gone to Toquerville
to deliver their steers.

Washington County News
June 22, 1909

Leeds, June 22 — Four fine orchards of high grade fruit trees and
one vineyard of seedless grapes have
been planted out here this season
which indicates that there are a few
people left in Leeds who have faith
in its future

Mr. and Mrs James Bleak and
little daughter of Salt Lake arrived
here last week and after visiting a
day or two with E C. Olsen and
family went on to St George to visit
Mr. Bleak's father and other relatives at that place

E C. Olsen returned from Lund
on the 16th bringing with him his
daughter Margaret, who has been in
Salt Lake City attending the L D.
S U. the past winter.

Mrs Lottie R. Carter and daughter Ellen came over from St George
Saturday. Ellen will remain here
for a few weeks the guest of Mr. and
Mrs. B Jarvis jr.

Several of our young people went
to St George Friday on a pleasure
outing and returned Sunday.

Harvesting has *commenced and
the wheat crop is reported exceptionally good.

Mr and Mrs Crecelius of Silver
Reef have left for the east to be gone
some time.

Leeds, June 29—Spend the Fourth in Leeds if you are looking for a good time. Horse racing and other sports will follow the usual meeting and program and plenty of refreshments will be at hand all day. A dance in the evening to finish the celebration. Remember, next Monday.

An excellent program was given by the L L society Sunday evening It is the most flourishing organization in town at present and the membership is steadily increasing.

Elder Thomas Cottam and wife of St. George spent Sunday in Leeds Elder Cottam is a member of the Stake Sunday School Board and came to visit our Sunday school

President Cornelia Brooks of the Stake Relief society and Mrs Mary Jarvis, one of the aids, held meeting with the local organization Sunday evening.

Miss Mayme Olsen of the L D S. Groves Hospital corps is here to spend a two weeks vacation with her parents

Annie and Clarence Cottam and Miss Asineth Jarvis came over from St. George this week to put up fruit,

Lynn McMullin and Henry Peterson have gone north with fruit and vegetables.

Everybody is busy these days with fruit picking and harvesting

Leeds Has Best Celebration in Years

Leeds, July 6—The Fourth was celebrated in true patriotic style under the direction of committees of the L L society. "The best celebration we have had for years," was the general expression of those who attended. The program consisted of a rousing meeting at 10 a. m , a children's dance and field sports in the afternoon and a ball in the evening An abundance of ice cream and mild drinks took the place of booze and the whole town had a jolly good time without an unpleasant circumstance to mar the spirit of the occasion

Ray Bentley and Don Carter came over from St George Saturday bringing with them the latter's mother, Mrs. Lottie R Carter, who will remain here for some time visiting relatives The boys return-

Rain at Leeds.
Shipping Tomatoes

Leeds, July 20.—We have had a number of refreshing showers, and everything is fresh and green. Tomatoes are ripe and a shipment has been made to Cedar.

Sunday, Will Macfarlane of Cedar City brought Mr. and Mrs. John A. Creeclius to Leeds They have been spending a month visiting the fair and other points of interest.

Mrs. Thos. Bleak and daughter, and Miss Maymo Olson, who have been visiting here, left Sunday for Salt Lake City.

Miss Etta McMullin returned Monday from California, where she has been attending Summer school and visiting

A number of teams have passed through here wending their way toward Panguitch lake to spend the 24th.

Some of the boys are planning to spend Pioneer day on top of old Pine Valley mountain.

Mr. and Mrs. Roy Harris left Monday for their new home in Idaho.

Leeds Spends Quiet Pioneer Day

Leeds, July 27.—Leeds spent a very quiet day on the 24th. However, on the night of the 23rd the young people of the town went out hay rack riding, and with shout and song made the would-be-sleeper aware of the approaching holiday.

Ephraim Webb of St. George, who was on his way to Kanarra, spent a few hours visiting here.

Misses Mable Jarvis and Mamie McAllister of St. George are here visiting friends and relatives

Mrs. Mary E Olsen's mother, Mrs Schlappy of Washington, is here visiting

Leeds Visitors Have Returned Home

Leeds, August 3 —Mr and Mrs Brigham Jarvis left last Sunday for St George accompanied by Miss Ellen Carter who has been visiting in Leeds for a number of days

Miss Maggie Olsen entertained a number of her friends Friday evening. Dainty refreshments were served and a jolly time is reported.

Mr. and Mrs. Thomas Perry of Cedar City have been spending a day or two in Leeds, the former being here on business

Miss Ellen McMullin has returned home from Parowan, where she has been visiting her sister, Mrs D. C. Parker

Mr. and Mrs Alex. Milne of St. George passed through Leeds Saturday on their way to Toquerville.

Washington County News
August 10, 1909

Leeds People Take In G. A. R. Celebration

Leeds, August 10 —David Stirling left Thursday for Lund to get freight for Stirling's store. He was accompanied as far as Lund by his sister, Miss Eleanor Stirling, and Mrs Ada McMullin, who will go from there on to Salt Lake City to attend the G A. R. celebration.

Truman Angell returned home last Saturday from Salt Lake City, where he has been working for T. M. Reese for some time

A crowd of the young people of Leeds went to Hurricane last Sunday to attend the Sunday School convention

Bp B. Y. McMullin returned home last Sunday from Cedar City, where he had been with a load of melons.

Leeds Will Build New School House

Leeds, August 17.—David Mc-Mullin and William and Joseph Stirling left last Sunday for Milford to get lumber for our new school house.

Mr. and Mrs. Thomas Stirling came down from Virgin yesterday. They expect to remain a week in this place.

Elder George Spilsbury of Toquerville was in Leeds visiting the Sunday school last Sunday.

The weather has been cloudy for a number of days, but so far we have had very little rain.

Charles and Truman Angell left last Wednesday for Moapa, where they expect to work.

Washington County News
August 24, 1909

Leeds, August 24.—Misses Ruth
Stirling and Edith McMullin returned home a few days ago from Salt
Lake City, where they have been
attending summer school.

Frank Sullivan and Lynn and
Dan McMullin returned home Saturday from Logan, Nevada, where
they had been hauling cantaloupes.

E I Hastings and O. A. Barry
stayed in Leeds a short time yesterday on their way from St. George
to Virgin City.

Charles Hanson returned home
Sunday from Salt Lake City.

Mrs. Ida Tullis of Pinto is visiting in Leeds.

Washington County News
September 7, 1909

Leeds Now Has ·
A Fruit Cannery

Leeds, Sept. 7.—Henry Peterson
returned home last week from Milford with a canning outfit for Brigham Jarvis jr. Mr. Jarvis has now
commenced canning his tomatoes
and so far seems well pleased with
the results he has had.

James Hamilton of Beaver spent
two or three days in this place loading up fruit to take north with him.

Donald Fuller and Henry Peterson have gone to Milford to get
more lumber for our school house

Mrs. Annie C. Angell has gone to
Hurricane to visit with her son,
Charles A. Angell.

Mrs. Naoma Hartley of Hurricane has been a visitor in this place
for some time.

Mr. and Mrs. Frank Batty of
Hurricane are here visiting relatives
and friends.

Mrs. P. J. Hamilton left Sunday
for Middleton to visit with Mrs. Ida
McDonald.

Attorney Beebee and wife of Junction are in town on business.

Mart McAllister of St. George was
here yesterday on business.

Work Commenced On Leeds School House

Leeds, Sept 14.—Thomas Perry of Cedar City, who has the contract for finishing our new school house, commenced work on it today.

We are waiting patiently for the threshers to come and commence threshing as most everybody is getting out of flour.

Mrs M. J. Hamilton is home again after visiting a short time in Middleton and taking in the fruit festival.

A large number of Leeds people went to St. George to the fruit festival. They report having had a jolly time.

Mark Parker and his sister Miss Nina Parker of Circleville are visiting with relatives in Leeds.

Marriage Licenses

Marriage licenses have been issued by County Clerk Woodbury as follows:

Sept. 9—Parley Leavitt and Miss Lovena Hafen, both of Bunkerville

Sept 13—John T. Jarvis of St George and Miss Rose E. Lee of Hinckley; Ernest Tobler and Miss Cecelia Ence, both of Santa Clara.

Sept 14—Frank Barber of Hurricane and Miss Ida Webb of St. George; Raymond Stewart of Alamo, Nevada, and Miss Ruth Paris of Leeds.

Sept 15—David A. Abbott of Mesquite, Nevada, and Miss Emma C. Gardner of Pine Valley; Calvin D Barnum of Mesquite, Nevada, and Miss Lucy Jepson of Virgin.

DIXIE FRUIT FESTIVAL AND FAIR A GRAND SUCCESS

(Special Correspondence.)

ST. GEORGE, Washington Co, Sept. 13.—The Dixie Fruit Festival closed Sept. 10, 1909, with a general reception and feast of fruits and melons on the tabernacle grounds at 8 o'clock p. m. The grounds were beautifully illuminated with electric lights, and the tables fairly groaned with the loads of fruits and melons. The weather was delightful and the 1,200 or more people who had gathered were entertained by musical selections and speeches by the visitors from the north and others.

In an interview with J. T. Taylor, state horticultural inspector, he made the following statement:

"It is seldom that one sees practically every variety of fruit, from the crisp apple to the fig and pomegranate, in the exhibit of so small a section as Washington county; and yet we have them here, showing perfection of development in all varieties." He further states that for size, color, quality and variety, it surpasses any fruit exhibit ever held in the state outside of the state fair.

The arrangement was very artistic, and a unit in design. Particular mention should be made of the apple exhibit of F. D. Gifford and Thornton Hepworth of Springdale; the pears and the dried figs from Toquerville; the melons from Rockville; the pyramid of peaches from Bloomington; the general exhibit from La Verkin, remarkable for size and color; the Hungarian prunes from Santa Clara; the pomegranates from Washington; the pyramid of fruit from Middleton; the melons and grapes from Leeds; the grape exhibit by G. F. Jarvis of St. George; and the general display of fresh and dried fruits from the southern Utah experiment farm.

The best present opportunity for a market lies in canning and drying fruits. Canned fruits were exhibited by Dixie Canning & Manufacturing company, and by B. Jarvis, Jr., of Leeds.

Leeds Young Lady Marries Nevada Man

Leeds, Sept. 21.—Last Wednesday. Sept 15, Miss Ruth Paris of this place and Raymond Stewart of Alamo, Nevada, were married in the St. George temple. They were accompanied to St. George by the bride's sisters, Mrs. Jennie Stewart and Mrs Dallace Hartman. A reception was given Thursday evening at the bride's home. A number of pretty and useful presents were given them Dainty refreshments were served to the guests during the evening and those who were present report an enjoyable time.

Born, on the 17th inst. a baby girl to Mr. and Mrs. William Sullivan; all doing nicely.

Leeds Has Had Some Nice Showers

Leeds, Sept 28 —We have had another nice shower which lasted just long enough for us to want it to clear up again

Willard, Mark and Edward McMullin and David Stirling left today for Pine Valley mountains, to get some horses.

Thomas Stirling and William Nickles have gone to Cannaan ranch on business

We are still waiting for the threshers

Washington County News
October 5, 1909

Albert Hartman Dead And Buried

Leeds, Oct 5.—Funeral services were held in the meeting house last Saturday over the remains of Albert Hartman, who was formerly a resident of Silver Reef. He had been working at Frisco for some time when he was taken ill with typhoid fever. Word came last Wednesday that he was very low and Thursday he passed away. The body was brought here for burial.

Mr. and Mrs Lenore Scott were in this place last week visiting with relatives and friends Mrs. Scott was formerly Miss Eleanor Stirling

Miss Ellen McMullin has gone to Pleasant Grove, where she will attend school this winter.

Truman Angell has returned home from Moapa, where he has been working for some time.

Miss Ivy Barlow left last Thursday for Richfield to visit relatives

Visitors At Leeds

Leeds, Oct. 18—Mrs Charles Bastian of St. George, Mrs. Benjamin Bradshaw and Mrs. Charles Angell both of Hurricane, and Mrs Charles Nichols of Lovell, Wyoming, are visiting with their mother, Mrs. Naoma Hartley.

Mrs. Lizzie Wilder, who was formerly a resident of Silver Reef, has been visiting a few days in Leeds with relatives and old friends, but she is at present visiting in Virgin City, the guest of Mrs Thomas Starling. She will remain there a few days before starting for her home in Lovell, Wyoming.

Mr. and Mrs H. Welte of Salt Lake City are the guests of Mr. and Mrs. Henry Peterson. Mr. Welte is here on business

Leeds School House Nearly Completed

Leeds, Nov. 9—Mrs Ann McAllister of Manti staved a short time in this place yesterday She was on her way from St George to Cedar City to visit her sister, Mrs. Jane Wilkinson, who is ill with pneumonia.

Henry Welte, vice-president and manager of the new company which has been formed to revive the mines at old Silver Reef, expects to go to Salt Lake City before the fifteenth of this month. His business there is connected with the Company.

George R. Lund, county game commissioner, and Charlie Bastian, both of St. George, and Frank Hamilton of this place have just returned from a short trip to Pine Valley mountain.

Our new school house is now nearly completed The carpenters will be through in a day or two and the painters are hard at work.

Miss Nell Andrus of Middleton is a visitor in Leeds.

H. W. Gubler and Arthur Webb of La Verkin arrived here last Friday to have the latter's eye treated by Dr Woodbury. They were both at Toquerville the previous day working on a molasses mill. Gubler was doing something to the mill, using a hammer when the head of it flew off and struck Webb on the left eye. The unfortunate man was wearing glasses at the time which the hammer smashed, driving pieces of glass into the eye. It is hoped that the sight of the eye can be saved.

To Receive Governor

The following are the committees appointed with respect to the anticipated visit of Governor Spry and party, which will be fourteen in number:

On reception—Ed H. Snow, Francis L. Daggett, James Andrus, David H. Morris, Albert E. Miller, Harry J. Doolittle, Thomas P. Cottam, Joseph T. Atkin and Ed. M. Brown, all of St. George; George A Holt, of Enterprise, J. S. P. Bowler, of Gunlock; James Ballard, of Grafton; Frank Prince, Harmony; Samuel Isom, Hurricane; B. Y. McMullin, Leeds, James Judd, LaVerkin; Heber E Harrison, Pinto; Reuben Gardner, Pine Valley; David Hirschi, Rockville, Ed R. Frei, Santa Clara; Freeborn D. Gifford, Springdale, John T. Batty, Toquerville; James Jepson, Virgin City, and Calvin Hall of Washington.

Appt. School Funds

Following is a statement showing the apportionment of county school funds to the respective school districts of Washington county, $1 50 per capita.

Place	School Pop.	Amount
Springdale	56	$ 84 00
Rockville	94	141.00
Grafton	32	48 00
Virgin	48	72 00
Toquerville	97	145 50
La Verkin	48	72 00
Hurricane	94	141.00
Leeds	54	81 00
Washington	177	265 50
St. George	588	882 00
Bloomington	18	27 00
Santa Clara	102	153 00
Gunlock	36	54 00
Pine Valley	47	70 50
Enterprise	102	153 00
Pinto	26	39,00
Harmony	44	66 00
Central	42	63 00
Total	1705	$2557.50

WILLARD O. NISSON,

Snow To Hay Mowing

New Harmony, Nov. 29 —The other day our mail carrier left here in about fifteen inches of snow and when he got to Leeds the farmers there were mowing hay—quite a little contrast.

RAILROAD BONUS $100,000.00

Division of $100,000 00 Bonus to Utah Southern Company divided among Settlements interested on basis of assessed valuation.

Place	Assessed valuation		Proportion of $100,000 00
Springdale	$12,860		
Rockville	41,815		
Grafton	16,610		
Virgin	41,105.		
Toquerville	67,535.		
La Verkin	22,740	$202,695 00	$23,745 85
Hurricane	$15,865, raised to	91,730 00	10,746.22
Leeds		49,015 00	5,745,65
Washington		74,530 00	8,731 26
St George		370,670 00	43,424 18
Bloomington		9,280 00	1,087.16
Santa Clara		50,380 00	5,890 34
Gunlock		10,715 00 cut to 5,372 00	629 34
			$100,000 00

DID CLARK SAY THIS?

Elsewhere in this paper will be found an article copied from the Deseret News giving Senator Clark's views of the Salt Lake route's position and the probable routes In this article appears the following paragraph

"In discussing the matter recently Senator Clark declared that it was certain that the road would not go by way of St. George, as it was too far."

If Senator Clark is correctly quoted, it is not easy to understand what is meant by the words "too far." If the Senator meant that it would mean a longer route than the one previously had, he is mistaken. A nearer route can be obtained through this county with a lesser grade than that which the Salt Lake route had through the Meadow Valley wash country. By leaving the present line at Thermo a straight shoot can be made for Las Vegas or Moapa via Cedar, Kanarra, Harmony, Leeds, St.

George and the "Narrows" The worst grade is between the "rim of the basin" and Leeds, where it is one and six-tenths as against two and four-tenths between Crestline and Caliente on the old route. By taking a look at any good map it will be readily seen that the St George route is the shorter route, and it would have a safe and solid roadbed all the way, secure from washouts, and it would run through a productive country that would furnish twenty cars of freight to each one that was had over the old route

The engineers now going over this route will find the facts as stated here, and we have no fears as to the result

Leeds, Jan 25—William Huntley, an aged resident of Silver Reef, was seriously burned and died from the effects of it He lived twenty-four hours after the accident He was buried on the 21st inst.

W. D Newton was arraigned before the Justice's Court on the 22nd inst. to answer to the charge of selling wine to the Indians. The verdict of Justice David McMullin was "Not Guilty."

The orchestra from Washington gave a dance here last night A crowd of young people came over from Washington with the orchestra A very enjoyable time was spent.

The railroad engineers who are looking up a grade for the railroad passed through here making the prospective grade a little to the north of Leeds

Leeds, Feb. 15 —The boys of Leeds have organized a base ball team and have sent a challenge to Hurricane for a baseball game, to be played on Washington's birthday.

Wm. Sterling had a runaway with his team hitched to a plough. They ran through a wire fence, but no serious harm was done

Men are busy hauling posts or working on the farm, for spring work is coming on and time for garden work.

Mrs Eleanor Scott and Mrs John Tellis, who were here visiting with relatives, have returned to their homes.

Home missionaries were here on the 13inst. from Hurricane. A very good meeting was held.

Mark McMullin, who has been sick, is around again

Leeds, Feb 28—Monday, the 21st of Feb was observed by the pupils of the Leeds school district as a "clean up" day. The girls cleaned the windows and the school house, while the boys cleaned up the yards A great improvement was made.

A game of base ball was played between Leeds and Hurricane on the 22nd of Feb Hurricane players were victorious People from settlements near by were in attendance and a very good time was spent.

Robert and Willard McMullin left last week for work on the road between Bellevue and Kanarra

Mrs Hamilton, who has been visiting relatives in Middleton, returned home last Saturday.

Leeds, March 8—A surprise party was given in honor of Miss Leonia McMullin's sixteenth birthday on the evening of Feb 28th.

A dance was given here last Thursday evening and an enjoyable time was spent.

Some of the people have been to St. George for conference.

Several people are suffering from bad colds and lagrippe.

Geo. R. Lund of St. George was in town yesterday.

Leeds, March 15.—Some of the Leeds boys are working on the county road between Bellevue and Kanarra

A surprise party was given last Wednesday evening in honor of Alex Sullivan's twentieth birthday.

A son was born to the wife of Wm. D. Sullivan, Jr., on the 10th inst

Mrs. Taylor and Mrs Kelsey were in town last week visiting relatives

The water has been turned out of the ditch for spring cleaning.

Mr. Caldwell of Washington is in town on business

Washington County News
March 22, 1910

Leeds March 22,—Elders M. M Harmon and George Lytle were here last Sunday as home missionaries A very good meeting was held and enjoyed by all present

Jesse Jepson and Miss Brenda Angell are in town visiting friends and relatives.

Frank McMullin and family were in town a day or two visiting relatives.

A water meeting was held last evening in the Leeds school house

Mr. Caldwell of Washington was in town on business.

Leeds, March 28 —A baseball game will be played here next Saturday between Leeds and Toquerville. The losing team will give a dance in the evening to the winning team

A crowd of young people went to Toquerville to a dance last Friday evening A very good time was had.

Mrs. George W. Worthen of St. George was in town last week to get some bees,

David Sterling has been to Lund after freight for the store.

Come and see the ball game next Saturday.

Leeds, April 4—A ball game was played in Leeds Saturday, April 2nd, between Leeds and Toquerville. Leeds lost the game and gave the Toquerville boys a free dance A very good time was enjoyed by all. The Washington orchestra played for the dance.

Mrs Hamilton has gone to Salt Lake City to conference, where she will meet her daughter. After conference she will go with her daughter to Montana to spend a few months.

George Spilsbury of Toquerville was a Sunday visitor. He greatly encouraged the Sunday school workers

County Attorney Paxman was in town a day or so looking up the case of Emett selling wine to minors,

Mrs Hattie W. Barnum and her husband are here visiting relatives.

Mr. Caldwell of Washington was a visitor here for a few days.

Leeds, April 11—The Springdale Dramatic company presented here last Saturday night the drama entitled "Dora Thorne." A dance was given after the play and a good time was spent by all present.

Willard McMullin left this morning for Caliente with a load of beans Truman Angell and Frank McMullin went with him. They expect to get work out there

Court for the Emett trial should have been held here last Wednesday but a jury could not be called, it was therefore dismissed and taken to St George

Leeds, April 19—Miss Ruth Stirling was very agreeably surprised last Thursday afternoon by the pupils of her school Games and dancing were indulged in after which a nice lunch was served.

Don Fuller, Mark McMullin and Charlie Angell have gone to haul wool from Gould's ranch to Lund

A surprise was sprung on Wm L Woodbury last Thursday evening A good time was enjoyed by all

Miss Isabel Stirling has gone to Modena to visit her sister, Mrs Eleanor Scott

William Stirling is putting up a new hay shed on his lot

Leeds, April 26—The Relief society members met last Thursday afternoon to sew rags for the benefit of helping to make carpet for the St. George temple. All helped willingly.

Wm D. Sullivan, Sr., Robert McMullin and Wm Nicholls, came in from the roundup with a bunch of cattle. Some of the boys were busy branding calves yesterday.

Henry Peterson, T. A. Sullivan and Frank Hartley left yesterday morning to haul wool from Gould's ranch to Lund.

Mrs David McMullin went to Parowan last week to visit with her relatives and friends.

Don Fuller, W. D. Sullivan and Charlie Angell, left this morning for Gould's ranch

Charlie Foster of St George was in town the latter part of last week on business

Nielson Bastian, of Washington was in town the latter part of last week.

Col. Woods has moved from Leeds to live in Harrisburg

The fruit crop is good this year.

Washington County News
May 3, 1910

Leeds, May 3—Andrew Sproul of Washington has been here taking the census. He visited our Sunday school and meeting and gave some very good instructions, which were very much appreciated

Wm E Woodbury of St George was in town the latter part of last week. Miss Annie Woodbury of St. George was in town also, visiting her friend, Mrs Verda Sullivan

Mr and Mrs Hyrum Thompson of St. George were here last Friday evening visiting with Mr. and Mrs E. C. Olsen.

The wool haulers returned yesterday evening looking rather dusty. There were eight teams all together

Frank Hartley came in last evening with a load of freight for Mr Emmett at Harrisburg.

Mr Caldwell of Washington is a business visitor here today.

Washington County News
May 11, 1910

Leeds, May 11—Mr and Mrs Ira McMullin are expected home today from Meadow Valley wash, where they have been visiting relatives, and also to bring home their daughter, Etta, who has been away the past winter teaching school.

A pleasant surprise was sprung on Mr. and Mrs Henry Peterson last Saturday evening After the music and singing, a nice lunch was served A good time was enjoyed by all

Duncan McArthur of St George was in town the latter part of last week buying cattle of Bp B Y McMullin

Mrs Minnie Harris of Salt Lake City is here visiting her parents, Mr, and Mrs Peter Hansen

Charlie Bastian of St George was in town yesterday buying cattle of Frank Hartley

Mrs Thomas Sterling of Virgin City is here visiting her sister, Mrs Mary Sullivan

Henry Peterson has sold his property at Grape Vine to Mr. Gower of Cedar City

Joseph Meeks of Virgin City was in town on business the fore part of the week

George Lund of St George was in town yesterday on business

Washington County News
May 17, 1910

Leeds, May 17—We had a terrific wind here Sunday afternoon, which did some damage blowing down barns and large trees. Garden stuff looks like a heavy frost had struck it. The barn of Don Fuller was blown to the ground. Albert Gowers' barn at Grape Vine is blown down and demolished, also Mr Wickes' barn. T. A. Sullivan's barn was partly destroyed.

Thomas Sterling and wife and family went back to Virgin Sunday after spending a few days here in town.

A crowd of young folks had a party last night at the home of Miss Georgania Angell. All had a good time

Wm D. Sullivan, Sr , is hauling wool from Gould's ranch to Lund.

Some of the farmers are busy cutting their first crop of hay.

Washington County News
May 25, 1910

Leeds, May 25—Born, to the wife of Wm Nicholls, a son, May 25th, mother and babe doing nicely

Some of the boys have been up to Pine Valley mountain with salt for their cattle.

Thomas Caldwell of Washington was in town the fore part of the week

Roy Barlow is out at Peter Anderson's ranch to work.

Wm E Woodbury of St George was a visitor here Sunday.

Leeds, May 30—The men have been busy the last few days gathering their cattle for the steer sale today at Anderson's ranch

Wm Nicholls has just returned from Buckskin mountain where he has been working the last few weeks.

Mr and Mrs Charlie Angell of Hurricane are here visiting relatives and friends.

Mrs Ed. Foster of St George is here visiting Mr. and Mrs. Oscar McMullin

Willard McMullin has gone to Caliente to work

Leeds, June 14 —Henry Welta and wife of Salt Lake City are living in Silver Reef   He is interested in some mines there.

Elders M L McAllister and Geo E. Miles of St George were visitors here Sunday.   Their remarks were very interesting and highly appreciated.

Frank McMullin of Hurricane is here for a few days, very much improved in health

Mrs Etta McMullin of Hurricane is here visiting with relatives and friends.

Joseph Sterling left this morning for Lund to bring in freight.

David Sterling's foot is improving very slowly.

Thomas Flynn of Virgin City is in town.

Killed at Caliente

Matt Wicks, a former resident of Silver Reef, is believed to be the man referred to in the following account, which is copied from the Deseret News:

Caliente, June 20—Matt Wicks is dead, Walter Murphy with his arm half shot away and the stump in a sling and James B Murphy in jail is the toll of a gun fight in the main street of this Nevada camp at an early hour Sunday morning. The direct cause is traceable to a protracted spree. The shooting took place on the tracks in front of Billy Noble's saloon in Clover avenue. Nearly one-half the population of the town was on the street at the time the loud quarrel began, but no one interfered. A stranger who started towards the spot where the dead man fell after the shooting was warned away by Murphy with his gun pointing to the spot the stranger occupied

Deputy Sheriff T. J. Harrington and Dr W. P. Murray were soon on the ground after the shooting. It was too late to give the victim any medical or surgical attention and the sheriff's deputy soon had Murphy in jail guarded by three stalwart men, for it was feared that an attempt to lynch him would be made Murphy said that the three men had come here from a bridge gang camp, and that as soon as they landed in town they began drinking. The dead man formerly lived in Utah and the Murphy brothers were formerly from Colorado

Leeds, June 21—A pleasant surprise was sprung on Mrs Henry Welta last Friday evening at her home in Silver Reef   A jolly good time was spent by all

Albert Gowers and Miss Grace Gowers of Grape Vine returned yesterday from Cedar City where they had been to attend the funeral of their grandfather.

Frank Hamilton has just returned from the Pine Valley mountains, where he has been on a pleasure trip for a few days.

Orin Kelsey of Harmony was in town last week getting fruit and visiting Mr. and Mrs Alma Angell

Neilson Bastian of Washington was in town the fore part of the week,

Elson Morris of St George was in town last week on business

Some of the farmers are cutting their second crop of lucerne

Peter Hansen is building a new addition to his house.

Leeds, June 28—Mrs Annie Angell fell last Thursday afternoon and severely bruised herself.

Miss Isabel Sterling returned home Sunday from Modena where she has been for some time.

We are all very glad to see David Sterling able to be out again.   His foot is improving nicely

Frank Hartley's little son was very sick last week but is on the improve now.

John Tullis and wife of Pinto were here Sunday visiting relatives and friends

Frank Hamilton has gone on the mountain again for a few days.

Thomas Caldwell of Washington was in town last week.

Oscar McMullin has gone to Panguitch with fruit.

Leeds, July 5—The Fourth of July was celebrated in a rousing good style Sports of all kinds were indulged in by young and old Much credit is due the committee for the good management; the day was well spent and enjoyed by all A crowd of young folks from Toquerville attended the dance in the evening. A jolly good time was spent

Miss Rebn Coates of St. George is here visiting with Mrs Oscar McMullin

Mrs. Marion Paris has sold her home to a Mr. Jolly of Long valley.

Mrs Thomas Sterling of Virgin is now making her home in Leeds

Wm. D. Woodbury of St George is a visitor for a few days

Neilson Bastian of Washington is here visiting friends

Much has been said of the Iron Mountain, St. George & Grand Canyon railroad, and now that the preliminary survey has been completed and the first map drawn, the details will be of interest. The line leaves the Salt Lake Route at Thermo and runs to Cedar City via Enoch. From Cedar it goes to Kanarra and at a point a few miles east of New Harmony it branches

The Kingman branch is projected to run through the following places Belleview, Silver Reef, Leeds, Harrisburg, Washington, Middleton, St. George, where it makes a turn up Santa Clara Creek to a point near Santa Clara and then makes another turn to the southwest, effecting an easy grade in crossing the Beaver Dam mountains, thence thence to Littlefield, Bunkerville, St Thomas. The Colorado river is crossed at Stone Ferry, a few miles west of Rioville. This is a pioneer landing in the old river steamboats, fully and interestingly described in Sunday's Tribune Then the line runs due south to Kingman, Ariz, where it connects with the Santa Fe

Returning to the point of divergence near New Harmony, the other line runs southeast through Virgin, Canaan Spring, Short Creek and east to Pipe Springs and Mangum Springs in Arizona. Between Pipe Springs and Mangum Springs the third branch runs to the rim of the Grand Canyon of the Colorado in Arizona, at a point about fifty miles south of Kanab That town is north of the railroad line between Pipe and Mangum Springs but a few miles.

A distinct feature of the whole project is that it penetrates an entirely new and virgin field and at no point after leaving Thermo does it compete or aim to compete with any other railroad or branch The entire region is rich in products of mines, the soil, of forests, of animals, while the scenic attractions, headed by the Grand Canyon, would make it the most wonderfully attractive railroad in the world As a retreat for campers, hunters and fishermen it would be a paradise

Engineer Burgess has completed a map which is a most thorough one in setting forth the exact geographical outline of the country, as well as the geological and industrial possibilities It shows one of the most extensive empires not reached by a railroad that can be found in the whole west —Tribune.

Leeds, July 19, 1910—Elders Frank Barber of Hurricane and John Judd of La Verkin were home missionaries here Sunday. They bore faithful testimonies to the truth of the gospel and give good counsel to the young men in regard to the use of tobacco and other injurious articles

Mrs. Caroline McMullin returned home the latter part of last week from Parowan, where she has been visiting for the past three months

Mrs S. J. Paris left last week for Alamo, Nev. Don Fuller has just returned from taking her to Lund.

Fault Not at Leeds

Editor Washington County News

Dear Sir —In your paper of July 14, you quote from an interview with the St. George postmaster wherein he explains that, "Toquerville is now the distributing office for points up the river instead of Leeds, as formerly, but that the second class mail sack is still made up by the railway mail clerks for Leeds, and labeled to that office," infering that the non-arrival of papers for up the-river points is caused by their delay at this office

This is a mistake, as Leeds suffers the same as other points in that way, owing to the change of time in the arrival of the mail train from the north.

It is true that the second class mail sack is still made up for and addressed to Leeds, but the mail is all looked over before the mail driver leaves here and is dispatched on the same day on which it arrives

Very Respectfully,

Post Master,

Leeds, Utah

Washington County News
July 27, 1910

Leeds, July 27—Pioneer day was celebrated with a meeting in the forenoon, ice cream and lemonade were the refreshments and sports were indulged in. A good time was had by all.

Sheriff C. R. Worthen of St. George was in town yesterday. He brought Mr. Newton over with him to get bondsmen and succeeded. Mr. Newton was turned loose.

Frank McMullin has returned home from Hinckley where he has been employed for some time

Miss Buelah Schmutz of St. George is a visitor at Mrs. C E. Olsen's for a few days.

Washington County News
August 2, 1910

Leeds, Aug 2—Born, to the wife of Francis Hartley, a daughter, July 30; mother and babe doing nicely.

Maggie Olsen has just returned home from Salt Lake City, where she has been at school the past winter.

Some of the boys went on the mountain yesterday to build a cabin and to look after their cattle.

David McMullin accompanied by his wife, went to Milford last week with a load of fruit.

Dr F. J. Woodbury of St. George was in town the latter part of last week.

Charlie hansen has returned home from Salt Lake City.

Leeds, Aug. 9—David Sterling, Frank Hamilton, Don Fuller, Lin McMullin and Charlie Angell returned Sunday from the mountain where they have built a good comfortable cabin, for the benefit of the cattlemen. They report the cattle looking fine.

Bp B. Y. McMullin returned yesterday from Cedar City where he went to meet his daughter, Mrs Mattie Harris and family of Salt Lake City. She is visiting her parents for awhile.

The little child of Mr. and Mrs. Hyrum Leany, that was seriously ill last week, is much better and able to be out again.

We had rather a wild storm last week, the wind blew very hard and the rain fell in torrents for a little while.

David McMullin has returned from Milford with some lumber for his house.

William Nicholls has gone to the Buckskin mountains looking after cattle

Wm Hartman went to Kanarra last week to work for Bp Berry.

Some of the farmers are busy cutting their third crop of lucern.

Edward Vincent has gone north with another load of fruit.

Leeds, Aug 16—Most of our young people, and some of the older one went to Hurricane last Friday to take in Elberta day. They all had a good time and were treated royally by the people of Hurricane.

Mrs Mary E Olsen has gone to Salt Lake City to visit her daughter Mamie, who has graduated as a trained nurse from the L D S hospital.

The fruit haulers are very busy, going and coming Dixie's fruit seems to be in the lead, some of the men are contracting their fruit

Prof J. E Hickman of the Beaver academy lectured here in school house the fore part of last week.

Henry Welte of Silver Reef returned home from St. George yesterday, where he went on business

Wm D. Sullivan, Sr , has gone north with fruit, his daughter, Estella, accompanied him.

Wm E Woodbury of St George was a visitor here the latter part of last week

*Mrs Emma Angell of Hurricane is visiting with relatives and friends here.

Leeds, Aug. 23—The Toquerville boys gave a dance here last Wednesday night, and a jolly good time was spent by the young folks

Bert McQuarrie and wife and family of St George were here last week visiting Mr and Mrs. Wm. Sterling for a few days

Charlie Angell of Hurricane was here Sunday visiting his mother, Mrs Annie Angell.

George Spilsbury of Toquerville was a visitor at Sunday school and meeting Sunday.

Robert McMullin has just returned from the north, where he has been with fruit.

Charlie Bastian and wife of St George were visitors here last week

Mrs Eleanor Scott of Modena is here visiting relatives and friends.

Mrs Ida Sterling Tellis of Pinto is a visitor here for a few days

Leeds, Aug. 30—Ira McMullin, Joseph Sterling, George Olsen, Edward Vincent and Hyrum Laney, Jr., went north with fruit the latter part of last week.

Mrs Mattie Harris returned last Friday to her home in Salt Lake City. She was accompanied by her mother, Mrs. Ada McMullin.

Frank Sullivan, Charles Angell and Don Fuller returned last week from Panguitch and Circleville, where they went with fruit

Peter Hansen is having a new porch put up in the front part of his house. Charlie Hansen is doing the carpenter work.

A committee has been appointed to select fruit for the coming fruit festival to be held in St. George on the 7th and 8th.

Miss Georgiana Angell left yesterday for Salt Lake City to visit her sister, Mrs. Bessie Reese, for a short time.

Miss Ivy Barlow left yesterday for Idaho, where she will spend some time in visiting relatives and friends

David McMullin and daughter, Myrtle, left for the north this morning with a load of fruit.

Woodbury---Sullivan

Mr William E Woodbury and Miss Verda Sullivan were united in wedlock in the temple here Tuesday The bride is a daughter of Mr. and Mrs. William D. Sullivan of Leeds, an estimable young lady, the groom is a son of Mr and Mrs John T. Woodbury of this city, an exemplary young man The bride and groom both came from good stock, and a host of friends wish them unalloyed happiness

After the ceremony, the young couple left for Leeds, where a reception was given Tuesday evening at the home of the bride's parents

Leeds, Sept 20---Thomas Sullivan and wife have gone north with a load of choice fruit. Tom has everything his own way now, most of the peddlers having been put out of commission by the hail storm.

Cupid is doing a rushing business here of late. During this month we have lost two of our young ladies through his pranks, and from the looks and shy blushes of another we judge that one other will soon be added to the list.

Cards have been received here announcing the marriage at Salt Lake City of Miss Mayme Olsen of this place and D. O. Beal of Ephraim, Sept. 14th.

Mrs B. Y. McMullin has returned from Salt Lake City, accompanied by her daughter, Mrs S. L Harris, who expects to spend the winter here.

Mrs Mark Miller is here from Salt Lake City visiting her mother, Mrs Oscar McMullin.

Chas. Hanson went to Cedar to attend the fair (?) by special invitation.

Leeds, Sept. 27—Mrs. M. J. Hamilton has returned from Montana, where she has been all summer visiting. She is much improved in health and enjoyed her trip both going and coming

Some of the boys have been on the mountain after their cattle. The cattle looked to be in pretty good condition. Ras Anderson was in town last week buying cattle that were in good order.

Some of the men are now busy making molasses. From the looks of the cane crop and the molasses barrels coming in town, there will be plenty of sweets

Chas Hansen, returned from Cedar last week He went there on business and also to attend the fair, which was a success in every way

Mrs M. J. Hamilton went to Middleton last week to visit her neice, Mrs Ida McDonald, returning home Sunday.

Miss Isabel Sterling has gone to Beaver to attend the Murdock school this winter

Mat Hartley of Hurricane was in town Sunday visiting his brother, Frank Hartley.

Mrs Annie Angell is on the sick list; we hope she will soon be out again.

Frank Hamilton went north yesterday after grain and potatoes.

Leeds, Sept. 27—Mrs. M. J. Hamilton has returned from Montana, where she has been all summer visiting. She is much improved in health and enjoyed her trip both going and coming

Some of the boys have been on the mountain after their cattle. The cattle looked to be in pretty good condition. Ras Anderson was in town last week buying cattle that were in good order.

Some of the men are now busy making molasses. From the looks of the cane crop and the molasses barrels coming in town, there will be plenty of sweets

Chas Hansen, returned from Cedar last week He went there on business and also to attend the fair, which was a success in every way

Mrs M. J. Hamilton went to Middleton last week to visit her neice, Mrs Ida McDonald, returning home Sunday.

Miss Isabel Sterling has gone to Beaver to attend the Murdock school this winter

Mat Hartley of Hurricane was in town Sunday visiting his brother, Frank Hartley.

Mrs Annie Angell is on the sick list; we hope she will soon be out again.

Frank Hamilton went north yesterday after grain and potatoes.

Leeds, Oct. 4—Mrs. Mary E Olsen has returned home from Salt Lake City, where she has been for the past seven weeks visiting relatives and friends, and also the Sunday schools and meetings, which she enjoyed very much.

Our school started yesterday morning with Chas. Hanson teacher of the higher grades and Miss Maggie Olsen as teacher of the primary grades

A bouncing big baby boy came last week to the home of Hyrum Leany at Harrisburg, reported that mother and babe are doing nicely.

David Sterling has returned home from Beaver where he went to take his sister, Miss Isabel, to attend the Beaver school this winter.

Mr. and Mrs Thos. Caldwell of Washington were visiting Mr. and Mrs. T A Sullivan the latter part of last week.

David McMullin and his daughter, Myrtle, came home last week from the north where he went with fruit.

Don Fuller has gone north with a load of fruit. The fruit season is about over here.

Some of the men are still busy gathering their cattle out of the mountains.

Mrs Annie Angell has recovered from her sickness and is able to be out again

Miss Libby Leany of Harrisburg is teaching school in Virgin this winter.

Leeds, Oct 11.—Bp B Y. McMullin went north the latter part of last week with a load of dried beans, also to take his daughter Ethel to Beaver, where she will attend school this winter.

Chas Hansen has been chosen as president of the Y. M. M. I A. He is an exemplary young man and is well respected by all the community.

Oscar McMullin and Don Fuller have returned home from the north where they went last week with fruit More fruit is the cry.

Ammon Jolly who was very ill last week, is able to be out and around at work again.

Frank Anderson was in town last week repairing the telephone wires

Thomas Flynn of Virgin was in town last week on business

Wm. Sterling has gone to Parowan after a load of flour.

New Harmony, Oct. 17.—A fare-well party will be given in honor of Elder J. L Prince, on Friday Oct 21. His field of labor will be in the Eastern States People from surrounding settlements are expected to attend.

Our district school started last Monday the 10th. Miss Sterling, the teacher from Leeds, reports every thing moving along all right.

We have had a nice rain which will fix the farming land in a good shape for plowing.

Leeds, Nov. 1.—Owing to the correspondent being sick, Leeds news has not been sent for some time

Mrs. Maud Miller has returned to her home in Salt Lake City after spending a month here visiting relatives and friends.

Mr. and Mrs. Crecelius of Silver Reef left last week for Los Angeles, Cal , where they expect to make their home.

Frank Hamilton came home Sunday from Hamilton's Fort, where he has been to get a load of potatoes

Robert and Edward McMullin left last week for Beaver, to attend school there this winter.

Willard McMullin is home from Caliente where he has been working all summer.

Born, a son to Mr. and Mrs. Will Hartman Sunday, Oct 23rd.

Some of the men are just hauling their last crop of hay.

Leeds, Nov. 8 —The young people are taking a great interest in their Sunday school and meetings especially their mutuals They all respond in taking their parts, when called upon to do so We feel as though there is a wakening up amongst the young and old and hope it will continue so.

Elder George Spilsbury of Toquerville visited our Sunday school and meetings Sunday. He spoke on different subjects which was very much appreciated by the people *

Miss Ann McMullin was chosen as president of the Y. L M I A. She is well qualified for the position and we all give her our hearty support

Mr and Mrs Thos Cadwell of Washington were over the latter part of last week visiting Mr. and Mrs T. A Sullivan

Miss Julia Ford entertained at a rag bee at the home of Mrs Susie Sterling last Wednesday. They all had a good time

We had political speakers here last week, their talk being mostly on state wide prohibition and local option.

Frank Hamilton and Will Nicholls have gone on the mountain to search for some horses that are missing.

Ira McMullin and David Sterling returned last week from Beaver, where they went on business

Wm Sullivan, Sr., returned from the north last week with a load of lumber.

Chas. Hansen is putting a new coat of paint on the Hansen residence

Andrew Gregerson, Sr , of Bellevue was in town for a short time today.

Miss Libby Leany of Harrisburg was visiting the schools here yesterday.

Owing to it being election day the schools are having a holiday today.

Leeds, Nov. 28 — The Y. M. and Y. L M. I A. had a dance for the benefit of raising means for the mutual expenses this winter. They sold lunches consisting of hot chocolate, cake and sandwiches All had a good time.

Bp B Y. McMullin is making quite an improvement on his place He has his house newly shingled, and is now having a neat picket fence put up His son Clarence is doing the work, with the help of Wm. Sterling and Wm Nicholls

Thanksgiving day passed off very quietly. The town boys had a game of base ball in the afternoon, and in the evening all the youngfolks had a pleasent time at the home of Miss Ethel Sullivan.

Oscar McMullin came home last week from the north with a load of lumber. He is going to make some improvements on his house

Bp B Y. McMullin has just returned from taking his son Robert and daughter Ethel back to Beaver to school.

Frank Hamilton has just returned from Salt Lake City, where he went as a witness on W. D. Newton's case.

Ammon Jolley has gone out to Tropic where he will have employment all winter.

The little son of Mr. and Mrs. Frank Hartley is still ailing with Bright's disease.

Molasses making will soon be over with here

Washington County News
December 6, 1910

Leeds, Dec. 6.—Died in St. George, Dec. 3, 1910, at the residence of Mr. and Mrs. John Schmutz, Lyle Olsen Sullivan, the infant babe of Mr. and Mrs. Wm. D. Sullivan, Jr., after an illness of three weeks. Funeral services were held here yesterday at eleven o'clock in the school house. The parents have the sympathy of the entire community in their sad bereavement. Mrs. Julia Andrus of Middleton, and Mrs. John Schmutz and John Sullivan both of St. George were here to attend the funeral.

C. F. Hansen closed school last Friday afternoon in order to clean the windows and benches. The large school boys and girls did the cleaning with a right will, Mr. Hansen doing his share.

The steam thresher from Washington was here last week threshing beans for C. E. Olsen, Bp B. Y. McMullin and Frank Hartly.

Mr. and Mrs Clarence McMullin returned to Calient last week, Joseph Sterling taking them to Lund station.

Charlie Angell came in from Milford last Saturday with a load of goods for Hansen's store.

Frank Sullivan left yesterday for Lund, after a load of flour.

Washington County News
December 13, 1910

Leeds, Dec. 13.—Bp. B. Y. McMullin went to St. George to attend conference Saturday and Sunday. He has his new picket fence completed, his son Willard did the work in place of Will Nicholls, as was stated by correspondent some time ago by mistake.

David Sterling, Don Fuller, Willard McMullin and Frank Hamilton came in with a bunch of cattle last Friday from the mountain.

Henry A. Jolley is very sick. His many friends hope that he will be better and able to mingle with them again before long.

Mrs Susie Sterling entertained her many friends at a rag bee last Thursday at her home; all had a good time.

Frank Sullivan came in from Lund yesterday with a load of flour.

William Sullivan has gone to Lund with a load of molasses.

Leeds, Dec. 27.—Last Friday evening Miss Maggie Olsen had a Christmas tree for her school children   A beautiful program was rendered and each little tot was heartily applauded by the audience. The tree was a pretty sight lighted up with Christmas candles and many a pretty present for the little ones hung on it.   They had a good time.

Last week Bp. B. Y. McMullin and his counselor, Hyrum Leany of Harrisburg, were round visiting the people in the ward, encouraging them to come to meetings and also to settle their tithing at the end of the year, and said the people would be blest by doing so.

The Primary officers had a dance and picnic Saturday afternoon for the little folks. The time was well spent in dancing by the little ones.

William Sterling, Sr., went to Harmony last Thursday, returning Sunday with his daughter, Ruth, her school being closed for holidays.

Edward and Robert McMullin came home last week for holidays, from Beaver, where they have been attending school.

Chas F. Hansen and Mark McMullin went to Cedar yesterday to spend holidays.

David McMullin has commenced the erection of his new residence

Edward Vincent has been hauling fence posts the last few days

Miss Libby Leany of Harrisburg is home from Virgin City.

Henry A. Jolley is still quite sick, improving very slowly.

At Silver Reef·

Henry Welte, manager of the Reef mining company, reports the outlook for the property as very favorable · He has had development work done during the past six months and states that at a rough estimation he could produce 200 tons of copper and silver ore per day had he the plant which his company has been figuring on installing to tread the copper ore. If things go as he expects, it will be pretty lively in the old camp of Silver Reef this coming year

Miss Agnes Lienhard of Salt Lake City, who has been with her sister, Mrs. Henry Welte, at Silver Reef all summer will remain for the winter.

Leeds, Jan, 3 — A crowd of young folks had a jolly good time on New Year's eve   They gathered at the home of Edward McMullin and played till twelve o'clock, when the people were aroused by ringing of bells from one end of town to the other.   Happy New Year rang out on the midnight air.

Miss Libby Leany of Harrisburg entertained her friends the fore part of last week.   Games were indulged in, after which a nice lunch was served, consisting of sandwiches, cake and pie.   The young folks all had a merry time.

Miss Maggie Olsen entertained at a party at the home of Mrs Lyle Sullivan last evening.   They played lively games during the evening after which refreshments were served.   They all had a most enjoyable time.

Mr. and Mrs. Ira McMullin went to Overton to spend holidays with their daughters, Mrs. Martha Fleming and Miss Etta McMullin.

Joseph Sterling, Carl McMullin, W. D Sullivan and Frank Hamilton came in from the hills yesterday with a bunch of cattle

The many friends of H. A, Jolley are very glad to hear that he is much improved in health.

Neils Bastian of Washington is a visitor here during holidays.

Leeds, Jan. 10 —Mrs Hannah Wilkinson was found dead in her door yard last Thursday morning. Funeral services were held in the school house Friday at two o'clock. She had been feeble for some time being eighty two years and eight months old at the time of her death. She was highly respected by all who knew her.

Mr. and Mrs Ira McMullin have returned home from Overton, Nevada, where they went to spend the holidays with their daughters. They had a pleasant time while there.

A suprise was sprung on Miss Ethel Sullivan last Tuesday evening. The time was spent in lively games, refreshments were served, and all had a jolly good time

George Spilsbury of Toquerville was over here and attended our Sunday school and meeting last Sunday. He gave some instructions which were much appreciated.

A crowd of young folks from Leeds and Harrisburg went over to Hurricane last Friday evening to attend a dance They all had a good time.

Charles Hansen, and Mark McMullin came home from Cedar City last week. They had a good time while there during holidays.

David Sterling returned yesterday from taking his sister, Miss Ruth, back to Harmony, where she is teaching school

Joseph Stirling, Frank Sullivan, Dan and Lin McMullin came in yesterday from the hills with fence posts

Mrs Ida McDonald of Middleton is here visiting her aunt, Mrs M. J. Hamilton, and friends.

Robert and Edward McMullin returned back to Beaver to school

Leeds, Jan. 17.—R G. McQuarrie and son, Bert, of St George are here putting up a lumber building for the forest ranger.

Mrs M. J. Hamilton has returned from Middleton, where she went last week to spend a few days visiting Mrs. Ida McDonald.

David McMullin has been busy the last week hauling lumber, doors and windows for his new house.

Born, to Mr. and Mrs. Donald Fuller a bouncing big boy Jan. 14th; mother and babe doing nicely.

David Forsha of St George was in town last week on business.

Leeds, Jan. 24.—Mr. Christensen of Manti, spoke to the Y. M. M. I. A. meeting Sunday evening He gave the young men good counsel and encouraged them to keep on doing good and attend to their meetings regularly and to cultivate good moral habits

Elders M. M. Harmon and George Lytle of St. George were missionaries here Sunday. They spoke on different subjects which was very interesting and highly appreciated.

Bp. B. Y. McMullin went to St. George last week on business, returning Friday with a load of lumber for the meeting house.

Charles Angell returned from St George, Saturday. Miss Connie Moss of St. George accompanied him.

Joseph Sterling, Frank Hamilton and Carl McMullin went in the hills yesterday to hunt for cattle

W. D. Sullivan, Jr., is making quite an improvement on his side walk.

Frank Seegmiller of St. George was in town last Saturday on business.

Leeds, Jan 30 —Frank Jones of Enoch and Mrs Farnsworth and daughter of Summit were on their way to St George yesterday. While the young man was watering his horses, while hitched to the buggy, the horses became frightened and started to run. The young lady jumped out, but her mother could not get out in time However, she had presence of mind to grasp the lines and hold herself in. The horses ran a distance of two hundred yards when the rig capsized, throwing Mrs Farnsworth out, bruising her arm considerably and completly demolishing the buggy The horses ran for another two hundred yards with the tongue and front wheels when they were stopped The party hired another rig and went on to St. George yesterday afternoon.

Miss Hazel Olsen went to St. George last week to visit with friends and relatives, returning home Sunday.

A crowd of young folks went to Hurricane last Friday evening to a dance. They had a real good time

Frank Anderson of Echo farm was in town last week on business

Some of the boys have been busy the last few days branding cattle,

Leeds, Feb. 14.—Bp. B. Y. Mc-Mullin has set Saturday as a regular cleaning day around the meeting house. Both the old and young men will turn out with teams, plows, scrapers and shovels to make a general cleaning up.

Willard McMullin, David Sterling and Mark McMullin have been appointed to try and find a piece of ground suitable for a ball ground and a place for amusements for the young people and report to the next P. H meeting.

Frank Hartly went to St George last Thursday returning Saturday with a load of shingles for the meeting house.

David Moss, Jr., of St George is busy working on the forest reserve house papering and painting.

Frank Hamilton, Joseph Sterling and Frank Sullivan went in the hills last week hunting for cattle.

The infant of Mr. and Mrs Donald Fuller has been very sick the last few days.

Assessor Heber E. Harrison of Pinto was is town yesterday on business

Joseph Sylvester of Washington was a visitor in town last Sunday.

Leeds, Feb 21 —Mr and Mrs Henry Schlappy and family of Washington were here visiting Mr. and Mrs C E Olsen Sunday.

Miss Marie McMullin entertained her young friends at an ice cream party at her home last Friday. All had a jolly good time

George Spilsbury of Toquerville was a speaker in our meeting Sunday afternoon, his remarks were very interesting

Mr. and Mrs. Bryant Jolley of Washington were here Sunday visiting their relatives, Mr. and Mrs H. A Jolley.

Rueben Jolley and Roy Pectol of Washington were in town the latter part of last week on business

W. D Sullivan, Sr , had the misfortune to cut his foot with a hay knife last week.

We are very glad to say that the babe of Mr. and Mrs Donald Fuller is much better.

Mr. and Mrs W. D Sullivan, Jr., went to Hurricane Sunday.

Mark McMullin left this morning for Parowan after grain.

Mrs. M J. Hamilton is on the sick list

Leeds, March. 7.—A pleasant party was held at the home of Bp B Y. McMullin last Tuesday evening in honor of Miss Leona's birthday. Music, singing, and lively games were indulged in after which a nice Lunch was served. They all had an enjoyable time.

Owing to the stormy weather we have been having, Bp B Y. McMullin has postponed working on the meeting house until the weather is more favorable

T. A. Sullivan, Ira McMullin and W. D. Sullivan, Sr, left this morning for Cedar City after seed grain.

Edward and Chester Slack of Toquerville were visitors here Sunday, also Eddie Dalton of Hurricane.

Miss Julia Ford who has been very sick with the grip for several days is now much better.

Charles Larson of St George is here working He expects to remain about a month.

J H. Lee of Harrisburg is putting up a new barn on his lot at Harrisburg

Leeds, March 14 —Mark McMullin of Leeds and Miss Grace Gowers of Cedar City were married last Thursday. March 9th, at Parowan. Their many friends wish them a long and happy life

The farmers are all busy getting their spring work done. We are having March weather indeed, sunshine and plenty of cold wind and a rain occasionally.

Our M. I. Assns. have closed after a very successful season's work. The attendance and home preparations have been better than usual

Thos Perry of Cedar City and his son, Raymond, are here for a few days. They are going to work on the meeting house here

Miss Ann McMullin returned home last week from Modena where she has been for the past few months with Mrs Eleanor Scott.

Miss Ellen McMullin returned yesterday from Parowan, where she went last week to visit friends and relatives

Bp B Y. McMullin was unable to attend conference at St. George Saturday and Sunday on account of sickness

The little babe of Mr and Mrs. Frank Hartly has been very sick the last few days with croup

Lawrence Marker of Cedar City is here visiting his friends for a few days.

We had a moving picture show here Saturday and Monday nights

Leeds, March 21 —The Primary officers, namely, Mrs Caroline McMullin, Mrs Susie Sterling and Mrs Miranda McMullin, gave a dance and lunch last Thursday evening in the Sterling hall, for the purpose of getting song books and other articles for the Primary here.

A pleasent party was had at the home of Mr. and Mrs. Mark McMullin, at Grapevine last Saturday evening by the young folks of Leeds The young couple received many useful and nice presents and the hearty good wishes of all for their future happiness.

Pres. C H. Snow and Pres Geo F Whitehead of St George were speakers here Sunday. They gave good instructions to the people, and encouraged them to build up and improve their surroundings and make their homes comfortable.

Thos W. Perry and his son, Raymond, returned to their home at Cedar City last Sunday, after working here a few days on the Meeting house

Frank Hamilton, Wm. D. Sullivan, Sr , Donald Fuller and Wm Nicholas went in the hills yesterday to gather cattle.

The farmers have been very busy lately getting their spring grain in, most of them are nearly through sowing grain

Mr and Mrs John Schmutz, Sr , of St George were here Sunday visiting Mr. and Mrs. E C. Olsen

Mr. and Mrs Charles Beams of Virgin City were in town the latter part of last week on business.

Thos. Caldwell and Earl Daniels of Washington were in town last week on business

Amos Workman of Hurricane was in town the latter part of last week on business

We are glad to say that the little babe of Mr and Mrs Frank Hartly is much better. ✱

Thomas Sterling and Chas Larson went to Virgin City last Saturday after lumber.

Leeds, April 4 —Mr and Mrs B Y. McMullin's little grandchildren left here yesterday morning for their home in Salt Lake City in charge of Miss Julia Ford, who is going to stay with them and keep house during the summer for L Harris and his family.

Wm Sterling, Jr , T. A Sullivan Don Fuller, Wm D Sullivan, Geo Olsen, Roy Barlow and Charles Angell donated two days' work each shingling the meeting house

The young folks had a dance last Thursday evening   They all had a merry time   The music was furnished by Frank Staheli of Washington

Wm Sterling, Sr , returned Sunday from Harmony with his daughter, Miss Ruth, her school being closed

Roy Barlow returned home last week from Idaho, where he has been working for several months

Mr. and Mrs Don Fuller went to Hurricane the latter part of last week, returning home Sunday.

Ammon Jolley returned home last Friday from Tropic, where he has been employed for some time.

Miss Ann McMullin left yesterday morning for Milford, where she expects to remain for awhile

Miss Verda 'De Mills of La Verkin is here visiting relatives and friends for a few days

M L McAllister and Alex Macfarlane of St George are here working on the reserve.

Frank Hamilton and Wm Nichols went in the hills this morning hunting for cattle.

George Spilsbury of Toquerville was a visitor here Sunday.

A. B Ballantine, the manager of the Southern Utah Experiment farm went up the river the fore part of the week to look into general farming and horticultural conditions of the settlements there.

8th Grade Graduates

Mammie Jolly, Washington
Francis Leaney, Leeds.
Stirling Russell. Springdale

SANTA CLARA
Edmond Gubler
Clarence Staheli
Milo Ence
Julius Wittwer

ST. GEORGE
Zoe Gates
David Woodbury
Irvin Carter
Genevieve Snow
Mathew Bentley
Mirriam Platt
Will Graf
Lyle Farnsworth
Nettie Whitehead
Camilla Woodbury
Laura Andrus
Millie Pendelton

Louis Woodbury, La Verkin.

HURRICANE
Alvin Hall
Elsie Stout
Sophia Langston
Lizzie Ballard

Genevieve Thornton, Pinto.

PINE VALLEY
Ivie Gardner
Irving Jacobson
Alma Jacobson
Vera Snow
Mira Snow

All who failed can try the examination in May by applying to Supt. in writing

Ass'd Valuation, County

County Assessor H E Harrison has completed the assessment of Washington County for this year, the returns showing an increase over last year's valuation. The following is the assessed valuation of the several precincts

Springdale	$13,055
Rockville	41,990
Grafton	9,655
Virgin	32,240
Toquerville	67,435
La Verkin	23,355
Hurricane	41,055
Leeds	33,150
Washington	74,670
St George	380,305
Bloomington	8,995
Santa Clara	46,425
Gunlock	9,820
Pine Valley	53,490
Enterprise	52,190
Pinto	18,420
Harmony	35,855
Central	10,845
Total	**$952,950**

Leeds, May 9 —Ward Jolley, the six-year old son of Mr and Mrs H. A Jolley, while trying to climb on a horse last Sunday, April 30, got hurt pretty bad. His foot slipped through the stirrup and he fell to the ground, frightening the horse which ran for a block dragging him and brusing his head very badly. He is getting along nicely

On the last day of school Mr. C F Hansen and Miss Maggie Olsen took their students and went to the Dixie canyon for a picnic and spent the day in having a jolly good time

Lawrence Marker of Cedar City gave two dances here last week, ice cream was served, the young folks of Toquerville were here and all had a real nice time

Born, a son to Mr. and Mrs Edward A Vincents April 19th; a daughter to Mr and Mrs T A Sullivan, all concerned doing well

Willard McMullin is laid up with a very severely sprained ankle, we hope he will be able to be out again soon

Mr. and Mrs Kelsey of Harmony were here the latter part of last week visiting Mr and Mrs Alma Angell

Don Fuller, Lynn McMullin and George Olsen have gone to Kolob after lumber for the reserve here.

Mrs Minnie Harris of Salt Lake City is here visiting her parents, Mr. and Mrs Peter Hansen.

Bert Gowers of Cedar City was here last week visiting his sister, Mrs Mark McMullin

Mrs Ethel Bastian and Mrs Verda Woodbury are home from Provo for the summer

Frank Sullivan returned from Fillmore yesterday after a two week's absence.

Joseph Sylvester of Washington was in town for a short time yesterday.

Washington County News
May 16, 1911

Leeds, May 16 —Sunday, the 14, was the day for our Missionaries to visit us, but for some reason or other they did not get here   Hope they will come soon as we always welcome visitors and like to have them come often.

Stake Aid George Spilsbury of Toquerville was a visitor here Sunday.   His remarks were very interesting   There was a good attendance at meeting, it being Mothers' day.

Oscar McMullin, George Olsen, Roy Barlow and Lynn McMullin have just got back from the sawmill with more lumber for the reserve

Some of the men folks are busy gathering their cattle for the spring sale, also putting cattle on the mountain for the summer.

Wm Sterling, Sr, is engaging teams here to go after freight at Modena for the Stake Academy, which they are in need of.

We are very glad to say that H. A Jolley is able to be out again; he has been very sick for the last two weeks.

Miss Emma Harradence of St George is staying with Mrs T. A Sullivan for a while

We had a beautiful rain here Sunday making everything look fresh and bright.

Frank McMullin of Hurricane was in town last week, on business

Leeds, May 23 —Elders Wm Gardner and Jos T. Atkin of St. George visited our Sunday school and meeting Sunday They spoke on different subjects which was very interesting both to the young and older people who all enjoyed the good instructions given

Mrs Wm Harris of Wyoming is here visiting her daughter, Mrs Susan Sterling She expects to remain for some time visiting her many friends and relatives

Frank McMullin came home last Thursday from Milford with a load of lumber for David McMullin's house and some dry goods for Hansen's store

A crowd of the young folks went to Toquerville Sunday evening after strawberries, they had a good feast, returning home after having had a good time

Frank Hartley went to Hurricane Saturday with his mother. She is moving from her home here to her new home at Hurricane

Edward A Vincent returned home yesterday from Harmony, where he has been working the last two weeks

Charles Angell and daughter, Kate, of Hurricane were in town the latter part of last week

Miss Etta McMullin returned home last week after being away all winter teaching school

Mr and Mrs John Tullis of Pinto are here visiting relatives and friends

Mrs Annie Angell is able to be out again after a very sick spell last week.

C E Olsen is making some improvements on his house

The farmers are busy getting up their first crop of hay

Some of the men folks are out on the cattle drive

Washington County News
May 30, 1911

Leeds, May 30 —Robert McQuarrie and his son Bert of St George are here putting up a barn on the reserve

The young folks had ice cream and cold drinks Sunday at the home of Mrs Lyle Sullivan, which they enjoyed very much.

David Sterling went to Beaver last week to bring home his sister, Miss Bell Sterling, who has been attending the Murdock school.

Earl McMullin and his sister, Miss Etta, went to Beaver last week Miss Leona McMullin accompanied them.

Robert McMullin returned home last week from Beaver where he has been to school all winter.

Mrs Maud McQuarrie and family of St. George are here visiting for a few days.

The first crop of hay is about all cut and in the stack

Washington County News
June 6, 1911

Leeds, June 6 —Edward McMullin, Miss Bell Sterling and Miss Ethel McMullin returned home from Beaver last week, they have been at school there.

Mr. and Mrs Edward A Vincent went to Harmony last Thursday to remain about two months. Mr. Vincent has been working there for some time past.

Mr. and Mrs Charles Angell and family of Hurricane returned to their home Monday after spending a few days here visiting relatives and friends

Mrs Ida McDonald of Middleton was here for a few days last week visiting with Mrs M. J. Hamilton, returning to her home yesterday.

Miss Grace Bryner, Miss Connie Moss, Munn Cannon and J. Duncan of St George were here Sunday visiting.

Mr. and Mrs Jessie Jepson of Hurricane were here Sunday visiting with their relatives and friends

Loraine Bryson of St. George is here working on the reserve

Miss Rachel Beebe of Hurricane was a visitor here Sunday

Leeds, July 11 —The Fourth of July was celebrated by a program in the morning consisting of patriotic songs, music, and recitations; in the afternoon there was foot racing and prizes for the little ones, and a dance in the evening for the older ones.

Mrs M Schlappy of Middleton is here visiting her daughter, Mrs. C E Olsen, for a few days Miss Nellie Andrus of Middleton is also a visitor here

The young folks had a dance here last Friday evening, some of the young people from Toquerville came over and all had a good time.

Mrs Charlotte Angell has gone to Lehi to spend the summer visiting with friends and relatives

Robert McMullin came in last evening from Milford with a load of freight for Hansen's store

Frank Hartley returned home last evening from the north after an absence of two weeks

Leeds, July 18 —Mrs. Thos. Sterling has returned home from Salt Lake City, where she went to have her baby attended to for gastritis, the child is on the improve

Mrs Wm Harris left for her home in Oregon Friday, after spending several weeks visiting here Wm Sterling Jr took her to Cedar City, returning home Sunday.

Mrs Mary Jarvis and Mrs Matilda Bleak of St George, were here last Thursday, and talked to the sisters that were present at the meeting

Donald Fuller left Tuesday for Milford, with a load of fruit, he will bring back freight for Hansen's store

Born, a daughter to Mr. and Mrs. Wm E Woodbury July 15th, mother and babe doing nicely.

Miss Alice Sterling left Friday for Salt Lake City to visit friends and relatives

Roy Barlow and Charley Angell have gone north for the summer, to work

John Tullis of Pinto was in town on business the latter part of last week •

Frank Anderson of Echo farm was in town Sunday.

Frank Hartly has gone north with a load of fruit

Leeds, July 25 —Pioneer day was not celebrated here. A good many of the young folks were away, some of them going to Toquerville, Hurricane and Washington for the day and a crowd went fishing.

Mr and Mrs David Moss, Jr , of St George have been here for a few days David was doing some painting for the reserve

Mr and Mrs M McArthur of St George are over here spending the 24th with Mr and Mrs Oscar McMullin

Some of the farmers are busy hauling their grain. We have had a nice rain here, doing a great deal of good.

• Mrs Mary Olsen went to Panguitch for a pleasure trip with Mr and Mrs B P. Wulfenstein of St George

Misses Ruth Sterling, Libbie Leany and Georgiana Angell have just returned home from Salt Lake City

Mr. and Mrs Henry Welte and family of Silver Reef left last Thursday for their home in Salt Lake City

W. W. Sterling, Sr., went to Toquerville and the up river settlements last week on business

Mrs Chas Westover of Washington was in town last week visiting relatives and friends

Donald Fuller came home last evening from Milford with freight for Hansen's store

Misses Connie Moss and Mamie McAllister were in town last week for a short time

Oscar McMullin is putting up a new wire fence in front of his place

David McMullin and family have moved into their new home

Washington County News
August 1, 1911

Leeds, Aug 1 — Bp B Y. McMullin and H A. Jolly are on the sick list; they are improving slowly

Mr. and Mrs Frank Batty, Mrs Charles Angell and Mrs Jesse Jepson of Hurricane were Sunday school visitors here Sunday.

Mrs Peter Hansen, Miss Annie and C. F. Hansen went to Salt Lake City last week for an outing

Wm. D Sullivan, Jr, Donald Fuller and Ammon Jolly went north last week with more fruit

Burt Gowers of Cedar City is here visiting Mr. and Mrs Mark McMullin for a few days

Mr and Mrs Joseph Sylvester of Bellevue were in town Sunday for a short time.

Miss Alice Sterling returned home last week from Salt Lake City.

Frank McMullin has gone to the Moapa valley to work

Leeds, Aug 9 —Mrs Charles Angell and Mrs Jesse Jepson of Hurricane returned to their home Sunday after spending a week here putting up fruit.

Mrs M J Hamilton has returned home from Middleton where she was visiting, she was very sick while there but is very much better now

The fruit peddlers have all arrived home from the north but Frank Sullivan, he went on to Newhouse with his load of fruit.

Willard Barlow and Mrs Kadie Luke of Junction were guests of Mr and Mrs Donald Fuller the latter part of the week

Miss Hazel Olsen returned home today from Cedar City, where she has been visiting with friends for several days

David Sterling and Lynn McMullin went on the mountain last week for an outing, they had a good time while there

Mr and Mrs John T. Woodbury of St George are over here visiting Mr and Mrs Hyrum Leany of Harrisburg

Frank Hamilton and Cleo Sullivan went on the mountain this morning with salt for the horses.

Leeds, August 29 —A pleasant birthday party was held at the home of Bp B Y. McMullin last Wednesday evening in honor of their son Lawrence's birthday The cakes, lemonade, and the fruit were heartily enjoyed by the little ones They spent the evening in games, singing and music

William D , Jr , and Frank Sullivan and Donald Fuller came in last week from Panguitch with lumber for their sleds and barns

Mrs Wm Pritchard of Parowan and her daughter, Golda, were guests of Mrs T. A Sullivan last Thursday.

Most of our town boys have come home, and are loading up with fruit to go right back north again

Stake Aid George Spilbury of Toquerville was a visitor here Sunday, he is always welcome

Miss Verda Demill of La Verkin is here visiting her friends and relatives for a few days

Arthur Cottam of St George was in town last Thursday for a short time

Hyrum Leany, Sr , of Harrisburg has gone to Kanab on business

Leeds, Sept 5.—Our town boys are sure rustlers, some of them have come home and loaded up and gone back north again taking Dixie's choicest fruits, the northern people think it is the most delicous fruit they have eaten for some time. The cry is "Bring us more just like it." David McMullin, Wm. D Sullivan, Jr., Donald Fuller, Frank Sullivan, Karl McMullin, George Olsen, Alex Sullivan and Lynn and Robert McMullin, are all gone north with fruit, some of them left this morning

Mr and Mrs Henry Schlappy of Washington and Mrs Julia Andrus of Middleton were here Saturday and Sunday visiting Mr. and Mrs C. E Olsen and their mother, Mrs. Henry Schlappy, Sr, who has been here for some time

A picture show was given in Sterling's hall last evening, it created quite a bit of amusement for the little ones and some of the older ones as well, after the show they had a dance

The threshers have been here the past week threshing our grain, they finished up last evening and leave here this morning for the Washington field

Mr and Mrs. Christian of Manti are here for a while putting up fruit, they are going to St George for the homecoming

Our town people are doing their best in regards to furnishing fruits and vegetables for the Dixie home coming

Some of the young people from Toquerville were over here taking in the show and the dance Monday night.

Miss Urie of Cedar City is here visiting Mrs. Mark McMullin for a few days.

Eddy Dalton of Hurricane was a visitor here Sunday.

Leeds, Sept 12 —Mr and Mrs Ira McMullin entertained Mr and Mrs David Chidister of Richfield Sunday, they were on their way to St. George for the home coming

Frank Hartley, Donald Fuller, Wm D, Jr., and Frank Sullivan Sullivan came home from the north last week with lumber

Wilford McArthur of St George was here Monday getting two or three loads of melons for which he had contracted.

James Larson and his son Willard of Bloomington were here last week buying two loads of grapes from W. W, Sterling

Edward McMullin and Joseph Sterling have gone on the mountains for a few days looking after their horses

Robert McMullin came home last evening with some new furniture for Mr. and Mrs B. Y. McMullin

Mr. and Mrs H. R Jolley left yesterday for Parowan, to be gone a few days on business

Mr. and Mrs Demills and family of La Verkin were visiting relatives here Sunday.

Mrs A Hartley of Panguitch is visiting relatives here for a few days

Leeds, Sept 19 —John Tullis of Pinto is a visitor here for a few days. He came down to take his wife and family home, who has been here for some time visiting and putting up fruit

Mr. and Mrs J. R. Christiansen returned Sunday to their home in Manti after taking in the homecoming and spending a few days here putting up fruit

Some of the boys have gone to Panguitch again with fruit; they will bring back lumber to finish their barns and sheds.

Miss Ruth Sterling left last Saturday for Price, Emery Co , where she is engaged to teach school this winter.

Charles F Hansen and Joseph Sterling have gone to Logan to attend the A. C. this winter.

Neils Bastain of Washington is here from Richfield where he has been working all summer.

Martin L McAllister of St George was in town yesterday on business

Alex Sullivan has gone to New Castle to work.

Leeds, Oct 10 —The school rooms were nicely cleaned Monday ready for school Tuesday morning. Every bit of rubbish was burned and things put in order. W. W. Sterling had the larger boys plowing and scraping the school yards and removing some of the large rocks out of the way. Misses Ada McMullin and Maggie Olsen with the aid of the larger girls did the cleaning

Mrs Susie Sterling to went St George Sunday to have her little daughter, Lucile's, finger attended to, which was crushed very badly some time ago by being caught in the cogs of the clothes wringer.

Mrs Bessie Reese of Salt Lake City has been here for some time visiting her parents, Mr and Mrs George Angell. She is going to teach school in Rockville this winter

Born, a son to Mr. and Mrs W D Sullivan, Jr , Oct 4th, a son to Mr and Mrs Neils Bastain, Oct. 9th, all concerned doing nicely

Edward and Lynn McMullin have gone north again with more of Dixie's good grapes

Leeds, Oct *17—Mrs Susie Sterling returned home last Saturday from St George, her little daugnter Lucile having to have a finger on the right hand taken off at the first joint Dr Woodbury attended it, and the finger is improving nicely.

J. H. Lee of Harrisburg is re-shingling his home Mrs Lee returned from St George yesterday, bringing her daughter, Mrs Larsen of Bloomington to spend a few days with her

The men folk were out in the hills last week gathering cattle and bringing them in to mark and brand the young calves

Miss Ethel McMullin went to Salt Lake City last Friday to take care of Lu Harris's children and keep house for them

Hyrum Leaney of Hairisburg went on the mountains Saturday looking after his cattle

Miss Nellie Andrews of Middleton is here working for Mrs W. D Sullivan, Jr , for a while

John T. Morse of St George was in town Monday transacting business

Stake Aid George Spilsbury of Toquerville attended Sunday school and meeting here Sunday.

Leeds, Oct. 24.—The farmers are busy cutting and hauling their last crop of hay and gathering in their corn and grapes; some of them have quite a lot of grapes out drying.

Mrs Eleanor Scott of Modena and her sister, Mrs. Ida Tullis of Pinto, were here last week visiting relatives and putting up fruit, returning to their homes Sunday.

Mr and Mrs. C E. Olsen received word here that their daughter, Mrs. M. E. Beal of Baltimore, has an eleven-pound boy, born Oct 18th.

Ira S. McMullin, Ammon Jolley, Charles and Truman Angell, and Donald Fuller left last week for the northern settlements with grapes.

Miss Lottie Hanson returned to her home at Bunkerville last Monday after visiting here for some time with relatives.

Leeds, Nov 14 —Charles and Truman Angell came home last Saturday evening with some fine deer meat Some of the other boys have gone on the mountain today to try their luck.

Willard Sorenson of St. George is here working on the reserve. The boys were having horse races yesterday (Monday) and Willard Sorenson got his arm hurt while riding one of the horses

Frank Hartley, Wm. Sterling and Frank McMullin have returned home from the Grass valley reservoir, where they have been working for some time

Charles F Hansen, Frank Sullivan, Willard McMullin of Leeds and Hyrum Leany, Jr, of Harrisbury have all received letters from "Box B"

Some of the farmers are busy getting in their corn and pumpkins. We have had quite a cold spell the last few days It is much pleasanter now

Bp B Y. McMullin has returned home from Beaver where he went to take his daughter, Leona, to study music lessons this winter.

Louis Harris of the forest reserve and Wm Nicholls have gone on the mountain to plant trees

Thos. Sterling has been making molasses the last few days, he will finish up this week.

Ira S McMullin left for the north last week with a load of grapes.

Ras Anderson of Kanarra was in town yesterday buying cattle

Leeds, Nov. 21 —A pleasant surprise party was held at the home of Mr and Mrs C E Olsen last Friday evening, it being their son George's twenty-first birthday. A good time was had in the early part of the evening, after which a delicious lunch was served. George had a fine gold watch presented to him by his parents as a birthday gift.

Your correspondent wishes to correct a mistake of last week. It should have said Thos Sterling was making molasses last week and that he would be through cutting and hauling cane in a few days, for he will be some time yet making molasses

H. A. Jolley has been very sick the last few days, he is feeling a little better now and we hope he will soon be out again.

Harmon Gubler of Santa Clara was in town the latter part of last week on business

Mrs Lamar Pearce of Washington was a guest of Mrs Susie Sterling last evening

Cattlemen from Panguitch were the biggest part of the day Sunday buying cattle

Mr. and Mrs. Donald Fuller went to St. George Monday on business

Leeds, Dec 5 —The school had a nice time on Thanksgiving day. In the afternoon a program was rendered which was very appropriate, the teachers deserve much credit for the interest they take in the children, and we, as parents should encourage them by getting out more and visiting the school and see how our children are doing in their studies; the teachers like to have any one visit their school.

Misses Ada McMullin and Maggie Olsen gave a masquerade ball last Friday evening for the school children, it was very amusing to watch the little tots in their queer costumes, for two hours they had an enjoyable time after which the older ones had a dance

Clifford Sullivan of St George has been here for a few days getting a boiler for the stake academy at St George Wm D Sullivan and William Sterling has been helping him, they had quite a time in getting it loaded on the wagon

William Nicholls and family have moved into the home of Mrs Charlotte Angell Last Friday while having nothing to do, William worked on the road in front of his place and made a good job of it as it was a bad piece of road

Miss Libby Leany and her brother, Hyrum, attended the dance here Friday evening They came home from St George to spend Thanksgiving with their parents at Harrisburg

Frank Sullivan came home last Friday evening from Cedar with a load of coal

Stake Aid George Spilsbury of Toquerville was a visitor here last Sunday.

Donald Fuller and Alex Sullivan have gone in the hills after wood.

Mrs Neils Bastian has gone to Provo to live this winter.

Leeds, Dec 12 —Pres E. H Snow and Thos P. Cottam were our speakers here Sunday The people expressed themselves as enjoying the meeting and the good talk from the brethren, hoping they will come again soon.

Born, a daughter to Mr and Mrs Bert Harris, Dec 9, also a daughter to Mr. and Mrs Wm Emmett of Harrisburg last week (date not known)

Miss Stella Sullivan entertained a few of her friends at her home last evening

Harmon Gubler of Santa Clara was here the latter part of last week on business

John Tullis of New Castle was in town for two or three days on business

C E. Olsen has put up a neat picket gate in front of his residence

W W. Sterling reshingled the back part of his house last week.

George Angell is making some improvements on his sidewalk.

George and Antoine Olsen have gone in the hills after wood.

Leeds, Dec 19 —We have had quite a snowstorm, about four or five inches of snow falling, the school children are enjoying themselves in having a good snow-ball game.

Robert McMullin returned from Milford the fore part of last week with some freight for Hansen's store

Wallace McMullin of Enterprise was here the latter part of last week visiting his relatives and friends

Wm. D. Sullivan, Jr , and Chas Angell went to St. George the first part of the week on business

The young men of the town are going to choose up sides and have a ball game here Christmas

Your correspondent wishes The NEWS force a merry Christmas and a happy New Year.

Bp B Y McMullin had some of the men working on the meeting house fence last week

Some of the boys are going to the Danish ranch to take hay and hunt for cattle this week

David Sterling left last Saturday for Lund with a load of beef hides

Donald Fuller has reshingled his house

Leeds, Jan 9 —The young folk have had a gala time here during the holidays; they have had dances, parties and skating on the ice; the boys had some horse races, foot races and ball games, everything passed off quietly and a happy New Year was ushered in by the young folk ringing bells at midnight from one end of the town to the other.

Mr and Mrs Lewis Harris of the forest reserve entertained the young folk New Year's eve, a jolly good time was had, the proceedings terminating with a very nice lunch.

Miss Bell Sterling returned to Beaver last Friday to attend school after spending the holidays at home, her sister, Miss Ruth, accompanied her

Mrs E. A. Vincent of Harmony is here visiting her parents, Mr. and Mrs. H A. Jolley, for a while

Mrs M. J Hamilton went to Middleton to spend the holidays with her neice. Mrs. J B. McDonald.

We have had quite a lot of bad colds and sore throats here, but nothing serious

Matt Wicks came in from Stateline this week and went on to Leeds. He will begin operations on his peach orchard as soon as he arrives at Leeds, and he is sanguine that he will have a lot of fruit this coming season that cannot be beaten for flavor and size. Matt's friends wish him well in his vocation as orchardist.

Leeds, January 16 —Stake Clerk David Forsha of St George was the guest of Bp B Y. McMullin the first of the week; he was here, attending to the settling of tithing

Donald Fuller, Wm. Sullivan, Jr, Wm Sterling, Frank McMullin, and Alex Sullivan are all going out on Little creek after posts and wood.

Edwin McMullin returned home the latter part of the week from Beaver, when he went to spend a few days visiting friends

Bp B Y. McMullin is having some work done on the tithing yard fence: T. A Sullivan is doing the work.

Some of the men are busy topping trees and cutting out old fruit trees and making old places look like new.

Mrs Ira S McMullin has been quite sick but we are very glad to say she is feeling some better.

Some of the men are rounding up their poor cattle and bringing them home to care for them

E A. Vincent came home Sunday evening from Harmony to visit for a few days

Leeds Jan 22 —An enthusiastic ball game was played here Friday afternoon by the girls the losing side giving a pleasant party Saturday evening The dainty lunch served showed that if the girls were not so proficient in ball playing they were not lacking in the culinary art

The Branch Normal basket boys passed through here Sunday afternoon after a successful game with the Academy boys The former Normal students here rejoiced to see the B N S colors and pennants so gaily flying

T Bert Harris arrived here last Wednesday from Eureka He will take Mrs Harris and their two small daughters back with him a fact very much regretted by Mrs Harris's many friends here

Truman Angell went to St George Friday bringing Miss Stella Sullivan back with him Miss Stella has been visiting in St George for the past week

Mr Wardell from Oregon is a guest of Mrs Peter Hanson this week Mr Wardell is a son in law of Mrs Hanson

Karl McMullin who has had a severe attack of quinsy is able to be around again

Leeds Jan 29 —Misses Alice Sterling and Maggie Olson were ho tesses at a delightful party at the Sterling home last Monday evening Mr and Mrs Bert Harris were the guests of honor A delicious lunch was served and and so pleasantly were the guests entertained that they stayed until the wee small hours

Born a daughter to Mr and Mrs Mail McMullin on the twenty f urth a son to Mr and Mrs Clair McMullin at Greenville Utah on the same date

The following left for Little Creel this morning for fence posts Will Sterling Donald Fuller Charles Angell Edward and Franl Mc Mullin

---

Lec ls Feb 5 —Frank Hatley Wm Sulhivan Jr M L Wills and Robert McMullin left last Friday for Phoenix Arizona

Willard McMullin and Truman Angell left this morning for Lund for freight

Mrs Tom Walelyn was a vistor lere last weel a guest of Mrs Lue Harris

---

Leeds Feb 13 —Our home mis
sionaries Elders Mathis and Bent
ley gave us some very interesting
and instructive advice Sunday after
noon

Miss Leone McMullin arrived
home Sunday from Greenville wl ere
she had been visiting with hei
brother for the past four months

Mrs Joseph McDonald of Middle
ton was a visit i here Sunday a
guest of Mrs M J Hamilton

The sch ol children and teachers
enjoyed a holiday yesterday

Leeds Feb 20 —The grain for
the convicts horses has arrived and
we are anxiously waiting for the
men to commence work on the
roads here

The children in the primary de
partment were the happy guests of
honor at a valentine party given at
school on the 14th The decora
tions were hearts the favors val
entines

Two linemen are here from Bea
ver today repairing the old Bell
Telephone line for the new company
that has recently bought it

M Wicks left Sunday morning
for Stateline on business He will
be gone about twelve days

I S McMullin and sons are put
ting up a fine fence in front of their
residence

Leeds Feb 27 —The following left yesterday to see the basket ball game between the Normal and the Academy boys Marie Myrtle and Leone McMullin David Stirling George Olson and Edward Willard and Lynn McMullin

Those who attended the basket ball game between Hinckley and the Academy boys are Maggie Olsen and Frank and Willard Mc Mullin

Miss Stella Sullivan entertained a number of her girl friends Friday evening Mr Truman entertained his gentlemen friends the same evening

Those who attended the opera Billy Taylor at St George last week are still singing its praises

Mat Wiel s was seen in town Tuesday He came up from Leeds and is on his way to Sateline where he has some business that needs his immediate attention —Iron County Record

E A Cripps of Hurricane passed through here last Thursday with a load of fruit trees which he was taking from Utah s Dixie Nursery Co to St Thomas Nevada Mr Cripps expects to stay at St Thomas this summer

Leeds Mar 5 — Work has commenced on the new Purgatory canal project William Stirling George Olson and Willard Edward and Frank McMullin left today to start work

Max McMullin had a pleasant birthday party Saturday evening progressive flinch was played Del bert Sterling and Willie McMullin receiving the prizes

Leeds Mar 11 —Miss Maggie Olsen s school room was closed last week after a successful winter s work A picnic in the canyon celebrated its closing

The stock men and farmers are rejoicing over the fine rain Though some are still loath to give up the idea of drouth

Home missionaries Elders Harmon and Atkin were very much appreciated

Miss Maggie Olsen is visiting friends and relatives in St George

Leeds Mar 19 — Our ward was given a rare treat Sunday evening when Mr Boyle gave his illustrated lecture on Utah and her industries The showing of the beautiful trophy cup and the hundred dollar wheel has aroused much interest in our boys in the potato raising contest

Mr and Mrs Lewis Harris were given a pleasant surprise party at their home Saturday evening when about twenty of their friends rather sudely roused them from their slumbers Mr and Mrs Harris leave soon for Diamond valley a fact very much regretted by their many friends

The seventieth annivesary of the Relief society was celebrated here Saturday An appropriate program was given at two o clock in the ward chapel at the conclusion of which a delicious lunch was served in the Relief society building

Those that attended stake conference from this ward were Bishop B Y McMullin and counselor Hyrum Leany and their wives and Elders Jolley and Lee

Leed April 19 — Mr and Mrs Frank Sullivan arrived here last Friday from Beaver where they have been the past winter Mr Sullivan has completed a missionary course at the Murdock academy

A mountain lion measuring eight feet from tip to tip was killed in Water canyon by Thomas Stirling and Frank Hamilton

Thomas Stirling and son Rex and Bob Barry arrived yesterday from Cedar City where they have been on business

Miss Stella Sullivan and Truman Angell left last week for Hinckley They were married at Parowan

Twelve teams from here left last week for Lund with wool

Born a son to Mr and Mrs Will Hartman

Iron County Record
April 19, 1912

Several marriages have been consummated here lately, among which are: Alma Trueman Angell and Miss Estella Julia Sullivan of Leeds, married in the clerk's office on the 6th; Lancelott Hyatt and Miss Della Decker of this place, on the 8th; Albert Mortenson and Disa Jackson of this city on the 12th; Victor Decker and Miss Reta Mortenson of this place on the 16th; Myron Robb and Miss Tophan of Paragonah, on the 13th.

Washington County news
April 30, 1912

Leeds April 30 —Ranger Moody called a meeting of the stock owners in his district Sunday to male ar rangements for the cattle on the reserve It was decided that all the cattle must be permitted and that gathering commences on the tenth

Ira S McMullin arrived home last Saturday from Santa Clara where he has been doing some work on the new school house

Glen the small son of Mr and Mrs Thomas Stirling fell and broke his arm Saturday evening Dr Woodbury set the limb

Alex Milne and sons of St George were seen in town yesterday They were on their way to Parowan

Utah Day was observed here Thursday by the district school

Fourteen teams left here last week with wool for Lund

Washington County Record
May 7, 1912

Leeds May 7 —The last of the wool hauler arrived home yesterday They are intending to leave again on the tenth

Mr and Mrs Frank Sullivan and Miss Myrtle McMullin went to St George yesterday to do some shopping

A crowd of boys from Santa Clara stayed in town last night They are on their way to Cedar City

Ranger Moody moved his family here from St George Saturday

Washington County News
May 14, 1912

Leeds May 14 —Willard and Clifford McMullin and George Olsen are at work on Bonanza flat They are fencing and plowing and from the energy and hours spent there we can expect to soon see this flat blossom as the rose '

Libby Hyrum and George Leany are home from St George Miss Libby has been teaching in the Woodward the past winter and Hyrum and George attended the Academy

Joseph Stirling arrived home Sunday from Logan where he has been the past winter attending the A C

Ammon Jolley arrived home Sunday from Cedar where he has been the past few months

Forest Supervisor Raphael was in town last night from St George

The district school closed here Thursday with a trip up the canyon

Leeds May 21 —Miss Etta Mc Mullin arrived home last week from Alamo Nev where she has been teaching school the past winter

Mr and Mrs Lee Scott and baby came in from M lena yesterday Mrs Scott and baby will spend the summer here

Mrs Ed Foster and children are visitors here guests of Mrs Oscar McMullin

Stale Clerk David R Forsha was was in town yesterday from St George

Overton, May 31 —Allen Martin Fleming who has been ill for some time died here May 28th Funeral services were held the following day the speakers being J P Anderson M D Cooper W L Batty and Bp W L Jones Wm A White head sang I Have Read of a Beau tiful City" and the choir sang I Need Thee Every Hour" and Some time Somewhere," also at the cem etery ' Nearer My God to Thee ' There were many beautiful floral offerings Deceased was born Dec 7 1861 at Olney Richland county Illinois and was the son of Robert Fleming and Christena Caley in Jan 1905 he married Martha Mc Mullin daughter of Ira and Helen McMullin of Leeds Utah they came to make their home in Over ton in Dec 1907 Mr Fleming was an honorable upright citizen He leave a wife and three children also his aged father and a number of brothers and sisters now living in Illinois as well as a host of friends who mourn his departure

Leeds June 4 —Mr and Mrs Charles Angell and Mr and Mrs Frank Batty and families of Hurricane were visiting relatives and friends here Sunday and Monday Elder Frank Batty occupied part of the time in the Sunday afternoon meeting his talk was very much appreciated by those who were in attendance

Clare Woodbury and Karl Snow of St George stopped over night in Leeds on their return trip from Cedar where they had been to attend commencement week

The Misses Ruth and Belle Stirling arrived home last Friday from Beaver where they have been attending the Murdock Academy

Miss Rachael Moody entertained a number of her friends at a candy pull Saturday night all present enjoyed a good time

Mrs William E Woodbury and baby of Mesquite are here visiting her parents, Mr and Mrs W D Sullivan

The Primary Assn celebrated Brigham Young s birthday with a program and picnic in Mr Wick's grove

Mrs Arthur Coates of St George was visiting here Sunday the guest of Mr and Mrs E C Olsen

Miss Reba Coates of St George spent several days last week with Leeds relatives and friends

Miss Edyth McMullin left last week for Salt Lake City where she will attend summer school

Mr Wills arrived here Saturday from St George to visit with friends

A number of the Leeds boys are gathering cattle for the sale

Mrs E C Olsen entertained her friends at a ragbee last week

Leeds June 10 —Mr and Mrs Niels Bastian are here visiting her parents, Mr and Mrs W D Sullivan Mr Bastian has been attending the B Y U at Provo the past winter

Co Sheriff Worthen passed through Leeds last Saturday from Toquerville where he had been on important business

Miss Edna Angell is visiting relatives in Harmony

Miss Verna Fuller is a Hurricane visitor this week

Wm F Woodbury was a Leeds visitor last week

Miss Hazel Olsen was a St George visitor last week

Leeds June 18 —A number of our people attended the conference at St George all report having had an enjoyable time and receiving valuable instructions

Forest Ranger Huff of Escalante is here for the summer to assist Mr Moody the forest ranger here

Two of our enterprising citizens have purchased new family buggies Now we want good roads

Mrs Milton Moody and family are visiting relatives and friends in St George this week

Miss Lila Harris of Arizona is in Leeds visiting relatives and friends

Niels Bastain has gone to Panguitch to spend the summer

Joseph Stirling left for Lund Saturday to drive cattle there

Leeds June 24 --Ira S McMullin returned Sunday from Modena where he had been to take his daughter Etta who will attend summer school at Reno Nevada

Mrs Julia Andrus of Middleton is visiting in Leeds the guest of her sister Mrs E C Olsen who has been quite sick but is improving now

B Jarvis Jr of St George spent a few days in Leeds last week in the interest of a canning factory We expect to have one in the near future

Forest Ranger Milton Moody arrived home yesterday with his family from St George where they have been visiting for the past week

Will Nichols Bob Barry and Frank Sullivan left Friday for Grass valley where they will spend the summer

Miss Alice Stirling spent a few days last week in New Castle visiting her sister Mrs John Tullis

Mrs Bert Coates of St George was visiting in Leeds Sunday, the guest of Mrs Oscar McMullin

J M Wicls arrived home today from Stateline where he had been for some time on business

Mr and Mrs Donald Fuller were visiting relatives and friends in Hurricane last week

Lyman McMullin arrived home last week from Little creek with a fine load of posts

Some fine trout are being caught in Quail creek by some of our good fishers

George Tullis of Pinto is in Leeds for a few days on business

Frank Hamilton has returned from the cattle drive

David Stirling went to Hurricane Saturday on business

Leeds July 3 — Mrs D O Beal and Miss Maggie Olsen arr ed here Sunday from Salt Lake ty to visit with their parent
Mrs D C Olsen Miss Grac of Salt Lake City accompanied them

Miss Bell Stirling entertained a number of her frien ls last Tuesday night at a lawn party games were played till a late hour after which ice cream and cake were served all present enjoyed a good time

Miss Clarissa Rappleye of I n guitch was visiting here at day the guest of Miss Maggie Jolley

W D Sullivan arriv d home to day from Milford with a load of freight for Hanson s store

Mrs Truman Angell of Hincl ley is in Leeds visiting her parents Mr and Mrs W D Sullivan

Miss Maggie Jolley spent several days last week in Washington vis iting relatives

Our town was well represented at the Summer School conver tion at Hurricane

Mrs William Stirling was visiting relatives in St George last week

Leeds July 8 — The Fourth of July passed off very quietly here A number of our townspeople went to Hurricane and St George for their time

George and David Spilsbury were here Sunday in the interest of the Sunday school They also occupied the time in the afternoon meeting Their talk was much appreciated by those who were in attendance

Mrs Niels Bastian entertained a number of her friends Wednesday night The evening was spent very pleasantly and a luncheon was serv ed

Mr and Mrs Frank McMullin of Hurricane were visiting relatives and friends in Leeds last week

Frank Hartley has returne l from a several months stay at Kingman Arizona

Edward F Vincent has returned from a stay of several months at Har m ny

Willard and Edward McMullin were visiting in Toquerville S nday

Mrs Beams of Virgin City was visiting friends in Leeds last week

Lee Scott of Modena is in Leeds visiting relatives

William Stirling Jr is building a fine barn

Leeds July 16 —A committee has been appointed for the 24th of July They seem to be an energetic bunch and we expect to have a rousing good time

Mrs Anna Angell one of our most repected citizens has been quite sick She is slowly improving we are glad to say

Lee Scott has returned to his home at Modena after visiting in Leeds for about two weeks with his wife and baby

Mr and Mrs Truman Angell arrived here Monday from Hinckley They expect to make their home here

Mr and Mrs John Tullis and family of Newcastle are in Leeds visiting relatives

The farmers are busy harvesting wheat and hay They report a good yield

Joe Stirling has gone to Milford for a load of freight

Leeds July 30 —We had an enjoyable time here on Pioneer day An excellent program was rendered in the morning beginning at 10 a m sports in the afternoon from 3 until 5 p m and a children s dance We were unable to get music for a dance at night and the young folks went to Toquerville

Misses Myrtle Spendlove Kate Wright Viola Holohan and Charles Spendlove of Virgin came down to spend the 24th and visit friends here

Mrs D O Beal has returned to Salt Lake City after visiting here for a few weeks with her parents Mr and Mrs E C Olsen

Mr and Mrs Frank McMullin of Hurricane were visiting friends and relatives in Leeds and Harrisburg last week

Miss Lila Harris of Ft Duchesne has returned to Hurricane after visiting here for a few days with relatives

Mr and Mrs Truman Angell have returned from Hinckley after an absence of about three months

Frank Sullivan has returned home from Grass valley after an absence of about two months

Lee Hafen of Santa Clara stopped over night in Leeds on his way to Cedar City

Miss Alice Stirling of Leeds is visiting friends in Pinto

Clair Woodbury of St George was in Leeds yesterday

Miss Rachael Moody was visiting in St George last week

Leeds Aug 6 —Mrs Lee Scott and baby left Wednesday for her home in Modena after visiting a few months here the guest of her father William Stirling

William Sullivan jr and George Olsen spent several days last week in Hurricane on business

Milton Moody forest ranger here is in Pine Valley for a few weeks on business

Matt Wiel s has returned from Stateline where he has been on business

Joseph Stirling spent a few days in Cedar last week on business

Frank Hamilton went to Pine Valley last week on business

Miss Hazel Olsen is the guest of Cedar friends

Miss Myrtle McMullin is visiting in Parowan

Peter Anderson, proprietor of the well-known Anderson fruit farm near Leeds, was in town Monday with a load of fine peaches. Mr. Anderson states that his crop is not as heavy this season as usual. He attributes the shortage to the fact that for seventeen years his trees have yielded an abundant crop each year, a record which is not to be expected under ordinary conditions. His trees have been over-bearing and the present shortage is a natural result, they are "taking a rest."

Democratic Convention

Headquarters Democratic County Committee St George Utah Aug 13th 1912

Notice is hereby given that there will be a County Convention of the Democratic Party of Washington County Utah held in the Court House at St George Utah on Saturday the 24th day of August 1912 at 10 o clock A M This Convention will elect Thirteen (1?) Delegates to the State and Judicial Convention to be held in Salt Lake City Utah August 29th 1912 for the purpose of nominating two Congressmen at large (and State and Judicial officers At the County Convention hereby called the Precincts of the County are entitled to Delegates as follows Springdale 1 Rockville 1 Grafton 1 Virgin 1 Toquerville 2 La Verkin 1 Hurricane Leeds 2 Washington 4 St George East 11 St George West 8 Bloomington 1 Santa Clara 5 Gunlock 1 Pine Valley 2 Enterprise 5 Pinto 2 Harmony 1 Central 1 Total 49

Democrats in the various Precincts are requested to hold primaries and elect Delegates to the County Convention hereby called It is suggested that all persons who favor the election of Wilson and Marshall be invited to attend and take part in the primaries with ut regard to previous political affiliations A full attendance of Delegates at this Convention is earnestly requested and desired

Washington County News
August 14, 1912

Leeds Aug 14 —Mr and Mrs Henry Schlappy and family Mrs Frank Price and Grandma Schlappy of Washington were here visiting last week the guests of Mr and Mrs E C Olsen

Lee Glockner a mining engineer, was in Leeds last week on business

Mrs Margaret J Hamilton of Leeds is visiting in Middleton

Mis E C Olsen is visiting in Harmony for a few weeks

Some of the farmers are cutting their third crops of alfalfa

O W Royce of St George was seen in Leeds yesterday

Washington County News
August 22, 1912

Mr and Mrs Jesse Jepson Mr and Mrs Matt Hartley Mrs Roy Barlow and Mrs Hartley of Hurricane were visiting a few days in Leeds last week with relatives and friends

Mr and Mrs Albert Formaster and Miss Lucy Sanders the two former from St George and the latter from Salt Lake are here visiting the guests of Mrs Milton Moody

The threshers have almost finished their work in Leeds The farmers report that their wheat crop is not as heavy as they expected

Mrs Bert Coates of St George is here visiting for a few days the guests of Mrs Osear McMullin

Karl McMullin has returned home after a three months stay in Moapa Nevada

Mrs Arthur Coates of St George is visiting relatives in Leeds

Alex Sullivan went to St George today on business

I S McMullin has gone to Harmony to work

Iron County Record
August 23, 1912

We are under obligations to Mr. Matt Wicks of Leeds for a box of large, delicious El Berta peaches, which he caused to be delivered at the home of the editor last Saturday. The fruit was the first year's crop, being harvested from young trees, but was equal in every way to the best we have seen this season. The peache were large, perfectly formed, rich in color, and their delciousness,—well, we would fail if we should attempt to describe it; there is but one way to fully appreciate their pleasant taste, and that is to eat them. Mr. Wicks is one of the most successful fruit growers in this part of the state, and if his peaches as a whole are as good as the sample sent the Record, he should experience no difficulty in finding ready buyers.

Leeds Aug 28 —A number of our townspeople attended Flberta day at Hurricane They report having had a nice time

George Spilsbury Dr Cox and Miss Ethel Jarvis members of the Sunday School board were visiting our Sunday school and meeting Sun day John T Woodbury of St George was also here to Sunday meeting in the interest of the Acad emey

Misses Grace Bergen and Mamie McAllister of St George spent a few days visiting here last weel the guests of Miss Leone McMullin

Miss Alice Stirling has returned from New Castle where she has been visiting with her sister for some few weeks

Victor Sullivan and Miss Meriam Platt of St George were visiting here last week the guest of Mrs Tom Sullivan

Willie Heartman has gone to Grass valley expecting to be away for some time

Will Nichols has returned home after a three months stay in New Castle

Born Aug 26 to Mr and Mrs Frank Sullivan a fine baby girl

Leeds Sept 11 —Mrs Watson and daughters of Parowan were the guests of Mr and Mrs B Y McMullin Sunday night They were on their way to St George where they will spend the winter

Mr and Mrs Mit Moody and family left for St George this morn ing for conference and the fruit festival The older children will remain to attend school at the academy

Miss Ethel McMullin who has been in Salt Lake City for some time is home again She brought her neice Ada Harris with her

Mr and Mrs Thomas Stirling have just returned from Salt Lake City where they have been for the past two weeks

Mr and Mrs Clair McMullin and baby of Beaver are here visiting their parents Mr and Mrs B Y McMullin

Miss Myrtle McMullin returned home from Parowan last week where she has been visiting for a few weeks

W D Sullivan is having his home remodeled Mr Christiansen of St George is doing the work

Miss Thaxton of Idaho is here vis iting her grandparents Mr and Mrs Henry Jolly

Mr and Mrs William Woodbury of Mesquite Nev are here visiting relatives

A son was born to Mr and Mrs Wm Nichols Tuesday, Sept 3rd

Mr and Mis Sam Mortenson of Tarowin were visiting and getting fruit in Leeds last week. They were the guests of the latter's mother Mis Peter Hanson

David McMullin and his son Frank left last week for Pioche, Nevada where they will spend the winter

Mrs Bert Harris and two children of Salt Lake City are here visiting with her mother Mis Peter Han son

Misses Linda Slacl and Florence Spilsbury of Toquerville were visiting in Leeds Sunday

Mis John Tullis and family of Into are here visiting relatives

Chas Angell and Lynn McMullin went to Cedar for the fair

Mis Lee Scott of Modena is visiting relatives in Leeds

Leeds Oct 2 —Dr and Mrs D O Beal of Idaho are here visiting Mrs Beal's parents Mr and Mrs C E Olsen

Miss Leona McMullin will leave the latter part of the week for St George to attend the Stake academy where she will study music

Mrs Lee Scott leaves tomorrow for her home at Modena after spending some time here with relatives

Mrs Neils Bastain left last week for Provo where her husband will continue his studies

A Democratic rally was held here today All those who attended enjoyed a treat

Mrs Jolley of Idaho is here visiting her daughter, Mrs Frank Hartley

Leeds Oct 8 —Robert McMullin returned home last week from Bakersfield Cal where he has been the past eight months

A surprise party was given in honor of Miss Leone McMullin All who attended report an enjoyable time

The Y L M I A commenced Sunday night The Y M M I A expect to commence next week

David M Mullin returned from Pioche last week He reports plenty of work in that district

Farmers and stockmen are rejoicing over the recent rainfall

Robert Barry has been visiting here the past week

Leeds Oct 15 —The Republicans enjoyed a rare treat yesterday afternoon at the rally Willard Done is certainly an able speaker

Miss Maneita Thaxton who has been visiting relatives here for the past few weeks left for Mt Carmel last week

Thomas Sullivan and Willie Hartman returned last week from Grass valley where they have been working

Dr Beal William Sullivan jr, and George Olsen have gone in the mountains to hunt deer

Our School started Monday with Misses Ella McMullin and Belle Stirling as teachers

Mr and Mrs Frank Sullivan left for St George this morning

Leeds Oct 21 —Miss Ruth Stirl ing was hostess Friday afternoon in compliment to Mrs D O Beal a dainty lunch being served The same evening Mr and Mrs William Sullivan jr entertained all the young people of the town for Dr and Mrs D O Beal The evening was delightfully spent in games and delicious refreshments were served

Sherman Hardy county game warden arrived here Saturday morning with eighty thousand fish for Quail creek The Leeds boys took them up the same day and put them in the creek Much cred it is due Mr Hardy for getting the fish here in such good condition

Mr and Mrs Frank McMullin are in town visiting relatives and friends before leaving for Arizona where they will make their home

Mrs Bert Harris will entertain tonight for Dr and Mrs D O Beal who leave soon for Salt Lake City

Deer hunting is the order of the day but deer killing is quite anoth er thing

Leeds Oct 29 — There is going to be a farewell dance for Frank Sullivan tonight He leaves on the fir t for the Southern States mission

Miss Ruth Stirling has gone to Wheeler where she intends teach ing school this winter

Mr and Mrs Willard Anlelin and Miss Jost gave a concert here last Thursday night

There was a Republican rally here last night David Hirschi being the principal speaker

Mrs Grace Beal Thompson of Cedar City has been visiting rela tives in Leeds

Bob Berry came in from Grass valley last week

Washington County News
November 12, 1912

Leeds Nov 12 —Leeds loys are still hunting deer Donald Fuller brought in a rice one weighing when dressed 200 pounds

Miss Leone McMullin who is attending the stake academy at St George spent Saturday and Sunday at home

Our school teachers were down to St George the latter part of last week taking the county examination

Oscar McMullin returned recently from the northern settlements where he has been on business

The mutual will give an old fashioned ball Friday night at which a good time is expected

Charles Angell returned home Friday from Grass valley where he has been working

Washington County News
November 26, 1912

Leeds Nov 26 —Presidents Snow and Whitehead were here Sunday to reorganize our ward David Stirling was put in bishop with Elders Henry Jolly and Edward McMullin as his counselors

The M I A amusement committee are preparing a Thanksgiving entertainment The old folks will enjoy dinner at six after which a suitable program will be rendered Dancing will be the feature of the evening

Seeing that the time was far spent some of our hunters got busy Frank Hamilton and Thomas Sterling brought in a fine buck the day before the deer season expired

Mrs M L Pains and son Alton came in from Caliente last week to visit with her daughter Mrs Willie Hartman

Born a twelve pound son to Mr and Mrs Donald Fuller all concerned doing nicely

Our old fashioned ball was well attended and proved a success in every way

Ammon Jolly returned recently from Parowan where he has been working

Born a daughter to Mr and Mrs Truman Angell all well

Leeds Dec 10 —Last Sunday Elder George Spilsbury and his son David were here and reorganized our Sunday school and gave us some good talks at meeting Willard McMullin was sustained as superintendent

The Mutual Amusement committee have cast a comedy which will be put on during holidays

William Sterling sr and Oscar McMullin are reshingleing their dwelling houses

David McMullin has returned from Jund with new toves for our school house

Charles Angell made a business trip to Harmony this week

Matt Wicks left for Stateline last week on business

Company Organized

The Leeds Packing Company will be the name of a company forming with the object of packing first class fruits and vegetables at Leeds Considerable stock has already been subscribed and at a meeting held at Leeds Saturday night it was decided that the company be incorporated with a capital stock of $5000 as soon as sufficient capital is subscribed for It is the intention to install a plant with a daily capacity of 10 000 cans Most of the stock so far subscribed has been taken by Leeds people but some stock is being taken by people of other settlements A temporary organization was effected Saturday with the following officers B Jarvis president Edward McMullin, vice president Etta McMullin secretary and treasurer Articles of incorporation were drawn up and adopted,

Leed Jan 7 — Ammon Jolley and Victor Angell came in from Grass Valley after a short absence

Miss Mamie Jones passed through here Sunday on her way to St George

Miss Ruth Stirling left for Grafton Sunday to continue her school work

Lorenzo Bringhurst is in town this afternoon on business

Maggie Olsen spent the last week of holidays in Cedar City

JULIA ANTONETTE SULLIVAN

Died last Saturday January 4 of a paralytic stroke which she received a short time ago

Deceased was born in Norbee County Mississippi September 18 1836 a daughter of Joseph and Rhoda Mathis She joined the church of Jesus Christ of Latter day Saints in her native state and came with her parents to Salt Lake City in 1847 with the first band of pioneers her father having the distinction of driving Pres Brigham Young's carriage on this memorable occasion Deceased was married to Archibald Sullivan Nov 6 1850 at Salt Lake City afterwards going through the End wment house Came to Dixie in 1862 and has resided here ever since

Four sons three daughters thirty four grandchildren and a number of great grandchildren survive her The sons are Jos John Sullivan St George Wm D Sullivan Leeds Thomas Sullivan Leeds and Chas C Sullivan St George The daughters are Mrs Chas R Worthen St George Matthew Gray St George and Mrs John M McQuarrie St George

Funeral services were held in the tabernacle Monday

Leeds, Jan. 28 —The work on the road, under forest ranger, Martin McAllister, is making rapid progress This road extends north up Quail creek and expects to reach what is known as the Danish ranch It will be a great benefit to the people of Leeds as well as to the stock owners Much credit is due Mr. McAllister and to the Leeds citizens who have been very generous in donating labor.

Some of the younger boys have proved to be successful trappers, as they have caught quite a number of foxes, coons, cats, badgers, etc

Mrs Bert Harris and children left for Burley, Idaho, Saturday morning, where they intend making their home.

Mis M. E. Paris who has been visiting her daughter in Leeds left a short time ago for Alamo, Nev.

Mr. and Mrs. Ira S McMullin are in Overton, Nev , visiting their daughter, Mrs Martha Fleming

Miss Leone McMullin left recently for St George to continue her studies at the Academy

Forest Ranger Mitt Moody has been here the last few days on forestry business

Leeds, Feb 4 —Mrs S H. Crosby of Eagar, Arizona, is the guest of Mrs B Y. McMullin. Mrs Crosby came over from St. George with her brother, E M. Brown, with whom she has been spending the winter.

Wm Sullivan, sr., Joseph Stirling and Robert and Lynn McMullin returned Sunday from the Bench Lake country where they have been after cattle.

Mr. and Mis Ira S McMullin have returned from Overton where they have been visiting

The work on the Danish ranch road has been discontinued for an indefinite length of time

The little son of Dr. and Mrs. D. O. Beal has been quite ill but is improving nicely.

Leeds, Feb. 11.—Mrs D O. Beal of Salt Lake City is here with her mother, Mrs E. C Olsen Mrs Beal will return to the city as soon as the health of her baby will permit.

Wm. Sullivan, sr., Francis Hartley and Wm Sullivan, jr., returned recently from Lund with freight for Leeds and neighboring towns.

The M. I A. will entertain all those over 16 years at a house party tonight at the home of William Stirling, sr.

Forest Ranger Mit Moody left for St George Monday.

Leeds, Feb 19.—The party given for the retiring bishopric at the home of Bp Stirling was a rousing success. The committee in charge did everything to make it go off nicely. Delicious refreshments, ice cream, chocolate, cake, etc, was a feature of the evening

Mr. and Mrs Joseph Thompson of Cedar City and Mrs. Thompson's father, Thomas Bleak of Salt Lake City, were here enroute to St George. Mr. Bleak came down on mining business

Last Saturday the school boys played the older ones a game of base ball. The score being 11 to 13 in favor of the youngsters

Jas. Booth came over from St George last week to get some views of the convict camp While here he gave us a dance.

Dr. McGregor passed through Leeds Monday evening, having been called to assist Dr. Woodbury in a very critical case.

Leeds, Feb 26 —Stockmen and farmers are rejoicing over the storm It has been raining steady for the past three days

Elders Snow and Sandberg were home missionaries Sunday Their talk was good and much appreciated by all who were present

Mrs Naomi Hartley and son Alpheus, old time residents of Leeds, are here visiting friends and relatives

William Nichols has recently returned from Grass valley where he had been working

Thomas Sullivan has sold his property here and will move to Washington soon

Leeds, Mar 11 —The weight ball that was given last Friday night under the M I A, urpassed all expectations A large crowd of young people came from Toquerville which added very much to the enjoyment of all Delicious refreshments were served.

The debate between the M. I A's of Toquerville and Leeds, was given to the latter, the Toquerville debaters failing to qualify.

Mrs D O Beal left Saturday for Overton, Nev , where she will join her husband Miss Hazel Olsen accompanied her.

A game of base ball was played between Toquerville and the convicts Sunday. Leeds expects to play the winners

A fine baby girl was born to Mr and Mrs Thos Stirling March 8th· all concerned doing nicely.

Leeds, Mar 18 —The trip from St George proved most to much for Elder George Spilsbury as he had a sinking spell on the road and arrived in Leeds in a very week condition

We had a picture show here two nights in succession The pictures were good and were shown to appreciative audiences

Quite a number of our young people attended conference and as always were well paid for their trip

Wm Sullivan, sr , and jr , came in Saturday with freight for the convict camp and Leeds store

B Jarvis, jr , of St George was in town last week in the interest of the canning business

Willie Hartman is home from Grass valley after an absence of several months

Leeds, April 1.—Thomas Sullivan and family are moving to Washington The people of Leeds regret losing such good citizens

Quite a crowd from Leeds was out to the convict camp Sunday to see the ball games

Myrtle McMullin returned home Sunday after spending a few days in St. George

McCune, the stock buyer, was in town last week contracting for cattle.

Mrs Mitchell of Parowan is the guest of Mrs N. J. Hamillon,

Iron County Record
April 4, 1913

Wm. D. Sullivan of Leeds passed through here today going to Lund for flour for the convict camp. He informs us that the convicts will stay until about the 1st of June. He says one can now travel the state road from South Ash creek to Grape Vine wash. Just think of the rocks and sand you will miss while traveling the road.

Washington County News
April 15, 1913

Leeds, Apr 15 —Miss Maggie Olsen entertained a number of her friends last Friday night Dainty refreshments and games were features of the evening

Elder George Spilsbury and son, David, were S S. missionaries Sunday. They also remained for afternoon services

Miss Bessie Crosby of Cowley, Wyoming, came up from St George last week to visit relatives here.

Robert McMullin and some Washington men have commenced to work on the Purgatory canal.

Willie Hartman came home from Grass valley yesterday on account of being ill

Mrs Rebecca Angell is in Salt Lake visiting her daughter, Mrs. I. M. Reese.

Wool hauling has commenced and several Leeds teams are on the road

Ira S McMullin came in from Lund last week with freight

Leeds, April 22 —Quite a crowd of Leeds people attended Elder Spilsbury's birthday celebration at Hurricane Sunday

Forest Ranger, Mit Moody, and several Leeds men are going into the hills today to get all cattle off the reserve

Mrs Rebecca Angell returned from Salt Lake City recently where she has been visiting for some time

Miss Ruth Stirling came down from Grafton, where she is teaching school, Saturday.

Mrs Lee Scott of Modena is here visiting her relatives

School will soon close and final exams are in order

Miss Hazel Olsen came home from Overton Sunday

Willie Hartman left for Grass valley yesterday.

Mrs Mary Sullivan is quite ill

Enterprise, April 28 —Things in general are commencing to look green and nice and it looks as though spring was here at last The season has been very backward and we are about three weeks behind former seasons but this seems to be a condition in the surrounding country If we could have another good rain or two the farmers would feel more hopeful as our reservoir is not as full as other years

Our town board has been busy of late and drafted and passed a number of ordinances for our good government and already it has had the desired effect of keeping cattle off the streets, and improvements in general.

Arthur Truman and Mary Morris were married in the St. George temple on Wednesday last and returned home yesterday. We join their many friends in wishing them a pleasant journey through life

J. Willard Canfield is home for a short visit, returning to Cedar City today to school.

A. R. Ivins and Bp George A Holt each lost a thoroughbred mare last week

Washington County News
May 1, 1913

Eighth Grade Graduates
SAINT GEORGE

Lola Andrus
Mary Lund
Lucile Schmutz
Helen Sturzenegger
Olive Dodge
Evadeen Higgins
Clio McArthur
Bert Riding
Paul Gates
Ruey Spencer
Vernon Worthen

Richard Miles
John Atkin
Rachel Atkin
Clara Savage
Grace Prisbrey
Ruth Snow
Jean McAllister
Vilate Sandberg
Alice Harmon
Grant Graf
Ann Picket

Harold Snow
Annie Worthen
Henry Miller
Vera Conger
Joseph Foremaster
Elizabeth Cox
Inez Snow
Kenneth Cannon
Douglas Cannon
Louie Fawcett
Edna Nelson
Myrtle Bryner
Philena Pickett
Edward Christian
Belle Scott
Laura Snow
Caddie Riding

WASHINGTON

George Thayne
Lillie Nisson
Hattie Nisson
Arnold Schlappy
Bert Covington
Bert Hall

NEW HARMONY

Rosalia Schmutz
Mildred Pace

HURRICANE

Stanley Bradshaw
Harvey Wright
Thomas Stratton
Delsey Workman
Jennie Wood
Hilda Hall

LEEDS

Max McMullin

PINTO

Rulon Knell
Merle Thornton

SANTA CLARA

Golden Hafen
Laura Staheli
Elsie Frei
L Reber
Samuel Gubler
Ernest Stucke
Erma Reber
Katy Stucke
Gladys Gray
Elmer Graf
Chester Graf
Andrew Laub
Harvy Staheli

ROCKVILLE

Arthur Terry
Mae Dalton
Gertrude Terry
Minerva Dalton

PINE VALLEY

Laura Gardner
Levi Snow
Rodney Snow
Flossie Gardner
Malin Cox

TOQUERVILLE

Walter Slack, jr.
Gladys Sylvester
Leo Bringhurst
Floyd Spilsbury

LA VERKIN

Winifred Gubler
Margie Naegle
Alberta Savage
Grant Woodbury
Mina Morrill

GIANT CAPS EXPLODE

Three Men Severely Injured at The Grass Valley Tunnel; Two Taken To Salt Lake Hospital

An explosion of dynamite caps at the Grass Valley tunnel Saturday injured three men, one severely. The injured men are Richard Oakley, severely, J. X. Gardner and William Hartman. Oakley's home is at Provo, Gardner, the engineer for the Newcastle Reclamation Co., is a native of Pine Valley, while Hartman's home is at Leeds.

The explosión occurred Saturday afternoon and a telephone message was rushed in to Dr. F. J. Woodbury of this city requesting his attendance. Dr. Woodbury was unable to go and Dr. McGregor left in his stead by auto, arriving at Newcastle one o'clock Sunday morning. The run from Newcastle to the tunnel was quickly made and the injured men attended to as speedily as possible, Mrs. Dr. Woodbury accompanied Dr. McGregor to administer anesthetics, if necessary, and to assist in dressing the wounds.

On examination it was found that Oakley was seriously injured. He is lacerated from head to feet, the left eyeball punctured, the right hand badly smashed, and pieces of copper driven into various parts of his body. If he recovers he will probably be minus an eye. Blood poisoning is greatly to be feared on account of the nature of the wounds.

Gardner was blown off his feet by the force of the explosion and whirled around several times. He was bleeding profusely from several gashes and from the mouth and nose. The others were also bleeding from the mouth and nose, due probably to the concussion. The worst cuts sustained by Gardner are on the lower abdomen and left thigh. His body is considerably bruised and pieces of caps are buried deeply in his flesh. He will recover unless blood poisoning should develop.

Hartman was not so seriously hurt as the others. He was blown off his feet and whirled around, receiving bruises and gashed eyelids, but fortunately the eye itself appears to have escaped injury.

Gardner and Oakley were taken to the L. D. S hospital at Salt Lake City for treatment, as the Southern Utah hospital in this city is not yet completed. Dr. McGregor accompanying them. Hartman is being treated here and is progressing nicely.

Dr McGregor had X ray plates made of the injuries received by the two patients at the hospital, the rays disclosing many pieces of copper embedded in the flesh of the patients. The doctor says that when he left the hospital the patients appeared to be doing as well as could be expected

Dr. McGregor returned home at 4 a m Wednesday, and from him The News learns the following particulars of the cause of the accident   It appears that Gardner and Hartman were in the black smith shop at the tunnel sharpening some drills when Oakly entered carrying a box of fuse in one hand and a box of caps in the other. The box of caps was uncovered and h sat down with them in his hands Just then Hartman drew one of the heated drills from the fire and Gardner struck it a blow with the hammer. The explosion immediately followed, a spark apparently having flown into the box of caps A gale was blowing at the time, and this probably accounts for Oakly, who is reputed to be a very careful man with explosives, entering the blacksmith shop

Dr. McGregor speaks highly of Supt John L. Seevey and others of the Newcastle Reclamation Co , who displayed much solicitude for the victims of the accident and gave every assistance.

Leeds, May 13 —Word was received here today that Willie Hartman and two other men were hurt in an explosion at Grass Valley. Mrs Willie Hartman leaves today for St. George to take care of him.

Mr. and Mrs William Woodbury of Mesquite left Saturday for their home after spending a few days visiting Mrs Woodbury's parents, Mr. and Mrs. W. D Sullivan.

Messrs Pearce and Gregerson of St George have been here for several days looking over mining property at Silver Reef.

Miss Ruth Stirling is home again after spending the winter in Grafton teaching school.

Will Nichols has been quite ill with a severe cough since he came from Grass Valley.

The stock men have been in the hills getting all the cattle off the reserve

Leeds, May 28 —B Jarvis, jr, is here from St George superintending the construction of our cannary. One of the buildings is nearing completion and all Leeds citizens are very much encouraged for they realize that it will be a great thing to them as well as being an important factor in bringing Dixie to the front

Will Nichols left this morning for St George to bring Willie Hartman and family home Mr. Hartman has been under the doctor's care since the explosion at Grass Valley.

Word was received here that Mrs Mark Miller, formerly Miss Maud McMullin, was operated on at a Salt Lake hospital recently.

Mr and Mrs Chas Angell and family of Hurricane were visiting here the latter part of last week.

Born, a daughter to Mr and Mrs. Leo Scott May 25, all concerned doing well

Most all the farmers are busy cutting alfalfa.

Leeds, June 2.—A strawberry festival was held at the home of Misses Ethel and Leone McMullin last Thursday evening which all the young people of Leeds attended The evening was delightfully spent in music and games The delicious refreshments were the principal feature. A poem contest proved very interestingly and showed that we were not lacking talent in this line.

Mrs Willie Hartman has returned home from St. George, where she has been taking care of her husband who was hurt in an explosion at Grass valley.

Oscar McMullin left Tuesday for Salt Lake City to bring Mrs Mark Miller's three children home Mrs Miller is sick in the L. D. S. hospital.

Misses Maggie Olsen and Libbie Leany went to St George Saturday to attend the genealogical lectures and take notes.

Miss Ethel McMullin left Tuesday for Parowan where she will join the Adam Stock company and travel all summer.

Joseph Wilkinson of Cedar an old time resident of Leeds was the guest of his sister, Mrs George Angell, last Saturday.

Mrs. John Tullis and children left Tuesday for her home in New Castle after visiting here with relatives

Mrs Taylor and Mrs. Prince of Harmony were the guests of Mrs H A. Jolley last week.

Miss Myrtle McMullin left Tuesday for Cedar to visit relatives and friends.

Miss Blanche Angell of Hurricane is visiting friends and relatives in Leeds

Forester Milton Moody has returned home from Grass valley.

Edward McMullin went to St George Saturday on business

Thomas Stirling of Leeds was a business visitor in the city Tuesday Mr. Stirling reports everything looking good around Leeds, crops are fine and prospects for a ready sale of same are excellent.

Charles Olsen of Leeds was a business visitor here Tuesday.

So. Utah Packing Co's Plant Makes First Run

On Saturday last, the cannery at Leeds opened its doors to receive the first consignment of Dixie's delicious fruits. The canned products consisted of apricots and currants.

The results were highly satisfactory for the efforts were to test the efficiency of some of the apparatus and to make a beginning, preparatory to the great amount of work to be accomplished during the peach, fig, grape, and tomato seasons.

The canned product is of the excellent flavor and superb quality attributable to the sunny clime of Utah's Dixie. These unexcelled packed products will do much to bring Dixie into its own among packing concerns of the State. The significant beginning bids fair as such.

Leeds is fortunate, indeed, to have installed a real, live necessary commercial enterprise. They are to be congratulated on the material support and interest they have been thus far been accorded.

The success cannot be accurately predicted at this time, it cannot be estimated at the first anniversary of the packing concern's installment. But when this substantial beginning has seasoned and aged as similar industries have, the success, judged financially and economically, will be enormous.

The cannery consists of the cannery proper and a large storage room. A cement floor has been put in the former division. As work has been temporarily suspended because of the on coming apricot crop, the cement work in the storage room is not complete. As time and convenience will permit, the building will be pushed to completion.

Mat Wicks of Leeds was in town Tuesday on his way home from Lund, where he contracted several thousand crates of Elberta peaches for himself and other growers of Leeds. Mr. Wicks will have for sale 60,000 pounds of luscious fruit of his own raising.

Leeds, July 8 —The 4th of July passed off very pleasantly in Leeds We had a fine program in the morning, sports and children's dance in the afternoon and a dance at night.

George Spilsbury and his son, David, of Toquerville were visiting Sunday school and meeting here Sunday and gave us some very good instruction.

A crowd of the young folks of Leeds, are leaving today for a two days' stay at the head of Quail creek. They expect to have a good time fishing

Miss Etta McMullin returned home last week from Las Vegas, Nevada, where she had been to take the teachers' examination.

Mrs. Lizzie McQuaid and children of Overton, Nev., are here visiting her parents, Mr. and Mrs I S McMullin

Ben Bringhurst of Toquerville was a Leeds visitor Sunday. Roy Andrus of Middleton is here visiting relatives.

Willard McMullin left Monday for Salt Lake City to visit relatives and spend the summer.

Lee Scott of Modena has returned home after a week's stay in Leeds with his wife and children

Joe Stirling returned home yesterday from Lund where he had been to drive cattle

Leeds, July 15 —B Jarvis, jr , of St George arrived here Sunday with his wife and family. They intend staying here the remainder of the summer while Mr Jarvis superintends the canning factory.

Mr and Mrs Donald Fuller and daughter left yesterday for St George to get dental work done

The Relief society left today for Quail creek to enjoy a fishing trip

Miss Mabel Jarvis of St George spent Sunday and Monday in Leeds

The primary officers are going to attend the convention at Hurricane.

Leeds, July 23 — Word was recieved here last week by Mrs Dallis Hartman that her brother, of Alamo, Nev., was dying of appendicitis

Mr and Mrs. Mattson of Idaho are here visiting, the guests of Mr. and Mrs Donald Fuller.

Misses Rowena Worthen and Anna Sturzenegger of St. George were visiting in Leeds Sunday.

Mr. and Mrs Charles Angell of Hurricane were visiting relatives here last week.

Mr and Mrs. Park Westover of Washington were here last week visiting relatives.

A crowd of the young folks are leaving today to enjoy fishing at Quail creek.

George Leany has returned from Newhouse, where he has been for som time

Dr. Frank Whitehead of St. George was seen in town yesterday.

Edward McMullin has gone to Glendale for a visit.

Miss Roxie Millet of Rockville is visiting in Leeds

Leeds, Aug 5.—Edward McMullin was the recipient of a pleasant surprise party last week. Many of his friends of Leeds and Toquerville were in attendance. Delicious refreshments were served and a jolly good time was had by all.

Miss Georgina Angell has returned from Rockville where she has been visiting for the past two months.

Charles Angell has returned from Buckhorn, Nev., where he has been for the past six months. •

Eight teams left yesterday for Lund to get cans for the Southern Utah Canning factory.

William Stirling, sr., left Monday for Salt Lake City to spend a month visiting relatives.

Mr and Mrs Roy Barlow of the Muddy valley are here in Leeds visiting relativs

Byron Millet of Rockville spent a few days in Leeds last week visiting

Mrs Pauline Hemenway of St. George is visiting relatives here.

Victor Angell has gone to Rockville on business

Edward McMullin left last week for moapa, Nev.

Matt Wicks has gone to State Line on business

Leeds, Aug 27.—President E H. Snow and G. F. Whitehead were here Sunday at our Sacrament meeting. Their remarks of encouragment were very much appreciated. Mr Jenson was also here in the interest of our religion class work. He gave the children a course in Religion class work which was very interesting

Dr Beal and wife left this morning for their home at Moapa, Nev., after a two weeks' visit with their parents, Mr. and Mrs. E. C. Olsen

Mr. and Mrs John Tullis and family of New Castle are here visiting, the guests of their father, William Stirling, sr.

Lee Scott came in last week from Modena for his wife and children who have been spending the summer in Leeds.

Miss Hazel Olsen has returned from Moapa, Nevada, where she has been all summer visiting with her sister.

William Stirling, sr., has just returned from Salt Lake City where he had been for a month's visit.

Mr. Roylance of Lund was in Leeds last week to pack a shipment of Elberta peaches

Vernon Worthen and sister, Annie, of St. George were visiting in Leeds Sunday.

Miss Frona Mortinson of Parowan is visiting relatives in Leeds

The canning factory is doing a flourishing business

Girl Fatally Burned At Leeds Cannery

Myrtle McMullin, the eighteen-year old daughter of Mr. and Mrs. David McMullin of Leeds, was burned so terribly by gasoline at the Southern Utah Canning Company's plant at Leeds about 9 o'clock a. m. Monday that she succumbed to her injuries at 10 o'clock Tuesday morning

Just how the gasoline exploded is not clearly explained, but no one blames the management of the factory for the unfortunate affair. It is supposed to have been caused by a defect in the gasoline tank of the heater used for heating the soldering irons for sealing the lids on the cans Manager B Jarvis, jr., had just started the soldering furnace and left the building when the ex-

plosion occurred. The small gasoline tank, holding less than one gallon, is charged with compressed air to force the gasoline out by a small air pump. The furnace is a short distance from the tank and it is supposed that a defect in the gasoline tank caused a leakage of gasoline that became ignited by the furnace. The end of the tank nearest the furnace was blown about half way off, the escaping gasoline being thrown in the direction of Miss McMullin, who was about eight feet away, burning her terribly. There were nine girls and a child between two and three years old, a daughter of the manager, in the room at the time, but all escaped serious injury except Miss McMullin, two or three other girls receiving slight injuries only. A sister of Myrtle stood beside her when she received the fatal burns, yet escaped almost without being touched. The heating furnace and tank was entirely new, having been put in straight from the manufacturers for the opening of the season's work at the cannery, and the manufacturers guaranteed it safe and sound. The explosion appeared to be mainly upwards, as most of the gasoline went on the ceiling. The fire that followed lasted until the gasoline was exhausted, a few minutes only, and no injury was done to the plant further than the destruction of the gasoline tank.

Dr. F. J Woodbury left here hurridly on receipt of the sad news and did all that was possible for the sufferer at the time. Miss McMullin was brought to St. George for further treatment, arriving between 8 and 9 o'clock Monday night

The father was working at Pioche, Nevada, and was reached by telephone with the sad news. He arrived here this forenoon.

The remains were taken to Leeds this morning, and interment was made there today.

Deep sorrow is expressed for the parents and relatives of the stricken girl

Washington County News
September 30, 1913

Leeds, Sept 30.—Mrs Mark Miller is here from Eureka visiting her mother, Mrs Oscar McMullin Mrs. Miller is slowly recovering from an operation.

Mrs. Bert Harris and children arrived here last Saturday from Salt Lake City to visit her mother, Mrs, A. Hansen.

Miss Ethyl McMullin is home again after spending the summer traveling with the Adams Dramatic Co

Several of our boys are in the hills building a drift fence, under the direction of Forest Ranger Mit Moody.

Mr. Victor Angell of Leeds and Miss Roxie Millet of Rockville were married in St. George, Sept. 27.

Frank McMullin left last week for Cedar City, where he will attend the branch agricultural college.

Mrs Niels Bastian and small son are here visiting her mother, Mrs Wm Sullivan, Sr.

Matt Wicks has just returned from Cedar City where he has been on business

Joseph Sterling left for new Harmony this morning after cattle.

Miss Leone Parker of Circle valley is here visiting relatives

Leeds. Oct 14.—Our schools commenced Monday the 6th with Donald Schmutz as principal and Miss Ruth Stirling conducting the lower grades.

The Misses Edyth and Leone McMullin and neice, Miss Ada Harris, left for Salt Lake City last week, where Edyth will attend the U. of U. and Leone will study music

Some of our townsmen have been in the mountains hunting deer The successful hunters are Mit Moody, Bp David Stirling and Charles Angell

Last Thursday evening the young people met at the home of Etta McMullin and enjoyed games and refreshments.

Miss Etta McMullin left Friday for Elgin, Nevada, where she will teach school the coming winter.

Mr and Mrs Leo Scott of Modena are here visiting relatives

Mrs Frank Hartley is in Salt Lake City visiting relatives

Leeds, Nov 3 —Max Parker of Circle Valley, who has been visiting relatives here, left for his home last week accompanied by his daughter, Leone

Miss Maggie Olsen left Friday for Overton, Nev., having received word that her sister, Mrs Dr. Beal, was ill.

Born, a daughter to Mr. and Mrs. Wm. Sullivan, jr, Nov, 2; all concerned doing nicely.

Ammon Jolly came home from his work at New Harmony on account of being ill.

Donald Schmutz spent Saturday and Sunday at home in New Harmony.

Andrew Price of St George was a business visitor the fore part of the week

Leeds, Nov. 18 —Y. L and Y.
M M. I. A. met last Sunday night
for the first time this year. The
young men's organization was completed. We hope and expect to
have a progressive and interesting
year.

Thomas Sterling is having a fine
bungalow erected. It will have
every modern convenience The
Worthen Bros of St George are
doing the rock and cement work and
it is well under way.

Elder George Spilsbury and son,
David were visitors Sunday. They
attended both Sunday School and
afternoon services and their remarks
were very much appreciated

George Olsen has bought Miss
Julia Ford's residence. Miss Ford
intends making her home in Enterprise

Born, a son to Mr and Mrs
Ammon Jolley, Nov. 15; mother
and babe doing well.

Matt Wicks came home from
Stateline recently where he has been
for some time

Willie Hartman is home from
Grass valley for a few days

Leeds, Dec 2 —Bp. Calvin Hall and Elder Tobler of Washington were home missionaries last Sunday afternon, and in the evening Frank Bentley and Mrs. Eva Webb, Stake officers of the M. I. A , visited our mutuals They seemed very well pleased with our mutual work. Their remarks were very much appreciated.

Pres Whitehead and Cottam were here Sunday, the 23rd ult , and held ward conference. Their remarks were very encouraging and those who were not out missed a rare treat.

Forest Ranger, Mit Moody, and men from Leeds, Toquerville and Washington left today to get all the wild cattle off the reserve.

Frank McMullin, who is attending the B A C. at Cedar, came home to spend Thanksgiving with his parents

Thomas Furguson of Salt Lake City is here inspecting the mines of Silver Reef and vicinity.

Bert Harris came in from Milford to spend Thanksgiving with his wife and children.

B Y. McMullin left for Parowan the latter part of last week to transact business

Will Nichols left Saturday for the Grand Gulch mine.

Frank Hamilton of Leeds dropped into The Record office last Tuesday on his way back from Milford. Mr. Hamilton had made a tour of this part of the country in the interest of Ralph Pitchforth of Milford, buying calves and young stock. About 400 head were picked up and shipped to Montana.

Leeds, Dec. 16 —Last Saturday afternoon the friends of "Aunt" Maria Wilkinson under the direction of the Pres. of the Relief society, surprised her on her eightieth birthday. They were all laden with good things and sat down to a bounteous repast. Aunt Maria is enjoying good health and was pleased to have her birthday honored by her friends.

The young ladies of Leeds met at the home of Miss Margaret Olsen last week to effect an organization for a ladies sewing club Plans were discussed and many good suggestions given. Delicious refreshment were served by the hostess

Quite a number of our townsmen attended conference at St George and we expect to hear an interesting and instructive report at our next Sunday meeting.

Amusement committees are busy getting out programs for holidays We anticipate a jolly good time both for children and grown ups.

Mrs. Mark Miller and children left for their home at Eureka last week.

David McMullin and Mat Wicks have left for Stateline

Anna Bell Schmutz and Donald Schmutz, one of whom is teaching school in Leeds and the other going to school in Cedar, aren't with us yet but we hope to see their smiling faces in the near future.

Enterprise, Jan. 5 —The holiday season closed last Friday night with a dance The two weeks were filled up with dances and our theatre, "Uncle Josh," which was presented in a very creditable manner by home talent; all the cast were strong and with Leo Higgins as "Uncle Josh" everyone enjoyed it fine. The town seems deserted now as all the young people have returned to their several schools

One of the social events of the season was an old folks dinner and social held at the home of Mrs. George Morris, where songs, recitations, and speeches were had and an elaborate dinner served to all the elderly people of the town. Another dinner of the same kind was given at the home of Mrs A. P. Winsor, jr.

Our school started this morning in all the grades except Miss Anderson's department Miss Anderson not being able to be here on time.

Mr. and Mrs Geo J. Woodbury returned home Saturday from St. George where they spent the holidays with relatives and friends.

T. A Johnson returned home from Salt Lake City on Friday where he has been on business.

Leeds, Jan 20 —The forest service men are up from St George and work was resumed this morning on the road to Danish ranch It was suspended for a time on account of the storm

Thursday, January 8, the Relief society met at the home of Mrs. Anna Angell All the members took lunch and an enjoyable time was had by them.

Niels Bastian came in from Enterprise last week. He expects to return to that place soon with his family.

Our farmers and stock men are rejoicing over the storm and think it was the right thing at the right time.

Charles Westover, jr , of Washington was a visitor in Leeds Sunday.

Leeds, Jan. 28.—Elder George Spilsbury and son David were Sunday school visitors last Sunday. Both poke words of encouragement to be a hool They were surely an example of "doing one's duty" as it was a ve y disagreeable day

Miss Maggie Olsen came down from Virgin last Friday to spend Saturday and Sunday at home but was detai ed here several days on account of the storm

Miss Ethel McMullin entertained some of her friends last Saturday vening. Games and refreshments were features of the occasion

John Tullis of New Castle has been here for some few days transacting busi ess and visiting relatives. He left for his home today

Donald Schmutz left Friday for St George and Santa Clara to attend the teachers' league

Ira S McMullin is making some improvements on his home

Leeds, Feb. 11 —Mr. and Mrs Lue Meeks and children of Lovell, Wyo , are visiting friends in Leeds, and are the guests of Mrs. Donald Fuller Mrs Meeks was formerly Miss Annie Chidister of this place.

Mr and Mrs. Donald Fuller entertained at an evening party on Tuesday for Mr. and Mrs. Lue Meeks Both old and young were in attendance and all had a jolly good time; refreshments were served by the hostess

The convicts are expected to move their head quarters to Harrisburg within the next ten days

The weather has been ideal since the storm and the farmers are busy preparing land for crops

William Sullivan, sr , left the fore part of the week for Lund to get freight for local stores.

Leeds, Feb 17 —Forest Rangers Moody and McAllister and a number of Leeds boys commenced work on the drift fence in the hills the first of the week

Those who were not out to the picture show that was given here last Saturday night by a traveling Co missed a rare treat. The films were good and the pictures plain

Last Friday night Mrs Bert Harris entertained at a valentine party The evening was spent in games An appropriate lunch was served by the hostess

Our school teachers are busy preparing a Washington's birthday program to be given next Friday night Dancing will follow

Andrew Gregerson of St George was a business visitor here the latter part of last week.

Miss Maggie Olsen came down from Virgin to spend Lincoln's birthday at home

Born, a daughter to Mr and Mrs Edward Vincent, February 11, all well ⚫

Leeds, Mar 3.—Last Saturday the Toquerville school boys came over and played the Leeds school boys a game of base ball. It was a live and interesting game, the score being fifteen to nineteen in favor of Leeds. The Leeds boys expect to go to Toquerville the latter part of the week and play again.

Mr. and Mrs. Lue Meeks, who have been visiting friends here for some time, left for Parowan on the second Donald Fuller took them as far as Kanarra.

On the evening of Feb. 22 Judge O. F. McShane gave a very interesting lecture here. It was well advertised and a large crowd was out

Pres Whitehead and Elder Richard A Morris were home missionaries Sunday and gave some very good instructions to the people

Frank Hartley and William Stirling, jr., have taken the contract for hauling wood for the convict camp at Harrisburg

Will Sullivan, jr., came in from Hurricane Friday He expects to move his family to that place soon.

Frank McMullin came down from Cedar City to spend Washington's birthday at home.

Quite a number of children and older people are sick with the grip

Leeds, Mar. 11.—Antone Olsen met with a painful accident last Saturday night on his return from a dance at Toquerville He thoughtlessly run into a new barbed wire fence and received several cuts on his face which necessitated him going to St. George for medical treatment

Last Sunday Wm. O. Bentley and Vernon Snow, Lena Nelson and Ethel Jarvis of the S. S board were Sunday School missionaries and by request remained for afternoon services In the afternoon the time was given to Elders Bentley and Snow and their talk was both interesting and instructive.

Mrs Josephine Kelsey of New Harmony was in town last week visiting relatives.

Leeds, Mar. 24 —Mrs Ida L Simmons will lecture here Saturday March 28, at the Teachers Improvement League meeting All those who enjoy something good cannot afford to miss it, whether a member of the league or not. Musical numbers will be furnished by the Leeds pupils Dancing will be the principal feature of the evening

The anniversary of the Relief society was fitingly celebrated on the 17th. An excellent program was rendered in the afternoon after which picnic was served In the evening a St Patrick's ball was given and was attended by a large and jolly crowd.

An oratorical contest was held here last Saturday evening between Toquerville and Leeds Bert Anderson represented Toquerville and Miss Libbie Leany, Leeds Both subjects were good and well handled The decision was in favor of Toquerville.

Monday the 16th was observed as Arbor day and the boys of both schools spent most of the day in cleaning up the streets The girls helped the cause greatly by serving the boys a delicious lunch.

James Booth of St. George is in town on business.

Leeds, Apr. 8 — Most of our townsmen with their teams turned out and helped the convicts with the road through our town last week. They worked two or three days and made a great improvement. Their work is very much appreciated by the Leeds people.

Forest Ranger Mit Moody and a number of men from here and surrounding towns left this morning to get all the cattle off the reserve

Born, a son to Mr. and Mrs. William Hartman, Tuesday, April 7. The baby died this morning, living only twenty-four hours

Mrs Sarah Paris came in from Nevada last week to spend some time with her daughter, Mrs. William Hartman.

Robert McMullin, Charles Truman and Victor Angel left for the Grand Gulch mine last week.

Mat Wicks left for Stateline the fore part of the week to stay most of the summer.

Leeds, April 15 —The Leeds people tried to show their appreciation of what the convicts have done and are still doing to our roads by serving them a dinner last Saturday afternoon. The tables were spread in the amusement hall and presented a pleasing picture Over fifty convicts and guards sat down and from their remarks we know that our efforts were fully appreciated

The convicts moved their camp from Harrisburg to a point north of Bellevue the fore part of the week ;

Mrs Sarah Paris has returned from St George where she has been on business the past few days

Mrs M. J. Hamilton is visiting friends in St George and Middleton

Miss Maggie Jolley left for Tropic last week

Leeds Apr 28 —Mr. and Mrs Charles Angell of Hurricane spent Sunday and Monday here with Mrs. Angell's mother, Mrs. Anna C Angell, who has been ill for some time and is still very feeble

Frank McMullin who has been attending the B A. C at Cedar City came home some few days ago after attending conference at Salt Lake City.

Miss Alice Stirling returned Saturday from St George, where she has been having dental work done.

David McMullin returned from Pioche the latter part of last weak where he has been the past winter.

The improvement in our roads is very noticable as autos are no hong er uncommon on our highway.

Miss Maggie Olsen is home again after spending several months in Virgin teaching school

Judging from our chilly weather one would think that winter had come again

Leeds, May 6 —Mr. and Mrs Wm. Sullivan, Jr , are preparing to move to Hurricane this week, where they intend making their future home The people of Leeds always regret to lose good citizens.

Word has been received here of the marriage of Miss Etta McMullin of Leeds to Vivian Mariger of Salt Lake City. They were married in Nevada, at a point near where she has been teaching school the past winter.

Mrs. Sarah Paris left some time ago for Caliente Nev., after spending some time here with her daughter, Mrs. Wm. Hartman.

Ammon Jolley left for New Harmony recently to drive mail from Harmony to Cedar.

Mat Wicks is in town again after spending the past few months at Stateline.

A number of Leeds teams are leaving today for Lund with wool.

Leeds, May 12 —On the evening of the 6th the townspeople surprised Mr. and Mrs Wm. Sullivan, Jr., before they left for Hurricane Games, music and refreshments were features of the occasion and all who attended spent a very pleasant evening.

Mr and Mrs Jesse Jepson, Mrs Charles Stratton and Miss Blanche Angell of Hurricane were in Leeds Sunday visiting friends and relatives.

Born, a son to Mr. and Mrs. William Stirling. Jr, Sunday, May 10, mother and babe doing nicely.

Forest ranger Mit Moody and son Milton, were business visitors here the fore part of the week.

Miss Annie Worthen of St. George passed through here Tuesday enroute to Bellevue.

Matt Wicks left Monday morning for Stateline to attend to his interests there

J. D Neilson of Harmony is giving a dance in Stirling's hall tonight.

The stockmen are busy gathering cattle and putting them on the reserve

Willard McMullin is home again after an absence of several months

OBITUARY

Leeds, May 26 —Anna C. Johnson Angell departed this life May 18, 1914, after a long and useful life She was born in Sweden seventy eight years ago, embraced the gospel there and came to Utah in 1862 She was the wife of Solomon Angell and the mother of four children, three of whom survive her They are Charles Angell of Hurricane, Phoebe McMullin of Idaho Falls, Idaho, and Vinnie Fuller of Leeds She has resided here the past forty-seven years, and could count her friends by her acquaintances She was a noble woman and her sweet face and kind disposition will be missed by all She died as she lived, a faithful Latter-day Saint

Last Monday, the 25th, our Relief Society officers went over to Hurricane to attend the Relief Society convention which was to be held on that date, but were greatly disappointed as the convention had been postponed and they had not been notified of the postponement.

We were pleased to have Presidents Snow and Whitehead with us last Sunday. They attended both Sunday School and afternoon services and their remarks were timely and instructive

Mrs Charles Bastian of St George and her mother, Mrs Naomi Hartley, were visiting friends and relatives here the fore part of last week.

A number of our boys returned Monday from the Hurricane valley country where they have been on the drive

Leeds, June 9.—Robert McMullin and Truman Angell returned home Sunday from the Grand Gulch mine, where they have been leasing for the past two months.

B J. McMullin left for Lund this morning taking with him his daughter, Ethyl who will spend the summer in Salt Lake City.

A dancing party was given last night by Prof James Neilson; all who were in attendance report a lively time.

William Sterling returned home from Lund Saturday bringing with him a player piano for their home

Miss Maggie Olsen left last week for Salt Lake City where she will attend summer school.

Willard McMullin expects to leave for a mission to the Netherlands on the first of July.

Forest Ranger Mit Moody is in town attending to forestry business.

Brig Jarvis, jr, of St George, is a business visitor here today.

Hansen-Perkins

Cards are out announcing the marriage of Mr. Charles F. Hansen and Miss Clara A. Perkins, at the Salt Lake temple, Wednesday, June 10, 1914.

The bride is a daughter of Mr. and Mrs. R J. Perkins, sr., of Taylor, Arizona, (Mr. and Mrs Perkins were among the earliest settlers of Taylor, being the first couple to be married from that place, coming to St George for that purpose, Mrs. Taylor, when Miss Hancock, lived at Leeds, this county, her husband was of Bountiful), a young lady who is highly esteemed by her many friends The groom is a highly respected and progressive young man who claims Leeds as his home, he has taught school at Taylor, Arizona, for the past three years, and was one of the leaders in the movement to establish a cannery at Leeds.

The announcement cards state that the young couple will be at home, Leeds, Utah, after June 30.

Leeds, June 16.—The fishing season is open and fisherman from St George. Washington and Toquerville were here on Quail Creek preparing to take advantage of the opening day. Judging from reports they were a band of disappointed fishermen.

The many friends of Charles Hansen are glad to see him home with a young wife and to know that he intends making his home here Leeds is badly in need of such people

Mr. and Mrs Mark McMullin and Alfred Grower of—— were visitors here Sunday. Mark is talking of moving back to this country

A farewell dancing party will be given for Willard McMullin Friday night. He leaves for a mission to the Netherlands soon.

B Y. McMullin arrived home from Lund Sunday with freight for Hansen's store and the Southern Utah Packing Co

Edward McMullin left Monday for Glendale 'Tis rumored and hoped he will bring a fair one back with him.

Mrs William Woodbury of Mesquite, Nev., is here visiting relatives and friends

A crowd of young people from Hurricane were visitors here Sunday.

Mat Wicks and Oscar McMullin have gone to Lund on business.

Miss Edna Angell left Sunday for Cedar City to visit

Cannery Working

The Southern Utah Packing company started up its canning plant at Leeds Monday morning with a full crew of workers The first run will be made on apricots. Supt B Jarvis, jr., informed The News before leaving for the plant that the company had already over double the amount of orders booked than was summed up in the whole business of a year ago, and that at least five times as many apricots will be canned this year. Mr. Jarvis said that every store in the county had ordered its canned goods from the factory this year—a mighty good showing from two points of view, first that the merchants of the county believe in and practice "support home industries," and, secondly, that the class of goods being put out by the Southern Utah Packing Co. must be of excellent quality, for our stores do not carry inferior goods

Washington County News
July 15, 1914

Leeds, July 15 —A committee has been put in for the Twenty-fourth of July. We are anticipating a great time.

The Misses Edyth and Leone Mc-Mullin and their nieces Ada, Melba and Lucile Harris arrived home from Salt Lake last week.

Mrs Hamilton returned from Middleton this morning where she has been visiting the past week.

Maggie Jolley has returned from Tropic after visiting there a month with friends.

Miss Josephine Kelsey of New Harmony is visiting relatives in Leeds

Miss Edna Angell of Leeds is visiting in Hurricane.

Donald Fuller is our new school trustee.

Washington County News
August 26, 1914

Leeds, Aug 26 —Dr R H Bradford, Professor of metallurgy of the U. of U., D. H. Lyon, Supervisor Bureau of mines, and Samuel L Areutz, mining Engineer, all of Salt Lake City who are examining the low grade ores of the state have been here the past few days examining the mines of Silver Reef

The Cox family who have been living here the past two months left for Orderville Tuesday morning where they will make their future home. They are refugees from Mexico.

Mrs Vivian Marager, formerly Miss Etta McMullin of Leeds, came yesterday from Elgin, Nevada She will visit with relatives and friends for two weeks

Miss Margaret Oleson returned from Salt Lake City last week where she has spent the summer attending summer school and visiting relatives and friends

Miss Ethel McMullin came home last week after an absence of two months She has been visiting relatives and friends in Salt Lake and Beaver.

Miss Olive Mortenson, who has been here for the past month visiting relatives and friends, left for her home in parowan a few days ago

Monday evening the friends of Mrs Cloven Cox gave her a pleasant surprise before her departure for Orderville

Mr. and Mrs Mark McMullin and small daughter of Cedar City were here visiting last week.

The Misses Amelia and Mildred Woodard of Panguitch are the guests of Mrs Francis Hartley.

Mr. and Mrs Roy Barlow of Moapa, Nev., are here, the guests of Mrs Donald Fuller

Mrs M. S Hamilton is home again after spending some time in Parowan

Washington County News
September 16, 1914

Leeds, Sept 16—Elder Frank Sullivan returned from his mission last week. He is the first missionary Leeds has had the priviledge of welcoming home for a good many years. The last year of his mission he was president of the East Tennesee conference and we feel that we are justly proud of his success.

Miss Owens and Miss Fox of Salt Lake City are here on business. They are also trying to organize an art class here this winter.

Our ward was given a rare treat last night when Oscar A. Kirkham, leader of the boy scout movement, held a meeting.

Mrs William Woodbury of Mesquite, Nev., has been here several days visiting her mother, Mrs W. D Sullivan.

Mrs Lee Scott and children of Modena and Mrs John Tullis and family of New Castle are here visiting

Mrs Bryron Millet, nee Georgiana Angell, came in from Salt Lake City last week.

Mrs. Wm Sullivan, jr., of Hurricane was a visitor here last week

Mrs Martha Fleming and family of Overton, Nev., are here visiting.

Mrs. Vivian Manger left for Elgin, Nev., last week.

Washington County News
September 29, 1914

Leeds, Sept. 29—A welcome home party for Elder Frank Sullivan was held here Friday evening The amusement hall was filled with friends of the young missionary. Dancing was enjoyed and cake and fruit were served.

Mr and Mrs Will Woodbury were visitors here. They came over from St George for Elder Sullivan's party. Mrs Will Sullivan from Hurricane was also in attendance

Joseph Worthen of Salt Lake City left for his home on Cox's auto this morning. He has been visiting here for the past two weeks

Miss Maggie Olsen left Sunday for La Verkin. She is one of the school teachers there this winter.

Frank McMullin left last week for Grass valley

Leeds, Oct 14 —Last Saturday night the people, under the direction of the parents class, entertained for our school teachers, Misses Edyth McMullin and Elizabeth Leany, at the home of Wm Stirling, sr Music, games and refreshments were features of the occasion and all had a jolly good time.

Mrs James Fleming and family of Overton, Nev, left for their home last Saturday They were accompanied by Miss Alice Stirling who intends spending some time in that place

Mr and Mrs LaVanger came up from St George last week and spent several days They were the guests of Mrs LaVanger's sister, Mrs Edward McMullin.

Deer hunting is quite the order of the day The season's most successful hunters are Mit Moody, Joseph Stirling, Edward McMullin and Truman Angell

John Tullis of New Castle came down last week to get his wife and family, who have been here some time visiting relatives

Miss Margaret Olsen, who is teaching in La Verkin, spent the week end at home here

Leeds, Oct 28 —Mr and Mrs B Jarvis, jr, left for St George Sunday morning with their baby, which needed medical attention Mr Jarvis returned Tuesday night and reports the baby doing nicely He intends to finish the season's work at the canning factory within the next few days

Miss Leone McMullin left Tuesday morning for Cedar City She intends spending some time visiting relatives and friends at that place and Parowan

Mr and Mrs Frank Sullivan are at Hurricane looking after their interests They expect to be permanently settled there soon

Our schools will close Thursday noon so that our teachers can attend the institute at St George Friday and Saturday

Mr McCune of the Panguitch Commission Co was transacting business here the latter part of last week

Mrs Flora Davis and Mrs Bryson of St George were visiting relatives and friends here the first of the week

Charles Angell returned recently from Grass Valley where he has been working the past few months

Mrs Edward McMullin is spending the week in St George visiting relatives

All the stock men are busy getting their cattle out of the hills.

Mrs W D Sullivan of Hurricane is a town visitor today

Leeds, Nov 17 —The following from here are taking the winter course at the Dixie Academy: Robert McMullin, Antone Olson and Cleo Sullivan

Dr. Beal came in from Overton, Nevada, Sunday evening. He left yestertay morning for Hurricane where he will join Mrs Beal who is there visiting her sister, Mrs. E. C. Olson.

Miss Ruth Sterling entertained some of the ladies of the town Friday afternoon for the purpose of organizing a ladies literary club for this winter.

Mrs John T Woodbury and Mrs Will Woodbury are visitors here from St. George, the guests of Mrs. Wm. Sullivan

The speakers Sunday afternoon were Elders Heber Cottam of St. George and Thomas Blazzard of Washington.

George Olson came in Saturday from Copper Mountain where he has been for the past few months.

A number of our boys are in the hills getting the cattle off the reserve for the winter.

Mr. and Mrs Frank Sullivan are in St George attending the mutual convention

Bert Harris came in last week from Grass Valley.

Leeds, Dec.2 —The Thanksgiving dance and supper was a huge success Both young and old were in attendance and all did themselves proud, eating turkey and dancing the latest steps

Milton Moody, Arnold Schlapoy and Misses Lucile Schmutz and Verna Schlappy of St George spent Thanksgiving here with relatives and friends

Elder George Spilsbury of Toquerville was a Sunday school visitor last Sunday. He also remained for afternoon services

Robert McMullin and Antone Olsen who are now enrolled in the Dixie Academy spent the week end at home here

Karl McMullin left Sunday for St George to attend the Dixie Academy the remainder of the winter

Washington County News
December 23, 1914

Leeds, Dec 23 —Ira McMullin went to Lund last week for Mrs McMullin's sister's little adopted daughter. The little girl is a welcome addition to the McMullin family and will make her future home with them as her mother died a few months ago

Mrs Alice Stirling returned home last week She has been visiting at Overton, Nev, for the past few weeks She returned via of Modena and visited there for a few days with her sister, Mrs Lee Scott

The M I. A. is preparing a program and dancing party to be given Christmas Eve. A testimonial for Elder Willard McMullin of the Eastern States mission.

The district school closed last Friday for the holidays A Christmas tree and program was given at school for the children Friday afternoon

The following are home from the Dixie academy to spend holidays: Robert, Karl and Clifford McMullin, Cleo Sullivan and Antone Olsen.

George and Francis Leany are spending the holidays at their home in Harrisburg They are attending the Dixie academy this winter.

Mrs Lee Scott and children of Modena are here spending the holidays with Mrs Scott's father, William Stirling.

Edward and Robert McMullin and Joseph Stirling are in the hills getting the last of their cattle off the reserve.

Ranger Moody got in from Harmony yesterday. He has gone to St. George to spend holidays with his family.

Mr. and Mrs. C. B McMullin and C R. Bunker of Beaver spent a few days here last week.

Mr. and Mrs Will Hartman are are home again after a few months spent in Pine Valley.

Born, a son to Mr and Mrs Bert Harris, Tuesday, Dec. 15; all concerned doing nicely.

Will Nicholls arrived home last week from Beaver.

Eugene Leavitt left here this morning for New Harmony where he will spend holidays.

Sherman Cooper and Jack Batty left Monday for Toquerville on business.

Washington County News
January 5, 1914

Thomas Sterling of Leeds came here during the week on business He engaged some men to do assessment work on the Downey oil property. Mrs Towley Beames accompanied him to Leeds where she will spend a week visiting

Iron County Record
January 8, 1915

Mining Revival at Silver Reef.

"Mining is also attracting renewed attention at Leeds both at the River mine and at the Silver Reef. Oscar McMullin is starting development at the first named property, a silver-lead proposition, and tests are being made at the tailings dump of the Silver Reef, where 100,000 tons owned by B. Y. McMullin are expected to yield large returns in both silver and lead.

Iron County Record
January 22, 1915

Silver Reef Tailings Valuable.

From time to time during the past summer a number of mining engineers representing widely scattered interests have examined the famous old Silver Reef property in the vicinity of Leeds with a view to working over the old tailings that are known to carry a high percentage of silver lost in the early methods of ore treatment.

This mine has a production record of some ten million dollars and was in the heyday of its prosperity about 1875. Owing to the fact that the ore was treated at a number of different mills in the vicinity of Leeds, the tailings are badly scattered and it is this fault alone that has held up active operations on the old reef. The reports have been so satisfactory in other respects, however, and the chances of fair recovery so good that there is every likelihood of the early installation of a treatment plant. The mine itself is still believed to hold large deposits of low grade silver ore which may be marketable with the dawn of transportation in Washington county and the looked for increase in silver demand.

OBITUARY

Leeds Jan 27 —Miss Mary Leiny of Harrisburg, Utah, departed this life Friday morning, the 22nd inst. after an illness of several weeks. though not being confined to her bed but a few weeks Her death was a shock to her many relatives and friends as her condition was not regarded as serious until the day before her death Impressive funeral services were held Saturday in the Leeds meeting house The speakers were Bp B Y. McMullin, Elders George Spilsbury, Sr , Wm Sterling. Sr., and David Spilsbury They were all life long friends of the deceased ard all dwelt on her faithfulness and devotion to the gospel Too much could not be said of her integrity, as her life has been an exemplory one She was a true Latter day Saint and the greatest desire of her heart was to live her religion The following musical numbers were very nicely rendered: "Unanswered Yet," "Oh My Father" and "My Father Knows " Interment was made in the Harrisburg cemetery

Robert McMullin came home from the Dixie Academy last week on account of being ill He is much improved

Karl McMullin, George and Francis Leany came up Saturday to attend the funeral of their aunt, Miss Mary Leany

C Valis of Circleville has been here the past week buying cattle.

Iron County Record
January 29, 1915

IF satisfactory bids are received for the carrying of the mails on the advertisements now posted, i, e., via Cedar City, Kanarraville, Leeds, Washington, to St. George, it will prove a very great convenience for eastern Washington county, which at present has next to no service at all. It is to be hoped that a satisfactory bid shall be submitted.

Iron County Record
February 12, 1915

KEEN INTEREST IN FARMERS' ROUND-UP

LECTURES ARE ALL WELL ATTENDED, AND ALL INFORMATION IS BEING EAGERLY ABSORBED BY THE LARGE CROWDS IN ATTENDANCE.

Registration Does Not Quite Come Up to Last Year, But the Average Attendance is Much Better—People Are Not Here Out of Curiosity, But to Enjoy the Benefits of the Lectures.

The big ten-days Farmers' Round-up and Housekeepers' Conference is drawing to a close, and tomorrow will witness the winding up scene. It is pronounced by the management and those most deeply interested an unqualified success. Every session of both departments has been well attended right from the opening by people eager for the knowledge that has

Leigh, Mrs. S. W.   Parry, Mrs. I. W.
Leonard, Dr. A. N.   Palmer, Mrs. E. J.
Lunt, Mrs. H. W.   Perry, Clayton
Leonard, Mrs.A.N.   Perry, Mrs.J.H.
Lunt, H. H.   Perry, Jos. M.
Leigh, S. T.   Pettigrew, Mrs.A.
Lunt, Oscar   Parry, Evelyn
Lunt, Randle   Parry, Mrs. Ev'lyn
Lunt, Mrs. H. H.   Perkins, Miss Delia
Leigh, Mrs. W. H.   Perry, Lauretta
Leigh, Mrs. F. W.   Perry, Miss Della
Langford, Mrs. L.   Perry, Abner

Williams, Mrs.R.J. Williams, Mrs.M.J.
Williams, Mrs.S.M Williams, Lorenzo
Willis, A. M.   Williams, Mrs. L.

PARAGONAH.

Abbott, Samuel   Robinson, Thomas
Barton, James W.   Robinson, J. M.
Jones, T. W.   Robinson, T. A.
Lund, Joseph H.   Stones, Ray
Openshaw, Mary   Topham, Karl
Prothero, Stanley   Topham, Thomas
Robinson, T. R.   Topham, Mrs. Thos
Robinson, Calvin   Topham, Mrs.S.S.
Robinson, Mrs. T.A

SUMMIT.

Chamberlain, Isaac Dalley, W. W.
Dalley, Mrs. J. B. Farnsworth, Mrs.
Dalley, Mrs. M.   Fife, Mrs. S. L.
Dalley, N. B.   Fife, S. L.
Dalley, Mrs. M. J. Pratt, Mrs. Ann
Dalley, Mrs. N.   Smith, Harold
Dalley, J. B.   White, Herbert

NEW CASTLE

Forsyth, Mrs. D.   Knell, Verna
Forsyth, Donald   Morrison, Hila
Forsyth, Miss Effie Morrison, Andrew
Jones, Willard   Nelson, Edward
Jones, Mrs. W.   Tullis, John H.
Knell, Jas. G.   Whitesides, Heber
Knell, Iva

PINE VALLEY.

Gardner, R. J.   Gardner, Mrs.R.J.
Gardner, Mary   Gardner, Jessie
Gardner, Miss Eva Gardner, Royal S.
Gardner, Mrs. R.S. Gardner, Mrs.R.B.
Gardner, Nat

ENOCH.

Gibson, David   Matheson, Wm.
Gibson, Mrs. D'd   Matheson, Dan E.
Jones, S. F.   Stevens, C. F.

been so freely disseminated by the speakers, each a specialist along his or her line of work.

The register this morning discloses approximately 525 names enrolled, and others are being added all the time, or at each session. While this does not quite come up to the registration of last year, at the same time the attendance at the lectures has been better, and it is known that there have been a number at the meetings who were not registered.

The deep interest shown by the auditors proves that they are not here this year out of curiosity, but for the benefit they are receiving.

The lectures have been excellent, and have contained ample food for thought, and instructions which if put into practice will keep all the farmers and homekeepers busy for the next year. During the next few weeks The Record will attempt to reproduce, in abridged form, some of the best lectures. This issue we are giving a pretty full version of the lecture of Professor Eldridge on Homes.

The following list shows the registration from the various towns up to this (Friday) morning:

Of course the students of the college, a great many of whom have attended the meetings, are not included:

CEDAR CITY.

Adams, Mrs. W.B.	Ford, Victor
Adams, Mrs. A.	Foster, S. J.
Anderson, J. E.	Fife, Jos. S.
Anderson, Mrs.J.E.	Fife, Arthur
Adams, J. A.	Ford, William
Adams, Mrs.J.A.	Fife, John H.
Arthur, J. H.	Granger, Walter
Bulloch, Peter	Granger, Mrs. W.
Bryant, Mrs. Chas.	Gower, J. T.
Bauer, John	Gower, Mary
Bell, Mrs. C. G.	Gardner, Mrs.R.S.
Barnum, Mrs.Lucy	Higbee, Mrs. E. J.
Bulloch, Mrs.J.T.	Higbee, Mrs. M.D.
Bladen, Mrs. J.M.	Haight, Sherman
Bulloch, David	Higbee, J. M. B.
Berry, Mrs. J. S.	Haight, John S.
Bulloch, Mrs.S.A.	Haight, David
Barnson, Mrs. F.	Haight, Mrs. E.M.
Bryant, Charles	Higbee, I. C.
Bulloch, Thos. D.	Houchen, Wm.
Bulloch, J. T.	Hunter, Miles
Bauer, Miss Pearl	Haight, Herbert
Bulloch, Mrs. Alice	Higbee, M. D.
Bess, Lawrence	Haight, Mrs. C.J.
Bauer, Roy	Hogan, H. D.
Bullock, Maria	Houchen, William

Leigh, Mrs. S. T.	Perry, Hyrum
Leigh, Webster	Perry, Hyrum
Leigh, Mrs. Ada	Rickards, J. R.
Leigh, Winifred	Root, Lewis
Lundell, Mrs. H.	Roche, Margaret
Leigh, Sam. W.	Rice, Mrs. C. S.
Lunt, Wm. W.	Rice, C. S.
Lundgren, Mrs. C.	Rosenberg, Angus
Leigh, Henry	Ryan, Mrs. E. H.
Leigh, Mrs.Henry	Rosenberg, Harvey
Lundell, Albert	Stephens, Mrs.Wm
Leigh, S. F.	Simkins, Mrs. W.
Leigh, Mrs. W. D.	Simkins, Wm.
Leigh, K. F.	Smith, Wm. S.
Lunt, Mrs. M. P.	Simkins, Adrean
Lunt, Wallace	Stanley, Mary J.
Leigh, Mrs. S. F.	Sharp, Patti B.
Lunt, Roy	Smith, Mrs. Flor.
Lundgren, Chas.	Smith, Stephen
Leigh, W. H.	Sandin, Mrs. Polly
Macfarlane, Dr.M.	Stephens, Dan
Macfarlane, Glen	Simkins, Corlett
Middleton, F. W.	Schoppmann, Mrs.
Macfarlane, Mrs.K	Smith, Mrs. Jas.
Mendenhall, Mrs.	Spendlove, Mrs. J.
Macfarlane, Nettie	Tweedie, David
Mackleprang, Hat.	Thorley, L. A.
Middleton, Sarah	Thorley, Mrs. T.A
Macfarlane, W. C.	Thorley, David
Medenhall, J. W.	Tucker, William
Macfarlane, John	Thorley, Mrs.L.A.
Mackelprang, Mrs.	Thorley, Frank
Matheson, Mrs.A.G	Thorley, Rd. A.
Macfarlane, E. H.	Thorley, Mrs. D.
Matheson, H. G.	Thorley, Thos. A.
Matheson, Gwen H.	Thorley, Mrs.Rd.A.
Macfarlane, Ivie	Thorley, Stewart
Matheson, A. G.	Thorley, Mrs.H.A
Mackelprang, Hy.	Thorley, Dr. R.A.
McConnell, T. F.	Thorley, Mrs.F.A.
McConnell, Mrs F.	Unthank, Mrs. L.
Macfarlane, Lil'n	Urie, Mrs. David
Melling, Mrs. S.	Urie, Mrs. G. K.
Macfarlane, Mrs.E	Urie, Mrs. Violet
Nelson, Miss Ivie	Urie, Mrs. Geo.
Nelson, Miss Helen	Urie, Thomas
Nelson, Mrs.Emma	Urie, John, Jr.
Nelson, Mrs. B.	Watson, Ralph
Nelson, Isaac A.	Webster, Francis
Nelson, Bengt	Wood, W. H.
Nelson, Sarah A.	Williams, M. J.
Parry, Miss Est'la	Walker, Karl
Perkins, Joseph	Walker, Wm. V.
Pryor, Thomas	Woodbury, J. S.
Perry, Arthur	Woodbury, Mrs.J.S
Perry, Raymond	Webb, Mrs. Emma
Perry, Miss Min.	Webster, Ada W.
Parry, Mrs. John	Walker, J. W.
Palmer, Jethro	Walker, Miss Mary
Pryor, D. E.	Wrigley, Ester
Perry, Fred	Williams, E. E.
Pryor, W. E.	Walker, Erwin
Perry, Caroline J.	Wood, Mrs. G. A.
Palmer, Mrs. Jef.	Walker, Fannie
Parry, James C.	Wood, Conroy
Perry, Mrs. Hy.	Williams, Rd.
Palmer, E. J.	Wood, Mrs. E. A.
Parry, J. G.	Webster, Herbert
Parry, John	Walker, Mrs. F.
Perry, Fred	Wood, Violet
Perry, Ether	Wood, Mrs. Agnes

Jones, C. E.	Stevens, Carlos
Jones, John Lee	Stevens, Margery

TOQUERVILLE.

Bringhurst, Leo	Spilsbury, W. R.
Naegle, George	Spilsbury, Mrs. M.
Naegle, Ray	Spilsbury, A. P.
Stapley, S. T.	Wallace, H. M.

ENTERPRISE.

Adair, Israel	Jones, D. L.
Adair, J. H.	Jones, Mrs. Seth
Esplin, Eva	Jones, Mrs. Dola
Jones, Seth	

NEW HARMONY.

Mathes, A. F.	Pace, Minnie
Pace, L. A.	Schmutz, Eldon
Pace, Ashby	Whipple, J. E.

HAMILTON'S FORT.

Brown, F. A.	Mosdell, Charles
Cox, E. A.	Urie, Wm. C.
Mosdell, Mrs. Chas	

HURRICANE.

Hall, Harvey	Spendlove, Wm.
Hall, Mrs. Julia	Workman, Amos
Hall, Alfred	

KANAB.

Hamblin, Benj.	Rust, D. D.
Hamblin, F. M.	Spencer, J. G.

ECHO FARM.

Anderson, Albert	Anderson, Mrs. D.
Anderson, Peter	

SAINT GEORGE.

Fawcett, Fred	Nelson, Jennie
Jarvis, E. L.	

ORDERVILLE.

Esplin, Charles	Foote, H. H.

TROPIC.

Bebee, Myron	Cope, Morris

LEEDS.

Stirling, David	Stirling, Ruth

SALT LAKE CITY.

Holt, Thomas	Sevy, J. L.

SCATTERING.

Smith, J. S., Idaho Falls
Lindell, Molly, Sandy, Utah.
Covington, Miss Mary, Short Creek, Arizona.
Jones, Kumen, Bluff, Garfield Co., Utah.
Barton, George, Greenville, Utah.

Bauer, John A.
Bracken, Lawr'nce
Bulloch, D. C.
Buloch, Mrs.D.C.
Bulloch, Warren
Burbey, Miss K.
Bauer, Alowis
Bell, S. C.
Bracken, Mrs. Ida
Bulloch, Mrs.T.D.
Bauer, Rachel
Clark, Mrs. J. H.
Corry, Winnifred
Coaslett, Gomer
Clark, Earl
Corry, Willard
Corry, E. M.
Corry, Mrs. M'rni.
Corry, Moroni
Cox, Mrs. E. C.
Cox, E. C.
Clark, Mrs. Law'ce
Corry, Mrs.E.M.
Chatterley, Chris'a
Dalley, Mrs. Parl
Decker, Mrs.G.W.
Decker, Ivan
Dalley, Hillman
Dix, Mrs. Dan.
Dix, Mrs. May
Dalley, E. B.
Dover, Horace
Dix, Wm. Jr.
Dix, Mrs. Wm. Jr.
Esplin, Mrs. Lottie
Esplin, George
Fife, Mrs. Arthur
Foster, Mrs. S. J.
Froyd, Mrs. A.
Fife, Mrs. Kate
Fife, Peter B.
Fretwell, Orson

Higbee, Mrs. M.F.
Haight, I. C.
Higbee, M. F.
Haight, Hattie E.
Haight, Conrad
Hunter, Mrs. Miles
Haight, Horton D.
Hallman, Mrs. J.
Hunter, Wm. P.
Haight, Leonard
Higbee, S. A.
Hansen, Andrew
Higbee, E. J.
Heyborne, Bert
Hansen, Mrs. A.
Homer, Mrs. R.F.
Higbee, Mrs. I. C.
Houchen, Mrs.Wm.
Isbell, Mrs. J. C.
Isbell, J. C.
Jones, Mrs. C. R.
Jones, Henry
Jones, Mrs. R. L.
Jones, K. L.
Jones, Lehi M.
Jones, Henry L.
Joseph, Jno. F.
Jones, Mrs. K.
Jones, Sam B.
Jones, L. W.
Jones, Mrs. U. T.
Jones, Mrs. L. W.
Jones, T. J.
Jones, Eva L.
Jones, U. T.
Jenson, Henry
Jones, Jeddie
Knell, B. F.
Knell, Mrs. B. F.
Leigh, D. T.
Leigh, Elias
Leigh, Peter

Wood, Mrs. Agnes

Palmer, W. R.
Perry, Mary E.
Perry, Stanley
Palmer, Mrs. W.R.
Perry. H. C.
Pendelton, Daniel
Parry, Isaac

Walker, Geo. D.
Wood, F. B.
Webster, Frank B
Wood, Geo. H.
Webster, Annette
Wood, W. H.

PAROWAN.

Adams, Mrs. C. D.
Adams, Mrs. Julia
Adams, John R.
Bentley, Frank
Benson, Libbie
Bayles, H. D.
Bayles, Mrs. H. D.
Benson, Alvin
Benson, Mrs. Alvin
Clark, Lelia
Dalton, Harrell
Dalton, Randall
Gurr, Miss Pearl
Gurr, John H.
Halterman, Millard
Hoyle, Ben
Hoyle, Mrs. E. H.
Halterman, S. A.
Halterman, Mrs.S.
Lyman, Mrs. W.H.
Marsden, L. N.

Mitchell, Walter C
Mitchell, William
Mitchell, Laurette
Matheson, N. C.
Mathesan, D. A.
Matheson, Mrs.D.A
Marsden, William
Matheson, S. A.
Morris, George
Morris, Miss
Matheson, Mrs. H.
Mitchell, W. W.
Mitchell, Miss Bell
Matheson, Flossie
Page, Robert G.
Paramore, J. K.
Rasmussen, Violet
Smith, W. W.
Taylor, Henry W.
Taylor, Mrs. H. W.
Wilcox, Miss Ray

KANARRAVILLE.

Aldous, J. H.
Berry, Mrs. And.
Balser, Mrs. H. J.
Berry, Mrs. J. W.
Berry, J. W.
Ford, Sam. T.
Ford, Mrs. S. T.
Ford, Jessie
Ford, Mrs. Jesse
Ford, Jesse

Hale, Grant
Platt, Rulon
Pollock, Emery M.
Platt, John W.
Reeves, Otto
Roundy, Joel J.
Roundy, Jas. L.
Reeves, Miss Jennie
Roundy, Mrs. S. C.
Williams, R. J.

For Sufferers by War

The following amounts were subscribed and turned into L D S Church headquarters from the several wards in St George stake for the relief of sufferers, (non combatants) of the European war. The Deseret News shows a total of $28,-411 52 subscribed by 73 stakes and missions, and shows St George Stake as having subscribed $583 48 The latter amount did not include the donations from St George West and Washington wards, which raised the total to $794.75 This shows St. George Stake to have donated the 5th highest amount out of 73 stakes and missions

Enterprise	$ 24 25
Gunlock	18 75
Hurricane	22 10
La Verkin	29 00
Leeds	27 85
Pinto	28 55
Pine Valley	48 60
Rockville	54 80
Santa Clara . . .	38 00
Springdale	13 60
St George East	257 50
St George West	183 60
Toquerville	20 45
Washington . .	22 70
Stake Primary Assns .	5 00
Total	794 75

Leeds, Feb 24 —The schools gave a character ball on the night of Washington's birthday. A large crowd was out and the affair was a financial success It was under the direction of the eighth grade boys and the proceeds will be used for trees for the school grounds

Mrs W. D. Sullivan and family of Hurricane are spending the week with Mrs. Sullivan's parents, Mr. and Mrs E C Olsen

Miss Rull Stirling stopped at New Castle on her way from the Round up at Cedar, to visit with her sister, Mrs John Tullis

Mr and Mrs. Jesse Jepson of Hurricane were visiting relatives and friends here the fore part of the week

Bishop David Stirling returned from the Cedar City Roundup the latter part of last week

Karl McMullin, who is attending the Dixie Academy spent the week end at home

Leeds, Mar 24.—Clifford McMullin, Antone Olsen and Cleo Sullivan returned from St George last Saturday, where they have been taking the winter course at the Academy. They have enjoyed their work and only regret that they were not enrolled for a longer term.

The Washington Dramatic Co, played "The Miller's Daughter" to a large and appreciative audience last Saturday night. The interpretation of most of the parts was good.

Harry W Klein and John P Kurten of the "Procture Metal Extracting Co" of California are here testing the minerals of Silver Reef.

Born, a son, to Mr and Mrs Ammon Jolley, March 13; all concerned doing nicely.

Max McMullin is slowly recovering from a severe attack of pneumonia.

George and Francis Leany were in town the latter part of last week.

Miss Maggie Olsen is home again after a few weeks stay in St George.

Miss Margaret Olsen spent the week end at home here.

Bud Jackson, J. P. Kurten and Harry J. Klein are a trio of mining men of Venice, Cal., who are investigating the mining fields of Washington county. They intend making a thorough investigation of Silver Reef, Bull Valley and other fields.—Washington County News.

Washington County News
March 31, 1915

Leeds, Mar. 31.—Mr. Stephens of tht Procline Metal Extraction Company arrived here yesterday from California He is investigating with Mr Klein and Mr. Kurten, the metals of Silver Reef. Mr Stephens is the discoverer of the process by which they expect to work the low grade ores there He is very favorably impressed with the conditions at the old Silver Reef camp and expects to commence operations there very soon

A baby girl arrived at the home of Mr and Mrs Wm Nicholls Monday evening; all concerned doing well

David McMullin has just completed a fine new fence in front of his residence

Frank Hamilton has gone to Cedar City on business

Washington County News
April 13, 1915

Leeds, Apr. 13 —Our winter theatrical season closed last week with "His Just Reward," commonly known as "Silas the Choreboy," played by the La Verkin Dramatic association. The season has been a successful one and we hope that when it opens again next fall the latent talent in Leeds will assert itself.

Miss Eva Chamberlain left last week for her home in Hinckley. She has been visiting in Harrisburg for the past few months

Miss Edna Angell arrived home last week from New Harmony, where she has been for the past few weeks.

Miss Marvel Wulfenstein of St. George is here visiting, a guest of Miss Hazel Olsen.

J. M. Wicks left this morning for Stateline on mining business

Max McMullin is around again after an attack of pneumonia

Miss Libbie Leany spent Saturday in St George on business

Forest Ranger Moody is in town today

Iron County Record
April 21, 1916

MAY UTILIZE SILVER REEF TAILINGS DUMPS

Quince K. Kimball passed through Cedar yesterday en route to Silver Reef, where Mr. Kimball goes to examine the old tailing dumps that were made when that noted silver camp was a large producer. In the past five or six years there have been a number of different experts examine and test these dumps with a view of installing a system that would extract the values that were lost when the mills were working. Up to the present time, no one has undertaken to recover these lost values in silver and mercury, partly on account of the low price of these metals. Now that silver has moved up at least ten cents an ounce and is likely to go still higher, and quicksilver has gone up more than six times its former value, the chances are that the tailings can be handled at a profit.

Mr. Kimball and associates have a system on the centrifugal plan that they claim will save as high as 98 per cent of the values. The matter of crushing being eliminated and the tonnage to be handled a large one, with reasonable values in the tailings it seems probable that there will be some activity in the old camp again.

If the examination is satisfactory, preparations for work will move right along.

COUNTY 8 GRADE GRADUATES

ST. GEORGE

Alice Cannon
Aieta Cox
Afton McNeil
Annie Sullivan
Ellen Seegmiller
Florence Woodbury
Josephine Savage
Viola Fawcett
Elizabeth Smith
Fern Bryner
Nellie Pymin
Mattie Pendleton
Clara McAllister
Hazel Atkin
Marion Gates
John E. Keate
Milton Cottam
Edward Miles
Karl Pace
Clarence Cottam
Philip Foremaster
Henry Miles
Mary Blake
Glenn Snow
Glenn Webb
Andrew Baker
LeRoi Bentley
Vere Whipple
*Julius Herman

Arthur L Riding
Delmar Blair
George E Miller

HURRICANE

Lois Bradshaw
Stella Wright
Hulda Sanders
Bessie Christensen
Maude Wright
Carrie Isom
Ruby Hall
Kate Spendlove
Burr Bradshaw
Whitney Spendlove
Clinton Hall
Samuel Wright
Herbert Isom
Thomas Eagar
Golden Langston
Clarence Cripps

ENTERPRISE

Milda Holt
Lela Simpkins
Netina Alger
Hazel Hall
Gertrude Hall
Arthur Crawford
Verneth Barnum

WASHINGTON

Irene Neilson
Verna Schlappy
Lena Jolley
Ella Tobler
Ellen Hall
Thelma Thayne
Nancy Prince
James Keate

SANTA CLARA

Ezra Tobler
Clement Gubler
Leona Stucki

PINE VALLEY

Mamie Gardner
Lizzie Snow

PINTO

Leone Eldridge

NEW HARMONY

George Schmutz
William Orren Taylor

TOQUERVILLE

Loren Higbee
Charles Bringhurst
Myrtle Klienman
William Dodge
Augustus Slack

LA VERKIN

Amelia Sanders
Joseph Hinton
Ovando Gubler
Walter Segler

LEEDS

Wilford Leany
Glen B Olsen
Willard McMullin
Delbert Sterling

GUNLOCK

Beatrice Hunt
Blanche Leavitt

ROCKVILLE

Melvin Petty
Warren Hirschi

VIRGIN

Alma Flanigan
Ada Beames

GRAFTON

Lenora Ballard
Edna Russell

Washington County News
May 6, 1915

LEEDS

Mrs Mary Ann Goddard died here suddenly yesterday at the home of her granddaughter, Mrs Frank Hartley.

Francis Leany expects to leave here today for Long Valley, where she will spend the summer

Mr. and Mrs George Olson have moved into their home

Bert Harris left last week for Salt Lake City

The wool haulers arrived home from Lund Saturday, after a long muddy trip.

Iron County Record
May 7, 1915

MRS. MARY C. GODDARD DEAD.

News was received here last Tuesday of the death at Leeds of Mrs. Mary A. Goddard, mother of G. C. and Sidney Goddard of this place and Harmony, the day previous. Her two sons at once set out to attend the funeral, but on account of the delay in getting the word, and the extremely stormy condition of the weather, with resultant muddy roads and swollen mountain streams intervening, were unable to get through by the appointed time, and were obliged to return home. Interment took place in the Harrisburg cemetery, where deceased has a daughter buried.

Deceased came to southern Utah in 1850, and has resided for the most part at New Harmony. She was the first white girl married in Payson, Utah, which town was named after her father, "Jimmie" Pace.

Three sons and one daughter survive her, a son and a daughter have gone before. The living children, in addition to those already mentioned, are William P. Goddard, residing in Mexico, and Mrs. Hannah Jolley of Washington, Utah.

Leeds, May 12 —Monday afternoon the S and E club entertained the mothers at the home of Mrs B Y. McMullin* An appropriate program was rendered, some excellent number being given by Mrs Bert Harris, Mrs James McQuard and Miss Ruth Stirling Leone McMullin gave a number of delightful piano selections. After the program a delicious lunch was served in the dining room

A surprise party was given Mrs. J. M. Hamilton at her home last Saturday afternoon, the occasion being her 77th birthday. The afternoon was very pleasantly spent Mrs Hamilton doing most of the entertaining with reminiscences of the early days of the church Dainty refreshments were served.

A social and economics club was organized here last week with the following officers· Miss Ruth Stirling, president, Hyrum Leany, vicepresident, Leone McMullin, secretary and treasurer.

Karl, Clifford, and Dan McMullin left this morning for the Buckskin Mountain. They will ride for the Bar Z this summer.

J. M. Wicks arrived home Sunday from Stateline where he has been looking after his mining interests.

Leeds, May 25 —The test plant that Messrs Klein and Kurten ordered for testing the low grade ores of Silver Reef has arrived and they expect to have it in operation soon

Mrs Maria Wilkinson left last Monday for Salt Lake City to stay indefinitely with Mrs Quist, an old time friend, She went with Mrs Quist's son and wife in their auto

Mrs M J Hamilton and son, Frank, left for Cedar City the fore part of the week, where they intend to make their future home

Charles Hansen returned home from Snowflake, Ariz, last week where he has been teaching school the past winter.

The home of Mr. and Mrs Edward McMullin was made very happy on May 31 by the arrival of a fine baby boy

Miss Margaret Olsen left for Overton, Nev , Sunday, where she will work in the new drug store there this summer.

· The stock men are busy gathering their cattle. The buyers are expected tomorrow.

George Olsen left recently for Copper mountain to spend the summer.

Iron County Record
June 11, 1915

Mrs. Rebecca Angell of Leeds was in Cedar City yesterday en route to Salt Lake City to spend a month with her daughter, Mrs. Tom Rees, who resides in the suburbs of that city.

Washington County News
June 17, 1915

Bad Mail Service

There is something radically wrong with the mail service between St George and points up the river. Letters bearing the postmark "June 8" from Hurricane, Rockville and Virgin were not received here till Thursday evening, June 10 The postmaster here can give no reason for the delay in transmission of these letters. Presumably the delay has occured at either the Toquerville or Leeds postoffice. The same thing occurred the week previously. That letters from the same places were delayed two weeks in succession makes it unlikely that they were detained at mailing offices

It is hoped this condition will be remedied without delay.

Iron County Record
June 25, 1915

Charles Hansen of Leeds was in
Cedar City last Wednesday looking
over the feasibility of establishing a
Ford automobile passenger line between Lund and Hurricane.

Leeds, June 30 —Preparations are being made for the celebration of the nation's birth day Energetic committees are working hard to make it a a real glorious Fourth as their are some "live wires" on this committee we are anticipating a rousing good time We will cole brate on Saturday, the 3rd

Wallace McMullin arrived here from Parowan last week where he went to take Mrs McMullin and children. Mr. and Mrs McMullin and children have been visiting relatives and friends here for some time past. Mr. McMullin intends to trip in the mountains this summer.

C F. Hanson went to Lund to meet his wife some time ago He brought her home in a new Ford car. Since then his neighbors and friends have been enjoying some joy rides

Mrs. Mark Miller and children arrived here from Salt Lake City some time ago They will spend the summer with Mrs Miller's mother, Mrs Oscar McMullin

Andrew Gregerson of St George and a Mr. Jackson from California are here on mining business They will look over the mines of Silver Reef this afternoon

Mrs Will Woodbury from St George who has been here the past few days visiting went home yesterday.

Mrs Schlappy of St George is here visiting her daughter, Mrs E. C. Olsen

Mrs Will Sullivan from Hurricane is visiting here this week.

Joseph McAllister is a guest at Sterling's hotel today.

Joseph Stirling has gone to Laramie, Wyoming, with cattle

Washington County News
July 21, 1915

Leeds, July 21.—Charles Hansen left with a party of young men from Washington for Salt Lake City this morning He will take them through in his car and expects to make the trip to Salt Lake in two days

Mrs George Angell and daughter, arrived from Salt Lake City last week They have been visiting Mrs Angell's daughter, Mrs T M. Reece, for the past few weeks.

Mrs Maria Wilkinson returned last week from Salt Lake City where she has been visiting an old time friend for the past few months

Wm Sullivan, jr, of Hurricane was a visitor here Monday He took Mrs Sullivan and children back with him.

Miss Alice Sterling left yesterday for New Castle where she will visit her sister, Mrs John Tullis, for a few weeks

Mrs Wallace McMullin and children arrived here from Parowan last week. They will stay here indefinitely

Ranger Moody took a party of men in the hills Monday to do some surveying.

Washington County News
July 28, 1915

Leeds, July, 28 —Pioneer day passed off rather quietly here on account of so many people leaving town just at the last minute The sports in the afternoon were a succees however, considerable enthusiasm being shown in the different sports and races A children's dance followed The day was unusually cool for this time of the year and everybody appreciated the change of the atmosphere

Frank McMullin left last week for Copper Mountain Mrs McMullin will stay in Harrisburg for the remainder of the summer.

Clifford McMullin and Antone Olsen left last week for Copper Mountain.

Andrew Gregerson of St. George was here yesterday on mining business

Leeds, Aug 4 — Mr. McGinnis from Salt Lake City was a business visitor here Monday. He was looking over the ores of Silver Reef

Mrs Dan Parker and children from Parowan arrived here Saturday evening They will visit here a few weeks, guests of Mrs Parker's mother, Mrs David McMullin.

Charles Hanson left Monday with a party of tourists for the Grand Canyon He was accompanied by Mrs Hanson

Frank and Karl McMullin left yesterday morning for Pine Valley mountain to spend a few days

Miss Etta Cox of St George is a visiter here, a guest of her aunt, Mrs Thomas Stirling.

Mr. and Mrs Wallace McMullin and children left Sunday morning for Parowan

Victor Angell arrived home yesterday from Moapa Valley.

Mr. and Mrs. Lynn Jarvis are here spending the summer

Leeds, Aug 11 — Judge Jackson of Los Angeles, California, and Andrew Gregerson of St George spent a few days here inspecting the ores of Silver Reef Mr. Jackson left Tuesday morning for Salt Lake City. He shipped about 200 lbs of ore there to be tested

The children of the primary and kindergarten classes visited Mrs Maria Wilkenson Sunday. They sing songs and each child gave her some flowers Mrs Wilkenson or "Aunt Maria" as she is known by all the children had been away for some time visiting in Salt Lake City which made the visit doubly appreciated

Mern Wulfensten and Wesley McArthur of St George were visitors here Saturday and Sunday, guests of their cousins, Glen Olsen and Willie McMullin, respectively.

The Milne Bros have completed painting Ranger Moody's house and barn and have returned to their home in St. George

Ranger Moody and family returned yesterday from St George where they have been while their house was being painted

Mrs Will Sullivan and family of Hurricane are here visiting Mrs Sullivan's mother, Mrs E C Olsen

Miss Leone McMullin returned last week from Beaver where she has been visiting

A dancing party was held here Friday evening, a pleasant time is reported

Mr. and Mrs Chas Hansen returned last night from the Grand Canyon

Mr. Taylor of New Harmony was here Sunday

Washington County News
August 12, 1915

Los Angeles Man Buys Goldstrike Claims

Col K M Jackson of Los Angeles, Calif, came in last Thursday evening from Goldstrike, where he bonded the Dora Jane and the Dora Jane No, 1 from Andrew F. Gregerson of this city for G H. Hayes of Los Angeles The amount of the bond was not given out The Dora Jane claims adjoin the Hamburg group in the Goldstrike district, and give promise of being equally as good Mr Jackson immediately made a contract with the Bryson Bros to sink a shaft on the Dora Jane claims

Mr Jackson is an experienced mining man, well known in the west from the Yukon and Klondike down to Mexico He is representing G H Hays, a mining capitalist of Los Angeles, in the Goldstrike district

Mr Jackson accompanied Mr Gregerson to Silver Reef Saturday to look over the old camp He sampled the tailings on the dumps there and sent about 200 pounds to Salt Lake City to be tested He has taken an option on the tailings owned by A F Gregerson of this city and B Y McMullin of Leeds, estimated at about 300,000 tons

Mr Jackson contemplates working the low grade ores at the Reef. He left for Salt Lake City Monday, Mr. Gregerson returning to his home here

Iron County Record
August 13, 1915

Mrs. Nan Parker and little ones are visiting in Leeds with their parents, Mr. and Mrs. McMullin.

Washington County News
August 18, 1915

Leeds, Aug 18 — Mgr. B. Jarvis of the Southern Utah Packing Co and Miss Ella Bentley arrived this morning on the mail auto from St George They expect to have the cannery running tomorrow.

Jack Kurten, Harry Klein and Bob McMullin spent a few days last week enjoying the cool breezes of Pine Valley mountain.

A number of girls from St George are here making arrangements to work in the cannery the remainder of the summer

Mrs Flora Davis and daughters, Mrs Whimpey, and Miss Hila, are here visiting, guests of Mrs Thomas Stirling

Mrs Oral Beal of Overton, Nev., are here visiting, guests of Mrs Beal's mother, Mrs E C Olsen

Mrs Lizzie Beams of Virgin was a visitor here this week

Woodbury Reunion

A number of St George citizens left Saturday morning to attend a reunion of the Woodbury family at the home of Mr and Mrs Hyrum Leany, Harrisburg. Among those present from this city were Mr and Mrs John T. Woodbury and the Misses Annie, Mary and Louie, Mr. and Mrs Geo W Worthen and family, Mr and Mrs Melvin Harmon and family, Mr and Mrs E D Seegmiller and family, Lawrence Woodbury, Miss Florence Woodbury; from Hurricane, Mr. and Mrs Clarence Woodbury and family, from Leeds, Mr. and Mrs Hyrum McMullin and family

49 guests sat down to the fine dinner prepared Saturday, after which a good sociable time was had. The fine melons and other choice fruit for which Harrisburg is noted were liberally partaken of and enjoyed

The party attended Sunday school at Leeds, and dispersed for their various homes later the same day after having spent a very enjoyable time together.

Leeds, Aug 25 —Mrs Byron Millett received word yesterday that her husband who is running a sawmill in Zion canyon, was ill with an attack of appendicitis He was taken to Hurricane yesterday to be operated upon. Mrs Millett left for Hurricane yesterday afternoon.

Mr. and Mrs John Tullis and children and Miss Alice Stirling arrived here Sunday evening from New Castle

The Misses Minnie and Mildred Pace and Ashby Pace of Harmony were visitors here the fore part of the week.

The cannery is putting up some very fine peaches this year A force of about 18 girls are working now.

A party was held at the home of Karl McMullin Saturday night. A good time is reported.

A very pleasant dancing party was held here last night

J M. Wicks left Monday for Stateline

School Population Washington County

The following is the school population of Washington County, showing the number in each of the five districts

Dist No 1	Boys	Girls	Total	
Springdale	30	29	59	
Rockville	33	38	71	
Grafton	8	8	16	
Virgin	22	28	50	
La Verkin	36	27	63	
Toquerville	54	47	101	360
Dist No. 2	Boys	Girls	Total	
Hurricane	114	132	246	
Washington	68	81	149	
Leeds	36	22	58	453
Dists No 3 & 4	Boys	Girls	Total	
St George	270	298	568	
Bloomington	11	9	20	
Santa Clara	55	42	97	685
Dist No 5	Boys	Girls	Total	
Gunlock	28	25	53	
Central	19	20	39	
Pine Valley	16	17	33	
Pinto	7	5	12	
Enterprise	68	87	155	
New Harmony	21	18	39	331
Grand Total				1829

Unofficial List of County School Teachers

Springdale, Marvin Terry, Florence Gifford. Rockville, C Walter Cottam, Anna Jennings. Grafton, one vacancy Virgin, Clinton R Burt La Verkin, Emil Graf, one vacancy Toquerville Morgan Edwards, Fannie Klienman Hurricane, Charles T Hansen, Robert P Woodbury, Josephine Spendlove, Augusta C. Wood. Leeds, Marcus Tegan, Margaret Olsen Washington, Israel Neilson, Val Hafen, Emily Sandberg, one vacancy St George, W. O Bentley, jr, W E Woodbury, A D. Allen, Jed Fawcett, H R Bentley, J Leslie Harmon, Lena Nelson, Metta C Morris, Mishie Seegmiller, Florence Foremaster, Mary Crosby, LaVerd Watson, Jos W. McAllister. Bloomington, J Gordon Riding. Santa Clara, Leland Hafen, Josephine Wittwer. Gunlock, Henry Graf Central, Gilbert D Hyatt Pine Valley, Estella Jacobson. Enterprise, William Staheli, J Willard Ganfield, Althea Gregerson, Rachel Moody New Harmony, Minnie Pace

Lee Scott Called

W L Scott of Modena died at the Washington County hospital last Thursday night, the 2nd inst, of uremia Mr Scott was brought in the preceding Tuesday afternoon from Goldstrike, where he had mining interests He was in a serious condition and despite all that could be done for him passed away

Mrs Scott arrived here from Modena very early Saturday morning, William Lund bringing her through in his auto during the severe storm that was raging on the desert The remains were taken to Leeds, Mrs Scott's home, for interment

Funeral services were held at Leeds at 2 p m Sunday, the speakers, Bishop McMullin, Elders Frank Sullivan and Geo R Lund, paying eloquent tribute to the deceased.

Mr Scott was a man who is very highly spoken of by all who knew him as an industrious, honorable citizen, and a good neighbor

Leeds, Sept 7 —Funeral services for W Lee Scott were held here Sunday afternoon The ward house was filled with sorrowing friends The speakers were Bp B Y Mc Mullin, Elders Frank Sullivan and Geo Lund of St George and H A Jolley The sudden death of Mr Scott was a severe shock to his many friends here and they deeply sympathize with the bereaved wife and children

Mrs Wm Farnes and Mrs Aug ust Kuhn of Salt Lake are visiting friends and relatives here, guests of Mrs Will Stirling, jr

Mark Miller and George Olson came in from Copper Mountain last week to stay until after the fruit festival

Born, a son to Mr. and Mrs. Will Sullivan, Sept, 2,

Washington County News
September 14, 1915

Leeds, Sept 14.—The following from here have enrolled in the Dixie Academy Hazel Olson, Thos Stirling, Verna, Cliton, and Stanley Fuller Others expect to commence soon

Mr. Hemming Mortenson of Salt Lake City visited his aunt, Mrs Hanson, for a few hours today. He came down from Parowan, where he has been taking in the fair, in Mr Hanson's car this morning. They returned to Parowan this afternoon

News of the terrible automobile accident on the Black Ridge has caused considerable excitement here this afternoon

A fine boy arrived at the home of Mr and Mrs Frank McMullin, Harrisburg, Monday morning the 13th inst.

Mr. and Mrs A. Hartley left to-day for their home at Hurricane They have been visiting here a few days

Ranger Moody has moved his family to St George for the winter.

Joe Stirling and Charlie Angell left today for Pine Valley mountain.

Alex Taylor of New Harmony was a visitor here Sunday

Mr Joseph M Worthen and Miss Leone McMullin were married in the St George temple Wednesday, Sept 22. The bride is a daughter of Mr and Mrs. B Y McMullin, highly respected residents of Leeds The groom is a highly respected young man of Salt Lake City.

Leeds, Sept 23 — Miss Leone McMullin was the guest of honor at a linen shower, given at her home last night by the young ladies of the town The boys received a rather belated invitation but it didn't make them late for the party and all spent a delightful evening A dainty lunch was served and Miss McMullin was the proud recipient of a beautiful linen table set

Mrs Eleanor Scott and children accompanied by Judge Leany, Miss Ruth Stirling and Joseph Stirling left Saturday for Modena. Joseph Stirling arrived home last night bringing with him his father, who has been looking after Mrs Scott's interests there Miss Ruth will stay with her sister indefinately

George and Francis Leany have returned home from Cedar mountain. They left for St George Saturday to attend the Dixie this winter. Wilford Leany is a new student at the Academy this winter

Mrs. August Kuhn and small son left on the stage last Saturday for her home in Salt Lake City She has been visiting friends and relatives here and in St. George for some time past

The Misses Liddie and Annie Hopkins of Glendale are visitors here this week, guests of their sister, Mrs Edward McMullin. They will attend school at the Dixie Academy this year.

The cannery is putting up some fine grapes now Miss Bentley expects to be here for some time canning They will can a number of beeves when the fruit is finished.

Mrs Thomas Stirling is the proud possessor of a fine new overland car Last evening her neighbors were enjoying some joy rides in it

Mrs L A Tomsik and children of Salt Lake City are here visiting friends and relatives, guests of Mrs. Frank Hartley.

Judge H. S. Leany of Salt Lake City has been visiting his relatives here, a guest of Wm. Stirling

Max McMullin and Maggie Jolley left Sunday to attend the Dixie Academy.

J. M. Worthen from Salt Lake City is a visitor here this week.

Mark Miller left Thursday for the Grand Gulch mine

Leeds, Oct, 6.—Our school opened this morning with Miss Margaret
Olsen and Herbert Milne as teachers   This is Miss Olsen's second
year here and the pupils are rejoicing over their good luck in being
with her again.   She taught a successful term in La Verkin last year
This is Mr Milne's first year at
teaching but he comes well recom-
mended and he is beginning with an
earnest determination that brings
success   The childr n are all enthusiastic over their work and we
anticipate a successful school year

John Tullis and son, Sterling, ar
rived Saturday evening from New
Castle   Mr. Tullis is loud in his
praise for the New Castle country
and says it offers splendid oppor-
tunities for a young man as there
is some fine land there that just
now can be procured on easy terms
Mr. Tullis will take Mrs Tullis and
children home with him

Wm Sullivan, jr ,from Hurricane
spent Sunday here   He left this
morning taking with him Mrs. Sullivan and children.

Mrs. J. Perkins arrived here yesterday from Taylor, Ariz.   She is
visiting her daughter, Mrs. Chas
Hanson.

A candy pull was held at the
home of Miss Alice Sterling.   A
pleasant time is reported.

Leeds, Sept. 29 —Mr. and Mrs
J M Worthen left Friday morning
for Salt Lake City where they will
make their future home.   Mrs
Worthen nee Leon McMullin will
be greatly missed here as she is a
young lady of unusual musical ability and has for some time past been
our ward organist.

W. A. Smith and John Alexander, mining men from Los Angeles,
have been here for the past two or
three days looking over the mines
of Silver Reef   They were very
favorably impressed with the conditions at the old silver camp and
feel that with the present good prospects of a raise in silver it will become a lively camp   They expect
to make another visit here in the
near future

Mrs. L A. Tomsek and children
who have been visiting friends and
relatives here and in Washington
for the past few weeks left last week
for their home in Salt Lake City.

Mr. and Mrs Frank Sullivan arrived home last week from Parowan
where they have been taking in the
county fair.

Miss Margaret McMullin is visiting in Cedar City.

Leeds, Oct 12 —Chas Wilkinson of Cedar City had the misfortune to break his car near Harrisburg yesterday while on his way from St. George to Cedar with his family. The machine was brought here for repairs and Mr. Hanson took the family on to Cedar City

Mr. and Mrs Mark McMullin and daughter, and Miss Marguerete McMullin arrived last week from Cedar City. Mr. and Mrs McMullin expect to make their home here.

Mr. and Mrs. C. F. Hanson have moved to St. George for the winter. Mr. Hanson has a daily passenger service to Cedar City. He works conjointly with B F. Knell

A. F. Gregorson of St George was here Saturday on mining business.

J. M. Wicks has gone to Stateline on business.

Molasses is being made here now.

Leeds, Oct 10 —The cannery factory is busy canning tomatoes Miss Bentley is not with them this week She left for her home in St. George Mgr B Jarvis has just received a letter from the Hotel Utah for prices on fruit They had seen the samples on exhibition at the State fair

The following students from the Dixie Academy spent the week end home Hazel Olson, Max McMullin, Thomas Stirling and Clinton Fuller.

A fine baby girl has arrived at the home of Mr. and Mrs. Will Hartman.

Wesley McArthur of St George spent Saturday here deer hunting.

Washington County News
October 26 & 27, 1915

Leeds, Oct 26 —Mr and Mrs Mark McMullin arrived this evening from Cedar City. They are home-steading some land at Grapevine Springs and expect to spend the winter here

Bishop David Stirling left this morning for Modena He will bring his sisters, Mrs. Scott and Miss Ruth, home with him

Mrs Taylor of Harmony and son, Alex, spent Sunday here visiting relatives and friends

Mrs Lynna McMullin is very ill with a bad cold and has symptoms of pneumonia

W O Bentley, jr , county super visor, has been visiting the schools here today.

Karl McMullin killed a fine deer last week

Will Stirling is very ill

Leeds, Oct 27 —Will Stirling passed away last evening after a lingering illness Although his many friends and relatives knew he could not live much longer his death came unexpectedly Funeral services have not yet been arranged

Most of the boys of the town are busy now getting the cattle off the reserve

Ranger Moody has just arrived from the foot hills with a fine deer.

Iron County Record
October 29, 1915

Alonzo Dalton of Hurricane was in Cedar yesterday with an Overland car that he has bought from Thomas Stirling of Leeds. The car was won by Mrs. Stirling in a voting contest put on by the Evening Telegram of Salt Lake City some little time ago. Mr. Dalton will use the car for carry-ing the mail between Leeds and Hur-ricane.

Leeds, November 2 — Funeral services over the remains of William Stirling, jr, were held here last Thursday afternoon Counselor A J Jolley of the ward bishopric had charge of the services The speakers were Elders B Y. McMullin, David McMullin, David Spilsbury and A J Jolley, all of whom spoke very highly of the integrity of the deceased Beautiful and appropriate musical numbers were furnished by the Toquerville ward

Our speakers Sunday in Sunday afternoon sacrament meeting were D H. Morris Principal Woodward and Prof Gourley of the Dixie Academy It has been some time since we have had the privilege of hearing Elder Morris and his talk was very much appreciated Pr f Gourley gave some instructions relative to the Mutual fair which aroused considerable interest among the Mutual members Prof Woodward urged the parents to send as many students as possible to the winter course The meeting was most interesting and it was regrettable that more people were not in attendance Mrs Woodward was with the party and after meeting she explained some of the requirements of the art department in the proposed Mutual fair.

Bishop David Stirling and Ammon Jolley left Saturday for Modena, Bishop Stirling started for Modena the fore part of the week but had to return on account of his brother's death

The sad news of the sudden death of August Kuhn of Salt Lake City comes as a great shock to his many friends here Mr Kuhn died of a severe case of pneumonia, being ill only six days

Mr and Mrs John Tullis came in from New Castle last week to attend Mr. Stirling's funeral. They left for their home Saturday.

Mr and Mrs Bert McQuarie of St George were here Thursday They came over to attend the funeral of William Stirling, jr.

Edward McMullin arrived home from Glendale last week Mrs McMullin stayed there to visit a few weeks.

Holem Mortenson of Colorado spent a few days here last week visiting his aunt, Mrs Hanson.

Thomas Stirling and Clinton Fuller spent the week end home from the Academy.

Lynn McMullin is improving and will soon be around again

Leeds Nov 9 —We have had a fine warm rain which is making the farmers rejoice In spite of the bad roads the mail auto comes bravely through every day Such a contrast to our last winter's rainy delays The weather here has been unusually fine this fall having had practically no frost yet The tomatoes have not yet been injured Owing to the lateness of the season it was feared that this crop would be a failure but they have matured far beyond expectation The cannery reports receiving unusually fine ones and that they are proud to put them on the market

The citizens are now working for a water system With our natural advantages this can be done with little expense, and with our excellent water and most urgent need for the system it should be done with little delay.

We regret to report the illness of Wm Stirling this week He arrived from St George this morning on the stage having been under the doctor's care there for the past few days

Miss Ella Bentley came over from St George last week She expects to be able to stay now until the cannery closes. This week finishes the tomatoes

Mr. Dalton brings the mail in a new Overland car. The storm doesn't interfere with his time, He comes at the usual hour via Echo Farm

Miss Ellen Carter was a visitor here today, a guest of Mrs J. M. McQuaid She left this evening on the stage for St. George.

A baby boy arrived at the home of Mr. and Mrs Charles Hanson at St George the 3rd of this month

Mrs. Frank McMullin and children have moved here from Harrisburg for the winter.

A fine baby girl arrived at the home of Mr. and Mrs George Olsen Sunday, the 7th.

Bishop David Stirling arrived home from Modena today.

Supervisor W. O Bentley visited the schools here Monday.

Washington County News
November 15, 1915

Leeds Nov. 15 —Our speakers in Sacrament meeting Sunday were Patriarch George Spilsbury from Toquerville and Elder George Spilsbury from Toquerville They both spoke very interestingly and their speaking was very much appreciated They were also Sunday School visitors.

Mgr. B Jarvis and Miss Ella Bentley left for St. George Sunday. The heavy frost that fell here last Wednesday night put an end to the tomato canning They will return later to can meat

Mrs. Elinor Scott and children, Miss Ruth Stirling and Ammon Jolley arrived here last Wednesday from Modena Mrs Scott and children will spend the winter here

Max McMullin left for St George today to continue his studies at the Dixie academy. He has been home for the past few days with an attack of the grip

Frank McMullin left today for St George. He will take the Midwinter course at the Dixie academy,

Edward McMullin left Saturday for Glendale. He will bring Mrs McMullen back with him.

William Stirling is still very ill.

Washington County News
November 22, 1915

Leeds, Nov. 22 —Threshing beans and molasses making keeps some of the farmers busy The molasses made here this fall is of very fine quality, but not enough has been made to supply the demand Those that have produced it have found it very profitable and people are planning to make more of it next year.

Some of the boys are trapping again this fall. Roy Hartley and Clyde McMullin, two of our youngest trappers, caught a large coyote last night, one of the largest caught in the vicinity for years

Mr and Mrs Chas Bastain of St George were visiting here last week. guests of Mr and Mrs Frank Hartley They came over mainly to see Wm Stirling who is still very ill.

The Purgatory Land Co. expect to have their canal finished very soon now From their reports we expect to see crops growing there next summer

Thomas Blazzard passed thru here today enroute for Cedar City with a load of turkeys from his farm in the Washington field.

Frank Hartley left today for his dry farm on Kolob Mountain He expects to spend some time there plowing his land.

Antone Olson arrived home this morning from Copper Mountain where he has been for the past few months.

Edgar Westover passed thru here Saturday from the Grand Gulch mine enroute for his home at Washington

Mr. and Mrs Edward McMullin and small son arrived home last week from Glendale

The M. I. A put in a committee Sunday evening to arrange a party for Thanksgiving

Prin Herbert Milne was visiting the St George schools last Friday.

Mark Miller came in last week from the Grand Gulch mine

Miss Ruth Stirling was a St George visitor to day.

Washington County News
November 29, 1915

LEEDS ·

OBITUARY

Leeds, Nov 29 —Funeral services for William Stirling, who passed away last Wednesday, Nov. 24th, were held Thursday afternoon in the ward chapel Stake President E H Snow had charge of the services Prayer was offered by Elder David Spilsbury The speakers were Bishop B Y McMullin, Pres. E H. Snow and Pres Geo F Whitehead, all of whom paid tribute to the sterling qualities of the deceased and his undaunted faith in the gospel Beautiful music was furnished by a quartette consisting of Viola McAllister. Nettie White-head, Pres Geo F Whitehead and Vernon Snow, with Nettie Whitehead at the organ The following numbers were given· "I Know that My Redeemer lives," sung by Viola McAllister the rest of the singers joining in the chorus, "My Father Knows" and "Tho Deepening Trials Throng Your Way," Viola McAllister sang the solo "Face to Face "

William Stirling was born in Forfarshire, Scotland, in 1840 He accepted the gospel in his native land and came to Dixie in 1862, driving an ox team from St. Louis right into this county He was one of the formost workers in the building up of this Dixie country His friends will remember him and miss him for his genial hospitality and optimistic nature. He leaves nine children, twenty grandchildren and a host of friends to mourn his loss His wife Sarah Ann Leany Stirling died just fifteen years ago this fall.

The following students from the Dixie spent the Thanksgiving holidays home. Hazel Olsen, Frank and Max McMullin, Thomas Stirling, Maggie Jolley, Verna Chislen, Stanley Fuller and Cleo Sullivan

Frank Anderson, his mother and Miss Laura Anderson from Echo Farm and Heber Neagle from Toquerville attended Mr Stirling's funeral, they came over in Frank's new Ford car.

The Misses Annie and Liddie Hopkins spent Thanksgiving holidays here, guests of their sister, Mrs Edward McMullin

A chicken supper was held at the home of Cleo Sullivan Saturday night; a pleasant time is reported.

A band of gypsies arrived in town today. They have pitched their tents in Hartley's lane.

Mr. and Mrs John Tullis left Friday for their home at New Castle

Leeds, Dec 6 —Mgr B Jarvis and Mrs Ella Bentley of the Southern Utah packing Co arrived here from St George last night They started the cannery this morning and expect to keep it running now until Christmas Pork and beans, beef, soup and sausage will be the principal things canned.

The Y L M I A are contesting with the young men for the highest average attendance. Considerable enthusiasm is being shown and a pronounced increase of attendance in both departments is noticed Last week a number of new faces were seen, mostly. married people The contest closes at the end of the month, the department having the highest average attendance by that time is to be entertained by the losing department, The competitive idea is carried out in the preliminary work. The departments take turns furnishing the programs Next week the young ladies give the program and the committee in charge of it promises us something out of the ordinary

Mrs Bert Harris and children arrived here Friday from Salt Lake City for the winter Mrs Harris is a valuable addition to our ward and her many friends here rejoice in their good luck in having her back.

The Kleiman brothers from Toquerville were here buying cows today.

Glen Olson enrolled in the Dixie Academy last week

Dan McMullin went to Cedar City today on business

Donald Fuller is suffering from the grip

Old People Called.

During the past few days a number of the old people of Iron and Washington counties have answered the last summons. Among the number, are William Stirling, one of the old land marks of Leeds, Utah, who is known to a wide circle of friends and acquaintances throughout the southern portion of the state; another figure no less familiar, is Rufus Allen of St. George, who passed to the other side of the river during the first of this week. Bro. Allen has a number of relatives and warm personal friends in this immediate locality; and Henry Houchen, an elderly and respected resident of Cedar City, who passed away the present week. On account of a lack of time and space we are obliged to defer publication of any extended obituary notices until next issue, when we will publish something in relation to their lives and careers.

Leeds, Dec 20 —The contest for attendance this month between the young men's and young ladies' M. I. A closed Sunday evening The young men winning by two The young ladies are making preparations for the party that they, as the losing side, have to give The competitive idea is doing much good in increasing the attendance and working up a lively spirit in the Mutual work New members are being enrolled each week who are taking an active part in the lessons The plan also insures the regular monthly party

The program for the M. I. A next Sunday evening promises to be a success The young ladies have charge of it and it will be suggestive of Christmas The numbers will be given by the Dixie students The Joseph Smith program given by the young men last week was a very good one The numbers being a talk on the Life of the Prophet by Elder David McMullin, and "The Unknown Grave" sung by Clyde McMullin

The cannery closes tomorrow until after holidays. It has been doing a rushing business for the past few weeks and has put up some very fine goods. This is the first year that it has attempted canning meat to any great extent, last year being largely experimental, but once getting the goods on the market the demand has exceeded all expectations.

Chas Hanson was sustained as president of the M I A Sunday evening. The former president, Frank Sullivan, having gone to Grand Gulch.

Ranger Moody and a party of men arrived home today from the reserve where they have been getting the remainder of the cattle.

The district school teachers are preparing a Christmas dance and program for their pupils which is to be given Wednesday night.

The Misses Anna and Liddie Hopkins are spending the holidays here, guests of their sister, Mrs Edward McMullin.

The following left last week for Grand Gulch: Mark Miller, Frank Sullivan and George Olsen.

Chas Hanson has moved his family here from St George for the remainder of the winter.

Nels Anderson is spending the holidays here, a guest of Mr and Mrs. Thos Stirling.

Forest Supervisor Raphael was here from St. George on business this week.

A. F. Gregorson was here today from St. George on mining business.

J M. Wicks left last week for State Line on business.

The Academy students are home again for the holidays.

Bert Harris arrived here Saturday from Salt Lake City.

Iron County Record
December 24, 1915

Matt Wicks came up from Leeds the middle of the week. Matt is like the prodigal son, but as far as a nice fatted calf was concerned, the home coming was a disappointment. But gentle reader, don't become discouraged, for there was a nice fat hog in Mr. Buehl's pen, awaiting for the occasion. Matt promptly rolled up his sleeves and attended to Mr. Hog.

Leeds, Jan. 3 —The holiday sea-son has been pretty lively here in spite of the fact that there has been so much sickness, most of the people are around again after their spell of the grip Mrs D S McMullin has almost recovered from an attack of pneumonia.

The snow storm was a delightful treat to the people here Coasting was indulged in by the grownups as well as the children New Year's day, and one lone bob sleigh with its sleigh bells (cow bells) made most of the night

Wednesday night a testimonial for Elder Willard A McMullin was held. In spite of the stormy night and so many people being ill a pleasant time was spent and a Christmas present of $20 was sent to Elder McMullin

Mr. and Mrs. William Woodbury of St George spent part of the holidays here visiting Mrs Woodbury's parents, Mr. and Mrs. Wm Sullivan.

Last week the young ladies of the M. I A entertained the young men at a dancing party Lunch was served and an enjoyable time was spent.

Mr. and Mrs. Wm Sullivan, jr., of Harrisburg are spending the holidays here, guests of Mrs Sullivan's parents, Mr. and Mrs E C. Olsen.

Miss Libby Leany entertained at a watch party at her home in Harrisburg New Year's eve A very pleasant time is reported.

The Dixie students have all gone back to school, most of them going this morning in Mr. Dalton's car.

Miss Edyth McMullin entertained at a party New Year's night.

LEEDS

Leeds Jan 18 — A committee consisting f Mr Bert Harris Lili Be t r an l Margaret Ol en has been app iute i t arrange for the m ntl ly party of he M I A The young ladies again have the pleasure of entertaii ir g the v ung men because of the lowest atten lance but un Hunted they have challenged the young men again f r the coming month The party will be a tie ind apron dancing party and will be given Frid iy night

George Church an a party consisting of his wife hi mother and their children trom St George had the misf rtune Sun lay to break his car in the mu l below town ind the party in cor sequence has h id to remain over here since Sun lay Thomas Stirling took them home in his buggy to day

Patriarch Geo Spilsbury ur d Elder David Spilsbury from Toquerville were visitors at Sunday school Sunday They als remained over and spoke in our Sacrament meet ir g By request Eld r David Spilsbury give curent events in Mutual Sunday night

The fine warm rain that we are having shows no sign of letting up The farmers are rejoicing and many of them no doubt wish ing they were dry farmers as the pr cipitation al ready insures success for the dry farmer this year

The cannery stock holders held two important meetings last week their annual meeting was held on the 11th and a special meeting held on the 18th

Mrs Donald Fuller is visiting her children who are in St George attending the Dixie this week

Lynn Jarvis came up Saturday from St George with a lo id of beeves for the cannery

LEEDS

Leeds Feb 1 —The M I A dancing party will be given here to morrow night instead of last Thurs day It was postponed on account of the stormy weather

Mrs J M Worthen, nee Leone McMullin arrived here list Satur day from Salt Lake City She will visit with her parents, Mr and Mrs B J McMullin for a few weeks

Robert and Karl McMullin went to St George today to take horses to the horse buyer

Mrs Charles Hanson is still in St George with her baby under the docter s care

Miss Hazel Olsen came home from St George yesterday to stay for a few days

Leeds Feb 15 — Robert McMul lin and Ammon Jolley came in from the Purgatory property Monday They bring favorable reports from the ditch there and say that it is holding water well and is going to be a complete success This is con trary to some predictions owing to the peculiar formation of the soil

Mr and Mrs George Angell re turned this afternoon from St George where they have been with their daughter Edna who was op erated on Monday for appendicitis They report a successful operation

Mark Miller arrived here last Saturday morning from the Grand Gulch mine He intends leaving in the morning with his family for Salt Lake City

Mr Sonnedecker of Salt Lake City spent a few days here looking over the mining property in the vicinity

The farmers are taking advantage of this fine weather and are prepar ing the ground for the season's crops

Mrs Joseph Jolley is here from Washington visiting with her daughter Mrs Frank Stirling

Miss Alice Stirling left Monday morning for Cedar City to attend the Farmers Round up

The Primary association is pre paring a program for Washington's birthday

Leeds Mar 8 — Mr Alexander of Los Angeles has been here recent ly and spent some time looking over the property at Silver Reef He was very much impressed with the possibilities and predicts a future for the camp

Miss Ethyl McMullin returned Tuesday from Moapa Valley Nev where she has been the last few months She reports that country in a prosperous condition with a promising future

A delightful affair of last week was that given at the home of Ira S McMullin in honor of Mr and Mrs Edward McMullin who left for Long Valley last week to spend the summer

Mrs Leon Worthen left for Salt Lake City last week accompanied by her sister Miss Edythe McMul lin who expects to remain there some time

Bert Harris returned Monday from a business trip to Salt Lake

Leeds Mar 21 —The Stake M
I A officers were here and held
meeting last Sunday night Al
though we have discontinued our
mutuals a very good crowd was
out to hear their excellent instruc
tions

Mr and Mrs Turley of St George
have rented Edward McMullin s
home and expects to remain here
this summer Mr Turley intends
doing market gardening

Mrs Eleanor Scott and family
left last Saturday for their ranch
near Goldstrike Miss Ruth Stirling
accompanied them and expects to
stay a short time

Frank McMullin Glenn Olsen
and Cleo Sullivan are home again
after taking the mid winter course
at the Dixie Academy

Misses Hazel Olsen and Maggie
Jolley who are attending school at
the Dixie Academy, spent the week
end at home

Mrs Julia Andrus of Weiser Idaho is the guest of her sister Mrs
E O Olsen

Tax Assessor Paxman was a busi
ness visitor here the fore part of the
week

Leeds March 4 —Some of the young people attended a theatre in Touquerville last night. They were delighted with the performance and think that their T querville friends have more than their share of talent along this line

Mrs Susie Stirling left Monday morning for Salt Lake to attend conference and visit relatives

Mr and Mrs Ira McMullin spent a couple of days in St George last week working in the temple

Charles Hansen was on the road again Monday with his car taking passengers to J und

Robert McMullin left the fore part of the week for Salt Lake City

LEEDS

Leeds April 11 —Mr and Mrs Henry Schlappy and family spent a day or two here last week visiting Mr Schlappy s sister Mrs E C Olsen They were on they way to Burley Idaho where they expect to make their home

Mr and Mrs Martin of Milford were at the Stirling house last week Mr Martin was looking over some mining property here

Last Friday night some of our young people met at the home of Mrs Marie Olsen and spent a very pleasant evening

Mrs George Crosby of St George spent the week end here visiting with her daughter Mrs Isaac Turley

Frank Sullivan came in from the Grand Gulch mine Sunday

Iron County Record
April 14, 1916

It is learned with regret by relatives at this place that George Angell of Leeds is quite seriously ill with rheumatism, and does not seem to be improving.

Mat Wickes came in from Leeds last week with a load of molasses and other eatables. And as usual, Mat rolled up his sleeves and is at work in dead earnest. At present he is helping George Tyron and Mr. Buehl on their ranches.

Washington County News
April 18, 1916

Leeds April 18 —The Dixie Opera Co passed thru here this morning enroute to Beaver and Iron counties They are billed at Hurricane for Friday night so those who have not already seen it may anticipate a treat

Last Wednesday evening Lynn McMullin and Herbert Milne entertained at an oyster supper Games and dancing were features of the occasion and those in attendance spent a jolly evening

Gaston Bastian a former Dixieite now of South Jordon was in town this morning visiting old time friends

Mr and Mrs Frank Sullivan left last Friday for the Grand Gulch where they expect to spend the summer

Mrs Susie Stirling returned from Salt Lake City last Saturday

Thomas Stirling left for Cedar Saturday on business

Washington County News
May 2, 1916

Leeds, May 2 —The following students are home again after a very successful winter at the Dixie Academy Hazel Olsen Verna Fuller Maggie Jolly Thomas Stirling Clinton and Stanley Fuller

The closing of our schools last week ended a very creditable year The eighth grade all graduated and attended the exercises at St George

Word has reached Leeds of the illness of George Crosby at St George and his many friends here are hoping for his speedy recovery

Leeds was well represented at the Track meet and M I A fair and all agree It was the time of their lives

Frank Hamilton of Cedar City was a business visitor the fore part of the week

Washington County News
May 9, 1916

Leeds May 9 —H H Clark of Reno Nev has been spending several days here looking over the mining properties at Silver Reef and is only one of the many mining men that think very favorably of the possibilities since silver has attained its present price

Mit Moody and family have moved on the Wicks farm from St George for the summer We are always glad to welcome new residents and only wish they would make this their permanent home

Andrew Gregerson of St George has been in Leeds the past few days in the interest of his mining property at Silver Reef

Joseph Stirling left Monday morning with cattle for his ranch that he recently bought on the Kanarra mountain

Mrs Mark McMullin of Grape Vine returned from Cedar City the latter part of last week where she has been visiting

George Lund and A B Andrus of St George were business visitors here the fore part of the week

Matt Wicks left for Stateline the latter part of last week

WILL FORGET ABOUT
SILVER REEF DUMPS

Failure of Residents to Accept Fair Offer for Holdings Queers Deal for Extensive Operations.

It is a wise man who knows when to let well enough alone. One of the greatest failings of we weak mortals is to let our desires get the better of our judgment. Because a prominent man of Leeds was not willing to take a good thing when it was offered, giving the other fellow a chance to realize something for his time and investment, it looks probable that he has not onl shut the door against a neat little fortune for himself, but has prevented a nice little boom for his section of the country which would have been a benefit to the entire region, and might have led to other and far greater developments.

For some time experiments have been progressing for the purpose of obtaining a cheap process for the treatment of tailing dumps from which not all the values had been extracted during the original operation, and recently some pronounced successes have been obtained along this line.

This has led again recently to the sampling and testing of the old tailing dumps at Silver Reef, which have been located by parties of that section of the country. The investigations appear to have been satisfactory, and interests represented by Quince K. Kimball, for whom S. A. Higbee of this city, made an offer of 25 cents per on royalty for the dumps, which it is estimated would have netted the locators something like $25,-000. Not satisfied to take this offer for these old dumps which have been lying unimproved or used ever since the demonetization of silver, the locators insisted upon the company going into the market and bidding for the dumps. The following letter from Mr. Kimball to his local representative, is the sequel:

Salt Lake City, Utah, May 10.

S. A. Higbee, Cedar City, Utah, Dear Friend.—I have been waiting to hear from McMullin. Today I received a letter from him, in which he calls off the offer you made him. It seems he wants us to make him a bid along with others, that he claims are becoming interested. We have too many good things coming to us now. We will forget the Silver Reef for the present, and let the other fellows handle the tailings."

Leeds May 23 —Last Friday night the ward gave a benefit dance for the purpose of procuring a sacrament set Although the weather man frowned with distavor a large and jolly crowd was out

J T Waldis of Goldfield Nev is spending some time here looking over some mining property at Silver Reef

The stock men have been busy gathering and counting cattle for the reserve

Bert Harris left this morning for Milford where he expects to remain some time

A B Andrus of St George was transacting business here the first of the week

Leeds May 30 —Elders George Miles and E B Snow were here as missionaries Sunday Elder Miles attended both Sunday school and afternoon services and his excellent remarks were both interesting and instructive

George Judd of La Verkin passed thru here Sunday enroute to Cedar City in his new car He had for passengers Dr and Mrs W C Cox and Mr and Mrs E B Snow of St George

Wm Nicholes Matt Wicks and Clifford McMullin left Saturday morning for Modena with steers to be delivered at the railroad

Clifford McMullin returned from Good Springs Nev last Wednesday where he has been the past ten months

Bp David Stirling returned from New Castle Sunday bringing with him Mrs Eleanor Scott and family

Messrs Brooks Cripps and Ross were here last week inspecting some mining property at Silver Reef

Leeds June 12 —J Wallis left for Milford the fore part of the week after spending some time investigating and developing some mining property at Silver Reef

Cripps and Lusk who have been doing development work at Silver Reef have a shipment of ore out and intend shipping it in the morning

Oscar McMullin and sons are the proud possessors of a new car Here's hoping that we may boast of several more in the near future

Mrs Susie Stirling and family returned from St George Sunday where she has been the past week working in the temple

Miss Margaret Olsen left last Tuesday morning for Salt Lake City where she will attend summer school

Albert Goer of Cedar is spending a few days at Grape Vine with Mr and Mrs Mail McMullin

Mrs Isaac Turley is visiting her mother Mrs George Crosby at St George

Alex Taylor of New Harmony spent the week end here

Leeds June 20 —Joseph Stirling returned last week from Denver and other northern points where he has been with cattle

George Olsen returned this morning from the Grand Gulch mine where he has been the past few months.

Karl McMullin and Thomas Stirling jr , left last Saturday for the Kanarra mountains with cattle

Mr and Mrs Lake of St George spent the week end here guests of Mr and Mrs Isaac Turley

George Jund of St George was a business visitor here the fore part of the week

Miss Mabel Jolley of Hurricane is visiting relatives here

Thomas Stirling left for Cedar City this morning

Dixie Cannery Has A Splendid Output

B Jarvis jr, was here from Washington county Saturday representing the Southern Utah Packing company, located at Leeds Mr Jarvis had with him samples of the products of the company, peaches figs pork and beans beef and vegetables all of very superior quality The company s market extends from Los Angeles to Salt Lake and is only limited by the ability to supply the demand —Provo Herald

Leeds June 27 —Some influential mining men of Salt Lake arrived here today to make preparatory arrangements for the working of the tailing dumps at Silver Reef

Sisters George Brooks and George Miles Stake Relief Society officers of St George held a meeting here Wednesday in the interest of their work Their instructions were timely and interesting

The different committees are at work on our fourth of July program and we are expecting a real live time from the raising of the flag at sunrise till the last strain of music at night

John T Batty and Martin Anderson of Toquerville were home missionaries Sunday Their encouraging remarks and good instructions were more than appreciated

Mrs Thomas Stirling expects to leave for Salt Lake City in the morning with her small son, Glen who is needing medical treatment

Mrs Hannah Jolley of Washington is spending a few days here with her daughter, Mrs Francis Hartley

Robert McMullin came home last week with a new car This is the second one for Leeds recently

Forest Ranger Mart McAllister is in town again after spending a few days in St George

Mrs W T Beams of Virgin City is visiting friends here

Leeds July 16 —Last Sunday morning our Sunday School was visited by Elders Nicholes Leo Snow Bert Macfarlane Wm Woodbury, and Miss Mabel Jarvis of the Stake S S board They give our officers and teachers some excellent instructions and ideas and we only wish they would visit us more often

Last Friday afternoon we witnessed a real flood in Leeds due to a local thunder shower It came up very suddenly and before we were aware of it a large stream of water was rushing thru town Some of our farmers suffered severe loses but as a whole the damage was small

Miss Anna Turley who has been spending some time here with her brother Isaac Turley left last Sunday morning for Provo where she will attend the second session of summer school

Word was recently received here of the birth of a son to Mr and Mrs Joseph Worthen of Salt Lake City Mrs Worthen was formerly Miss Leone McMullin of this place

Alex Milne and son Herbert left last week for St George after papering and painting the residence of David McMullin

J T Wallis was a business visitor here last week from Beaver City

Bert Harris is home again after spending several weeks at Milford

Miss Lucile Alger of St George is the guest of Miss Verna Fuller

Leeds Aug 1 —Elders John T Woodbury and George Webb were missionaries at our services last Sunday afternoon Prohibition Sunday ' and both talked very interestingly on that subject

H Lapadaire of San Francisco Cal is spending some time here in the interest of his mining property in this locality

Winifred Moody of Thatcher Ariz spent several days here last week the guest of Mr and Mrs Milton Moody

Miss Ruth Stirling returned Saturday from Newcastle where she has been the past few months

Mrs Bert Harris and children are visiting relatives and friends in Parowan

Miss Edna Angell is visiting her sister, Mrs Byron Millet, at Rockville

George Olsen has left for the Grand Gulch mine

Leeds Aug 14 —Edwin Higbee with a force of men and teams will commence work in the morning on the road just north of Leeds This is one of the worst pieces of road along the line and its completion will be a time of rejoicing for the public in general

Dr and Mrs D O Beal and Misses Margaret Olsen and Mallie Beal arrived here from Ephriam last week After visiting Mrs Beal s parents Mr and Mr E C Olsen they will motor to Overton Nev accompanied by Miss Beal

A capping machine has been installed in our canning factory which together with the water system that has recently been put in is a wonderful improvement and affords us the conveniences of a larger factory

B Jarvis jr and Miss Ella Bentley of St George are here overseeing the canning of fruit at the cannery

Misses Etta Cox and Lucile Alger of St George are the guests of Mrs Thos Stirling

Mrs Frank Sullivan came in from the Grand Gulch last week

Truman Angell of J ab is visiting relatives here

Leeds Aug 22 —A mass meeting was called last night by some of our citizens to decide what could be done about moving the telephone poles out of the center of the street   It was decided to move them to the west side   This will enable them to get a better grade for our improved road north of town

Mrs Niels Bastian of Idaho and Mrs Wm Woodbury of St George are here visiting their mother Mrs W D Sullivan

Mr and Mrs A Tomsick of Bing ham were here the latter part of last week visiting the latter's sister Mrs Frank Hartley

Bishop David Stirling has just re turned from Kanarra mountain where he has been looking after his cattle

Miss Edna Angell is home after spending several weeks with her sister Mrs Byron Millet at Rock ville

Leeds Aug 30 —A large crowd of relatives and friends gathered at the home of Hyrum Leany at Har risburg last Saturday to celebrate his birthday   Relatives from Mil ford Newhouse St George and other places were there altogether numbering about fifty   Melons and fruit were features of the occasion and all report having had a jolley good time

Word has been received here of the release of Willard McMullin who has been laboring in the East ern States mission since his transfer from the Netherlands

William Nichols was called sud denly to Cowley Wyo to the bed side of his mother who is seriously ill   He left yesterday morning

Mrs Frank Sullivan and small daughter Irma returned to the Grand Gulch mine Sunday

Miss Reta Hartley left for Bing ham last week where she will attend school the coming winter

Leeds Sept 26 —Alex Colbath of Salt Lake City has been here for the past few days getting samples from the tailing dumps of Silver Reef He left yesterday morning for Salt Lake City

Elder W G McMullin returned on the 14th inst from the Holland and Northern States mission Mr and Mrs J M Worthen and Miss Edyth McMullin accompanied him from Salt Lake City Elder McMullin has been twenty six months in the mission field being first called to Holland where he was allowed to remain but 2½ months on account of war conditions The last 13 months were spent in Detroit He occupied the time in meeting Sunday giving an interesting account of his mission

Our district school has been in session two weeks with Chas Hanson and Margaret Olsen as teachers We will have an eight month term this year

Edward McMullin came in from Glendale for a short visit he expects to move his family back soon They spent the past summer in Glendale

Thos Bleak of Salt Lake City left yesterday for his home after spending a few days visiting Mr and Mrs E O Olsen

Mgr B Jarvis of the S U Packing Co has been here for the past few days finishing up the heath peaches

Mrs Sam Mortenson of Provo visited her mother Mrs Andrea Hanson a few days last week

Mrs Frank Sullivan and daughter Irma arrived home Sunday from the Grand Gulch mine

A F Gregerson of St George was here the latter part of last week on mining business

H Lapadaire left Sunday for his home in San Francisco

Mrs Neils Bastain left last week for her home in Idaho

Some of the farmers are busy making up their molasses

GEORGE H. CROSBY, SR., DIES AT SAINT GEORGE

Tidings were received last Wednesday by friends in this city of the death at St. George of George H. Crosby, Sr., who made his home there something less than a year ago, moving there from Wyoming.

Deceased is a well known figure in southern Utah, in the Mormon colonies of Arizona, and also in Wyoming. He has served as bishop in a number of places, including Hebron, in the early settlement of that place, before the present town of Enterprise was thought of, in Leeds, during the palmy days of Silver Reef, and in one or more towns in Arizona. He was a man universally liked, and had a happy faculty of making friends, which gave him a very extended acquaintanceship.

George was the eldest of a family of four brothers—the others being Jesse, for a number of years president of the Panguitch stake, Samuel, who also resided in Panguitch, and Joshua, of St. George. All his brothers preceded him to the other side. Mrs. Elida Snow, a sister residing in St. George, survives him.

He is also survived by a number of sons and daughers, most of whom reside in Arizona, and some of whom are prominent in business and politics there. The funeral has been postponed to Sunday afternoon in order to give the members of the family an opportunity to attend the services, which will also be attended by a number of people from this place.

Deceased was 70 years of age, and his health had been on the decline for the past two years, though it was not regarded as serious until within the past few months.

George Crosby was an honorable and upright citizen, and did his full share for the uplifting of humanity while on earth. He will be greatly missed by all who have had the pleasure of his acquaintance.

Leeds Oct 17 —Messrs Gourley Webb and Woodbury, the stake presidency of the Y M I A and scout master Guy Halen were our speakers Sunday evening 1 Mutual Sister Libbie Cox of the stake board of the Y L M I A was also a speaker

Mrs Will Sullivan and children will leave this evening for their home in Hurricane after spending a few weeks here with her mother Mrs E C Olson

Joseph Wilkenson of Cedar City was a visitor here yesterday He was on his way from St George where he went to attend the funeral of George Crosby

John Tullis from Newcastle was a visitor here Sunday He left for his home yesterday morning taking Mrs Tullis and children back with him

Mrs Chas Hanson and small son arrived here last week after having spent a number of months with her parents in Taylor Arizona

J M Moody and son Milton.
each brought in a deer Monday A
number of men are still in the
mountains hunting

Prin Chas Hanson and Miss
Margaret Olson attended the teach
ers institute at St George Friday
and Saturday

Bp B Y McMullin and Isaac
Turley attended the funeral of
George Crosby at St George Sun
day

Miss Rita Hartley arrived home
last week from Bingham where she
has been attending high school

Miss Frona Mortensen from Par
owan is here visiting her grand
mother Mrs Andrea Hanson

Miss Myrtle Cottam of St George
was a visitor here yesterday

Hon D H Morris is a visitor
here today from St George

Supervisor Bentley visited our
schools here yesterday

Washington County News
October 19, 1916

Useful Life Ended

George Henry Crosby died at his
home in this city Tuesday Oct 10
of heart failure His health had
been failing for some time and he
expired suddenly after eating his
midday meal

George Henry Crosby had a long
active and interesting career He was
born in Kennebec county, Maine
Oct 26 1846 a son of Jesse W
and Hannah E Crosby and came
to Utah with his parents Sept 26,
1847 and to St George in 1861
When 17 years old he crossed the
plains under Capt Daniel D Mc
Arthur to bring in a company of
immigrants and again in 1866
performed this service under Cap
tain Thompson He served as dep
uty sheriff of Washington county

under sheriff David H Cannon and at the August election of 1867 was elected sheriff of Washington county taking the oath of office some time later when he reached his 21st birthday He was a member of the troop of cavalry that went out under Capt James Andrus to recover the bodies of Dr Whitmore and Robert McIntyre, who had been killed by Indians near Pipe Springs while out near a ledge of rocks one of the Indians covered him with his rifle from behind these rocks and was detected by one of the cavalrymen who fired just in time to save Crosby as the Indian fired about the same time his shot however missing its mark In 1869 Bro Crosby was appointed bishop of Hebron he being the first bishop of that place It was while living at Hebron that he antagonized the Ben Tasdell gang notorious cattle robbers who ravaged that section and adjoining portions of Nevada in his position as sheriff he was continually thwarting the evil ways of this gang and finally drove them out of the country some of the gang under Mart Moore taking advantage of Crosby's absence in the fall of 1887 set fire to his home and store in the middle of the night evidently intending to burn his wife and children The smoke awoke Mrs Crosby who broke the windows and saved the children and herself, though her feet were so badly cut by the broken glass that she still feels the effects On Crosby's return home he took up the trail of Mart Moore and chased him as far as Lee's

Ferry on the Colorado river where he lost his track, Moore never returned to the scene of his hideous work and years later when apprehended by U S Deputy Marshall Charley Reed of Globe Ariz talked of the deed and how Crosby chased him saying Crosby was the best fighter he had ever met Bro Crosby served as bishop of Hebron for eight years and was then called by Pres Erastus Snow in Jan 1878 to be bishop of Leeds the mining camp of Silver Reef near requiring that a strong man hold this position he served in this capacity at Leeds until 1886 when he was called by Pres Erastus Snow to go to Nutrioso Ariz arriving there April 17, 1886 He was made bishop of Round Valley 10 miles from Nutrioso June 17, 1886 and founded the town of Eagar there he lived there until 1899, being a prominent figure in political and social life, he served as a representative in the 18th legislative assembly, and in a speech to prevent the division of Apache county held the floor for seven hours He moved to Torrey, Wayne county, Utah in 1899 and was appointed bishop there which position he held for two years until he moved to Big Horn county as a colonizer in 1901 Bro Crosby served 32 years as a bishop in the four places In the Big Horn basin he helped to found the towns of Lovell and Cowley He lived at the latter place until the fall of 1915 when he moved back to St George to spend the remaining days of his life

Bro Crosby is survived by one sister Mrs Elida Snow of St George two wives Mrs Sarah H Crosby of Eagar, Ariz and Mrs Mary L Crosby of this city and the following children Benjamin B of Eagar Ariz , George H St Johns Ariz Mrs Sarah A Wiltbank Eagar Ariz Jesse T Holbrook Ariz , John A Ramah N

Mexico Charles W, Eagar, Ariz Albert W Eagar, Ariz Frederick, Cowley Wyo, and Mrs Elizabeth Partridge Cowley, Wyo There are 20 grandchildren surviving and all the children are married except Charles W and Albert W

Funeral services were held in the St George tabernacle Sunday Oct 15 Pres Ed H Snow eulogized the life of the departed brother and reviewed the good work he had done Bishop B Y McMullin of Leeds spoke of Bro Crosby s work as bishop at Leeds and his associations with him Pres David H Cannon spoke of the useful and faithful life of deceased how stedfast to duty he was as his deputy sheriff etc, etc Charles Wilkenson of Cedar City was the last speaker and told of the high esteem in which Bro Crosby was held as a bishop of Leeds to whom the speaker was a counselor The singing was very fine and the attendance at the services was very large   •

Interment was made in the city cemetery _____

Washington County News
October 24, 1916

Leeds Oct 24 — The M I A gave an excellent program to a well filled house Sunday evening The mutual work is commenceing with much enthusiasm which if carried out will insure a successful season

Joe and Thos Stirling left this morning for Kanarrah Mts to bring in their cattle from the summer range

A baby girl arrived at the home of Mr and Mrs Bert Harris yesterday all concerned doing nicely

Mrs Elinor Scott returned home from Modena Sunday evening where she has been on business

The M I A amusement committee is busy planning a Halloween social to be given next week

Mrs Lucile Alger of St George is a visitor at the home of Mr and Mrs Thomas Stirling

Lynn and Dan McMullin each brought a fine deer in from the mountains last week

Mrs Isaac Turley is visiting with her mother Mrs Crosby at St George

The cannery is busy canning beef today _____

Leeds Nov 14 —Mrs Joseph Jolley from Washington is visiting her daughter, Mrs Frank Hartley She is on her way home from Salt Lake City and surrounding points where she has been visiting her children

Our home missionaries Elders Arthur Paxman and Israel Neilson from Washington gave us some very good instructions in Sacrament meeting Sunday

The regular routine of work is being followed now after a rather exciting election most of the people being well pleased with the result

Mgr B Jarvis and Miss Ella Bentley are here working in the packing factory

A baby boy was born to Mr and Mrs Will Booth at Harrisburg last week

R G McQuarrie from St George is a business visitor here today

A F Gregerson of St George is a business visitor here today

Leeds Nov 29 —The telephone men have finished moving the telephone poles from the center of the street to the hills west of town This adds much to the appearance of the street and the safety of the public

Utah product week was observed in the schools last week and the schools and M I A united with a fitting program Sunday evening

Pres E H Snow and Elder John T Woodbury were here and held ward conference Sunday afternoon

Clifford McMullin arrived home from Blackfoot Idaho last Sunday where he has been for the past summer

A F Gregerron of St George was here Saturday on business

Leeds Dec 5—The Primary Assn and the district school united and gave an entertainment here Thanksgiving night The proceeds will be used to buy books for the primary Home made candy and bags of popcorn made by the primary members and sold by the children helped to increase the funds

The following students came home from the Dixie Academy for Thanksgiving Delbert Stirling, Marguerite McMullin Leland Sullivan Lawrence McMullin and Rex Stirling

The Misses Venice and Lydia Hopkins spent the Thanksgiving holidays here with their sister Mrs Edward McMullin They are attending the Dixie college

Mgr B Jarvis and Miss Ella Bentley are here from St George working in the Southern Utah Packing House

Miss Ethel McMullin spent Thanksgiving home from the business college at Salt Lake City

Miss Margaret Olson spent the week end at Hurricane with her sister Mrs Will Sullivan

A I Greger on was here today from St George on mining business

Miss Leta Hartley is spending a few weeks in St George

Washington County News
December 26, 1916

Leeds Dec 26 —Christmas was very fittingly celebrated here with a Christmas tree and program Christmas eve and a dance Christmas night The snow which fell during the night gave everyone the real Christmas spirit altho there was not enough for sleighing

The Misses Margaret and Hazel Olsen returned today from Salt Lake City where they have been attending teachers convention and visiting relatives and friends

The following men came in from the Grand Gulch to spend holidays with their families David McMullin Frank Sullivan and George Olsen

The following students are spending the holidays home Ethel McMullin Leland Sullivan Rex Stirling and Marguerite McMullin

The Misses Venice Anna and Lydia Hopkins are here spending the holidays with their sister Mrs Edward McMullin

Mr and Mrs Will Sullivan came over from Hurricane yesterday to spend Christmas with relatives and friends

Mr and Mrs Bert Harris moved into their new home on their farm near Grapevine Springs last week

Frank Hartley and Charlie Angell left t day for Bull Valley to do assessment work

Chas Hanson attended the State teachers convention at Salt Lake City last week,

Mrs Alice Stirling left last week for Salt Lake City

Washington County News
January 9, 1917

Leeds Jan 9 —The Adah Copper Mining Co is empl jing a number of men at the old Emily Jane property at Silver Reef which it recently bought

Hartley Woodbury of La Verkin, a member of the hospital corps who just recently returned from Nogales has been visiting friends and relatives here for the past few days

The high price of silver and copper is causing considerable locating in the surrounding country

All the students went back to school after spending the holidays here

Thomas Tolbert and family have moved here from Panguitch for the winter

The Southern Utah Picking company is canning beans t day

A dancing party was held in Stirling's hall last evening

A B Harris of St George is here t day on mining business

Leeds, Jan. 24 —Wm Sullivan had the misfortune while on a freighting trip to Lund to have one of his fingers frozen. He went to St George Monday to receive medical treatment.

An oyster supper was held at the home of Mr. and Mrs George Olsen Monday evening. An enjoyable time is reported.

Miss Lucile Alger who has been visiting here for a few weeks returned to her home at St George yesterday.

Miss Reta Hartley returned home from St. George last Friday where she has been for the past few weeks.

Mrs Andrea Hanson is celebrating her seventy fourth birthday with a family dinner today

Ben Granger from Salt Lake City was here Sunday on mining business.

A B Harris of St George was a business visitor here Sunday.

Leeds, Jan. 6 —Lesle McMullin from Idaho Falls. Idaho, returned to his home Sunday after spending a week here visiting relatives

Miss Reta Hartley is visiting her grandmother, Mrs. Joseph Jolley, in Washington this week

Cleo Sullivan left last night for the Grand Gulch. He expects to be gone for some time.

Bp David Stirling is visiting in Salt Lake City after attending the round-up at Logan.

J M. Lauritzen from Short Creek, Ariz, is a visitor at the Stirling hotel today.

Alex Colbath from Salt Lake City is a visitor here on mining business

Leeds, Feb 20 —The recent snow storm has brought much rejoicing among the farmers here Besides the assurance of an abundance of water for the coming season it comes in an opportune time for the spring plowing Snow ball fighting was indulged in the greater part of yesterday and a cow hide used as a sleigh afforded much pleasure for some of the young people

The stork has been a very busy bird here for the past few days, leaving a baby girl at each of the homes of Mr and Mrs. Antone Olsen, Mr and Mrs Ammon Jolley and Mr and Mrs. Edward McMullin

Mrs. Brown from Harmony was a guest at the Stirling hotel yesterday enroute for St George

Ben Granger from Salt Lake City was a business visitor here yesterday

Leeds, Feb 27.—Most of the farmers, taking advantage of the fine weather, are plowing and preparing their land for the season's crops

Rehearsals are being held now for a play to be given in the near future, the proceeds to be used for the M. I A and S S. needs

The M I A gave a very interesting and instructive Washington program last Sunday evening

Mrs Roy Barlow and two small daughters are visitors here, guests of Mrs Donald Fuller

A B Harris was a mining visitor here yesterday.

Indian War Veterans

Springville, Utah, March 7, 1917
Hon D H. Morris, St George, Utah

Dear Friend·—Senator Smoot's bill has become a law to pension the veterans of the Black Hawk war and their widows   Will you please publish it in your county paper and tell all those who wish me to file their claims to send me their name and address at once as I have a copy of all the records   I write this to you as I do not know if you have a commander in your department since the death of our friend, James Andrus   J M. Westwood,
Commander

The following list of Indian War veterans and their widows has been sent to Mr. Westwood by Hon. D. H. Morris

ST GEORGE

Charles F Foster, Schuyler Everett, Alexander Fullerton, Edward M. Brown, Thomas R Forsythe, James B Bracken, David H. Cannon, George F. Jarvis, Richard Prince, Andrew Sorenson, William H Thompson, William G. Miles, George Brooks, Neils Sandberg, William Gardner, James L Bunting, Brigham Jarvis, Walter R. Pike, Horatio Pickett, Anson P. Winsor, Haden W. Church, Joseph S Worthen, H · Joseph Burgess, Andrew F Gregerson (Ferdinand), Elizabeth A Hardy, widow of Agustus P / Hardy; Hattie R Snow, widow of Mahonri M. Snow; Mary E L Crosby, widow of George H. Crosby; Isabell Wilson, widow of Ephriam Wilson; Almira Adams, widow of Samuel L Adams; Mary S Maudsley, widow of Henry

Maudsley, Sarah H Riding, widow of Henry H Riding, Mary Ann Rogers, widow of David Rogers; Ann C Macfarlane, widow of John M Macfarlane, Selena Nelson, widow of Aaron Nelson; Martha Alice Woodbury, widow of John S Woodbury; Abigal Walker, widow of Charles L Walker, Susanna Bryner, widow of Casper Bryner.

HURRICANE

James A Stratton, Morris Wilson, James M Ballard, James Humphries, Alice Isom, widow of George Isom; Mary D Spendlove, widow of John Spendlove; Harriet E Lee, widow of Erastus F Lee; Sophia A. Langston, widow of John F. Langston.

WASHINGTON

Jacob Bastian, H P. Iverson, Israel Neilson, Robert Covington, Hyrum Boggs, Pernella S Nisson, widow of Neils Nisson.

SANTA CLARA

Samuel Wittwer, Casper Gubler, Mary Ann Leavitt, widow of Lemuel S. Leavitt; Laura L Knight, widow of Samuel Knight; Lina Ence, widow of John Ence.

OTHER PLACES

John Batty, Toquerville; J. H. Jennings, Rockville; J. H. Harrison and Neil D. Forsythe, Pinto; Thomas Flannigan and John Elmer Dennett, Virgin; William Spendlove, Kanarra; Brigham Y McMullin, Ira McMullin and Hyrum Leany, Leeds; Cornelia Crawford, widow of Wm. R Crawford, Springdale; Henretta Cox, widow of Isaiah Cox, Hinckley, Joseph Sylvester, Mesquite, Nevada; Mary A Beebe, widow of Leroy Beebe, St. Thomas, Nevada, Melissa Lee, widow of John M. Lee, Panaca, Nevada, Rebecca Coates, widow of Benj F. Coates, 120 South, 10 East St. Salt Lake City; Joseph Fish, Beaver City; George M Burgess, Alpine; Benj Brown, Springerville, Arizona

Washington County News
March 28, 1917

Leeds, Mar 28 —Mr Colbath and A B Harris are still here in the interest of the mines and mining business of Silver Reef We are in hopes that something of a substantial nature will soon be in evidence Ben E Granger of Salt Lake City is also here in the interest of the mines and mining business, looking up and securing everything by location that is open to location, for the people he represents.

The M I A's put on a play called "Pocahontas" last Saturday night which was a complete success, all parts being well rendered, and much credit due those who coached them A sum of about $18 was collected for the benefit of the Mutuals and Sabbath school.

William G McMullin one of the Purgatory canal owners is now, with the other members of the company making a great effort to complete the canal and put the water on their land this spring

We have had a very cold, bleak winter and backward spring until today, which appears to indicate that spring has at last come

Miss Edyth McMullin has gone to Salt Lake City, having been sent for by her sister on account of sickness

Washington County News
March 29, 1917

Bishop B Y McMullin of Leeds was a city visitor Wednesday, on business He reports much interest being taken in mining property near Leeds and prospects good for much activity this summer

Iron County Record
March 30, 1917

SILVER REEF TO ENJOY BIG BOOM

Old Silver Camp in Dixie to be Scene of Much Activity Coming Season.

BIG REDUCTION WORKS WILL BE INSTALLED

New Electrical Process Opens Possibilities for Treatment of Low Grade Ores—Tailing Dumps Also to be Utilized.

Indications are excedingly promising for the old mining camp of Silver Reef to regain at least part of its one time life and prominence as a producer of the precious metals. Not only are there a great many of the rich silver ledges that have not been exhausted, and the old tailing dumps which carry enough in the white metal to make it very profitable to treat them by a new electrical process that has been discovered since the palmy days of silver reef, but with copper at its present high price, there are many ledges of the red metal that offer a fortune to those who will engage in its mining and reduction into concentrates.

Ben Granger, manager of the Dixie Mining and Development Company, who spent a day or two in Cedar City this week, gave a glowing account of conditions at the old camp. He says that four or five big companies will operate there the present season and that California capitalists and prospectors are picking up every available promising prospect, either with an option or a location notice.

The Ada Copper Company, of which A. H. Dahle is president and George Aelrad secretary, has possibly the biggest proposition in the district, in the shape of a huge vein of low grade copper ore, and they are even now figuring on large reduction works to reduce the ore into concentrates for economy in shipping. This vein is several hundred yards in extent, and carrys more than twice as high a percent of copper as the great Utah Copper mine at Bingham. Other copper veins run as high as fifty to sixty per cent copper, but are of course much smaller.

A wagon shipment of copper and silver ore from the Dixie properties represented by Mr. Granger passed through here en route to the smelter last Wednesday. S. W. West of Salt Lake City is president of this company, and Roy T. McFadden, chief chemist for the Utah Copper company, is secretary and Mr. Granger manager.

Photographer R. D. Adams accompanied Mr. Granger to the camp last week and made a number of fine views of the properties with his swinging lens camera, which give a good idea of the geography and location of the mines.

The shipment of ore which Mr. Granger was sending to the smelter for the purpose of giving it an actual test, is from the Old Blue Ribbon and New Shaft — properties purchased from Andrew Gregerson.

Grant Snyder, at one time manager of the Dixie Copper company near St. George, and well known in mining circles throughout the state, with Mr. Colbath, has formed a company and purchased the old tailing dumps at the Reef from Bp. B. Y. McMullen of Leeds, making a substantial cash payment and agreeing to pay a certain royalty on each ton of the material handled. It is their intention to put in a plant for treating these tailings in the immediate future.

Taking it all together, the outlook is exceedingly encouraging for the old camp, and if Silver Reef enjoys a substantial boom again it will mean a great deal, not only to the Dixie country, but also to Cedar City and Iron county, which forms the gateway to that section of country.

Washington County News
April 4, 1917

Leeds, Apr 4 —There are good reasons to believe that there will be some activity here in the near future in the mining business, both in the working over of the tailings and the developing of the mines, giving employment for some of our surplus labor

Donald E Fuller had a good strong working force out Monday cleaning the canal and is continuing with all lateral ditches.

Robert P McMullin has gone to Salt Lake to attend conference and have a visit with his relatives

A B Harris is here from St George in the interest of developing the mines of Silver Reef.

Born, a son to Mr and Mrs Frank Sullivan, April 6, all concerned doing nicely

Ben C. Granger, manager of the Dixie Mining and Development company, operating at Silver Reef, passed through Cedar Wednesday on his way back to the workings.

Washington County News
April 11, 1917

Leeds, Apr 11 —A B Harris who has charge of the Adah Copper Co's business here has been having a few hands making a road leading to the site where they are intending to install their copper plant which is expected to soon be in course of construction

Home missionaries, Tanner and Blazzard of Washington held meeting here Sunday. The boys spoke well but the turnout to the meeting was not as good as it should have been. All who were not there certainly missed some good talk

James M Wicks has gone to Stateline, as we are informed, to spend the greater part of the summer in developing his valuable mining interests in that district

Dr Beal and his wife of Overton, Nev, have been spending a few days here with Mrs Beal's parents, Mr and Mrs E C Olson, and expect to leave for home today.

Washington County News
April 19, 1917

FOR SALE —One traction engine with six plows for $600 (six hundred) Enquire of Mrs Elinor Scott, Leeds, Utah —Adv. a12 26

Iron County Record
May 4, 1917

SOUTHERN UTAH COMING TO THE FRONT AS A MINING REGION

ANTIMONY DEPOSITS AT GOLDSTRIKE CHANGE HANDS AND WILL BE VIGOROUSLY DEVELOPED, WITH PROSPPECTS OF EARLY SHIPMENTS.

Copper Properties South of St. George, and Silver Reef Ledges to be Penetrated to the Lower Levels in Virgin Ground With Aid of the Diamond Drill.

St. George, Utah, April 27.—Mr. Wright of San Francisco has just left St. George. His business here as a diamond drill operator was to tie up a contract with Mr. Kenhue, manager gf the Hidden Lake Copper Company, for $5,000 worth of drilling south of St. George. He made satisfactory arrangements and will return immediately with his diamond drill and start work.

he three comanies organized in the Silver Reef district—the Adah Coper Co., Dixie Development Co., and Rainbow Mining Co., have partially arranged for a number of holes to be drilled on the different companies' ground. The silver reef, after which the camp took its name, dips 35 degrees and has four distinct veins. It is the intention to drill back on the dip 1000 feet all in virgin ground with thousands of tons of carbonized ore on the apex. In penetrating the mineral zone at this depth they will no doubt find a sulfied ore. All old time Silver Reefers have longed to see a deep shaft in this location.

In the mean time the Adah Copper Co. are going ahead with their leaching plant and within a short time we look to see considerable activity in this part of the country.

A. B. HARRIS.

County Military Census is Completed

Co Assessor Herman W. Stucki has completed the census of all males of Washington county between the ages of 18 and 45 which shows a total of 1028, 220 of whom are between 18 and 22 years of age, and 808 between 23 and 45.

From the list the Co Assessor has kindly sent the NEWS, we are unable to give the number that will be liable for service under the selective draft for the big army to be raised which takes in all males between 21 and 30 inclusive

The numbers shown in the various towns follows· Virgin, 28, LaVerkin 30, Rockville 29, Enterprise 111, Leeds 81, Pine Valley and Central 34, New Harmony 29, Springdale 34, Gunlock 16, Hurricane 135, Washington 86, St. George 333, Santa Clara 59 Toquerville 7, Pinto 5   Total 1028.

Mrs May Harris went to Leeds Monday to spend the week visiting

Iron County Record
June 1, 1917

SAYS MAIL SERVICE IS VERY UNSATISFACTORY

Mr. W. W. Wylie of the Wylie Way Camps being installed in the Little Zion Canyon, and who was in Cedar City yesterday completing some of the arrangements for the opening of his camps to tourist travel, stated that one of the greatest handicaps he was having to contend with was the very unsatisfactory mail service, by reason of which it requires three days for their mail to reach Lund from the camps, whereas it should take but one. Of course, when the transportation line goes into operation on the 15th of this month, their mail, so far as practicable will be sent via their own automobiles and will eliminate the two day's delay, one of which is at LaVerkin and the other at Leeds, and which is due to a hitch in the existing schedules, which breaks the connection at each point only by an hour or two.

In the mean time Mr. Wylie has taken the matter up with the Post-office department at Washington, D. C., and hopes for an early adjustment of the matter, which if continued to remain as at present would be a serious handicap to his business.

Iron County Record
June 8, 1917

Miss Margaret Olsen of Leeds was the guest of Miss Ethyl McMullin Wednesday. Miss Olsen was on her way to Salt Lake City, where she will attend the summer school at the University of Utah.

Mr Leonard Dalton of Rockville and Miss Edna Angell of Leeds obtained a marriage license this morning, 14th, and intend being married at the St George temple

Mr. Clifford Hartley McMullin and Miss Verna Fuller, a highly respected couple of Leeds, obtained a marriage license here this forenoon and intend being married in the St George temple

ACTIVITIES AT SILVER REEF

A. B. Harris, the Well Known Mining Man, Enthusiastic Over Conditions at Old Camp.

Mr. A. B. Harris, who is playing a prominent part in the reopening of mining operations at Silver Reef, was in Cedar City the fore part of this week en route to Salt Lake on mining business. Mr. Harris reports that matters are a little quiet just now at the camp, but expects that they will get to moving at a lively pace in a short time. The diamond drill that was recently shipped into that part of the country is now operating at Hidden Lake Copper Company's holdings, having a hole down something more than 100 feet. As soon as the drill finishes there it is expected that arrangements will be made to have it taken to the Reef for exploring the lower levels of the old camp, below where any of the former workings have yet reached.

Mr. Harris has a plan for the draining of the old workings which are full of water, and at the same time the development of an irrigation project for the Harrisburg bench which would alone pay the expenses of driving a tunnel approximately a mile long in the soft sand stone, from the old Stormant to tap the reef at a very low level. The undertaking is meeting with favor among the residents of that region, and there seems to be no reason why it would not be a big money-maker.

Mr. D. M. Parker, who is associated with Louie King at Hidden Lake in the operation of the diamond drill, was in Cedar City at the same time as Mr. Harris.

Leeds, June 27.—The officers of the S S entertained at a garden party at Bishop Stirling's The lawns were beautifully decorated in the national and allied colors, which together with Japanese lanterns made a very pleasing effect Music, games and refreshments were features of the occasion, punch being served throughout the evening A large crowd was in attendance.

Mrs Vera Hatton and small daughter Virginia left this morning for Salt Lake City, after spending some time here visiting her sister. Mrs. A H. Dahle.

Judging from the many fishermen going to and from Quail creek one would naturally suppose it to be a very attractive place They report big catches

Joseph and Rex Stirling and Lawrence McMullin returned from Lund last Saturday, where they have delivered a bunch of cattle

Frank and Max McMullin left last Wednesday for the Grand Gulch, where they expect to stay the remainder of the summer.

Mrs. A. H Dahle entertained at a dancing party Tuesday evening in honor of her sister, Mrs. Vera Hatton of Salt Lake City

Mrs Margaret Schlappy of Washington spent the fore part of the week here visiting her daughter, Mrs F. C Olsen.

Miss Ethyl McMullin arrived here last Thursday after spending the past winter and spring in Cedar City

Bert Harris left for Salt Lake City Sunday morning on a hurried business trip

J M Moody reports a severe hail-rain and windstorm at Leeds Tuesday evening which did considerable damage The storm only lasted five minutes, yet during that short time it filled creeks and laid grain low.

FATAL ACCIDENT
WOMAN KILLED

Mrs. Chas. Bastian of St. George Meets Tragic Death on Dixie Black Ridge.

(Washington County News.)

A terrible accident which threw gloom over this city and Washington occurred on the Washington black ridge about 8:45 Tuesday morning, Mrs. Charles Bastian being killed and her son injured in a runaway.

Mrs. Charles Bastian and her son, Arvil, were returning home from Leeds, where they had been visiting at Hartley's. On coming down the west side of the Washington black ridge one of the tugs became unhooked causing the horses to bolt and become unmanageable.

Arvil was driving; he is about 16 years old, and on account of a gun accident last Thanksgiving day, whereby a part of his left shoulder was blown away leaving him in a weakened condition, he was unable to exercise the same control over the horses that he otherwise could have done.

Judging from scattered articles, the horses ran down the ridge about 200 yards, when, near the point about 200 yards above the bridge across the wash, the buggy went over the dugway, going down about 40 feet. Mrs. Bastian was instantly killed and her son rendered unconcious. The buggy was upside down the top being smashed at its side; one of the horses had two legs broken.

In this condition the party and the outfit were found about five minutes after by J. M. Moody and family and Miss Hazel Olsen of Leeds, who were coming to the home of Mr. and Mrs. Moody in this city to spend the 4th. Mr. and Mrs. Moody, daughter, Miss Rachel, and the younger children were in the auto, their sons following in a buggy. Immediately one of the sons, Schuylar, saw the dead woman and her apparently dead son, he fainted, falling under the horses with the reins in his hands. Fortunately the horses stood still. Schuyler was for a long time in a serious condition of health here, sometimes critical, with leakage of the heart, and he is rather delicate in consequence. The shock completely unnerved him, and was nearly as severe on his mother who is also a sufferer from heart trouble, but who did her utmost for the injured Bastian boy.

The Moody party at once set to work to extricate the victims of the accident from the wreckage. Mrs. Bastian was found with her feet in one of the buggy wheels and her body bent over the axle; she was dead and had a large cut on the head from which a large quantity of blood had flowed and her neck was broken. Arvil was found tangled up in the top; his head was cut and he was badly bruised. He recovered consciousness soon after being found, his first words being "Where is mother, is she hurt?" He said his back hurt him and was spitting blood. Moody asked him to go to Washington but he said he could not stand the ride. Moody then went to Washington and phoned to Dr. Wodbury, this city, who responded in a remarkably short time, being at the scene of the accident about 45 minutes later.

The horse with the broken legs was shot to end its misery.

The people of Washington were all out in holiday attire and were just about to ring the bell for their Fourth of July program, instead of which they went to the scene of the accident to see if they could be of service. It cast a gloom over the town as it did here and the program was abandoned.

The grief-stricken husband and his two daughters arrived on the scene as quickly as possible after receiving the sad and terrible news.

The body of Mrs. Bastian was brought in, and the son was taken to the local hospital. Dr. Woodbury said this morning that Arvil shows no unfavorable symptoms and is doing as well as can be expected.

Besides her husband and the son, Arvil, Mrs. Bastian leaves two daughters, one about 20 the other years old. Needless to say that these sorrow-stricken fellow citizens have the fullest sympathy of the community.

Funeral services for Mrs. Bastian will be held in the Stake Tabernacle at 3 p. m. today. (July 5.)

Interment will be made in the family grave at the Washington cemetery.

J. M. Wicks of Stateline was in the city last Tuesday. Mr. Wicks has important mining interests at that place, in addition to his extensive fruit orchards at Leeds, and predicts important developments at the camp this fall.

Leeds, July 10 —Several Presbyterians, who are making a tour of this country, held open air meetings here last week. Their music was exceptionally good and was quite a drawing card

Mrs D O. Beal of Overton, Nev, and Mrs Wm Sullivan of Hurricane are here visiting their mother, Mrs. C E Olsen

Mr. and Mrs A. H Dahle were business visitors in Cedar City the fore part of the week

Miss Lydia Hopkins of Glendale is the guest of her sister here, Mrs. Edward McMullin.

Cleo Sullivan is home again after an extended stay at the Grand Gulch mine

Alex Colbath and George R. Lund of St George are business visitors here today.

Most of the boys of the town are enjoying a trip on Pine Valley mountain

Mrs Mary McArthur of St George is the guest of Mrs Oscar McMullin

Iron County Record
July 13, 1917

————— X —————
Mrs. Thomas Stirling of Leeds spent Friday and Saturday of last week in town, en route to Salt Lake City, where she accompanied her husband on Saturday morning. While here she was the guest of Mrs. M. J. Hamilton.
————— X —————

Mrs. Susie Stirling Dead

Mrs Susie Stirling of Leeds died at the local hospital Sunday of spinal meningitis. Mrs Stirling underwent a very critical operation at the hospital on the 9th inst and was apparantly making a very good recovery until the disease developed that carried her off despite all that skilful medical aid could do

Mrs Stirling is a widow and leaves seven children, the oldest a boy of 17 and the youngest child three years old   Much sympathy is felt here for the stricken family.

The remains were removed to Leeds for interment

S. S. Red Cross Fund

The loyalty of the St. George Stake Sunday Schools is evidenced by their generous contributions to the call for S S. Red Cross donations, as shown below. The Stake Board greatly appreciates the efforts of the local officers in this work.

Springdale, $9 30, Rockville, $6; Virgin, $5 60, Toquerville, $1.60; LaVerkin, $10 25; Hurricane $12; Leeds, $8 40. Washington, $16.80; St. George East, $29 50, St. George West, $26 05; Bloomington, $3.60; Santa Clara, $11 45; Pine Valley, $8 25; Enterprise, $11.50; Central, $6.35; Glen Cove, $3 50.

OLD SILVER REEF GRAVES DESECRATED

Cemetery Plowed Up and Converted Into Farm for Production of Corn.

HEADSTONES REMOPED AND THROWN INTO PILE

J. R. Rickards Brings Revolting Tale of Sacrilige and Ghoulish Deed; Leeds People Incensed.

J. R. Rickards returned from Silver Reef and Leeds in Washington county last Tuesday with a revolting story of how the old Silver Reef cemetery, once a beautiful, well-kept spot, is being desecrated and destroyed by a local farmer who has turned the Bonanza Flat, where the race track and other familiar land marks besides the cemetery were located, into a field of alfalfa, corn and grain.

This in the main, is along the line of increased food production, and is commendable. But the cultivation of the cemetery, by the removal of the headstones to a pile in one corner of the partial enclosure, and the plowing up and planting of the graves on the western side to corn, is a piece of sacralige and inhuman conduct that would not be expected except, possibly, in Germany.

Mr. Rickards, who was a resident of the old silver camp in its palmy days has a wife and chi'd buried in the eastern side of the old cemetery, and when he heard of the desecration of the spot he made haste there to see if his graves were included in the despoiled region. It is perhaps fortunate for the man who has converted the cemetery into a field that they were not, for had they been Mr. Rickards states he would have been very likely to have taken a gun and shot the offender.

In company with two men from Leeds, he visited the spot, and could plainly see by the dicerence in the color of the soil brought from the lower level, where a number of graves had been. Some of them had fallen in now, due to the running of irrigation water over them, and a pile of head and foot stones had been carried off a short distance to clear the way for the plowshare. Mr. Rickards remembered the position of and was well acqainted with some of the decedents whose graves had been dessecrated. Some of them were prominent and influential people at the Reef.

Above the graves corn higher than a man's head now waves, and sends its roots down to pierce the mold of those who were presumed to have found a permanent resting place.

Mr. Rickards has now gone to remove the remains of his wife and child to this place for burial, as he is convinced that the spot occupied is no safe resting place for them.

Mr. Rickards mentioned the name of the person guilty of the depredations, but as he is well known to the people of that locality and can easily be learned by any person interested, we will refrain from publishing it. He ought, however, to be prosecuted for his inhuman conduct.

Iron County Record
July 27, 1917

The price of silver is now the highest it has been since the demonetization in 1873. From present appearances if the war continues it will be only a matter of a short time until the law of supply and demand will reinstate silver in its former relationship to gold at a pardiy of 16 to 1. With the white metal in such great demand and commanding so high a price it seems strange that the promised activity at Silver Reef is so long delayed. Certain it is that the old camp still holds millions in the white metal for those who have the courage and determination to go in and wrest it from its long resting place among the sandstone reefs.

Leeds, July 31 —Mrs Susanne Harris, who has been here with her grandchildren since the death of their mother, Mrs Susie Stirling, left for St George the latter part of last week to spend some time before returning to her home at Salt Lake City.

Mr. and Mrs A H Dahle and family left for Milford last week where they expect to stay indefinitely. The Dahles have been here for some time and will be greatly missed by the friends they have made

Mr and Mrs S. L Harris of Salt Lake City spent the week end here visiting relatives and friends They left Monday morning for the Grand Canyon.

Mr and Mrs Thomas Stirling returned from Salt Lake City recently in a new auto which they purchased while there

David McMullin who was operated on at Cedar City last week for appendicitis is improving nicely.

Miss Wanda Nicholes left for Milford this morning where she expects to stay this winter

Frank McMullin arrived home from Milford last week

Miss Ruth Stirling is visiting relatives in Uintah.

Can This Be True?

The Iron County Record in its issue of July 20 contains an article which says that the cemetery at Silver Reef has been plowed up and the headstones removed and thrown into a pile The Record quotes 'J. R Rickards of Cedar City, a former resident of Silver Reef, as its informant and says Mr. Rickards had gone to Silver Reef to remove the remains of his wife and child from Silver Reef to Cedar City for reburial.

The desecration is alleged to have been done by a farmer, who has turned the cemetery into a corn field.

It is hard to believe that anyone would be guilty of such vandalism, almost sacrilege, as this. The amount of land could not have been great, and he must be a poor man, indeed, who would desecrate the resting place of the dead and bring sorrow into the hearts of surviving relatives by such action.

We hope the report is not as stated. Perhaps our Leeds correspondent, or some of our friends at Leeds will kindly furnish The News with particulars

Since the foregoing was set up the editor had a talk with Alex Colbath, of this city, who has recently been at Leeds Mr. Colbath says the report made by Mr. Rickards is perfectly true, that the people of Leeds are feeling shocked at the action of the perpetrator of the outrage, whose name is given by Mr. Colbath as Vincent

Some action should be taken against the man. We understand that the offense is a punishable one.

The people of Leeds should see that the county attorney is informed and action taken.

Shoes Forwarded

The News forwarded 10 pairs of boots and shoes, Tuesday, to the collection depot at Salt Lake City The shoes, the first to come into the office for the war stricken sufferers of France and Belgium, were donated by the following people· Mrs R A Morris, city, five pairs; Mrs Thos Stirling, Leeds, one pair; Bishop I C. Macfarlne, city, two pairs; Mrs. J. R Wallis, city, two pairs

Those having shoes to spare for this humane cause are asked to please send them in as early as possible to the News office, as they must be forwarded from here not later than Aug. 10.

Washington County News
August 9, 1917

Denies Desecration

Under Leeds date of Aug 5, Edward A. Vincent denies that he has desecrated the Silver Reef cemetery, as he was accused of doing by J. R. Rickards, in the Iron County Record, the article being republished in this paper last week. Mr. Vincent's letter follows

"Editor Washington Co. News

"Dear Sir.—An article appeared in your issue of August 2 which accuses me of desecrating the Silver Reef cemetery at Leeds, the foregoing being copied from the Iron County Record and qualified by a Mr. Alex Colbath of St George. I will say in reply that both Mr. Colbath and J. R Rickards are poor judges of the truth. I stand ready to back and prove my statement to be correct now. I am one of three poor men who are farming near the cemetery, Bishop H. A. Jolley and Robert P. McMullin, the latter a son of Bishop B. Y. McMullin, of whom I—the only offender—purchased the land, and I own it and I farm it, and I intend to as long as I am able to And I can further say that my plow has never turned one ounce of dust from the top of a grave, nor have my hands or hands of others removed the slightest mark from a single grave Now, there are three graves on my land which I have protected by waste ditches, so that the moisture from irrigation would not disturb them, and the graves that the investigators are so interested in are unmolested as they have been for a number of years, not even having a head board with a pencil mark of whom they were

"I will inform the public to investigate the condition now termed vandalism and then be fair enough to give those interested an honest decision It don't cost any more to spell the truth and it may cost less, for public slander is a more punishable misdemeanor than the charge I am falsely accused of.

"I will give the name of our most reliable man in Leeds, who has lived here for sixty years and who hauled and cast for use the few rocks which the Iron County Record terms "removed head stones" His name is J. S. McMullin, our present justice of the peace.

"I will further inform the Washington County News to inquire from Judge D. H Morris and Co. Atty. Leo Snow and publish truth and not trash such as Messrs Colbath and Rickards have furnished the editors with.

"I will kindly ask the News to please publish and sign my name, as I am standing on solid foundation and am not ashamed to have my name signed to the truth

"Thanking you in advance, I am,
"Very Respectfully,
"EDWARD A. VINCENT."

Complying with Mr. Vincent's request, the editor spoke to Judge D. H. Morris and asked him what he knew about the matter. Judge Morris replied that while in Leeds he was informed by two people that the graves had been desecrated and by one person that the graves had not been disturbed. Further than this Judge Morris says he knows nothing of the matter.

County Attorney Leo A. Snow when seen by the editor said that when he heard of the alleged grave desecration he wrote to the justice of the peace and the constable of the Leeds precinct to make an investigation On Sunday last he received their reports which were to the effect that the graves had not been disturbed, that the pile of rocks referred were not head stones but rocks that had been collected to form a base for a monument on one of the graves The justice of the peace is Ira S. McMullin, the constable, Robert P McMullin.

Leeds, Aug. 14 —Our drafted boys were down to St. George last week taking their examinations. Those who passed are Cleo Sullivan, Robert McMullin, George Leany and Francis Leany.

Mr. and Mrs. Leonard Dalton, nee Miss Edna Angell, who have been visiting relatives and friends here, left for their home at Rockville this morning.

Mrs H. A. Jolley, who has been having quite a serious time with blood poisoning, is slowly improving but is still under the doctor's care at St. George.

Miss Lydia Hopkins who has been visiting her sister, Mrs Edward McMullin, the past few weeks has left for her home at Glendale.

Mr. and Mrs E. D. Lewis and A Bringhurst of Salt Lake City were business visitors here Monday

Ward Gillies and Mr. Orton of Beaver City were business visitors here the fore part of the week.

Miss Reita Hartley returned from Washington Sunday where she has been spending some time.

Milton Moody, jr., left for St. George this morning to undergo a slight operation.

Miss Margaret Olsen is home after an extended visit to Salt Lake City.

Miss Fay Stirling is in St. George receiving medical treatment.

The Draft

Washington county failed to furnish its quota of men out of the first 101 called. There is a surprising number of exemptions, 30 alone being shown as physically unfit Exemptions for other causes number 44; these we have not been able to get from the clerk for publication in this issue; they will appear in next A call has been made for 75 men from which to complete the quota, and physical examination of these will commence next Monday 27 only of the first 100 called made no claim for exemption, their names follow

THE HONOR ROLL

PHYSICALLY FIT AND CLAIMING NO EXEMPTION

Albert Lang, St George
Eldon L Schmutz New Harmony
Robert Parker McMullin, Leeds
Otto Jennings Rockville
George Pollock, Hurricane
Frank Judd, St George
O Pratt Miles, St George
Robert Miles, St George
John Woodruff Averett, Washington
Samuel Brooks, St. George
Lester Dalton, Rockville
Stanley Snow Ivins, Enterprise
George Woodbury Leany, Leeds
Nelson Glenn Hunt, Enterprise
Leo Larson, St. George
Moroni Jarvis Cottam, St. George
Calvin Dalton, Hurricane
Ray C. Coleman, Enterprise
Francis Scarce Leany, Leeds
Floyd Spilsbury, Toquerville
Herbert Milne, St George
Leslie Adams Morris, St George
John Franklin Pymm, St. George
George Spendlove, Hurricane
Charles Asplin, St George
George G. Felter, St George
Archie Cleo Sullivan, Leeds

Washington County News
August 23, 1917

H. A Jolley was here from Leeds the fore part of the week, visiting his wife, who has been here several weeks suffering from blood poisoning in her hand and arm   Mrs Jolley is reported to be improving.

Iron County Record
August 24, 1917

VINCENT DENIES PLOWING GRAVES

Says Only Graves on His Land Protected by Fence, and Not Been Molested.

J. R. RICKARDS REPEATS DESECRATION CHARGE

A Number of Prominent People of Leeds are Sighted to Prove Mr. Rickards' Statements.

Under date of August 4th, The Record received a communication from Mr. E. A. Vincent of Leeds, in which he makes reply to the article published in The Record some little time ago in relation to the desecration of the Silver Reef grave yard. We have withheld publication of Mr. Vincent's communication pending an opportunity of investigating the matter further. We now publish the salient and pertinent portions of his communication, together with such other information as we are able to obtain. What The Record desires to do is to get at the facts in the matter, and if Mr. Vincent has been wrongly accused we desire to see him vindicated. If he is guilty as a number of people charge, he ought to suffer the consequences of his unfeeling act.

Here is what Mr. Vincent has to say in his own behalf:

Leeds, Utah, Aug. 4, 1917.

Editor Iron County Record.— In your issue of July 20th, there is an article about the Silver Reef grave yard being plowed up for the production of corn and headstones removed and thrown in a pile. Said article is reported to you by J. R. Rickards of Cedar City.

I, the undersigned, am the one who your article refers to, and in answer will say, and I am also very able to defend the same, that who ever misconstrued the stuff has falsified to a very great extent, as to there even being any grave removed or "desecrated," for I challenge anybody to prove that the same has been done.

There is not one word of truth in your article except that there is corn higher than a man's head growing there, which is west of the grave yard. Said land is owned by me and I hold the deed to it, and it was sold to me under a clear title by Bishop B Y. McMullen of Leeds, Utah.

I have three graves on my land and they are protected from desecration by fence, and though the owners have not lived here for many years they pay for the upkeep of their graves, and they are honest enough to themselves and others to be broader-shouldered than to cry before they are hurt.

Your article stated that Mr. J. R. Rickards was going to remove his loved ones to a better resting place. Now if the same money was expended for permanent identification it would seem to the public a more humane act.

Now, Mr. Editor, please note that Bishop H. A. Jolly, R. P. McMullen are also farming on the border of the grave yard, east and south of me.

As to the pile of rocks near by Mrs. Hardie's grave, I will state that I. S. McMullen, a justice of the peace and stone mason, hauled and used and left what he didn't use on the ground, and that is what Mr. Rickards supposed was head stones. Because we live here in Leeds we are not either Germans or anarchists nor inhuman. We are proud to say that we are superior to any act of which we have been wrongfully accused."

The town constable regards that Mr. Rickards has cooled off now, and that he is going to leave his property here.

You further state that the offender ought to be prosecuted. Why don't they?——

Kindly publish this answer as I would appreciate an even break for the truth. Kindly sign my name. EDWARD A. VINCENT.

The above was shown to Mr. Rickards, who made the following statement for publication:

There is just one assertion in my original statement as published in The Record in which I may have been in error. That is in regard to the pile of stones,

believed by me and the two gentlemen who accompanied me to the graveyard—Mr. Don Fuller and Mr. Oscar McMullen—to have been used for the purpose of marking the graves that had been plowed up for a corn patch. We could all three see clear evidences of the presence of graves in the corn field, which extends from 50 to 100 feet into the west side of the cemetery. While residing in

Silver Reef I personally witnessed the burial of not less than half a dozen persons in the portion of the cemetery now being farmed. None of these graves are being protected in any way whatsoever, and beyond the cultivated area the water has been allowed to flow into and sink a number of other graves.

As to the ownership of the land embraced in the old Silver Reef cemetery, will say that it is unpatented mineral land, and was held under location by Capt. Lubbock at the time the cemetery was located there, the Captain having given the ground with such title as he possessed for this purpose. If Mr. Vincent has a deed for the property, as he states, it can be nothing more than a quit claim deed from a locator, and is subject to the requirements of the laws governing the holding of mineral locations. I presume that the farming operations being done are certified as annual assessment work on mineral land.

On my arrival in Leeds a number of persons, among them being members of the family of I. S. McMullen, justice of the peace, reported to me the condition of the Silver Reef cemetery. Since the report published in The Record I have received communications both verbal and written, from persons who were willing to testify to the truth of the statements contained in the article.

Mr. Bert Connell volunteered the information that he had remonstrated with Mr. Vincent over the destruction of the graves, and stated that if I need a witness to prove that the facts are as stated to call on him.

The following letter was received from Mr. J. M. Moody, well known throughout southern Utah, and will speak for itself:

"Leeds, Utah, Aug. 10, 1917. Mr. J. R. Rickards, Cedar City, Utah. Dear Mr. Rickards.—You will find enclosed a clipping from the Washington County News, answering your letter, which you can read. The people here are getting stirred up quite a little, and if you can swear that there are graves where he has plowed we have a clear case against him and will have him sent, which by all means should be done; and I don't think we should let the thing rest now until he is sent over the road. If you know where there are any graves he has gone over we will dig down and find out. Then we will have a clear case.

"With best wishes,

"J. M. MOODY."

Leeds, Aug. 28.—A reunion of the Woodbury family was held last Saturday at the home of Hyrum Leany at Harrisbury. Relatives gathered from all points as far north as Salt Lake City and a large crowd was in attendance.

Willard McMullin returned Thursday from Salt Lake City where he has been the past two weeks visiting relatives and friends

The ice cream and candy shop of Mr Minnie Harris now under construction will soon be ready for occupancy.

Miss Ruth Stirling is home again after spending most of the summer visiting friends at northern points

Victor Angell and Frank McMullin left last week for Milford where they expect to work for some time

Mrs J M Worthen of Salt Lake City is here visiting her parents, Mr. and Mrs B Y. McMullin.

Jediah Adair and family of St George were visiting friends here the fore part of the week.

J. M. Wicks was a business visitor here from St. George the fore part of the week.

Frank Hamilton of Cedar City was a business visitor here Monday.

The Second Call

The 75 men of the second call are accounted for as follows.

THE HONOR ROLL

ALREADY IN ARMY

120, John Kaze
150, Daniel W. McMurtrie
158, Brigham D Randall

PHYSICALLY FIT AND CLAIMING NO EXEMPTION

Andrew Godfrey Laub, Santa Clara
Ether Stucki, Santa Clara
Robert Worthen, St George
Warren James Graybill, St George
Lee Andrus, St George

John Talmi Miles, jr, St George
LeRoy Cox, St George
Ferdinand Stucki, Santa Clara
George Everett Owen, Enterprise
Joseph Edgar Carpenter, Central
Nelson A Empey, St George
Israel Abbott, Mesquite, Nev.
Harold Bunting, St George
William Charles Staheli, Enterprise
Samuel Melvin Wittwer, Santa Clara
David Thatcher Ballard, Hurricane
Karl Alfred McMullin, Leeds
D. Leslie Spilsbury, Toquerville
Joseph Harvey Wright, Hurricane
Isaac Heber Langston, Springdale
Perry Demill, Rockville
Olaf J. Scow, Hurricane

Leeds, Sept 11.—Our soldier boys were guests of honor last Thursday evening at a dancing party given by Miss Margaret Olsen and Miss Ethyl McMullin at the home of Bp. Stirling The porch and lawns were effectively decorated in the national colors which, together with the beautiful lighting effects, made an attractive picture Over fifty invitations were issued and a large crowd was in attendance Dancing was enjoyed till the wee hours of morning, a delicious lunch being served in the meantime. Punch was served througout the evening.

Mr. and Mrs Thomas Stirling entertained at a social affair at their new bungalow last Wednesday evening in honor of our drafted boys. The large porch was bright with flags and bunting and the patriotic colors were used in various other details An appropriate program and dancing were features of the occasion, after which ice cream and cake were served by the hostess.

Mrs. Henry Jolley is home from St George where she has been receiving medical aid for a serious case of blood poison. She is improving nicely.

Mr and Mrs S. J. Harris of Salt Lake City have been visiting here the past few days, Mr. Harris being interested in a mining venture near here

Mr. and Mrs C. B McMullin and Mrs. Jack Murdock motored down from Beaver last week to visit relatives and get some fruit.

Mrs J. M. Worthen left for her home at Salt Lake City last week after a brief visit here with relatives and friends

Miss Ethyl McMullin expects to leave Wednesday morning for Salt Lake City to spend some time.

It is to be regretted that so much exceptionally good fruit has gone to waste in Dixie this year J. M. Moody of Leeds lost over 100 tons of beautiful peaches and his experience has been that of many others. Probably thousands of tons have been lost altogether. There appears to be no help for it The fruit ripened so rapidly that it was absolutely impossible to get help to take care of it. This and the long haul to markets are responsible.

RICKARD'S STORY IS CORROBORATED

Leeds Citizens Sign Statement that He Did Not Lie About Desecration of Cemetry.

MATTER IS NOW UP TO THEIR COUNTY OFFICIALS

D. A. and Bert Connell of Washington Also Submit Deposition in Regard to Vincent's Acts and Admissions.

Mr. J. R. Rickards is in receipt of the following statement bearing the signatures of a number of the prominent residents of Leeds, Utah, bearing upon the controversy over the desecration of the old Silver Reef cemetery, in which the statements heretofore made by Mr. Rickards and published in The Record are verified.

The statement and signatures, which are published at the request of Mr. Rickards, are as follows:

"To Whom it May Concern:

"We the undersigned, having read a statement by J. R. Rickards, published in the Iron County Record, and reproduced by the Washington County News, together with the denials published over the signature of Ed. A. Vincent, who is accused of desecrating the graves of persons buried in the old Silver Reef cemetery, we wish to and hereby do verify the statements made by Mr. Rickards in relation to the plowing over of a number of graves, and the permitting of waste water to run into and sink a number of others. We further wish to state that we abhor such ghouldish work and insist that the Washington County authorities investigate this matter and see that the offender is dealt with as he deserves. We do not feel like remaining passive and permitting such things to go unpunished in our midst.

CLIFFORD MC MULLIN
GEORGE E. ANGELL,
DAVID MC MULLIN
W. D. NEWTON
J. M. MOODY
J. J. MC DONALD
GEORGE OLSEN
OSCAR MC MULLIN
WILLIE MC MULLIN
F. M. HARTLEY
WM. HARTMAN
LYNN MC MULLIN
THOMAS STIRLING
W. S. NICHOLLO
D. A. CONNELL
ROBERT CONNELL

The foregoing signed statement is supplemented by the following deposition made before a notary-public by Messrs. D. A. and Robert Connell:

"State of Utah, County of Iron, ss.

"D. A. Connell and Robert Connell, being severally duly sworn, each for himself deposes and says that he is a citizen of the United States, over the age of twenty-one years, and a resident of Washington, Washington County, State of Utah.

"That he has known and been acquainted with the Silver Reef cemetery in said Washington county for several years last past and knew the location of many of the graves in said cemetery; that during the month of July, 1917, affiant was at said cemetery and at said time about one-third of said cemetery had been plowed and cultivated to corn and other crops; that the mounds and graves in several instances were then visible where said crops had been planted; that affiant was at said cemetery again about the 8th day of September, 1917, and plainly observed where several of the graves had sunken on account of the land being irrigated where said crops were planted.

"That affiant, while at said cemetery, in July as aforesaid, talked with one Ed. Vincent, of Leeds, Utah, and who had plowed and cultivated said cemetery as aforesaid, and on said occasion affiant spoke to said Vincent about plowing and cultivating said cemetery and on said occasion said Vincent admitted that he had plowed up several graves but that the people who were buried there would know nothing about it.

"Affiant further says that while at said cemetery in July, 1917, as aforesaid, he observed several head-boards from the graves of those interred in said cemetery thrown in a pile on one side and the graves desecrated as above stated.

D. A. CONNELL,
ROBERT CONNELL.

Subscribed and sworn to before me this 17th day of September, A. D., 1917,
E. H. RYAN,
(Seal)   Notary-Public.

My commission expires July 22nd, 1921.

Washington County News
September 27, 1917

Big Time Given Our Soldier Boys

Our Boys who left for Camp Lewis Wednesday morning were given a big sendoff Tuesday. A parade was formed shortly after 4 o'clock in the afternoon near the Tabernacle, which was led by the Stars and Stripes, followed by the Dixie Silver band, then the College faculty, the College students, District school grades led by their teachers, and citizens afoot. The parade was about four blocks long, arriving at the courthouse, where the Boys were receiving final instructions.

The band played as the boys formed up on the steps after registering. After the band ceased playing, Mr E. S. Romney called for three cheers for the Boys which were heartily given. The 8th grade girls sang "Good Old U. S A." Sheriff Worthen appointed Stanley Wanlass as Captain of the Boys with Merkins Winsor of Enterprise and Cleo Sullivan of Leeds as his two assistants The crowd gave cheers for these three.

The parade then reformed with Captain Stanley Wanlass bearing the flag and his two aides leading followed by the rest of the Boys, then the band, and the remainder of these taking part following in the original order. They marched through the principal streets and then formed up in front of the Tabernacle, where the Boys mounted the steps. The band played a patriotic selection. The crowd sang "The Star Spangled Banner" accompanied by the band. Cheers were lustily given for the Stars and Stripes and for the Boys The children saluted the flag, pledging alleg ience. Principal H. M. Woodward of the Dixie Normal college responded to the toast "Our Boys," and Captain Wanlass responded to the toast "When we come back." The crowd sang "America." A large national flag, a gift of the Dixie Normal college, was presented to the Boys by Elson Morris. Captain Wanlass thanked the college. A selection was played by the band and the crowd dispersed.

A party was given in honor of the Boys on the lawn of the residence of Dr. Woodbury at night. Games were played, orchestra selections rendered, a nice lunch was served and the Boys and their relatives were made to feel good. A short speech was made by Mr. L S Romney just before lunch. The crowd dispersed about 9 30 to attend a dance given in the Boy's honor at the new gymnasium, which had been splendidly decorated for the occasion. The dance adjourned at a late hour, the Boys having had a delightful time

The Boys left about 7:30 o'clock next morning in cars decorated with national colors. Sad indeed were the good-byes, but the Boys bore themselves bravely though it was readily seen that they felt the parting keenly. They are a fine looking lot of boys, and will give a good account of themselves when the occasion requires it. Dixie is proud of them and they carry the love and heartfelt good wishes of all Dixieites for safe return after honorable service.

The names of our Boys going to Camp Lewis at this time follow:

6, W. H. Anderson, Toquerville
8, Stanley Wanlass, St George
10, Eldon Schmutz, New Harmony
12, Moroni M. Bigelow, Los Angeles
13, Robert P. McMullin, Leeds
15, S W Turnbeugh, Washington
22, Elmer F. Wood, Hurricane
37, John W. Averett, Washington
48, Merkins T. Winsor, Enterprise
50, Lorenzo Spendlove, Hurricane
53, Nelson Glenn Hunt, Enterprise
57, Cleon J. Reber, Santa Clara
66, Calvin Dalton, Hurricane
76, Floyd Spilsbury, Toquerville
82, George Spendlove, Hurricane
93, Archie Cleo Sullivan, Leeds
102, Andrew G. Laub, Santa Clara
111, Ether Stucki, Santa Clara
113, Robert Worthen, St. George
128, John T. Miles, jr., St George

Of these Robert Worthern, Stanley Wanlass, C J Reber, A. G. Laub, Ether Stucki, M T Winsor, Glen Hunt, A. C. Sullivan, Robert McMullin, John Averett and Steve Turnbeaugh took part in the doings here. John T. Miles, jr and Calvin Dalton joined the party at Salt Lake City, and the rest enroute to Lund

Leeds, Sept 27 —Francis and George Leany left for Salt Lake City to join Uncle Sam's forces. They will be greatly missed by the younger set, as their jovial dispositions and sterling qualities have made them social favorites. A host of friends here wish them God sped and a safe return home when they have fulfilled their call to duty.

Mrs Arthur Nicholls and Mrs James Wilder left Saturday for their home in Lovell, Wyo, after visiting friends and relatives in this section Mrs Wilder and Mrs Nicholls were both prominent people of the Silver Reef. Their many friends wish them a speedy and safe trip home

Will Pace and family motored in from Delta. While here they are the guests of Mrs. Pace's sister, Mrs F. M. Hartly

Mrs Etta Mariger (nee Miss Etta Mc Mullin) is here from Salt Lake City visiting her mother, Mrs Mc Mullin

Miss Ethel McMullin has gone to Salt Lake City where she will be employed as a stenographer.

Milton Moody has accepted position as principal at Springdale for the ensuing school year.

School began here on the 17th with C F. Hanson and Miss Margaret Olsen as teachers

B Y. McMullin is home after attending the local hospital at St George.

Miss Racheal Moody has accepted a position as teacher at Hurricane.

Washington County News
October 9, 1917

Leeds, Oct 9 —Cleo Sullivan and Robert McMullin left Wednesday for Camp Lewis. We are surely proud of the boys who go to fight for us, and our only wish is that we as citizens at home will prove ourselves worthy of "their fight" Physically and mentally they are well equipped and these with all the best sent out from each town, surely our success is secure.

The "Uncle Sam" boys were met here, by all the town's people and the teachers and school children who met at the postoffice to do honor to the two boys who went from here. The boys and all other passengers were feasted on delicious grapes.

Miss Rachael Moody left for Hurricane Sunday. She came home ill and was compelled to miss the week of school.

Mrs Edna Dalton (nee Miss Edna Angell) of Rockville is here visiting her mother, Mrs, G. E Angell.

Mr. and Mrs Charles Hanson and Annie Hanson were visitors in St. George on Saturday.

Andrew Gregerson of St. George passed through Leeds today enroute to Bellevue

Mrs Mary Olsen returned from Hurricane Saturday.

Bishop B. Y. McMullen of Leeds was here the first part of the week. He intended returning home Monday afternoon, but the stage auto was too crowded, and refused to take him, so that he was obliged to remain until Tuesday. Brigham is living in hopes of something being done in the matter of the Silver Reef mines, concerning which there has been considerable talk and agitation the present season, but at present the place is very quiet and practically nothing is being done. With silver selling at above a dollar an ounce we can see no reason in the world for the famous old silver camp, which was never half depleted, lying dormant.

Leeds, Oct. 23 —The speakers at the Sabbath meeting were C G Y. Higgins and John T Woodbury. Mr. Higgins explained in a very excellent way the meaning of the 2nd Liberty Loan Mr. Woodbury appealed in his remarks to the patriotism of the people, and his discourse was certainly excellent

Word has been received that Robert P McMullin has been assigned duties as corporal and that Cleo Sullivan has been transferred from Washington to the National Guard at California.

The school children and teachers raised the fifty dollars and this, it is understood, will be applied on the Leed's allotment of $1,000 of the Liberty loan

Mrs Minnie Harris has moved into her new confectionary. The building is still incomplete, but Mrs Harris is able to handle her customers.

Miss Margaret McMullin has gone to Cedar City to attend her sister, Mrs Mark McMullin, who underwent an operation at that place

Vere McMullin was taken to St George for medical treatment, a case of blood poison in his hand. He is getting along splendid.

Mr. and Mrs Leonard Dalton of Rockville will make Leeds their home this winter.

Miss Stella Angell has returned home after a prolonged visit in Salt Lake and Idaho.

The district teachers enjoyed an interesting and educational institute.

Supt. Bentley visited schools here last week

Leeds, Oct. 30 —Molasses making is still in operation, though slow; it seems to be difficult to obtain men to handle the crops. The crops are all mature and heavy and laborers are few.

Mr. and Mrs Edward Dalton of Hurricane are now located at the Harris homestead. We are surely glad to have these people belong to our ward.

Joe Stirling, Karl McMullin and Tommie Stirling have just returned from the mountains • where they have been gathering horses

Mrs Lizzie McQuaid took her young son to St George on Friday to receive dental treatment

The S. U. Packing Co will soon begin to can meat. They are now waiting arrival of cans.

Frank Sullivan returned from Lund Saturday bringing freight for Hansen's store

The Relief Society' ladies have been collecting funds for the 2nd Liberty Loan.

Matthew Batty and son left for Hurricane Valley this morning.

Edward McMullin was a business visitor to St George on Friday.

All Women Register

Saturday, Nov 10. is registration day for women 16 years of age and upwards all over the nation. The State Relief Society has requested local branches at the following places to undertake this work:

Hurricane, including La Verkin, at Hurricane; Rockville. including Virgin, Grafton and Springdale. at Rockville; Toquerville and 'Leeds, at Toquerville; Washington; Santa Clara; Central and Gunlock, at Central; Enterprise; St George

Registration will commence at St. George in the Public Library at 10 a m. Saturday. There will be two registration officers working so that registrants may not be delayed.

Every lady over 16 years of age is urged to register.

Leeds, Nov. 20 —S. L. Harris was in town the fore part of the week Mr. Harris reports that he has succeeded in turning the Virgin River. This task has been accomplished under great difficulty, as Mr. Harris stood alone in his opinion that such a gigantic task could be realized. With the installation of his new gasoline pump he can soon begin to see his ambition realized. There was at the time the Stormont mill was in operation, 100 tons of quick silver lost. This is what Mr. Harris is striving to obtain.

Joe Stitling, while coming from Lund loaded with freight for Hanson's store, came very near suffering a fatal accident The break block became deranged, which started the horse to run, giving a turn the rear wagon went down grade, also the front wheels of first wagon. Joe in some manner jumped from off in time to save his own life The merchandise was scattered and broken, but neither Joe nor his teams suffered anything except fright

The Misses Ada, Melba and Lucile Harris arrived here from Salt Lake City last night; they are at the home of their grandparents, Mr. and Mrs B. Y. McMu'lin.

Mrs. Wm Sullivan visited at St. George and Hurricane the early part of last week.

Mrs. Lyll Sullivan of Hurricane visited her parents here last Saturday and Sunday.

David McMullin returned from a commercial trip in Iron Co yesterday.

Mr. Colbath, a mining expert, was a visitor here part of last week,

Mrs. Etta Manger left for Salt Lake City this morning.

William Emett of Harrisburg is out on $500 bonds charged with being in illegal possession of wine, a barrel containing 35 gallons of which was found in his cellar by Sheriff Worthen, other barrels apparantly recently emptied, and apparatus for wine making. Emett has been suspected for a long time

Mr. and Mrs Oscar McMullin of Leeds were business visitors here Tuesday.

Washington County News
December 4, 1917

Leeds Dec 4 — The Thanksgiving dance given under auspices of the M. I A was a splendid success Refreshments were served, a short program given, the music was exceptionally fine so altogether a well spent evening for both old and young

The Thanksgiving program given at the District school was along Puritian ideas and the little actors handled their parts with skill

Rex Stirling spent Thanksgiving day with his parents, Mr. and Mrs. Thomas Stirling Rex is in attendance at the Dixie college.

Lawrence McMullin has returned home from the Grand Gulch mine where he has been employed the past four months

Ed Tullis of Newcastle spent Thanksgiving at Leeds While here he was a guest at the Stirling house.

Mr and Mrs W D Sullivan and Miss Stella Angell left today for Salt Lake and Idaho points.

Bert Harris and Frank Hartley have gone to Purgatory to do a piece of contract work.

The Misses Venice and Ann Hopkins of St George spent the Thanksgiving vacation here

A dancing party was given in the local hall last night by some of the younger set

A. E Gregersen of St. George was here Wednesday on mining business

Mr. Dahle is here from Milford to transact mining business.

Edward McMullin went to St. George on business

Iron County Record
December 14, 1917

Miss Ruth Stirling of Leeds tarried a day in Cedar the first of the week on her way to Newcastle, where she will visit with her sister and family.

Washington County News
December 18, 1917

Leeds, Dec 18 — Word has been received here that Robert McMullin. now at Camp Lewis, has been transferred to the aviation corps

Don Fuller returned from Lund on Tuesday bringing freight for Hanson's store, also finishings for Harris' confectionary store.

Chas Hanson took a party to Harmony last week Mrs Minnie Harris was employed in the school room in his absence

The conference visitors were Mr and Mrs H. A. Jolley, Mr and Mrs C F Hanson, Maggie Jolly Olsen and Hazel Olsen.

Frank McMullin returned from Beaver, Sunday He has been employed there for the past four months

Willard McMullin returned today from Purgatory where he has been doing additional work on his land

Messrs Colbath, Grigerson and Granger, mining experts, were in Leeds the fore part of the week

A committee has been appointed to arrange for special social functions during the holidays

Glenn Olson returned today from Lund with a load of lumber to remodel their home

Mr. and Mrs Davis of Salt Lake are here to spend the winter

H A Jolley has just purchased a Ford car

Iron County Record
December 21, 1917

J. M. Wicks of Leeds and Stateline was in town the fore part of this week hobnobbing with Lon Higbee, another inveterate miner. We believe they have a vision of wealth ahead from the development of a large body of oil shale, which they are busy locating.

Deal Closed For Silver Reef Tailings

W. F. Snyder, R. G Edwards and Alex Colbath of Salt Lake City have closed a deal with B. Y. Mc-Mullin of Leeds and A. E Gregerson of this city for the tailings at Silver Reef and a certain amount of money passed to close the deal

It is understood that a leaching plant will be put in as early as possible to treat the tailings, which are said to contain a good percentage of silver.

Income Tax Notice

Word to the chairman of the C. C of D is to the effect that officers connected with the Internal Revenue Dept. will be at Leeds Feb 16, St George Feb 18 21, Hurricane Feb. 22, Springdale Feb. 23, Toquerville Feb 25, and 26 M. Spencer is the name of the visiting officer to this section The object of his visit is to instruct taxpayers how to make their returns, and also to collect the tax thereon. People are advised to make their returns as soon as possible

Leeds, Jan 22 —A party of Iron Co men passed through Leeds on Friday; they are now encamped at Harrisburg This party of men are putting in a bridge at Cotton wood and expect to put in six or seven before they are through.

The 10 year old son of Mr. and Mrs Matthew Batty died at their home at Silver farm, Friday of appendicitis The entire community extend their sympathy to the sorrowing family. The entire fifth grade, of which he was a member, attended the funeral Riley C Savage, H. A Jolley and Ira McMullin were the speakers.

Dr Parley Harris of Salt Lake, formerly of this place, and brother of S L and Bert Harris, was a visitor here last week Dr Harris spent a very pleasant time going over scenes and places of his first recollection Mr Harris was born here but left Dixie about 15 years ago, graduated at Union, Oregon, and has since filled a mission.

About ten men, surveyors representing the U. S government survey, are encamped at the lower end of Leeds, they are now doing work at Harrisburg.

Miss Ruth Stirling returned Thursday from Newcastle, where she has been staying with her sister, Mrs. John Tullis

A children's recreation party was given last evening The little folks enjoyed themselves dancing until 10 o'clock.

Bert Harris and Francis Hartley are in town again, they report the completion of their shaft sunk at Purgatory.

Mr Rappley and family of Sevier Co are here to stay, indefinitely They are located at the Sullivan house

Margaret Olsen attended the M I A convention at Hurricane, she reports excellent meetings.

Ward, son of H A Jolley is suffering from an attack of pneumonia

Silver Reef to Wake Up

Andrew F. Gregerson of this city received a letter from Cleveland, Ohio, last night informing him that Alex Colbath and associates have bought out the Brundage property at the Silver Reef and intend working it as soon as the machinery necessary can be installed. The letter was written by Bishop B Y McMullin of Leeds, who is at Cleveland on this business

Leeds, Jan 28 —A mining deal has recently been consummated between the northern company represented by Alex Colbath and B Y McMullin, agent for the Brundage Co , whereby operations to reclaim old Silver Reef will be begun as early as March 1st, and we understand that Virgin City promises to furnish 25 barrels of oil that will be necessary to run the new plant that will be used to handle the ore

B Y. McMullin and daughter, Miss Edyth returned home Tuesday The former has been to Cleveland. Ohio, on mining business, and the latter has been to Salt Lake the past year

Mr and Mrs Leonard Dalton who have spent the winter here have moved back to their home near Rockville

Wm. Batty of Toquerville 'and Mr Stringham of Salt Lake City are in town

Ward Jolley is much improved He has been ill

Bert Harris of Leeds was a city visitor Monday

Miss Fannie Kleinman of Toquerville, and Miss Maggie Olsen of Leeds were here Friday. They came to attend the game.

Leeds, Feb 12 —One of the most successful social functions of the season was given at the the home of Mrs Thomas Sterling, in honor of the soldier boys The rooms were tastefully decorated in red, white and blue A generous lunch was served to about fifty guests, after which the spacious upstairs rooms were thrown open to dancing, and the jolly party stayed until morning The out of town guests numbered fourteen. Mrs Sterling was assisted by Miss Margaret Olsen.

The first of the series of special programs of the M I A. was given Sunday night, by Miss Edyth Mc Mullen and Miss Melby Harris. Miss Edyth handled the piece "There Were Ninety and Nine," with much credit to herself, and little Melby did credit in a character part' The Old Fashioned Choir'

Oscar McMullen, Donald Fuller and Bishop Stirling attended the part of the roundup held at St George yesterday

Miss Anna Hopkins was a visitor here, from St George, the latter part of the past week

Mrs Elinor Scott left, on business, for Central and Newcastle districts, last week

Mr and Mrs Bert Harris were business visitors at Toquerville, Saturday

Miss Ethel McMullen returned home from Salt Lake, last Friday.

Mr. and Mrs. Antone Olsen motored to St George yesterday.

Leeds, Feb 19 —The M. I A enjoyed a special program Sunday night The following parts were enjoyed by those present. Talk, "Washington and Lincoln," R. C Savage; Song, "Don't Bite the Hand," etc, W. G McMullin; ' Incidents in Wilson's Life," Ruth Stirling; Song, "The Tea Party," by four junior girls dressed in colonial costume; Reading, Mrs. Hazel McMullin.

Mrs A. Hanson and Charles Hanson and Charles Hanson were business visitors at St George on Sat-

urday, also Mrs. Elenor Scott and M J. Moody, being called to court, as parties interested in the Hale case

The Misses Ethel and Edith McMullin returned from a pleasure outing to Grand canyon Saturday

Frank McMullin returned home from Copper Mountain last Friday.

Mr. and Mrs H A. Jolly were visitors at Washington Saturday.

Bert Harris and Antone Olsen left for Salt Lake City last Tuesday.

Leeds, Mar 5,— We surely are enjoying delightsome weather. Already the fruit trees are bursting into blossom, plowing has commenced and it looks as if we were on the eve of another growing season.

We are indeed sorry to learn of the critical illness of Mrs. Thomas Stirling Dr. McGregor, of St George was called on Sunday, and he is here again to day to make a second visit to her.

The "Bridgers" of Harrisburg entertained Leeds younger set Friday evening, at an oyster supper The contractor's wife of Salt Lake acted as hostess

The M I. A enjoyed an "Evening with Burns," Sunday night, given by Mrs. Minnie Harris,

Mr and Mrs S L Harris returned to their home in Salt Lake, on Tuesday.

B Y. McMullin returned from a business trip to Salt Lake last Sunday.

Leeds, Mar. 12 —The Sabbath meetings, both Sunday school and the Sacramental meeting, boast a larger attendance than for months past We take this as encouraging and feel that Leeds people are on the eve of awakening to their church duties which they have hitherto neglected

The S. S. officers received complimentary invitations to attend the Lyceum number Saturday night. We take this opportunity to extend our thanks to the official body at St. George

Leland Sullivan received injuries by being kicked on the leg by a horse His injuries though painful are not serious.

The M I. A enjoyed an evening with Riley, given by Margaret Olson and W. G McMullin

Mrs. Thomas Stirling who has been suffering from a bad attact of sciattca is much improved

Mrs Wm Sullivan of Hurricane is here visiting her mother, Mrs. E C Olson

We have received another delightsome rain.

Leeds, Mar 19 —Special Easter services will be held next Sunday, together with visiting missionaries and special musical numbers, we surely expect an extra fine meeting

About a dozen young people attended the opera at Hurricane Sunday evening They report it "fine "

The speakers at the regular sacramental meeting Sunday gave an excellent report of the conference

Application has been made for a chapter of the Red Cross to be organized at Leeds

A special "Thrift Stamp" program is being arranged for next Sunday evening

Charles and Triumah Angell left for Salt Lake last Monday

Frank McMullin left for Beaver last Saturday.

Leeds, Apr 2 —A very pleasant surprise party was tendered to B Y McMullin Thursday evening, the occasion being his 67 birthday The Misses Ethel and Edith McMullin acted as hostesses The rooms were decorated with pink blossoms Games and musical numbers preceded a dainty lap lunch. The older set lingered until a very late hour, the bishop received many congratulations and many "happy returns of the day."

The Sacramental service on Easter Sunday was fine, those present enjoyed a very instructive meeting, those who did not come out missed a fine treat The young missionaries showed ability in their delivery, in the manner their papers and talks were worked out, and showed "success" as a result of effort. We extend a hearty invitation to come again

Mrs Lizzie McQuaid has been chosen to act as chairman of this Red Cross unit, with Ruth Stirling as secretary Mrs. Thomas Stirling has offered one of her spacious new rooms to the Red Cross as a work room

Mrs Karl Snow of St George, was a visitor at our Sabbath meeting

Mrs Ada McMullin left for a visit to Salt Lake City, today

Iron County Record
April 4, 1918

ADVISORY BOARD AT PROVO TO PASS UPON DRAFTED MEN

The following boys from Washington County passed through Cedar Wednesday enroute to the Medical Advisory Board at Provo before being assigned to the various training camps: Wm. J. Squire, Donald C. Macfarlane, R. F. Riding, Frank Kelsey, Ed. Minder and John Atkin of St. George; Joseph Stucki, Byron Oviatt, and Hyrum Gubler of Santa Clara; Samuel Bradshaw, Harvey Dalton and George Spendlove of Hurricane; Clarence Stahli, Enterprise; Dan McMullin and Ray Batty of Leeds; Nathan Gifford of Springdale; and Stephen Jennings and Perry De-Mills of Rockville.

Washington County News
April 9, 1918

Leeds, Apr 9 —Mr. and Mrs Oscar McMullin went to St George today to take their son Dan, who leaves for Provo tomorrow where he will take an examination relative to joining the army

Ben Sorensen and family and Mrs Coates of St George were the guests of Mr. and Mrs Oscar McMullin, Sunday.

E C Olsen is having his home remodeled, George Prisbrey of St George has charge of the work.

Little Legrand Stirling, who broke his arm while playing with other children is getting along nicely.

Mrs Ruth Paris Stewart, formerly of this place, is here from Alamo, Nev, the guest of her sister.

Miss Venice Hopkins spent Saturday and Sunday here with her sister, Mrs Ed McMullin.

Bert Harris returned from Salt Lake Thursday.

Thomas Stirling left for Salt Lake on Wednesday.

Leeds, Apr. 22 —Herbert Haight of Cedar City, who has just returned from a mission to England, spent a few days here last week.

School will be out this week, the children in the upper grades are busy with final examinations

Mrs Oliver Coast of Parowan spent Friday and Saturday with Mrs A. Hanson

Mrs Don Fuller has returned from Hurricane, where she went for medical advice ·

Antone Olsen returned last Saturday from Salt Lake where he has been employed.

Mrs. Thomas Stirling was removed to the hospital at St George on Saturday

Miss Ruth Stirling has been in St George receiving dental treatment

Matt Wicks who has spent the past winter at Modena, has returned

Victor Angell and Karl McMullin came home from Washington today·

Dan McMullin returned from Provo and Salt Lake last week.

Leeds, May 7.— The Primary Assn assisted by Mrs Minnie Harris, Edyth and Ethel McMullin and Sebra Neagle gave a most excellent entertainment on Tuesday hight Tourists from Denver who attended said they had never seen a group of children handle their parts so well The prceeds go for the Primary Red Cross work.

A splendid program was tendered Karl McMullin A short program was given and refreshments consisting of sandwiches, cake and punch were served Karl is one of Leeds' most highly respected young men He arrived at Camp Lewis and in a letter to his mother describes the country around Camp Lewis as most beautiful

Mr Talbot of Harrisburg was called to Panguitch hurridly, on hearing of the death of his eldest son, who was killed by lightening

Mrs Ada McMullin returned home a few days ago after attending conference and visiting friends in Salt Lake and Beaver,

LEEDS

Leeds, May 14 —Milton Moody suffered a relapse last evening following a serious operation on nose and throat trouble undergone some time ago Milton being an ambitious and thrifty young man, tho still weak, supposed he had sufficiently recovered to be at work again The ride from St George to Leeds in the hot sun proved too much and started a flow of blood from the nose All aid possible was given him until the arrival of a doctor who came as quickly as possible, yet was only just in time to render assistance Milton is better at this writing, but still in a serious condition He has the best wishes of the entire community for a speedy and complete recovery.

Stirling Through a grieveous mistake the telephone operator did not leave Leeds connected with the doctor tho requested to do so All Leeds cars but two which were disgruntled were out of town, hence this necessitated a runner dispatched on horseback for medical aid, a distance of eighteen miles We feel far removed from a doctor at a critical illness time, and we feel that the telephone is our only satisfaction, this time central was instructed to connect Leeds with the doctor but failed to do so This error has been committed before, several times, hence we feel we are justified in making this little complaint

Dr D A. McGregor was called to attend Mrs Matthew Batty of Silver farm. The nature of her illness at this writing we are unable to state

The entire community was aroused it its sympathies over the sudden and critical condition of Mrs Thomas

Victor Angell and Stanley Fuller left for Delta today

Mrs Lizzie McQuaid of Leeds was a city visitor Monday.

Mr and Mrs Oscar McMullin of Leeds were in town Monday on business

Mr. and Mrs J. M. Moody and family left Tuesday for their fruit farm at Leeds, where they intend to spend the summer.

Eighth Grade Graduates

SPRINGDALE
Leland Russell, Francis Crawford, Nancy Christenson, Eva Gifford.

GRAFTON
Lula Ballard, Louie Ballard, Alton Jones, Monroe Russell

VIRGIN
Estella Wilcox, Eleanor Lee

TOQUERVILLE
Leona Naegle, Ethelga Batty, Lula Ingler, Afton Sullsbury, Rex Naeg, Daniel Kleinman, Lyle Bringurst, Delbert Jackson, Fern Slack

LA VERKIN
Thora Wilson, Irvin Webb, Wendell Christenson, Wilma Martineau, Whitney Jones, Rosalba Gubler, Alvin Hardy.

HURRICANE
Leona Hinton, Kathleen Isom, Lena E Isom, Annie Isom, Ida Isom, Nora Hall, Minnie Hall, Juanita Bradshaw, Lamond Stratton, Reece Jacobson, Girnzy Stratton, Cadmus Ruesch, Mary Sanders, Morelis Eager, Bernard Isom, Tennessee Spendlove, Florence Wheeler, Reed Langston, Otto Stanworth, Myron Stout, Eula Stratton, Blanche Petty.

LEEDS
Ada Harris, Alta Stirling.

WASHINGTON
Joseph Judd, Roy Neilson, Golden Paxman, Hilda Sullivan, Jesse Averett, Vilate Adams, Hilda Staheli

ST GEORGE
Mary Atkin, Alice Barlow, Blanche Bentley, Ellen Cannon, Evelyn Carter, Jennie Empey, Nellie Riding, Ruth Walker, Maurine Whipple, La Verna Webb, Henrietta Belnap, Helen Moody, Effie Empey, Helen Gardner, Vera Harmon, Verna Harmon, Grace Hemmway, Lorna Kemp, Lewis Christian, Vernon Miles, Joseph Pearce, Glenn Prisbrey, Bertram Sullivan, Karl Winsor, May Linder, Blanche Mathis, Helen Miles, Anna Miles, Alice Pendleton, Lois Parker, Ruth Riding, Zola Hatch, Rose Walker, Emma Blair, Ruth M Fawcett, Veilla Bastian, Alberta Hardy, Lee Bryson, Alan Wallis, Mary Defrieze, Paul Worthen, Van Prisbrey, Henry Crosby.

SANTA CLARA

Lorine Staheli, Vilate Staheli, Fern Reber, Emma Reber, Max Hafen, Walter Hafen, Newell Frei

GUNLOCK

Erma Bowler, Lillian Jones.

CENTRAL

Murray Bracken, Ruby Holt.

ENTERPRISE

Sylvia Emett, Lila Hunt, Anina Hall, Mabel Terry, Thelma Truman, Edna Barnum, Minnie Crawford, Marva Crawford

NEW HARMONY

Juanita Davis, Max A Pace, William H. Prince, Lester Taylor

PINTO

Minnie Knell, Lewis Eldridge, Karl Knell

Dr D A McGregor went to Pine Valley Monday morning on receiving word that Bishop Jeter Snow was very ill He is reported to be seriously ill

---

LEEDS

Leeds, May 20 —Private George Leany returned home on furlough from Camp Kearney, bringing with him his lady The young couple left for St George and were married in the St George temple The groom is the son of Hyrum Leany of Harrisburg and is a highly esteemed and capable young man The bride is from northern Utah, a stranger in these parts, but knowing whom she married we are perfectly secure in giving her safe anchorage They most certainly have the best wishes of this community for their future welfare.

Charles Angell left Sunday for Salt Lake City, he and Frank P McMullin leave with the next quota of drafted boys from Utah We are indeed sorry that no public demonstration could be tendered Charles, as no one knew he was leaving so soon; he had just come home from Salt Lake City. Frank McMullin at present is at Eureka

Mrs Matthew Batty of Silver farm was removed to the St George hospital in a very critical condition. At this writing we are glad to know she is much improved Our other sick people, including Mrs. Thomas Stirling, Milton and Schuyler Moody are much improved

Joseph C. Wilson, recruiting officer, spent a little time in Leeds, urging young men to volunteer for the army.

Milton E and Schuyler Moody were removed to St George where conditions for medical aid are more efficient.

Mr. and Mrs Will Sullivan of Hurricane spent Sunday in Leeds Will has just purchased a new Ford car.

Lynn McMullin is home again; he has been employed in Hurricane for some months past

We are glad to say that Leeds went "over the top" in the last Red Cross drive.

Mr. and Mrs Edward McMullin were business visitors to St George Saturday.

Leeds, June 11 —On May 28th the residence of Charles Hanson was completely destroyed by fire Mrs. Hanson was at the home alone, there being no water available except in a well, and a strong wind blowing, Mrs Hanson was unable to fight the flames and all household effects were lost

Mrs Elinor Scott, Mrs A. Hanson, J M Moody and Clarence Hanson were called to St George Saturday as principal witnesses in the Hall case.

Mrs Matthew Batty was removed to her home at Silver farm after spending some time at the St. George hospital She is much improved

Mrs. Mame Beal came in last night from Salt Lake, she will spend some time with her parents, Mr. and Mrs E C Olsen.

Mr. and Mrs Will Woodbury of Caldwell farm spent Sunday with W D Sullivan and family

Mrs Edward McMu'lin has gone to Glendale to spend some few weeks

Antone Olsen is home again after spending some time in St George

Mr. and Mrs John Schmutz of St George spent Sunday in Leeds

Joe Stirling was a business visitor to St George on Monday.

Valla Angell has been very ill the past two weeks.

Miss Margaret Olsen and Herbert Haight were married in the Salt Lake temple June 12 The bride is an esteemed young lady of this place The groom is the son of Mr and Mrs Isaac Haight of Cedar City, a young man of splendid character Their many friends here join in congratulations

Wallace and Mark McMullin motored from Cedar City on Friday, to spend a short time with friends and relatives Wallace has spent the past few years as teacher at Nephi and has lately been admitted to the bar as lawyer. He is an ambitious and self sustaining young man and is the son of David McMullin of this place.

M. L McAllister and daughter of St George, Mary Sanders of Hurricane. Lynn McMullin and J. M Moody were a party to go fishing on Saturday They report a splendid catch

Among those who attended conference at St. George are, Bp Stirling, H. A Jolly, C F Hanson, Mrs Ada McMullin and W. G. McMullin.

J. M. Moody returned yesterday from St George bringing with him part of his family. Schyler and Milton are both improving.

Mrs David McMullin left Monday for Iron Co She will spend the summer with her children at Cedar City and Parowan

Mrs Mamie Beal and son, Glen, will spend part of the summer here Dr Beal is "Somewhere in France," in the medical corps

Miss Rheta Hartley has left for Delta, where she will spend the summer

Mr and Mrs Wm Sullivan of Hurricane spent the week end at Leeds

MAIL CONTRACT TO ST. GEORGE IS LET

W. H. Perry and Gordon Whitehead Awarded Contract on Terms Safe and Satisfactory.

The Star Route mail contract between Lund and St. George, via Cedar City, Hamilton's, Kanarra, Leeds and Washington, a distance of 88 miles, has been let to W. H. Perry and Gordon Whitehead. There is a consideration of $9,500 per annum, intended to cover the carrying of the first, second and third class mail, of a minimum of 600 pounds, parcel post mail in addition to this, will be paid for in addition at the rate of 1¾c. per pound to St. George, and pro rated to the other stations along the route. According to careful estimates made by the bidders, the route is expected to pay approximately $19,000 per annum.

The new contracts are supposed to go into effect July first, but arrangements have been made with the present carriers to continue the service until such time as the new contractors can get fully equipped and ready for the work.

Mr. Perry informs us that Ford trucks will be used in transporting the mails. The contract calls for a ten hours through schedule between terminals for all but fourth class mail and is allowed a six day limit for the delivery of parcel post mail, not being required to load it until 2000 has accumulated at the railroad.

Mr. Perry, prior to leasing the Cedars Hotel, was engaged in the mail contracting business for many years in this state and Nevada, and knows the game from a to z. He says it will be necessary to erect a depot here for passengers, freight and equipment, that will receive attention at an early date.

It is the intention of the contractors to conduct a through passenger auto stage over their route in addition to the mail conveyances.

A splendid social was given Monday night in compliment to Lynn and Clifford McMullin who left with the last quota of boys for Camp Lewis

Visitors to Leed for this week and last are Mrs John Fife of Cedar City guest of Ethel McMullin, Mrs C D Peace of Los Angeles at Stirlings, and Mrs P. E Harris who is on her way home to Salt Lake City

Mrs Hazel McMullin has returned home after a two weeks' visit to Glendale

Leeds, July 16 —We are expecting an extra good time on the 24th The general plan is to hold the entire celebration in the Moody grove, an old time celebration A meeting has been arranged for, after which people will partake of lunch. Sports will be conducted here also At 5 o'clock a children's dance, finished at night with an adult dance We promise plenty of shade, the best water and ice cream in the county. Our general committee takes this means to extend a hearty invitation to our neighbor towns Fishing parties can be arranged for if our friends will come and inform us before hand

Visitors to Leeds this week and last are, Mrs Edna Dalton and Mrs Georgina Millet of Rockville; Mr and Mrs John Tullis of Newcastle, Mr. and Mrs Will Sullivan of Hurricane and Mrs S. A. Harris of Salt Lake.

A miscellaneous shower was given in compliment to Mrs Margaret Haight at the home of Mrs George Olsen. Mrs Haight left on the 3rd for Cedar City which place will be her home

Mrs Helen McMullin left last week for Salt Lake in hopes of bettering her health. A letter to her home states she is already much improved.

M J Moody, Rachel Moody, Mrs Mame Beal and Mrs. Minnie Harris were a party to St George on Monday.

Miss Edith McMullin is home again after a few days stay in St George.

Leeds, Aug 6 —As the result of a ride in a one horse cart, Reed Fuller is suffering with a fractured skull and severe cuts about the face He was taken to Hurricane but the Dr. there advised he be taken to Salt Lake City for medical aid He and his father left on Monday for Salt Lake

Mr. and Mrs Thomas Stirling, Fay and Tommie left in their car for a few days stay in Salt Lake.

Mrs George Leaney received word from her husband that he "had landed safe."

Miss Emily Larson of Hurricane spent several days here last week.

Mr and Mrs Will Pace of Delta were visitors here on Sunday.

Mrs Oscar McMullin has just received a new player piano

Mrs Ada McMullin has left for a month's visit at Beaver.

J. R Richards of Cedar City was a visitor here last week

We had a fine rain last night.

Leeds, Aug 20 ---Threshing here is just about completed, in most cases the output being greater than anticipated Farmers are pleased over this and taking all things in consideration, nature has yeilded abundantly in the line of fruits, grains and garden produce Large quantities of fruit is being shipped from here daily. Though the sugar question has necessarily placed orders smaller and it is feared that much of our choice fruit will waste unless the sugar situation is relieved Leeds was granted only 50 lbs for August, this, however, we feel is a mistake, on the part of the distributor, and not our full allotment

Reed fuller who was suffering from a two piece fractured skull is improving, he and his father are expected from Salt Lake today.

* Mr and Mrs Thomas Stirling returned last week after a few days' visit in Salt Lake

Word has been received that Cleo Sullivan landed safely,

Mrs Geo Angell left for Salt Lake City last Saturday.

———

Iron County Record
August 23, 1918

George Angell of Leeds came up Tuesday evening with a load of fruit for the community market.

Don Fuller and son of Leeds are back from a Salt Lake hospital, where the boy was operated on for fractured skull.

Soldier Boys Leave

A large number, 44, of our boys left last Thursday morning for Camp Kearney, Cal The silver band and the martial band were both out and discoursed lively music while the boys and their friends gathered and took leave of each other There was a great turn out, most of our citizens being there to give the boys a final handshake before leaving The boys were in the best of spirits, and departed with a determination to do their duty manfully and cheerfully

The following left from this point Alma H Jacobson, Dilworth Beckstrom, W Malin Cox and Rodney H Snow, all of Pine Valley, Joseph Stirling, of Leeds, Richard Henry Atkin R Louis Hinkston, William Carter, Junius J Duncan, Neal Dee Keate, Levi Atkin, Lorin Church Miles, Earl Worthen, Sherman Lamb, Levi Empey and Rolland Whitehead, all of St, George, George A Lemmon, Virgin, Edwin Stucki, Lorin Reber, Ernest E. Stucki and Walter P. Gubler, Santa Clara The boys from Washington, Leeds, Hurricane, Toquerville, Springdale, Rockville, and New Harmony joined the party as the cars went through Rodney Snow of Pine Valley was appointed captain of the company

LEEDS

Leeds, Sept 17 —Mrs Ira S McMullin of this place died in Salt Lake last week We will give obituary next week

School has begun for this year with Miss Edith McMullin of this place as principal and Miss Pearl Larson of Bloomington as assistant

Charles Hanson and family left for Arizona last week, where Mr. Hanson will teach school

Ethel McMullin left last week for Camp Lewis

OBITUARY

Leeds, Oct 1 —Helen Elizabeth Leany McMullin, wife of Ira S Mc Mullin of Leeds died at the home of her daughter, Mrs Etta Mariger in Salt Lake, Sept 7th, where she had gone in hopes of inmpoving her health which had been poor for some time She was born Sept 4 1850, in Salt Lake a daughter of William and Elizabeth Leany, pioneers of 1847 to Salt Lake, in 1851 to Parowan and to Harrisburg in the winter of 1863 Deceased was married to Ira S McMullin in the temple at Salt Lake Dec 7, 1874 She was the mother of seven children, two having died in their infancy She moved to Leeds with her family in 1877 and when the first Primary was organized in the ward by sister Eliza R Snow she was made president, was also the first president of Y L M I A organized in the ward and at the time of her death was president of the Relief Society which office she held for the past 15 years Deceased is survived by five children and seven grandchildren all of whom attended the funeral but her youngest child, Karl who is somewhere overseas with Uncle Sam s forces The funeral services were splendidly attended, remarks were made by Elders Cottam and Atkin of St George and B Y McMullin of Leeds, all paid glowing tribute to the busy and useful career or sister McMullin, and we as a community already feel the loss of her greatly Her life has been one of good events always ready to assist the needy and unfortunate

A beautiful floral offering was sent by the Mariger Bros of Salt Lake Solos was rendered by Prof J. H McAllister, Miss Polly Kemp of St George and Mrs Minnie Harris of Leeds, with Miss Evlyn Thurston of St George and Miss Ruth Stirling of Leeds at the organ The community extends its sympathy to the family in the loss of wife and mother.

BRIGHT PROSPECTS FOR THE SOUTH

H. B. Westover, Veteran Mining Man, Predicts Great Awakening for This Section.

SILVER REEF MINING CAMP TO BE REVIVED

Oil Fields Give Great Promise and Iron Industry Will be Developed in This Country

In the opinion of H. B. Westover, an old and experienced mining man of long and varied experience in the western country, an era of remarkable prosperity is at hand for southern Utah, which will include silver and copper mining at the old Silver Reef camp, oil gushers in the Harrisburg, or Pergatory domes, the mining and manufacture of iron in this county, the construction of a railroad and the construction of a cement plant near Cedar City.

ANOTHER GOOD RECORD

Last week we called attention to the proud record made by Toquerville with nine per cent of its population in Uncle Sam's srvice This week our Leeds correspondent points out that this pretty little village has seven per cent of its population in Uncle Sam's service

Leeds, Oct 18 —Seven per cent of our little town s population is with Uncle Sam's forces We are proud of this and are justly proud of our boys We are indeed glad to say that we have no complainers, their letters are cheerful and full of good humor These boys realized that conditions would not be just like they are at home, but are too manly to make mention of a few distasteful things All except two of our boys are overseas

Dr. P. E Harris and family have spent the past two weeks here visiting friends and relatives, Dr. Harris has also been looking over some business interests

Mrs Mame Beal came home from Cedar City on Saturday where she has been assisting Dr Macfarlane, she left for Hurricane Sunday at which place she will help Dr Wilkinson and assist in the drug store

Letters have been received from Ethel McMullin who is at Camp Lewis, describing the scenic beauty of that part of our country

Mrs Margaret Haight (formerly Margaret Olsen) of Cedar is visiting relatives and friends at this place

Willie and Max McMullin went to St George last week to take the physical examination relative to joining the army. They are in the last draft

Molasses making is in full operation.

Washington County News
October 28, 1918

Leeds, Oct 28 — A victrola is installed in our district school building The children are indeed fortunate to get such excellent music for their dances marching, games, etc Mrs Lizzie McQuaid has been very generous in giving the use of her Victrola for the parties that have heretofore been given by the district school

The Liberty Loan committee is to be congratulated on their excellent work in raisinng the last Loan, of $2700. They failed only in $200 of going "over the top"

All public gatherings have been closed for a week, as no Spanish Flu devoloped, school reopened yesterday

Bishop Stirling has left for Lund with a carload of hogs to be shipped to Salt Lake

M J Moody has moved his family to St George for the winter.

Washington County News
November 18, 1918

Leeds, Nov, 18 — We are indeed gratified over the war news, and sincerely hope that "Bad Bill" will get all he deserves, though it is bad policy to speak ill of one after he is dead Public demonstrations were kept as quiet as possible owing to our town quarantine,

Bishop Sterling is out again after being confined to the house with a case of influenza, contracted while in Salt Lake We have no other cases

P E Harris of Salt Lake and R S Gardner, instructor at the A. C. U of Cedar City, were business visitors here last week,

Mr and Mrs Mark McMullin of Cedar City are guests of Mr and Mrs David McMullin,

C E Colbath and party of Salt Lake were business visitors here last week

Edith McMullin left Saturday for St George to receive optical attention

GETS PLENTY OF CLOTHES

France, Nov 11, 1918.

Mrs W D Sullivan,
Leeds, Utah

Dear Mother and All

I will try and write a few lines to let you know I am well I received your letter of Sept 30 and one from Leland of Oct 21 and maybe you think they didn t look good I was shure surprised to know that there was so many of the boys from home over here

You asked me if I needed any woolen clothes over here We don t need anything like that It is a fellow s own fault if he don t get all the clothes he wants, for they are here for him There must not be any fellows in Leeds now, I was counting them last night and couldn t count many I guess the next draft will take the rest of them

This isn t a very comfortable place to write, so won t write a very long letter I am laying on my side writing this letter in a German dugout that we drove the Germans out of about three weeks ago

Will close hoping to hear from you soon and to hear that you are all well, the same as this letter leaves me

Your Afft son,
A O Sullivan,
Bat E, 119, A
A E F, France

Leeds, Dec 3 —The friends and relatives of Karl McMullin were greatly pleased and relieved last night on learning that a letter had been received from Karl the first except one, since he landed overseas in July. Great fears as to his safety have been entertained by his family At present he is in a base hospital in France recovering from gas wounds He reports he is getting along nicely except for burns on his body Karl spent his 45th birthday in the first line trenches and four days later was gassed

Joe Sterling, Robert P. McMullin and Victor Angell are still in the U. S ready and impatient to go as soon as Uncle Sam was ready for them we are waiting impatiently for the speedy return of our soldier boys

Geo Sullivan, another victim of wounds, left the hospital and has been again in the trenches the extent of nature of his wounds is not known but he was in the hospital three weeks

Francis and George Leany have been indeed fortunate, they too, have been in the trenches, and were the pioneer boys to leave our town, last report they were feeling splendid.

Clifford McMullin also has been an inmate of the hospital suffering from influenza and as a result some lung trouble. Last report he was recovering

Lyman McMullin has had the misfortune to lose a finger caused from a felon, from which he was suffering when he left the U. S

Mr and Mrs Edwards are located at the Wm Sullivan residence Mr. Edwards is here looking over mining interests.

Alex. Colbath, David McMullin, William and Oscar McMullin were business visitors to St George on Monday,

Frank P. and Charles McMullin are in France, their regiments had not as yet been called into active service.

School reopened on Monday, Nov 25. the school faculty gave a splendid thanksgiving dancing party.

Washington County News
January 2, 1919

Reported Killed
Found in German Prison

Storrs, Utah, Dec 25.
Editor Washington County News
Dear Sis ——It will be of interest to the people of Washington County to know that one of our soldier boys, Corporal Geo. D McMullin, who was reported killed in action has been found in a German prison camp and is in France in good health Mr McMullin is a son of Mrs Flora Davis of Cleveland, Emery Co, and a grandson of Mrs Olivia Bryson of St. George He was born in St. George and is well known there and has relatives there and in Leeds

Yours respectfully,
Sam C Bryson,
Storrs, Utah.

Leeds, Jan. 7—Holidays passed pleasantly, house parties and dancing have been chief sources of amusement School has recommenced and most everybody has settled themselves down to serious work Among holiday visitors are Mr. and Mrs, Wm Woodbury of St George, Mrs Wm. Sullivan, Miss Venice Hopkins of St. George, Dr. and Mrs P. E Harris of St George, Ida Jolley of Washington and Mr and Mrs Milton Moody, Jr, of St George

Leonard Dalton, who recently returned from a U. S. training camp and family have gone to Cane Beds on a short visit.

Word was received Sunday evening that Frank P, McMullin had arrived safely in New Jersey from overseas

Mr Sodaquist of the So Utah Bee Co has located here, having purchased a residence of G. E Angell

Born, a daughter to Mr. and Mrs Ammon Jolley, Dec 25th all concerned doing nicely.

Miss Edyth McMullin was a business visitor to St George on Friday

Thomas Sterling left Monday for Salt Lake with a bunch of cattle

LEEDS

Leeds, Jan 14 —Max McMullin and Marguerita Hartley were married at St George last Wednesday, Max is the son of B Y. McMullin of this place, an honorable, upright young man, Marguerita is the daughter of Francis and Maggie Hartley, a very highly esteemed young lady. This young couple have the very best wishes of this community for a happy and prosperous future life

Our Mutual commenced Sunday evening with a very interesting program and a very fine attendance A very instructive feature of the program was a Talk on Marine Life by Mr Andreson of Beaver who has just returned from overseas duty

The friends and relatives of Clifford McMullin were certainly relieved and glad to know that all is well with him. Clifford was last heard from about Oct 6th, so much fear for his welfare had been entertained

Robert McMullin, one of our soldier boys, has returned from Camp Lewis, Wash Robert looks splendid and we are surely glad to have him home again.

Ira S McMullin, Bp Stirling, Mrs. Thomas Stirling, Mrs Lizzie McQuaid and Libbie Stirling were business visitors to St George last week

An ice cream party was given by the Junior set at the residence of Thomas Stirling on Sunday evening.

A shower was given in compliment to Marguerita Hartley by Mrs Clifford McMullin. ·

J. M. Wicks came in from Stateline a few days ago and is paying a visit to his fruit farm and other interests at Leeds. Mr. Wicks states that the camp of Stateline is beginning to pick up again. The Liberty Leasing company, he states, are making good progress in the sinking of their new shaft.

Leeds, Feb 3 —On Friday evening a very successful soldier party was given Dancing, games, a short program and refreshments occupied the evening An interesting feature of the program was a talk by Dr. D O Beal who has just returned from England where he has been doing hospital work in connection with the war.

Joe Stirling another of our soldier boys arrived from Camp Kearney last night; our soldier boys certainly look splendid dressed in their uniforms and it is no surprise to hear (from the other young men of the village) "gee, wish I had gone "

Ira S McMullin has received official notice that his son Karl was badly wounded in his legs; Karl was gassed some time in early Nov. and has been in a hospital in France ever since

Frank P. McMullin returned from France Thursday Frank expressed the opinion that "France is just fine, but he is glad to be in Dixie " He belonged to the 145th Utah artillery.

Dr. D. O Beal, Mrs Beal and Dr's parents motored from Ephriam Utah last week. They left for Overton, Nev , today.

Mr. and Mrs Frank Sullivan of Hurricane are spending a few days in Leeds

Robert McMullin of Leeds spent Sunday in town visiting

Pvt Karl A McMullin

Karl A. McMullin
Wounded in Both Legs

The father of Karl A. McMullin, Ira S McMullin of Leeds, has received word, officially from the government, that Karl was wounded slightly in both legs, and gassed, October 13, 1918. He was still in the hospital in January, but expected soon to be sent to the United States.

Karl was originally in the 91st division, but was one of the cases detained on account of measles when the 91st division left Camp Lewis When he did leave Camp Lewis he expected to join his company at Camp Merritt, but it had sailed for France and he was transferred to Co B, 56th Infantry, 7th division, and left Camp Merritt on Aug 1, 1918, for France, He was sent to the fighting line on October 9th and was in the fighting near Metz

Ut to the 3rd of December he had received no mail from home, although letters were written to him every week, and had not had a pay day since leaving the U. S.

Leeds, Feb 25 —The townspeople need be proud of the improvements effected by the So Utah Bee Co , both in remodeling the house and the work done on the outside premises Others who are doing improvement work in and around their homes are B Y. McMullin, Ammon Jolly and W. D Sullivan

Antone Olsen has just purchased a new Ford car, he expects to carry mail from Leeds to Hurricane The route formerly run by Dalton Bros

Many of our townspeople attended the "Welcome Home" for soldiers, at St George

Mrs Caroline McMullin left for Cedar City last week returning home Sunday

Born, a son to Mr and Mrs Bert Harris, February 3rd, all doing fine

M J Moody left with a party Monday to explore Zion canyon

Mrs Lyle Sullivan was a visitor to Leeds last week

Quite a number of our people are on the sick list.

Karl McMullin Still in Hospital, Doing Fine

Base Hospital 85, A E F
Jan 25, 1919

Mrs Helen McMullin,
    Leeds, Utah
Dear Mother

I will try and write one more letter, but it is sure hard when I never get a scratch from anybody.

I am well and feling fine, leading a good, easy life, and getting plenty to eat, I can go to a picture show two or three times a week, so you see it aint so bad   If I could only just hear from home and know you were all well and that the 'flu" had not hit you, I would feel better.

There is a big bunch leaving here in the morning who expect to go home   I would like to know what they intend to do with me, whether they intend to send me back to my company or to the U S

I saw George Dodge a while back, he came over with Lynn and those fellows, but he didn't know anything about them, whether they got up to the front or not or what outfit they were in   Tom Wilder is here and I see him nearly every day   He told me there were some Dixie boys in his outfit and that one named Gray of Santa Clara was killed

I was in hopes of having some money to send home to pay my insurance in the Intermountain insurance company, but I haven't been paid in five months; I think Uncle Sam is good for it

It is getting dark, so will close with love   *

Your affectionate son,
    Karl

NOTE —Karl has been in the hospital several months with wounds received in action   His mother, to whom he wrote the foregoing letter, died Sept 7th last; he has not been getting his mail, therefore did not know this when he wrote.

The Boys Long For Home Now War is Over

Somewhere in France
Jan 21, 1919.

Mrs John Tanner, Leeds, Utah

Dear Sister —Just a few lines to let you know how I am   I am well and feeling fine, hope this finds you all the same   I got the little pack you sent me all o k. I have still got it   I think I will try and get a furlough in a little while and then I will need it, that's what I'm saving up for. There has been quite a few of the boys on furloughs but I haven't tried to get one yet   Well, Mattie, I will try and finish your letter

I just got a letter from mother which I was sure glad to get; she said that Geo Felter died and that Haven Paxman got wounded. How bad did he get wounded?

Well, Mattie, I guess it will be a few months yet before we get back Believe me the boys are sure sickened about it, it is sure hard to get any work out of them, they say the war is over and they are through and you can t blame them   I am still a chambermaid at the stable   Tell John that I will drop him a few lines in a day or two. Have been sporting the last few days and haven't written very much.

Last Sunday a French family invited me up to their place to have dinner with them; believe me it was sure sqme feed, I would like to go every day if they would feed me like they did last Sunday.

Well, I have told you about all I can think of this time, will close hoping to hear from you soon

Your loving Bro John
Pvt John W. Everett,
28th Co 20th Eng
American E F , France

"I'm Ready to Go Back"

Stigny, France,
Dec 28, 1918.

Mrs B Y. McMullin,
   Leeds, Utah
My dear Mother

I guess you are beginning to think I've forgotten you or got bumped off But I didn t get killed nor have I forgotten you, but I am about as homesick a boy as ever lived. Still it does no good to get homesick here I am getting along fine but we are longing for the time when we can sail for the U S It rains here in this country nearly every day

Well I wish I were home right now but I ought to be thankful I am here and alive and don't have to go back in the lines again and what I mean is I went into them too   I went over the top the morning of the 5th of Nov but we were fortunate in not losing many men

Well, the last letter I received was written the 17th of Sept. so you can see I would enjoy reading a letter myself

Today is Sunday and we don't drill on Saturday nor Sunday

I am so anxious to hear about my boy You know I have never heard a word about him

I certainly did think of home and the kids on Xmas morning and at dinner time I won't mention what we had for dinner but it was what we get every day

They say the army is the best place in the world as long as you are in it and I guess it is   I am just as loyal to my country as I was the day I joined the army with all I went through, but now I'm ready to go back.

I suppose Bob is home now isn't he?

I hope you are all well.

Praying the Lord to bless you all as well as my wife and baby.

From your loving son,
Cliff

Leeds, Feb 4 —A very serious accident was narrowly averted at school the other day when 8-year old Eugene Leany was hit just above the eye unintentionally, by his chum playmate We feel that the sling and flipper are dangerous weapons; we would urge parents, teachers, and superintendents to cooperate in urging the doing away of these playthings; indeed, we believe we should legislate against them ' as dangerous weapons."

Our Relief Society was recently organized with Ruth Caroline McMullin as president, Rebecca Angell as 1st Coun, Mary Leany 2nd Coun, Vinnie Fuller Sec and Treas and Elizabeth McQuaid as class leader The M I A was organized with Ruth Sterling president, Lizzie McQuaid 1st Coun, Edith McMullin 2nd Coun, Hazel McMullin class leader and Ada Harris Sec. and Treas Thus far both organizations are taking a lively interest in their work

Ada Harris returned Sunday morning from St George where she has been receiving chiropractic treatment

"Matt" Wicks is home aga'n, after spending the winter at Modena and surrounding towns

Alex Colbath a mining man of Salt Lake, is here on a business visit

Georgia Baxter of Milford is the guest of Fay Stirling

Enterprise has our sympathy in her new "flu" attack

What our Leeds correspondent says about the danger of the flipper is perfectly true No child should be allowed to have one, for they are a dangerous weapon Many eyes have been lost through them, and other injury to the person suffered Property damage, broken windows, etc, when the flipper was allowed to be used, was very great Many of our best and most useful songbirds have been killed by them. The flipper is forbidden in this city; its use should be forbidden everywhere.

LEEDS

Leeds, Mar. 11 —Francis Hartley while returning from Lund with freight was unfortunate enough to mash his foot He left for St George Saturday to receive medical treatment

Miss McAllister and Supt W. O Bentley spent one day last week visiting our schools

Mrs Ada McMullin and Mrs Elinor Scott were visitors to St George Saturday

Parker Bros , of Joseph, Utah. are developing their land at Silver farm

G . E Angell is reshingling his home

CHARLES ROSS SWINGS DEAL ON SILVER MINE

Interests Edward Bradsley, Well-Known Mining Man of Milford, in Silver Reef Group.

Charles F. Ross, a mining man who has spent the past year or two in Cedar City and vicinity and is interested in various properties hereabouts, left for Milford yesterday to close up a sale of a group of six silver claims in the ownership he is associated with the Cripps Bros. and Mrs. E. A. Cripps, the property being located on the White Reef, near Harrisburg, in Washington county, and adjacent to the Silver Reef district.

Mr. Ross and Mr. Cripps visited the property the first of the week to see that there was no flaw in the titles.

The purchaser of the group is Mr. Edward Bradsley of Milford, and the consideration is $11,000.

It is understood that the purchaser, who is a successful mining man and an ex-mayor of Milford, will commence developing the property as soon as arrangements can be completed for placing a crew of men there.

Mr. Ross and the Cripps boys also have promising silver properties in the vicinity of Newcastle, this county, on which they are now working.

Leeds, Mar. 25 —A spirit of "home improvement" has taken hold of our people here. Those who have already had work done are So. Ut. Bee Co, B Y. McMullin, Ammon Jolley, G. E Angell and Mrs Clifford Mc-Mullin Others are contemplating new buildings The new cement walks certainly are a big improvement.

Bp Stirling, H. A Jolley and W. G McMullin attended the recent conference at St George. At the regular meeting last Sunday they reported a splendid conference

Word has been received that Karl McMullin who was gassed in the front line trenches in Nov. and who has been in a hospital ever since, is on his way home.

There is a general epidemic of colds, bordering on pneumonia here, also one case of mumps reported.

This unit of the Red Cross is busy collecting clothes to ship to grief stricken Europe.

Wants to See Paris

Valdahon, France,
Feb 22, 1919

Mrs Beckie Angell,
Leeds, Utah

My dear Mother, and all:

Your most welcome letter came yesterday. I was glad as ever to hear from home once more, and also glad to hear that all is well at home

Today is Saturday, we don't usually have anything to do on Saturdays or Sundays, except inspection every Saturday morning, but most of the battery is out on the range today firing, I was lucky enough to stay in camp myself so will do a little writing

We are having plenty of rain as usual, the ground never gets entirely dry here at all; it's seldom we have a clear day.

I sure would like to have been with the 145th F. A. when they went home I have an idea they were a happy bunch. I think the 148th is lost; I never hear anything about when they're going home.

I can picture Wayne and Virginia with the mail and I can see ma with her glasses waiting in the door.

Well, if you could see us boys when the mail is called off here you might laugh too, we are just as anxious for the mail I think as anybody, at any rate I am.

I went to a picture show last night; it wasn't very good, but it don't take very much to please a soldier; they can make amusements for themselves out of most any thing.

Well I haven't gone on my furlough yet and am not sure that I will but if we stay in France much longer I want to go to Paris We will have a chance to go to Paris and stay there three days whether we take our furlough or not I think I would like that trip as well as to have a seven day leave, because on the seven day leave we don't see Paris

Well, I will be glad to get my feet under the table at home once more We have plenty of "slum gullion" to eat, but I would like to eat some white mans' chuck once more

I will close now hoping this finds you all well.

I am, as ever,

Charles.

Dixie Boys Reach New York From France

Specials to the Salt Lake papers state that the 348th field artillery of the 91st division arrived at New York early on the morning of Mar. 30 after ten months spent in France, Belgium and Germany. Most of the men in the regiment have been with it since the training days at Camp Lewis, Wash. On debarkation the 348th went immediately to Camp Merritt, N. J., where they will be divided into detachments according to their homes and sent to the nearest demobilization camps for their release from the service, which usually takes between 10 days and three weeks.

The Dixie boys shown as having arrived this side of the Atlantic are: Corporal Francis S Leaney, Leeds; Pvt Andrew C. Laub and Pvt Ether J. Stucki, Santa Clara; Corporal Elmer F. Wood and Pvt Lorenzo Spendlove, Hurricane, Pvt Nelson G Hunt, Enterprise; Pvts. Orson Pratt Miles, Frank Judd, Moroni J. Cottam, Samuel Brooks, Ralph W. McAllister, Leslie A. Morris and Leo Larson, St. George

Leeds, Apr 8 —A number of mining men whose names at this writing we are unable to give have just been here looking over "old ' Silver Reef It looks very favorable for a revival of mining activities in this noted old mining camp. We all certainly hope so, a payroll every month would certainly mean much to people here

Business visitors to St George last week included, Misses Edyth McMullin and Pearl Larson, Mr and Mrs B Y. McMullin, Bp Stirling, Mr Williams, T. G Sterling, M J. Moody and Oscar McMullin

Mrs Dick Williams of this place was operated on at the St George hospital last Friday. Last report she was getting along splendid.

Mr Anderson returned from Beaver last week bringing with him Mrs Anderson; they left for St George Tuesday on business

Mrs Margaret Haight of Cedar City and Mrs Hazel Moody of St George are here visiting relatives and friends

Mrs Max McMullin left Saturday for Overton, Nev, to join her husband who is employed there

Mr and Mrs Leonard Dalton have gone to Cedar City for an indefinite stay.

"Aunt" Marie Wilkinson has been confined to her bed for some time.

LEEDS

R C. Savage and family have removed to Silverlee farm (about a mile from Leeds) The house formerly occupied by them at "old" Grape Vine springs will be the home of John Parker and family of Joseph City; for an indefinite time

A dozen or more of our young people attended the play given by the D N C of St George at Hurricane on Saturday night They report the play as being very fine

Visitors to Leeds this week are Misses Venice Hopkins of St George, Genevieve Anderson of Beaver and Mrs Georgana Millett of Rockville

Bert V. Harris left on Tuesday to resume work on the St, George-Modena road.

Mrs W. C. Cox of St George was a visitor here last week.

R. C. Savage was a visitor here last week.

A. B. Harris, the well known mining man from Washington county, who is interested extensively in the Silver Reef district, was in Cedar City yesterday on his way back from Wyoming, where he went to bury his father, who died at the ripe age of 88 years. At the funeral Mr. Harris met brothers and sisters whom he had not seen for thirty years. He states that prospects are good for an active season at the old silver camp this coming summer.

Washington County News
April 28, 1919

Leeds, Apr. 28 —Among visitors to Leeds the past week are Mrs Leone Worthen and Mrs Stella Mansfield of Salt Lake, Mrs S A Harris, Mrs Bert McQuarrie, Mrs W. Worthen and Mr. and Mrs Milton Moody, Jr, all of St George Business visitors included Wallace Worthen, contractor and builder of St George, A B Harris, St. George, Engineers Beesam and Nelson of Salt Lake and Mr Coons, here on mining business

A number of our towns people have been ill the past week, two of the So. Ut. Bee Co, employees were removed to St. George hospital in quite a serious condition Mr. Soderquist is much improved and able to return home, but the other patient is still in the hospital.

"Aunt" Marie Wilkinson, after an illness of several weeks, died at her home on the 24th of April. Obituary next week.

Francis Leany of Harrisburg, one of our first boys to join Uncle Sam's forces, returned from France on Sunday,

Mr and Mrs. Donald Fuller, spent several days in St George last week

Washington County News
May 5, 1919

Leeds, May 5 —At the close of school, on Friday, the teachers, parents and students enjoyed an old time picnic in the grove Swinging, dancing, games and picnic occupied the afternoon, music was furnished by the school Victrola; Miss Larson was school photographer, so many interesting pictures were taken

Among those who attended the theatre at Hurricane last night are Bp and Miss Ruth Stirling, Mrs Elinor Scott, Mr. and Mrs G. E Olesn, Willie and Dan McMullin

Prominent among our visitors this week are Drs McGregor and D O Beal, also Mrs D. O Beal and Mrs Lizzie Bleak of Salt Lake.

Fay Stirling was unfortunate in running a needle into her knee. It was necessary to take her to the hospital to have it removed.

We are heartily in sympathy with ideas of Mr. Tippitts and urge people to read his article in issue of The News of May 1

R C. Savage has just received a new piano Victrolas have come to W .D. Sullivan and Donald Fuller,

W W. McMullin is suffering an acute attack of appendicitis He is reported much better today

Word has been received that A Cleo Sullivan has landed safely from overseas

Mrs Stella Mansfield left for Salt Lake today.

Leeds, May 27 —Dr and Mrs D O. Beal have returned to their home at Tremonton, Utah. They were accompanied by E C Olsen, who will remain there for some time to be treated for an affliction that has made him a sufferer for years. Glenn Olsen accompanied them to Salt Lake.

Those leaving for Salt Lake, Idaho and other northern points are Edyth McMullin, Lawrence McMullin, Mrs. E C Olsen, Mrs. Georgia Millet and Ross Angell

Arrivals to Leeds include A. Cleo Sullivan from France, Charles F. Hanson and Mr. and Mrs Andrew Perkins of Taylor, Arizona

Mr. and Mrs Wm and Frank Sullivan and families were Sunday visitors at Leeds from ———.

Leeds, June 10 —Social honors given in compliment to A. Cleo Sullivan, George and Francis Leany The affair, a dance was a splendid success The house was tastefully decorated, the color scheme being red, white and blue. The hall was a perfect jam, Hurricane, Toquerville, La Verkin, Washington, Harrisburg furnished their quota of young people Among the married visiting friends were Mr. and Mrs Albert Anderson, Mr and Mrs Edwin Dalton, Mr and Mrs Wm Woodbury, Mr and Mrs. Will Sullivan, Mr and Mrs Frank Sullivan, Mr. and Mrs R C Savage and Mr. and Mrs. John Parker and Mr. and Mrs. Hyrum Leany.

Thomas Stirling and sons, also Richard Williams were business visitors to St George Monday.

A meeting was called Sunday by Y. L M I A officers to elect officers for Bee Hive work

Ammon Jolley, Francis Hartley and Delbert Stirling have gone to Lund for freight.

Ann Hopkins of Glendale is visiting her sister, Mrs Edward McMullin.

Oscar McMullin is taking down his house, preparatory to rebuilding

Clifford McMullin is expected home from overseas any day

Bert Harris of ——— was in town a few days last week.

Georgia Baxter of Milford is the guest of Fay Stirling.

Mrs E C Olsen returned from Cedar City Saturday

Leland Sullivan left for Idaho Monday

Washington County News
June 15, 1919

Leeds, June 15 —Leeds surely enjoyed a treat in form of the street sprinkler in operation last week We deeply regret that we are not allowed this privilege every day We feel like we should begin to date history from this event

Clifford McMullin arrived home from France Saturday He is glad to be home and is looking fine after enduring some very trying experiences.

Wallace McMullin of Nephi is here combining business with pleasure He is at the home of his parents, Mr. and Mrs David McMullin.

Fishing season opened Sunday, many of our leading people and those from St George enjoyed an outing and a "good catch "

Mr and Mrs. V. Mariger are here for an indefinite stay, they are guests of Mrs Mariger's father, Ira S McMullin,

Mariger Bros of Salt Lake are here with three large auto trucks to look over Dixie and her resources

Mrs Thomas Sterling is home again from the hospital in St. George, much improved.

Washington County News
July 14, 1919

Leeds, July 14—Charles Angell returned from France last week, bringing with him Miss Reese of Salt Lake This couple left for St George on Saturday to be married Charles is the son of G. E and Rebecca Angell of this place, a highly respected young man, has just returned from France where he was called to serve his country. Miss Reese is the daughter of Brigham Reese of Salt Lake; she is an accompolished young lady, They have congratulations of a host of friends here Leeds will be their home for an indefinate time

Helen, the two-year old daughter of Edward and Hazel Hopkins McMullin of this place, died in St. George on July 3rd of spinal meningitis. She was a beautiful and much beloved little girl Much sympathy is felt by the parents in the loss of this child Funeral services were held here on July 4th.

Arrivals in Leeds this week from France, Salt Lake and other points Karl and Lynn McMullin, Mr. and Mrs Ed Mansfield, Mrs Leonard Dalton, Misses Venice and Anna Hopkins and P. E. Harris.

A cloudburst occurred at head waters on Friday, taking out the dam This is the worst of its kind in 60 years Discussion as to probability of a cement dam to replace the old one is current

Leeds is certainly fortunate in the safe return of all her soldier boys A reception will be given them tomorrow night.

Leeds, Aug 5 — Mr and Mrs Hyrum Leany of Harrisburg accompanied by Dr and Mrs W C Cox of St George have returned from a two weeks outing on Cedar mountain

Mr and Mrs Ed McMullin have returned from a ten days outing at Panguitch lake where they went to escape some of Dixie's heat

A party of surveyors who are working on the state highway are camped at Moody's grove

Mrs Donald Fuller and daughter, Mrs Clifford McMullin, left for Idaho early last week

D C Olsen returned from Tremonton, Utah, last Saturday greatly improved in health

Ralph Harris three-years old, was taken to St George Monday for medical treatment

Charles Wright returned from a month's outing in Iron Co.

M L McAllister of St. George was a visitor here Tuesday

Oscar McMullin is erecting a cement bungalow.

J. M Moody was here from Leeds Wednesday, Mr Moody says the fruit crop about Leeds is very good this year. 　*

Mr and Mrs Will Emmett and family of Harrisburg were visitors here the latter part of last week.

ACTIVE USEFUL CAREER IS ENDED

Death Calls Joseph T. Wilkinson at Early Hour This Morning—His Active, Unique Life.

By William R. Palmer.

Joseph T. Wilkinson, one of Cedar's aged and most respected citizens, passed peacefully away at an early hour this morning. In his demise the community and the church of his adoption lose a unique and useful character.

Joseph Thomas Wilkinson was born in Manchester, England, March 26, 1847. He, in connection with his parents and other members of the family, became members of the Church of Jesus Christ of Latter-day Saints and emigrated to Utah when Joseph was nine years of age. From this early period he has been associated with the Mormon people in all their struggles and hardships in establishing themselves in this country.

December 31, 1868, he was married to Elizabeth Emily Wells in St. George, Utah. To this union five children were born, four of whom still survive. These are Mrs. Emily Mc Connell, Mrs. Sadie Buckwalter, and Editor Charles S. Wilkinson, all of Cedar City, and Joseph T. Wilkinson, Jr., of Cane Beds, Arizona.

In July, 1880, his wife died and was buried in Leeds, Utah, which was then the family home.

Later Bro. Wilkinson married Jane S. Wells, a half sister of the first wife, and with her he has been blessed to live out the remainder of his days. Nine children have been the result of this union, eight of whom still live. They are Dr. H. H. Wilkinson, Percy N. Wilkinson, Gerald Wilkinson and Elizabeth Wilkinson of Cedar City, Raymond A. Wilkinson of St. Joseph, Arizona, Stephen R. Wilkinson of Milford, Utah, Jane W. Wilkinson of Salt Lake City, and Marion Wilkinson of Hurricane, Utah.

From the two unions he leaves behind him a large and respected posterity to perpetuate his name on the earth.

Bro. Wilkinson has lived an active and useful life. Civilly and ecclesiastically he has filled many important and responsible positions and his duties have always been discharged with fidelity and ability. He possessed a legal mind and was admitted to the Bar of Utah. Before coming to Cedar City he served as justice of the peace for years in Leeds, through the turbulent days of Silver Reef. In his court many a lawless character was given his lesson in respect for the magesty of the law. He permitted nothing but the orderly processes of law and when the bully attempted to override the proper regulations of his court he departed from it a sadder but a wiser man.

Since his residence in Cedar he has held the positions of mayor of Cedar City, justice of the peace, prosecuting attorney for Iron county, city recorder, and others.

Ecclesiasticallf he was first counsellor to Bishop Crosby in Hebron and afterward held the same position to the same Bishop in Leeds, Utah. He was for a long time Sunday School superintendent in Leeds and held the same position in Cedar after his removal here.

He was also a faithful and beloved member of the High Council of the Parowan Stake for a number of years, only resigning from that office a year ago on account of his rapidly declining health. Perhaps, however, it was as assistant stake superintendent of Sabbath Schools, associated with Jos. H. Armstrong, that he became best acquainted with the people, and particularly the children, of the Parowan Stake. In church circles he is revered for his faithful devotion to 🙼 and for his conspicuous ability as an exponent of church doctrines. As a logical and thoughtful public speaker he had few equals.

It can truly be said of Bro. Wilkinson that he was "a self-made man;" and I might go a step further and say that he was a self-educated man. The only scholastic training he received was in the schools of England prior to the time he was eight years of age ,and six weeks spent when a young man in a private night school. Yet when eight years of age he had read the Bible from cover to cover to his mother who unfortunately lacked this acomplishment, and before his death had accumulated a library second to none in the county and was perhaps the most copious reader in Cedar City, possessing a world of information on nearly every subject. Books were his hobby, and he would deny himself anything else to obtain the works he coveted. Notwithstanding the fact that he had so little schooling he was himself a very successful school teacher for a number of years in Leeds, and it is related of him that his pupils never failed to make rapid progress in their studies. A sequel to this progress may have been found in the ample hickory stick which was never lacking his desk, and was marked "exhibit one." Yet while he was exacting in the discipline within his school, on the playground he never failed to lead the boys in their athletic sports, such as ball, steal-sticks, "old sow" guinnea peg.

Failing health has ripened him for the separation which death must inevitably bring, but has not effaced the recollections of happy days spent with a fond and indulgent parent, who could play as well as work, from the minds of his family.

The funeral services over the remains of Bro. Wilkinson will be held in the Cedar City tabernacle next Sunday afternoon at 2 o'clock.

Washington County News
August 12, 1919

Leeds, Aug 12—An excellent meeting is reported at the regular sacrament services Elders Arthur Paxman and Wm Tobler of Washington were speakers and gave excellent talks

Mrs Elinor Scott and family, Bp and Miss Ruth Stirling went to Newcastle, Monday Bp and Miss Ruth returned Saturday

Mrs Rebecca Angell was called to Cedar City on account of the critical illness of her brother, Joseph Wilkinson.

J. M Moody shipped two hundred crates of peaches to Salt Lake City yesterday.

Iron County Record
August 15, 1919

Mrs. George Angell of Leeds, was in Cedar City last Saturday and Sunday to be present at the obsequies of her brother, Joseph T. Wilkinson.

LEEDS

Mrs Etta Mariger entertained at an informal afternoon party on Saturday The invited guests were Mrs John Kemple and Mrs George Comilley of Good Springs, Nev, Miss Iva and Mrs Margaret Haight of Cedar City, Ruth Stirling, Mrs Hazel McMullin, Mrs Minnie Harris and Mrs Lyle Sullivan of Hurricane, and Dalyce Hartman of Leeds

Arrivals this week and last include John Kemple and family, George Cormelly and family, all of Good Springs, Nev, Charles Harrison of Taylor, Ariz, Mrs Hartley of Hurricane, Mr and Mrs John Farer of Los Angeles, California.

Mrs Francis Hartley left for Los Angeles, in company with her sister, Florence, Tuesday.

Local men are constructing an auto road from Leeds to Silver Reef.

Alex Colbath arrived last night from Salt Lake City

HAND GRENADES FOR SCHOOL

This county has been apportioned 75 hand grenades to be given to the children for the purchase of War Savings Stamps during the 1919 campaign They have been apportioned to the various schools as follows,

Springdale 2, Rockville 2, Grafton 1, Virgin 2, Toquerville 3, La Verkin 2, Hurricane 12, Leeds 2, Washington 6, St George 24, Bloomington 1, Santa Clara 3, Gunlock 2, Veyo 1, Central 1, Pine Valley 1, New Harmony 1, Enterprise 6.

LEEDS

Leeds Sept 30 —Mr and Mrs R S Edwards are residing at the old Silver Reef mining camp where they expect to build soon A group of men have been working on the road to these mines removing boulders, etc

We are fortunate in having Mr Robert miles and Miss Pearl Larson for the Leeds school this year

Mr and Mrs Charles Hansen of Taylor, Arizona, expect to spend the winter in Leeds

Mrs Alice Singleton and Mrs John Tullis are visiting relatives here

THE CROSBY FAMILY OF ST GEORGE— A LIFE SKETCH

Contributed by a family member

The death of Elida Crosby Snow removes the last of the family of Jesse W. Crosby and his wife, Hannah E Baldwin Crosby, who were among the first settlers of St George. The Crosby family has played an important part in the life of Utah, Arizona and Wyoming, and particularly in the history of Washington County

Jesse W Crosby was a native of Novia Scotia and in early life joined the Mormon church in western New York In Nauvoo, Illinois, he met and married Hannah E Baldwin, who had been converted to Mormonism and had left all her people in New Hampshire They came to Salt Lake City with the second company and reached there on the 25th of September, 1847 Jesse W Crosby spent seenteen years of his life preaching Mormonism and his wife Hannah worked very hard to keep the family provided for during the years he was in missionary service His converts numbered well past one thousand and some of them were the most prominent people of Utah In Salt Lake City he was known as the early day molasses maker, so when St George was settled he was selected and sent for that purpose He came in 1861 and in St George his family grew to maturity His oldest son was George H who was an early day sheriff of Washington county and afterwords served as a member of its county court In 1869, just after marrying Sarah Brown, he was sent to be Bishop of the Hebron ward, (now Enterprise), and in 1878 to be Bishop of the Leeds ward In 1886 he moved to Arizona and was later Bishop of two other wards and assisted in the settlement of the Big Horn Basin, Wyoming, returning to St George and dying in 1916 He was the father of fourteen children

Jesse W Crosby, Jr, grew to maturity in St George and there married Sarah Clark He left St George to live by his brother George at Hebron and from there he moved to Panguitch where he became the financial leader of that part of Utah and where he also served as president of the Panguitch stake from 1882 till 1900 He then went to the Big Horn Basin in Wyoming and was the financial backbone of the Mormon colonies there and served for a number of years in the Stake presidency He had two large families and died at Cowley, Wyoming, in February, 1915

The third son was Samuel O Crosby who is remembered in early day musical circles as a leading baritone singer of St George He married Hannah Adelia Bunker who he met at Santa Clara and with her they pioneered Panguitch and Bunkerville, and he was prominent in business, political and ecclesiastical circles. He had a large family of whom seven grew to maturity. He died of blood poison in Panguitch in 1903

The oldest sister of the family was Elida Snow who married Erastus B Snow at St George in the middle seventies Her husband was prominent as an early day missionary in Mexico and together they were prominent in the life of St George He was a member of the Stake presidency for a good many years, and in 1885 helped start the present E B Snow Furniture company He died in 1900 and left Mrs Snow to raise the family and she did it remarkably well and proved an excellent father and mother both She seemed well preserved and her friends expected her to be with them for many years yet when her recent unexpected death came

The other sister was Amelia who married Allen Frost in 1882 They made their home in Kanab until 1887 when they went to Arizona and during the greater part of their time there they lived at Snowflake She was left a widow in 1902 and followed her husband in 1905 as a result of a stroke of apoplexy She left a family of seven children who are still living in and around Snowflake

The two younger brothers were Joseph and Joshua Joseph learned the carpenter trade when a young man and went to Arizona and lived at St Johns for ten years where he sold furniture and carried on a contracting business In 1890 he went to live in Salt Lake City and was killed in a runaway accident in Bingham Canyon in August, 1896 His wife was Maude Johnson, one of the sweetest and most loveable of the earlier St George girls She is now Mrs Maude Knowles of Nephi, Utah They had a family of eight children of whom six survived the father.

Joshua Alma Crosby knew no other home but S George In boyhood he came to love Lena Mathis whom he married in 1884 They made their home at the old Crosby home in St George and there he died twenty-five years later, leaving a family of eleven children who are well known in this community. He was one of St George s substantial citizens and left an impress on the town history and a remarkably good family

But it is around the dear old mother who lived in St George from 1861 till 1907—forty-six years, that the love of this branch of the Crosby family clustered, and while she lived the old house was a shrine It is hard for the Crosby descendants to believe that there was any dearer woman in all Utah's life than was she Her last thirty ears were spent in temple work in which she took a deep interest

President Joseph F Smith often remarked that Jesse W Crosby, Sr, was the hardest worker he ever knew His children followed in his footsteps and were hustlers in business life or as farmers or as ecclesiasts and now the last of the family has gone Of each it may be said that life was lived to a purpose, they have done their parts well and although their lives are ended, their history lives on

Leeds, Oct 14 —R L Edwards, general manager of the Silver Reef Mining company is in Salt Lake for a few days attending to business

Charles Hansen and family with Mrs Minnie Harris motored to Parowan where they spent a few days visiting relatives

The new home of Oscar McMullin has been completed with modern equipment throughout

Bishop B Y. MacMullin has returned to his home from a visit in Salt Lake City

Claus Anderson is a visitor here for a few days

Leeds, Oct 28 —We were fortunate in having two good speakers in meeting here Sunday Mrs McGreggor and Dr Cox Dr Cox gave an efficient talk on the life of former President Roosevelt and told many things about his life which we had not known before Indeed we prize the memory of this great man Mrs McGreggor spoke to the point saying we must live our religion not only profess, but above all practice it in our every days " She also said "we must gain more spiritually if we would progress '

Mr. Crane, geologist from Eureka, has been here several days looking over the mining possibilities in this district

Mutual officers were appointed Sunday and the first mutual service for this year was held Sunday night

Bishop Sterling has returned from Ogden having delivered a car load of hogs in that city.

Washington County News
November 4, 1919

Leeds, Nov 4 —Mrs Minnie Harris is leaving Leeds to spend the winter in Salt Lake Mrs Harris has been a faithful worker in this ward and we regret that she is leaving us

Bishop B Y MacMullin is having his home remodeled and a sleeping porch built on His son Lawrence is home from Idaho where he has spent the summer.

Matt Weeks has returned to Leeds to spend the winter. He has been working on his gold mine at Stateline during the summer months,

Edward MacMullin and J. W. Woodbury are home from a hunting trip having bagged a deer apeice

Washington County News
November 18, 1919

Leeds, Nov. 18 —Charles Hánsen is building an addition to the Harris home He expects to reside here with his family this winter and has just purchased a new truck

R S Edwards and Mr Wandel left for a business visit to Salt Lake City this morning

The farmers here have a goodly supply of sorghum from their cane this year.

Sam Williams is here looking over mining interests

Washington County News
December 2, 1919

Leeds, Dec. 2 —A school entertainment was given in the Leeds hall The children gave a very good program of recitations and the Leeds quartet sang two songs The entertainment was followed by a dance

Charles Hansen has returned with a new Ford truck

Mr. Lyons is visiting Tom Sterling here.

Leeds, Dec 15—We have been without water the last few days owing to a leak in the dam   The men folks are busy trying to repair it

Thé Milne Bros of St George are repapering and painting the home of B Y McMullin   A little paint wouldn't hurt the rest of us

Mr. and Mrs R L Edwards, Mrs Daisy Nicholes and Miss Pearl Larson were business visitors in St. George last week.

Mrs E C. Olsen returned today from Hurricane where she has been visiting her daughter, Mrs W. D Sullivan

Bishop David Stirling and Willard McMullin returned from St George where they attended stake conference

Floyd, the little son of Mr. and Mrs Edward McMullin has been quite sick but is on the improve

Mrs Leonard Dalton of Cedar City is here visiting her parents Mr and Mrs Geo E Angell

R C Savage with his family has moved to town for the winter.   We need more like him

Mr and Mrs D Estill of Boonville, are the guests of Mr. and Mrs Frank Hartley

Primary commenced last Friday after being discontinued for some length of time

Sam Williams was in St George last week on business

C F. Hansen has been to Lund on business.

Leeds, Dec 23—Miss Mary Elizabeth Edwards of Salt Lake is visiting with her parents, Mr. and Mrs A. L. Edwards.

The school gave an entertainment last Friday which was very good.

Robert Miles has returned to his home in St George to spend the holidays

Robert P McMullin has been to Lund and returned with a new car

There was quite a number of Leeds people in St George Monday.

Mr and Mrs Dee Estill are in Washington visiting Mrs Jolley.

Mr and Mrs Don Fuller were in Hurricane last Saturday.

Mr. and Mrs Haight of Cedar were in town yesterday

David Stirling and H. A Jolley are in St George today.

Mr. and Mrs P. E Harris of Kanab are in town

Joe Stirling has a new house on his homestead

Sam Williams has gone to Salt Lake City.

E C Olsen has had his home painted

Clyde McMullin is home for a while

J. M. Moody of St. George is in town

Washington County News
December 30, 1919

Leeds, Dec 30 —Miss Valla Angell has returned from Randolph and Salt Lake where she has been the past few months.

Visitors from St George were Mr. and Mrs Harold Snow, Benny Hopkins and Mr and Mrs Milton Moody

The M I A has been a great success this winter with a splendid attendance

Mr. and Mrs Max McMullin are home again after being absent for some time

The young people went to St George and Hurricane for Christmas night

Mrs Thomas Stirling has gone to California to be treated for rheumatism

Hazel Moody and Mrs E C Olsen were in Hurricane Sunday.

Mrs Ellen Sullivan of Hurricane spent the week end here

Miss Ada Harris has been quite ill but is feeling better

A party of young folks spent Monday in Zion Canyon.

Clifford McMullin has purchased a new car.

Robert McMullin has put in a new gasoline tank

Ella Batty of Toquerville is in town.

Leeds, Jan 6 — Mrs C C Anderson has returned from California where she spent the holidays

Mr and Mrs Milton Moody have returned to St George after spending the holidays here.

Mrs W. D Sullivan of Hurricane spent the week end here with her parents

Edith and Clyde McMullin have gone back to St George to attend school

Wm Hartman has gone to Good Springs, Nev, to find employment

Robert Miles has returned from St George to continue his school.

We were surprised to find snow on the ground this morning

The Misses Libbie and Ruth Stirling have gone to Enterprise

Dee Estill has returned to his home in Boonville, Calif

Last Saturday a party was given for the married folks

Francis Leany is home after being absent for some time

Miss Reah Sullivan spent last week in St George

Max McMullin has gone to his home in Nevada

Miss Ethel Isom of Hurricane was here Saturday.

Leeds, Jan 13 — A shower was given Mrs C C Anderson at the home of I S McMullin Saturday evening

Mrs B D Estill has gone to Hurricane to visit her grandmother, Mrs Hartley

The stockholders of the canning factory held a meeting here yesterday.

Miss Mary E. Edwards has returned to her home in Salt Lake.

Some of the school children are bothered with sore eyes.

Born, a son to Mr. and Mrs. Edward McMullin, Jan 9.

Leeds Jan 20 —Miss Pearl Perkins of Taylor, Ariz, is here visiting her sister, Mrs C F Hansen

Word has been received here that Mrs S A Harris, who is now living in S L C is seriously ill

Afton, the baby daughter of Mr and Mrs A P Olsen, received a terrible burn on the hand

Ellen Sullivan has been here visiting her parents, Mr and Mrs David McMullin

Misses Gladys Taylor and Emma Seegmiller of St George spent Sunday here

A party of young folks spent Saturday at the hot springs near La Verkin

Geo E Angell has been to Hurricane and has returned with a new car

Miss Ethel McMullin is home after spending some time in Seattle, Wash

R C Savage and family spent the week end in Toquerville

Mrs Wm Sullivan of Hurricane spent the week end here

The Primary gave a dance which was very successful

Jos Stirling returned from St George today.

Mrs Reita McMullin has gone to Moapa, Nev.

The Milne Bros of St George are in town

The Stirling home is being repaired.

Leeds, Jan 27 —Mrs Margaret Hartley has gone to Moapa, Nev, where she was called to care for her daughter, who is seriously ill

Misses Reah Sullivan and Fay Stirling spent several days in St George last week

Mrs Richard Williams left this morning for some point in the state of Washington

Harvey Ross of Salt Lake was here Saturday visiting his sister, Mrs Eva Savage

Mrs Hazel Moody of St George was here several days last week

Mrs B D Estill left for her home in Boonville, Cal, yesterday.

Joseph Leavitt has returned to his home at Joseph City.

Mrs Belle Jolley has been to St George on business.

Leeds has gone dry once more The dam is broken

Clinton Fuller is home from Good Springs, Nevada

Mr and Mrs Harold Snow spent Sunday here

Wilard McMullin is home from St George

Washington County News
February 3, 1920

Leeds, Feb 3.—School has been discontinued on account of the flu. We have one case here

Mr. and Mrs Leonard Dalton of Cedar City are here visiting friends and relatives

Mrs Thos Stirling is home from California where she has been for her health

Edith and Clyde McMullin are home from St George

Mrs D C Olsen has returned from Cedar City.

Dr Tolhurst of Salt Lake is in town

Iron County Record
February 6, 1920

DIXIE POWER LINE MAN MEETS DEATH

Touches Live Wire With Hand and Falls on Rock Embankment 25 Feet Below.

William Baxter, an employe of the Dixie Power Co., met death last Friday through falling from an electric light pole. He had been putting a fuse in a transformer some little distance from the plant and had just started to descent the pole when he touched a live wire with one of his hands, causing him to fall backwards. He fell about twenty-five feet and landed on a rock embankment, striking it with his face, breaking both jaws, a leg and causing other great injuries. This happened about ten a. m. and the unfortunate man survived his terrible injuries until 1:20 p. m. the same day. He did not recover consciousness. The remains were brought to this city.

William Baxter was born at Silver Reef, this county, 42 years ago last April. His mother, Mrs. Eliza Le Baron, is living somewhere in California and could not get here in time for the funeral. His wife died about a year ago. Two sisters are also living in California, and another sister, Mrs. Ella Oxburrow, who lives at Lund, Nevada, was at the funeral. His father died several years ago. He is survived by three sons, Fred, 18 years old, David 16, and Albert 12.

William Bazter was a man who was highly respected, honest, industrious and upright in all his dealings.— Washington County News.

Leeds, Feb 17 —Rodney Leany who is in the training camp in Texas is seriously ill

Mrs Margaret Hartley is home after spending some time at Moapa Nev

C C Anderson stopped here a few days on his way to Pioche Nevada

Mr and Mrs Leonard Dalton have gone to their home in Cedar City

Mrs Frank Sullivan of Hurricane spent last week here

Randolph Andrus of Washington was in town today

Karl McMullin has gone to St Thomas, Nev

R L Edwards has returned from Salt Lake

Cleo Sullivan has returned from Lund

After another serious interruption in the electrical service, the power being off all day Saturday until evening. The Record is going to press more than 24 hours late. At the same time, it appears that the Power company is doing everything possible to locate and correct the trouble, but the condition of the roads and the inadequate telephone service supplied at the plant end of their line, are serious handicaps. From present appearances the service will not be free from these interruptions until the line is completed between Kanarra and Leeds, the poles for which are already up.

Washington County News
February 26, 1920

Leeds, Feb 26 — Mrs Thos Stirling is troubled again with rheumatism

Dr Tolhurst is here He has just returned from St Thomas, Nev

Mr. and Mrs A P. Olsen were in Cedar City last week on business

Geo E Angell is having some repairing done about his home

Mrs Hazel Moody of St George was in Cedar last week

Mrs Donald Fuller has been quite ill but is recovering

Marguarite McMullin was in St George last week

Washington County News
March 9, 1920

Leeds, Mar 9 — Mrs C. C. Anderson has just returned from Bloomington where she has been visiting her parents She will leave here tomorrow for Pioche, Nev, to join her husband.

'Meg, The Outcast" was staged here Saturday night by Toquerville Bee Hive girls It was very good.

Miss Eythel McMullin has taken Mrs. C. C Anderson's position as primary school teacher.

Harold Snow and Ben Hopkins stopped here on their way to Cedar City from St George

Mark McMullin of Cedar spent the week end here Frank McMullin returned with him.

Robert Miles, our school principal, spent the week end in St George

The Southern Utah Bee and Honey Co has commenced work here again

Ammon Jolley has had some repairing done about his home

Mr. and Mrs Edward McMullin were in St George Saturday.

George E Angell and family are in Cedar visiting relatives.

David Stirling is in Cedar City on important business

Born, a son to Mr. and Mrs Clifford McMullin.

R C. Savage and family are in Toquerville.

Leeds, March. 16—The men folks have spent the past two days cleaning up our streets. They certainly are doing fine work

Several of the young people attended the theater given by the D N C Juniors at Hurricane It was very good

David Spilsbury of Toquerville attended our M. I A Sunday evening He gave us a very interesting talk

Miss Callie McAllister who is teaching school at La Verkin spent the week end here

The M. I. A. is planning a trip up Zion canyon We hope our plans are carried out

C F. Hansen took a car load of people to St George to attend conference

Mr and Mrs Craine of Salt Lake are here in the interest of the Silver Reef

Frank Hamilton of Cedar was in town Monday.

The water is being piped to the school grounds

Miss Ada Harris has gone to La Verkin

Mrs. E. C Olsen is in St George.

Leeds, Mar 31—A M I A dance was given Friday evening under the direction of R C Savage, Eythel McMullin and Mrs Edwin Dalton They certainly did well in entertaining the town We hope they are called on again soon

Dr Steiner and Atty Dalby were here Saturday on the State Educational campaign We certainly enjoyed their talk and wish they were coming again

Wilma, the baby of Mr and Mrs Wm Hartman, had her arm badly hurt some time ago It was thrown out of place and fractured

Visitors to Hurricane Tuesday were Mr and Mrs C F. Hansen, Pearl Perkins and Mr, and Mrs Edward McMullin

Dellas Sullivan returned home Saturday from St George where he has been under the doctor's care

Edyth and Clyde McMullin who are staying in St George this winter spent the week end here

Mining men who have been looking over Silver Reef returned to Salt Lake yesterday.

The electric power men are busy putting up the wires through town

Misses Fay Stirling and Margaret Savage went to Toquerville Tuesday

Francis Hartley is having a new fence erected in front of his home

Miss Ada Harris who is staying at La Verkin spent Sunday here

Leeds, April 6 —The Schmutz family of St George and Mrs Wm Sullivan of Hurricane were the guests of Mr and Mrs E C Olsen Easter Sunday

Mrs Geo E Angell returned home Saturday from Salt Lake City where she has been visiting her children

Mrs R L Edwards is in St George where she expects to remain for a short time

Mrs John Jenkins of Alamo, Nev, is here visiting her daughter, Mrs Wm Hartman

R L Edwards, Alex Colbath and Mr Worth left this morning for Salt Lake City

John Lavanger of Glendale spent Friday with Mr. and Mrs Edward McMullin

Miss Eythel McMullin and Robert Miles spent the week end in St George

Wilford Cox of Delta is here visiting his aunt, Mrs Thomas Stirling

Mr and Mrs. W D Sullivan and family spent Sunday in Hurricane

Mrs W. D Sullivan left this morning for Salt Lake City.

Dan McMullin went to Cedar last Thursday on business

Our peaches, apricots and almonds are all frozen.

F C. Hansen left here yesterday for Lund.

Leeds, Apr. 14 —Karl McMullin returned from Good Springs, Nev, yesterday where he has been employed

William Hartman was called home from Good Springs, Nev, on account of his son, Merwin, who is very ill with appendicitis

A basket dance was given Tuesday evening which was a great success Several young people came up from Washington.

Misses Callie McAllister and Ada Harris came over from La Verkin to attend the dance.

Levon McQuaid had the misfortune to break his arm while trying to crank a car.

Mr. and Mrs C. W. Angell have gone to Salt Lake to spend the summer.

Glen Olsen left this morning for Pioche, Nev, to get employment

Mrs B Y McMullin spent the week end in St. George.

Washington County News
April 20, 1920

Leeds, April 20 —Mrs J P. Jenkens and granddaughter, Arlean Stewart, have returned to Alamo, Nev, after spending some time here with Mr. and Mrs Wm Hartman

Evan Sullivan of this place is quite sick with pneumonia He was taken ill at Hurricane

Mr and Mrs. Clifford McMullin and William Hartman have been to St. George on business.

Karl and Hazel McMullin and Lizzie McQuaid were business visitors at Hurricane Tuesday.

Mrs Harold Snow of St George is here visiting her sister, Mrs. Edward McMullin.

Lawrence McMullin, Joseph and Delbert Stirling are at Piercen flat planting crops.

Mat Wicks is slowly recovering from a very serious case of pneumonia.

Mrs A Hunt of St George is the guest of Mrs La Venia Fuller.

Mrs Bual of Stateline is here on business.

Willard McMullin left Monday for Salt Lake City.

Washington County News
May 5, 1920

Leeds, May 5 —Rodney Leany, our youngest soldier, who has been training in Texas returned home Sunday Rodney was a volunteer and spent a year in training While in camp he had flu followed by pneumonia He is feeling fine now and we are certainly glad to have him back

Mrs Minnie Harris and family returned from Salt Lake Tuesday where they spent the winter.

Mrs R L Edwards is in St. George Mr Edwards left this morning for Salt Lake City.

Mrs Ellen Sullivan of Hurricane is here visiting her parents, Mr. and Mrs David McMullin

Misses Jessie Averett and Emma Atkin of Washington spent Monday and Tuesday here

Twin boys were born April 29, to Mr. and Mrs Elbert Parker.

Irvin and Alton Parker of Joseph, Utah, are in town.

Leeds, May 12.—Those attending ' The Beggar Student" in St. George were Mr. and Mrs. Edwin Dalton, Mr and Mrs Edward McMullin, Mrs. Claire Hansen and Miss Evelyn Savage They report having a very good time and all say the opera was fine. Good for the D. N. C.!

Mr. and Mrs Wm Hartman left yesterday with their son, Merwin for the St. George hospital where he will be operated on for appendicitis.

Week end visitors to St George were. Tom and Miss Fay Stirling. Lawrence McMullin and Delbert Stirling.

Ben Hopkins of Glendale stopped here on his way to St George to get his son who has been attending the D. N. C.

Misses Libbie and Ruth Stirling are home from Enterprise where the latter has been teaching school

Tom Conley and Louis Harris of Good Springs, Nev, stopped here Monday night.

Edyth and Clyde McMullin are home again after spending the winter in St. George.

School closed last Friday with a walk in the afternoon and a dance in the evening.

The members of the M. I A will spend the 15th in Zion canyon.

Mr. and Mrs Milton Moody of St. George are here on business

Ross Angell left here Saturday morning for Salt Lake City,

Mrs E C Olsen is in Cedar under the doctor's care

Miss Reah Sullivan is in Hurricane visiting relatives.

Mrs. E. C. Olsen of Leeds returned home Thursday after spending some time with her daughter, Mrs. H. P. Haight of this place. Mrs. Olsen was taking medical treatment from a local physician while here.

Leeds, June 2 —Elders Jos T Atkin and Melvin M Harmon of St George were home missionaries here Sunday They gave us some very interesting talks and we hope they will come again

Mrs D O Beal left here Sunday for New York City where she will join her husband

Mrs Joseph Jolley of Washington is here visiting her daughter, Mrs Frank Hartley.

Bert Harris arrived here Monday after spending the winter in Salt Lake City

Ward Jolley returned home Monday after spending some time in Cedar City

A party of young people attended the dance at Hurricane Saturday evening

Mrs. H. A Jolley has been to New Harmony visiting relatives and friends

George E Angell and family spent Sunday in New Harmony visiting

Lawrence McMullin was a business visitor to Hurricane Monday

Frank McMullin left for Salt Lake City Monday on business.

Leeds, June 9 —Rudolph Miller of Salt Lake City is here visiting his grandparents, Mr and Mrs Oscar McMullin

Mr and Mrs Edwin Dalton and Miss Margaret Savage left here Monday for Salt Lake City

Mrs Lyle Sullivan of Hurricane is here visiting her parents Mr and Mrs E C Olsen

Mrs Sam Mortenson of Parowan is here visiting her mother, Mrs Andrea Hansen

Miles Miller of the Southern Utah Bee and Honey Co is back again

Frank Weaver and Othal Judd of Washington were in own Sunday

Mrs Isom of Hurricane is the guest of Mrs Thomas Stirling

Joe and Delbert Stirling left this morning for Joe's ranch

Miss Ada Harris is here from La Verkin for a short visit

Mr and Mrs Milton Moody left Sunday for Cedar City

Leeds, June 23 —Leland Sullivan of this place and Miss Lola Ballard of Hurricane were married at St George, June 21 The groom is the son of Mr and Mrs Wm Sullivan, the bride the daughter of Mr and Mrs James Ballard A reception was given last evening at the home of the groom well attended by all Several relatives and friends came from Hurricane and St George Ice cream and cake were served and a very enjoyable time was had

No meetings were held here Sunday on account of so many of our people attending stake conference at Hurricane.

Mrs E C Olsen has gone to Hurricane to visit her daughter, Mrs Wm Sullivan, Jr

Mrs Herbert Haight returned to her home at Cedar City Sunday.

Mr and Mrs Miles Miller of Beaver are here

SILVER REEF LOOKING UP

B. Y. McMullin of Leeds was a business visitor here Wednesday. Mr. McMullin says a small force of men have started work at the famous old Silver Reef and are preparing the property to again open up the field. He thinks the field will soon be again to the front as responsible people are at the helm.

Washington County News
July 7, 1920

Leeds, July 7 —Mrs E. C. Olsen returned home Sunday from Hurricane where she has been visiting her daughter, Mrs W. D. Sullivan.

A fine celebration was given Monday under the direction of the Sunday school superintendency.

Harry Bringhurst and family of Toquerville spent the Fourth of July here.

Karl and Lawrence McMullin went to Washington Monday evening

Alex Cobath has gone to Salt Lake City on business.

Several men are here repairing the telephone line.

Charles Wright left for Cedar this morning

Washington County News
July 13, 1920

Leeds, July 13 —Mrs. Ernest Nelson and Mrs. Leila Atkin of St. George were here Thursday in the interest of the Primary. They held a meeting at the home of Mrs. Hazel McMullin, giving us some very interesting instructions We certainly appreciate their visit and hope they will come again

Willie, Laurence and Karl McMullin made a trip to Washington Sunday evening, while David Stirling and Wilford Leany went to Hurricane

Wm Nicholls with his daughter, Miss Wanda, have gone to Zion national park on business

Miss Anna Hopkins of Glendale is here visiting her sister, Mrs. Ed. McMullin.

The Bee Hive girls went on a hike Thursday up Quail creek

Washington County News
July 20, 1920

Leeds July 20 —— Mr and Mrs Chas Angell returned home from Salt Lake City where they spent several months

Clyde and Bernice Miller of Salt Lake City are here visiting their grandparents, Mr. and Mrs Oscar McMullin

William Hartman returned home Monday from Nevada where he has been employed.

Mrs Harold Snow of St George has been here visiting her sister, Mrs Ed McMullin

A fine program is being planned for Pioneer day Everybody is invited

Mrs Elenor Scott was a business visitor to St George yesterday.

Mr and Mrs William Sullivan and family spent Sunday here.

Bert Harris came home from Parowan Saturday.

Washington County News
July 27, 1920

Leeds, July 27 —— Mr and Mrs Ed McMullin, Mr and Mrs John Lavanger, Mr and Mrs Harold Snow and Miss Anna Hopkins went to Zion canyon Sunday

Mr and Mrs Frank Sullivan returned to their home in Hurricane today after spending some time here

A crowd of young people left this morning for the mountain where they expect to fish

Irving Isom of Hurricane and Miss Gene McAllister of St George spent Monday here

The Bee Hive girls spent Thursday afternoon in the swimming pool at La Verkin

Ward Jolley is home again after spending some time in the Cedar garage

Wilford Leany was a business visitor to St George Monday

Mr and Mrs Victor Angell of Salt Lake City are here

Leeds, Aug 3 —The Bee Hive girls were entertained Tuesday at the home of Mrs Lizzie McQuaid Refreshments were served and a very enjoyable time had

Alex Colbath and F. H Ball returned to Salt Lake City on business

Ward Jolley and Reed Fuller left for Cedar City Monday

A crowd of young folks went to Washington Sunday, Miss Ida Jolley returning with them

Misses Jessie Averett and Emma Atkin motored from Washington Friday evening

Clifford McMullin has returned from Nevada where he has been employed

Loren Higbee of Toquerville was a business visitor here Monday

U. S MARSHAL'S SALE

IN THE DISTRICT COURT OF THE UNITED STATES, DISTRICT OF UTAH.

Silver Reef Consolidated Mining company, a corporation,
Plaintiff,

vs

The Brundage Mining and Reduction company, a corporation,
Defendant

NOTICE

To be sold at United States Marshal's Sale on the 14 day of August, 1920, at the front door of the Washington County Court House in St George, Utah

The following described mining claims situate, lying and being in Harrisburg Mining District, Washington County, Utah to-wit

The Tecumseh Lode Mining Claim, U S Lot No 40,

The Pride of the West Lode Mining Claim, U S Lot No 41,

The Walker Lode Mining Claim, U. S Lot No 42,

The Barbee Lode Mining Claim, U S Lot No 43,

The Silver Flat Lode Mining Claim, U S Lot No 45;

The Silver Point Lode Mining Claim, U S Lot No 49,

The Chloride Chief Lode Mining Claim, U S Lot No 50,

The Silver Crown Lode Mining Claim, U S Lot No 51,

The Maggie Lode Mining Claim, U. S Lot No 52;

The Jumbo and Wonder Lode Mining Claims, U S Mineral Survey, No 4807A;

The Wonder and Brundage Mining and reduction Company Millsites, U S Mineral Survey No 4807B,

Also 29¼ feet of the Leeds Water Company, a corporation of Utah,

Also all of Lot 4, Block 7, of the Harrisburg townsite Survey, Washington County, Utah.

Dated this 13 day of July, 1920.

Aquila Nebeker,

United States Marshal for the District of Utah

By D S Dorrity, Jr,

j15a5
Deputy.

Washington County News
August 10, 1920

Leeds, Aug 10 —Delbert Stirling and Stanley Fuller came Sunday with some loads of lumber for Silver Reef

Mrs Elinor Scott and her three children left Tuesday for Illinois expecting to be gone about a month visiting her mother-in law

Alex McFarlane and Lorin Miles of St George are here looking after the cattle on the range

Arthur Webb and family of La Verkin were Sunday visitors of R C Savage and family.

Miss Ida Jolley returned home Wednesday to Washington after visiting friends here

Francis Hartley and his two sons, Louis and Calvert have gone to their ranch on Kolob

Mr and Mrs R L Edwards and children were in St George Monday on business

Harold Snow of St George is the guest of Edward and Mrs Edward McMullin

Mr and Mrs J L Sevey were visiting friends here Thursday

J W Hartman came home Tuesday from southern Nevada

Mrs B Y McMullin left Thursday for Salt Lake City to visit

Ward Jolley returned home Sunday from Cedar City.

Milton Moody came home Sunday from Cedar

Iron County Record
August 13, 1920

Many Patients Lose Appendixes

A near epidemic of appendicitis is on in Cedar. Last week Wilford Bergstrom was operated on and this week Dr. Macfarlane has removed three troublesome appendixes, those of Ray Robinson of Paragonah, Miss Evelyn Prothero of the same place, and Mr. Fuller of Leeds who has been employed here by U. T. Jones.

Other operations at the hospital this week are, one on Mrs. F. M. Fuller of Kanab for abdominal trouble, and on Mrs. Andrew Olsen of Glendale for the same sort of trouble.

Dr. G. W. Middleton is due to arrive in Cedar tomorrow to do some operating for goitre. After doing what work of this sort there is in Cedar, he will go into Dixie to do some of the same sort of work .

Leeds, August 17.—Word has been received here that Reed Fuller was operated on at Cedar City for appendicitis

Mr and Mrs Naegle of Toquerville spent Sunday afternoon with R C Savage and family. R C Savage arrived Wednesday from Salt Lake City

Evan Sullivan returned home Monday from Weston, Idaho, where he has been working for about three months

Alex Colbath and friend arrived here Saturday and left Monday for Zion canyon

Delbert Stirling and Stanley Fuller have gone to Beaver for freight.

Mrs John Tullis of Newcastle is here visiting friends and relatives

Wallace McMullin is here visiting his mother, Mrs David McMullin

Bishop Parker, of Joseph, is here visiting his son, J E Parker

R L Edwards and family left Monday for Salt Lake City.

J. W Hartman left Friday for Lund

OBITUARY

Funeral services over the remains of Pearl Larson Anderson, who died at Salt Lake City Aug 18 following an operation for childbirth, were held in the Tabernacle last Saturday, Bishop James McArthur conducting The speakers were Pres D H Cannon, Pres Edw H Snow and Bishop McArthur, each of whom spoke of the exemplary life of the departed sister The singing was beautiful The casket was covered with a pro-fusion of beautiful flowers and wreaths, some of which were brought from Leeds, where deceased taught school for some time Interment was made in the city cemetary.

Pearl Larson Anderson was a daughter of Mr and Mrs L J and Olena M P. Larson of Bloomington; born at Bloomington Utah, Nov 18, 1894 She graduated from the Richfield high school and attended the B Y U in 1914 She taught school at Fruita, Wayne Co, 1914-15, at Bicknell., Wayne Co, 1915-16; at Bloomington 1916-18, and at Leeds 1917-20 She also clerkd at the Petty Merc Co store and Hurricane Drug store at Hurricane She was married to Claus Childera Anderson of Beaver City, Dec 17, 1919, and is survived by her husband, parents, and the following brothers and sisters Mrs G H Fullerton of St. George, Aaron, Willard, Reuben, Charles, LeRoy, Ellis, Mrs A A Carpenter, and Miss Beth all of Bloomington, and Mrs. E. L. King, of Salt Lake City.

CENSUS, WASHINGTON COUNTY, 1920

Minor Civil Division	1920	1910	1900
Washington County.	6,764	5,123	4,612
Bloomington precinct	48	50	75
Central precinct	121	110	
Enterprise precinct, including Enterprise town	*	350	100
Grafton precinct	46	106	98
Gunlock precinct	115	112	100
Harmony precinct	157	105	119
Hurricane precinct coextensive with Hurricane town,	1,021	866	*
La Verkin precinct	173	120	*
Leeds precinct	211	148	248
Pine Valley precinct.	*	113	251
Pinto precinct	*	89	100
Rockville precinct	208	189	214
St George precinct, including St George city	2,271	1,769	1,600
Santa Clara precinct, including Santa Clara town	*	293	358
Springdale precinct	204	186	144
Toquerville precinct, including Toquerville town	*	314	307
Veyo precinct	79		
Virgin precinct	212	136	269
Washington precinct, including Washington city	464	465	529
Shivwits Indian Reservation	68	97	
Hebron precinct			100
Incorporated places	**1920**	**1910**	**1900**
Enterprise town	*		
Hurricane town	1,021		
St George City	2,215	1,737	1,600
Santa Clara town	*		
Toquerville town	*		
Washington city	200	424	529

* Not returned separately.

LEANY-LE BARON

Mr Wilford Leany and Miss Leota Le Baron were married in the St George temple Wednesday, Sept 1

The bride is a daughter of Mr and Mrs B F Le Baron of Hurricane, a charming young lady who is very highly regarded by a large circle of friends in her home town and elsewhere The groom is a son of Mr and Mrs Hyrum Leany of Leeds, an exemplary young man who stands high as a citizen and is possessed of excellant qualities

The news joins their many friends in all good wishes

Looks as if the old mining camp, Silver Reef is going to be active once more There is a large force working in the mines and they are getting out some very fine ore The boarding house is now running and the shift boss, Mr Doyle is here

Leeds, Sept 21 —The grandchildren of Mrs Oscar McMullin, Rudolph, Clyde, and Bernice Miller left for their home in Salt Lake City after spending the summer here

Mrs J White and sister-in-law, Miss Ella White 'eft for their home in Salt Lake City after spending some time here

Mr and Mrs B Y McMullin and son Willard took Miss Ada Harris to St George where she underwent an operation

J. M Wicks is back from Cedar and Stateline where he has been for his health and is very much improved

Milton Moody and wife have gone to St George to spend the winter Mr Moody is teaching school there

School started here on the 16th inst with Mrs Minnie Harris and George Miles as teachers

Mrs Elenor Scott has returned home from Illinois where she spent a six weeks' vacation

George Miles returned Sunday from a trip to St George.

Reed Fuller returned home Sunday from a peddling trip

STIRLING-ISOM

Mr David Stirling and Miss Ethel Isom were married in the St George temple today

The bride is a daughter of Mr and Mrs Thomas Isom a young lady who is very highly respected in her home town The groom is the bishop of Leeds, a young man of sterling good character and estimable qualities

The News joins their many friends in congratulations.

Washington County News
September 28, 1920

Leeds, Sept 28 —The latter part of July a number of the parents of our town met and organized a Parents club for the purpose of taking a course in child training and to handle any subject that might come before them for the betterment of our children   The books to be studied were "Practical Child Training " We now have our little club permanently organized and are receiving the benefits of it   Through the club we have a 9th grade in our school and are reaching out for extension work from the Dixie college, State university and Branch Agricultural college and have taken over the work of the Parents-Teachers association

Iron County Record
October 1, 1920

Bishop B. Y. McMullen of Leeds has been in Cedar City a few days this week locating his daughter Ethel and son Clyde for the winter. The children will attend the B. A. C. Bishop McMullen says that Leeds and vicinity sees a big future ahead in the growing activity of the mining company at Silver Reef, where a power line is being run to furnish energy for the mining machinery to be installed.

Washington County News
October 7, 1920

Mrs Jennie Naegle spent the week end visiting at Leeds

Leeds, Oct 12 —The Silver Con have their new hoist on the ground at the old Leeds mine Morgan Anderson the electrician is now putting in the transformer on the company ground and expects to have the hoist in running order soon

A dance was given on October 5, at Silver Reef for the opening of the boarding house The Dixie band furnished the music Cake, ice cream and coffee were served and a good time was had by all The dance was given by Alex Colbath.

Mr and Mrs Joseph Worthen of Salt Lake City are here visiting Mrs Worthen's parents, Mr. and Mrs B Y. McMullin

Edwin Dalton returned home Saturday from St George after leaving Mrs Dalton under the doctor's care

Andrew Gregerson who has been spending a few days in Silver Reef left today for his home in St George

Alex Colbath, Mr and Mrs Lewis and Mrs Lewis' sister left this morning for Salt Lake City on business.

Mr. and Mrs Wm Sullivan and family of Hurricane were Sunday visitors here

The miners have opened up some nice streaks of ore in the old mines

Born, Sept 28, a son to Mr. and City Mrs. W. S Nicholls.

Mrs Leland Sullivan is visiting her folks in Hurricane.

Leeds, Oct 26 —The hoist is installed and the gallice frame is up at the Leeds mine   Everything is ready now to start to hoist as soon as they get the electricity

Mr. and Mrs Leonard Dalton have movd back to Leeds from Lyndyll, Utah, where they have been for some time

Mr. and Mrs David Stirling went to Cedar City Saturday to take Mis Alice Singleton; they returned Saturday

Mrs. G E Porter and family has returned home again   She has been visiting in Salt Lake and Ogden

Mrs Alice Singleton has returned to her home in Springville, Utah, after spending the summer here

Mr and Mrs Francis Hartley and children, Roy and Thelma, returned home Saturday from Kolob

Margaret McMullin has returned home from Hurricane where she has been for some time

W J. Hartman has returned home to visit a few days   He has been employed at Lund

W G McMullin went to St George Sunday and returned home with a player piano

Mr and Mrs Milton Moody have returned to their home in St George

Veir McMullin and George Olsen were Tuesday visitors in St George

Miss Audrey Angell of Hurricane is here visiting Mrs Donald Fuller,

CERTIFICATES FOR SOLDIERS

The State of Utah has had engraved certificates made for each of the boys who served in the World War. They are of large size suitable for framing, and each certificate has the name of the soldier for whom it is intended on it

The certificates for the Washington county soldier boys have been sent to Lester Keate Post No 90, and the secretary, Lorin C Miles, is ready to deliver them on application

All certificates not delivered by the end of November must be returned, so it is important that the soldiers named in the following list make application before that time

Abbott, Israel	St. George
Adair, Josiah H .	Enterprise
Adams, Claude,	Washington
Alexander, Samuel L	Washington
Alger, Willard . .	Enterprise
Anderson, Walter H .	Toquerville
Andrus, Lee .	St George
Andrus, Moses W .	St George
Angell, Charles W. . .	Leeds
Angell, Victor . .	Leeds
Asplin, Charles S.	St. George
Atkin, John P	St. George
Atkin, Levi	St George
Atkin, Richard Henry	St George
Atkin, William T . .	St George
Averett, John W . .	Washington
Baker, Andrew W. . .	Central
Ballard, Afton . . .	Grafton
Ballard, D Thatcher .	Hurricane
Ballard, David Waldon	Hurricane
Ballard, Sheridan . .	Grafton
Barnum, William T. .	Enterprise
Beckstrom, Dilworth .	Pine Valley
Beebe, Edgar	Hurricane
Beebe, Fay H . .	Hurricane
Beebe, Franklin F. .	Hurricane
Beebe, Leroy A . .	Hurricane
Bentley, Arthur R . .	St George
Bentley, Mathew M . .	St George
Bigelow, Moroni M . .	St. George
Blair, Ethel	St. George
Blair, Tarlton	St. George
Booth, James Kay. . .	St George
Bradshaw, David Burr	Hurricane
Jacobson, Alma H . .	Pine Valley
James, Wilkes Elton	Nada
Jennings, George S	Rockville
Jennings, Otto M	Rockville
Jolley, James W .	Washington
Johnson, Charles R .	St George
Johnson, Edward R	Heber City
Jones, Alvin . .	Rockville
Jones, Clarence A	Veyo
Jones, Ellis W .	Veyo
Judd, Frank .	St George
Keate, Daniel Lester . .	St George
Keate, James .	Enterprise
Keate, Julius R.	St George
Kemp, Milo . .	St George
Keate, Neal D	St George
Kleinman, George .	Toquerville
LaBaron, Grover C	Hurricane
Lamb, Sherman . . .	St. George
Lang, Albert .	St George
Larson, Newell . . .	St George
Larson, Clinton .	St George
Larson, Leo .	St George
Larson, Reuben . . .	Bloomington
Laub, Andrew G	Santa Clara
Lauritzen, Marion M	St George
Leany, Francis S .	Leeds
Leany, George W.	Leeds
Leavitt, Franklin D	Gunlock
Leavitt, Josiah Henry	Gunlock
Lemmon, George A	Virgin
Levi, William D	La Verkin
Liston, Joseph C .	Enterprise
Lund, Bryan J	St. George
Lund, Thomas . .	St George
McAllister, Ralph .	St. George
McArthur, Ezra .	St George
McDonald, John B .	New Harmony
McMullin, Clifford H	Leeds
McMullin, Frank P	Leeds
McMullin, Robert P	Leeds
McMullin, Karl Alfred	Leeds
McMullin, Oscar L .	Leeds
McMurtrie, Daniel . .	Central
Mathis, Gordon . .	St George
Miles, George J . .	St George
Miles, Ivan	St George
Miles, John T	St George
Miles, Lorin	St. George
Miles, Pratt	St. George
Miles, Raymond W. . .	St George
Miles, Richard W. . . .	St. George
Miles, Robert	St. George
Miller, Henry W.	St. George
Miller, Raymond L .	Washington
Miller, William H. . . .	Washington

Bradshaw, Ellis D .. ...Hurricane
Bradshaw, Stanley.. ... . Hurricane
Bringhurst, Leland . . .Toquerville
Bringhurst, Samuel ....Toquerville
Brooks, Edward P........... St. George
Brooks, Llewellyn .. . .St. George
Brooks, Samuel . .. . St. George
Bryner, George Karl .. St. George
Bunting, Harold . ... .. St. George
Burgess, James H.. . ....Veyo
Button, Grant . .. .La Verkin
Canfield, David Lester ..Enterprise
Canfield, James Willard, Enterprise
Canfield, Marcus . ...St. George
Canfield, Milo ....St. George
Cannon, Amprose M .. .. St. George
Cannon, Douglass .. .. .. St. George
Cannon, Kenneth M.. .. St. George
Carpenter Joseph E ...... .Central
Carter, Don S . . ..St. George
Carter, William ... ... St. George
Chadburn, George A .. Central
Christian, Edward C. ...St George
Christian, George .. St. George
Cline, L. J. (Groveland, Cal) St. Geo
Coleman, Raymond . . ..Enterprise
Cooper, Sherman . ...Washington
Cottam, Milton .. ..St. George
Cottam, Moroni J... .. ..St. George
Covington, Robert L Jr. Washington
Cox, LeRoy H .. . . St. George
Cox, William Malin ... . Pine Valley
Cox, Warren Lee .. St George
Crawford, Arthur L .... Enterprise
Crawford, Squire . ..... Springdale
Crosby, Franklin M.... St. George
Dalton, Arthur . ... .Rockville
Dalton, Calvin ....Hurricane
Dalton, Leonard .... Rockville
Dalton, Lester ....Rockville

Day, John Jr .. ..Enterprise
Delameter, Edward H .. St. George
Dodge, George Samuel ...Toquerville
Dodson, Charles V. ..... St George
Drake, Thomas Z . . ...Enterprise
Duncan, Junius J... . .St George
Dyer, Walter . ... St. George
Elicker, John .... Enterprise
Emply, Levi .. . . St George
Empey, Nelson A ... .. St George
Empey, William . . St George
Ence, Milo J.. ... . .Santa Clara
Fackrell, Israel H . .. Enterprise
Farnsworth, Lewis F. .Washington
Farnsworth, Ronald ...Washington
Felter, George . ...St George
Mr Owen Felter,
Pleasant Place, Ohio.
Fordham, George A ... Santa Clara

Milne, Herbert . . ..St. George
Milne, Vivian .. . .St. George
Morris, Clarence .. . ..St George
Morris, Leslie A ....St. George
Morse, Leone .... St George
Moss, Edgar J.. . .... St. George
Moss, Edgar J. .... . St George
Murray, Robert M ... .Enterprise
Naegle, George A ....Toquerville
Naegle, Hans M. . ...Toquerville
Naegle, John W........ ....Toquerville
Naegle, Raymond B .Toquerville
Naegle, Roland . . . . Toquerville
Neilson, Joseph A ..... .Gunlock
Neilson, Vernal . ... Washington
Nelson, George T............Enterprise
Oakden, Clarence ....Enterprise
Owen, William C.. . Enterprise
Palmer, Asael . ... St. George
Payne, Rutherin A .... .Enterprise
Paxman, Charles H. .....Washington
Pearson, John R..... New Harmony
Petty, Edgar .. .. Hurricane
Pickett, C. E. .... St. George
Pickett, Henry .. . .. St. George
Pollock, George .. . Hurricane
Presley, Earl . ... .Hurricane
Prince, George E.... .New Harmony
Prince, John . ...Washington
Prince, Theodore ....Washington
Prisbrey, Grant .... St. George
Pymm, Donald ....St. George
Pymm, John Franklin... St. George
Randall, Brigham D ... St George
Randall, James Reid...... .Central
Reber, Cleon J............ Santa Clara
Reber, Loren .... Santa Clara
Riding, Arthur .... St. George
Riding, Robert S ... ...St. George
Rockwell, Ronald F .. St. George

Ruby, Alfred A .. .. .Washington
Ruesch, Hyrum .... Springdale
Russell, Eugene . ... .Grafton
Sandberg, Enos .... St. George
Schmutz Eldon L . . New Harmoney
Sshmutz, Walter .. . ...Washington
Scow, Olaf ....Hurricane
Seegmiller, Chas. Roscoe, St. George
Slack, Arthur ... .Toquerville
Slack, Edwin K. .. ... .Toquerville
Slack, Leon Lamb..... ... .Toquerville
Slack, Walter H Jr . .Toquerville
Snow, Eldon S . St George
Snow, Karl Nelson .. St George
Snow, Rex Bleak . ... St George
Snow, Rodney H ... Pine Valley
Spendlove, George . .. Hurricane
Spendlove, Lorenzo .. ..Hurricane
Spilsbury, Floyd ... . . .Toquerville

Fordham, John Eugene Santa Clara
Forsyth, Donald P. .... .Toquerville
Frei, John C .... Santa Clara
Fullerton, Harry P. .. St George
Gardner, Clarence S. ..Pine Valley
Gardner, Fenton . .. . Pine Valley
Gardner, Jeter X .. . .. .Pine Valley
Gardner, Rex ... ...Pine Valley
Gardner, Thurlow .. .. Central
Gates, Paul H. .. ..St George
Gibson, Henry Melvin .. Hurricane
Gifford, Cyrus . .. . .Springdale
Gifford, Freeborn . .... . Springdale
Graff, Milton . .. . Santa Clara
Graff, W. H .. .. St George
Gray, Wallace . .. . . Santa Clara
Gray, LaMar .. . . .. St George
Graybill, James W. . ... St George
Gregerson, Grant . . St George
Gregerson, James ... . St George
Grimm, Arthur O. .. .... St George
   St. Louis, Missouri.
Gubler, Hyrum . ... Santa Clara
Gubler, Louis . . .. . . Santa Clara
Gubler, Walter P . ..Santa Clara
Hafen, Guy .. . . Santa Clara
Hafen, Leland .. . .. . Santa Clara
Haley, Roscoe M.. . ... Enterprise
Hall, Bert .. . . .Washington
Hall, Desmond . . .. .Enterprise
Hall, Harvey . .. .Hurricane
Harmon, Frank N .... .. St George
Harmon, Irvin W. . .. .St George
Haycock, Joseph B . ... .St George
Haycock, William D . St. George
Herman Milton .. . . St George
Hiatt, Alton .. ..Enterprise
Hiatt, N. Frank . .... . Enterprise
Higbee, Lorin Summers Toquerville
Hinkson, Robert Louis . St George

Hirschi, Claudius .. . Rockville
Hirschi, George .. . .Rockville
Hirschi, Heber .. . . .Rockville
Holt, James Leroy ... Central
Holt, Heber M .... Enterprise
Hughes, Clayton . . .St George
Hunt, Amos .. . .Enterprise
Hunt, Clarence J.... . .... Enterprise
Hunt, Nelson G.. ... . Enterprise
Hunt, William L .. .. St George
Huntsman, Emery J... Gunlock
Isom, Herbert ... .Hurricane
Isom, Owen .. . . Hurricane
Iverson, Victor . ...Washington
Ivins, Stanley Snow..... ..Enterprise
Jackson, Harry Earl....... Toquerville
Jackson, Harvey A ....Toquerville
Jackson, James F .... Toquerville

Spilsbury, Leslie D . . ... .Toquerville
Sproul, Elmo C.,. . ... .Washington
Squires, William J..... ... St George
Stahell, Edward . .. .. St George
Stahell, William C ....Enterprise
Stewart, John W.... ..... St George
Stirling, Joseph ....Leeds
Stucki, Edwin . ... .Santa Clara
Stucki, Ernest Edwin ... Santa Clara
Stucki, Ether J...... ....Santa Clara
Stucki, Karl Ferdinand, Santa Clara
Sullivan, Archie Cleo .. Leeds
Sullivan, Gordon . . .. St George
Taylor, Elmer .... New Harmony
Tegan, Marcus . . . .Washington
Terry, James A. .. .. .. Rockville
Thaynd, Chester . ...Washington
Thayne, George D ... . .Washington
Thomas, Chauncey . ... St George
Thompson, David W. Jr., Enterprise
Thompson, Ezra ....St George
Thompson, F. O . .... . Enterprise
Turnbeaugh, Stephen ... .Washington
Turner, James E. Jr..........Washington
Walters, E J. . .. . St George
Wanlass, Stanley A ... ..St George
Waring John .... St. George
Webb, Wilford J. ....St. George
Westover, Ralph .. . . .Washington
Whitehead, Erastus C., St George
Whitehead, Morris . ... St George
Whitehead, Roland N...St. George
Whitney, Ralph E. ... ...St. George
Winder, Enos Elmer.. ... ..Springdale
Winsor, Murkins Terry, Enterprise
Winsor, Andrew Leon . St. George
Wittwer, Julius .. .. Santa Clara
Wittwer, Samuel M. ..... Santa Clara
Wood, Elmer ....Hurricane
Woodal, Walter . ... St George

Woodbury, Arthur H. Jr., La Verkin
Woodbury, David O. . ..St. George
Woodbury, Louis . . ... Hurricane
Worthen, Robert .. ..St. George
Worthen, Vernon . . St George
Wright, Jos. Harvey Hurricane
Yett, Ernest . St George
Zamalloa, Angelo ... . St. George
Zimmerman, William, New Harmony
Forsyth, Kenneth F.. :...Toquerville
Graff, Grant . . .. . . .St. George
Hunt, Isaac C . .. .St. George
Laub, Eugene McGinnis, St. George
Randall, Brigham D........ St. George

_____

Happiness comes to those who
seek it, but trouble creeps in una-
wares.

Leeds, Nov. 16.—Born, a daughter to Mr and Mrs C F. Hanson

Kathleen Isom is here from Hurricane visiting her sister, Mrs David Stirling

Mr and Mrs Geo Coast are here visiting Mrs Andrea Hanson

E C Olsen has been sick the last week but is much improved

Mrs Ellen Sullivan of Hurricane is here visiting relatives

Francis Hartley left Monday for his ranch at Kolob

Wm. Carlow's family is here to spend the winter

George Miles spent the week end in St George

C F. Hanson is recovering from a sick spell

Washington County News
November 30, 1920

Leeds, Nov. 30.—The Silver Reef Co has in its other hoist at the Thompson mine. They are sinking a shaft and have started to run night shifts.

David and Mrs. Thomas Stirling and Mrs. Elenor Scott were Monday visitors at St. George.

Mr. and Mrs. Thomas Isom and daughter Jean were Sunday visitors here from Hurricane.

Mr. and Mrs. Edward McMullin and Mrs. George Olsen spent Saturday at St. George.

Miss Ethyl and Clyde McMullin were here to spend Thanksgiving from Cedar City.

George Miles returned Sunday from St. George where he spent the week end.

Lamar Pearce and Ralph Westover were in town today from Washington.

Mr. and Mrs. E. C. Olsen and son Glenn spent Thanksgiving in Hurricane

Bill and Lynn McMullin were Monday visitors at St. George

Miss Melba Harris left Nov. 19, for Salt Lake City.

Mrs Leland Sullivan went to Hurricane Sunday.

Joseph Stirling went to St. George Tuesday.

Leeds, Dec 7 —Your correspondent of Leeds wants to know why the
paper always goes to Cedar City befor we get it here we do not get it
until Friday night

Mrs Linnie Naegle, Mrs Minnie
Harris George Miles and C F Hanson attended the teachers' institute
in St George last week

Mrs Mamie Beal is here visiting her
parents, Mr and Mrs E C Olsen
She had just returned from New
York.

Mrs Leland Sullivan returned
home Saturday from —————
where she has been visiting her parents.

The Silver Reef Con Mining Co
now has electric lights in the mines

Morgon Anderson returned to Silver Reef Sunday from St. George

Alex Colbath left for Salt Lake
City last week

Leeds, Dec 22 —Ethel and Clyde
McMullin came home Saturday to
spend the Christmas holidays with
their parents, Mr. and Mrs. B Y. Mc-
Mullin. They have been going to
school at Cedar City.

After being gone about six weeks
at northern points, Thomas Talbot,
Donald Fuller and son Stanley returned home Thursday.

Mrs Thomas Stirling, Ammon Jolley and Delbert Stirling were business visitors to St. George Wednesday.

Quite a number of our town's people attended conference at St.
George Saturday and Sunday.

Karl McMullin returned home
Monday from Cedar City where he
has been on business.

Valla Angell left Sunday morning
for Cedar City where she intends to
work for some time.

Antone Olsen and wife were business visitors to St. George Saturday.

Charles Hanson has much improved from a serious illness.

James M Wicks returned home
Sunday from Hurricane.

Evan Sullivan left for Cedar City
Wednesday morning

George J Miles came back Sunday
from St George.

Leeds, Jan 4 — Ethyl and Clyde McMullin have returned to Cedar City, they have been spending holidays here

Stanley Fuller and Lawrence Mc-Mullin have gone to Cedar City to go to school.

Mart Woolsey was a visitor here Tuesday on his way from St George

Geo Miles has returned here and school has started again

Born, a daughter to Mr. and Mrs R C Savage, Dec 27.

Will Carlow's mother is here from Beaver visiting him

C T. Hansen has moved his family to his farm

J M. Wicks is home again from St George

CHARLES WESTOVER DEAD

News has just been received here of the death of Charles Westover of Washington. Mr. Westover is well known to the older and iddle-aged class in southern Utah. In the old prosperous days of Silver Reef he was a conspicuous figure, and for a number of years conducted a butcher business there. For the past thirty years he has resided at Washington, and has reared a large family, mostly boys, one of whom, Park Westover, has resided in Cedar City for the past few years, but has now leased a large dry-land farm near Santaquin and removed there.

Leeds, Jan. 18 —Mr and Mrs B Y. McMullin have returned home from Washington, where they attended the funeral of Charlie Westover.

Mrs E C Olsen returned home from Cedar City. She has been there visiting her daughter, Mrs Margaret Haight

J. M. Wicks is slowly recovering from the injury he received in going to St George

Miss Kathleen Isom of Hurricane is here visiting her sister, Mrs David Stirling.

Ruth Sterling, Mrs E C. Olsen and son Glenn went to St George Monday.

Geo. Webb of St George is here as one of our home missionaries.

Born, a daughter to Mr. and Mrs. Ammon Jolley, January 14.

There is one case of measles in town.

Leeds, Jan 25 —Mr and Mrs George Olsen, Glenn Olsen and Mrs. Mamie Beal attended the theatre at Hurricane given by the Walters Co.

The 9th grade girls entertained at the home of Miss Fay Stirling Friday night A good time was had

Elders R C. Savage and George Webb went to Toquerville Monday as home missionaries

Mrs. E C. Olsen has returned home from St George where she has been visiting

The school gave a dance Thursday for the benefit of the European and Near East relief.

Miss Ruth Stirling has returned home from St George

Matt Hartley is in town visiting

Leeds, Feb 1 —Cleo Sullivan has returned home from Cornish, Utah, where he spent the summer

Mr and Mrs. Leonard have returned home from Rockville where they have been visiting

Mrs E C Olsen is in Hurricane visiting her daughter, Mrs William Sullivan

Alex Colbath and Thomas Homer have returned from Salt Lake City.

Charles B Petty of Hurricane was a business visitor here Monday.

Born, a son to Mr. and Mrs Leland Sullivan, Jan 28.

Miss Valla Angell has returned home from Cedar City

B Y. McMullin has returned home from St. George.

The 9th grade took a hike up the creek Monday.

PROGRESS AT SILVER REEF

B. Y. McMullin of Leeds was a business visitor here the fore part of the week

Mr McMullin tells of the work being done at the old silver camp, Silver Reef, by the Silver Reef Con Mining Co , and feels very optimistic concerning its future He says there are 30 men employed there taking out ore and prospecting

The ore, which is said to be high grade, is being stored until the property is further developed when it will be decided what capacity mill to infall to treat the ore.

Leeds, Feb 15 —Mrs Mamie Beal went to Hurricane to tend to her sister s child which has the pneumonia

Mrs Ada McMullin has gone to Cedar City to spend a few weeks with her children, who attend school at that place.

Thomas Stirling, Jr , was operated on for appendicitis Monday at St George, he is doing as well as can be expected

Mrs Carlow who has been here visiting her son, Will, has returned to her home in Beaver.

Sabra Naegle and Dave Foremaster of St George, spent Sunday with Mrs Edwin Dalton

Born, a daughter to Mr. and Mrs Max McMullin, February 4; all concerned doing nicely.

George Miles came back from St. George Sunday morning.

Forest Supervisor Mace was in Leeds Wednesday in attendance on hearing wherein a boy was charged with taking wrongful possession and disposing of ten axes belonging to the forest service.

Leeds, March 1 —The five-year old daughter of Mr. and Mrs J. W. Hartman has had an attack of appendicitis

Mrs Joseph Jolley was here last week from——— visiting her daughter, Francis Hartley.

A crowd of young folk went to the springs and a dance at Hurricane Friday night.

Thomas Stirling, Jr, is home from the hospital and is much improved.

Mrs. Margaret Haight of Cedar City is here visiting her parents

Mrs. Jane Perkins and C. F. Hanson were in St George Tuesday.

Alex Colbath and Thomas Homer have returned from Salt Lake.

J M Wicks is in Hurricane visiting.

Leeds, March 15 —The infant of Mr. and Mrs R C. Savage which has had pneumonia is slowly improving

J M Wicks is in Cedar City visiting.

Mrs R. C. McMullin left last Wednesday for Circleville to tend to her daughter, Mrs. Dan Parker, who has pneumonia.

A number of men from Richfield who have been here working on their farm have returned home

Mrs Margaret Haight returned Sunday from Hurricane where she has been visiting

Mr. and Mrs William Sullivan, Jr,, of Hurricane were Sunday visitors here.

Mr. Moorhouse and Mr. Ball are at Silver Reef.

Lawrence McMullin is home from Cedar where he has been attending school.

Leeds, Mar. 23 —The dance and supper given in honor of Messrs Colbath, Morehouse, and guests, was a big success A large crowd was in attendence Good music was furnished by the Hurricane orchestra

Mrs Hazel Moody of St George, Mrs Margaret Haight of Cedar, and Mrs Lyle Sullivan of Hurricane have been here visiting their mother, Mrs Mary Oleson

Bishop Stirling and wife, Henry Jolley, Edward McMullin and Chas Hansen attended conference at St George Saturday.

Mrs Dave McMullin has returned fromOrderville where she has been tending to her daughter.

Mrs Grace McMullin of ————— has been here visiting her mother, Mrs Dave McMullin.

J. M. Wicks has returned from Cedar City where he has been visiting.

Leeds, April 19 —The parents Teachers' League met at the home of Mr. and Mrs Edward McMullin, April 13 A review of the past month's work was given by Frank Anderson, the subject being, "Natural and Corporal Punishment" This being the night for reorganization Frank Anderson was unanimously sustained as president with Mrs Minnie Harris vice-president, Albert Anderson and William Nicholls as members of the executive committee Mrs Hazel McMullin was retained as class leader and Mrs Maggie Olsen as secretary. A splendid sentiment was given by Mrs L K. Naegle entitled "The Plea of the Child to be Understood" Refreshments were served by the host and hostess.

On April 8th a chicken supper was served for the Boy Scouts in town. Stake Scoutmaster W. C. Cox and Co Supt of Schools, W. O. Bentley were in attendanc. A Scout organization was partly affected.

Some time past a petition was gotten up by the members of this club to the county board of health requesting that the animals be kept off the streets and from polluting our drinking water.

The club is anxiously looking forward to the promised visit of Mrs May Ward Hunt.

Leeds, Apr. 19.—Mr. and Mrs Wilcox and daughter Thelma, Mrs Thomas Stirling and W. S Nicholls spent Friday in St George,

Miss Rhea Sullivan returned Sunday from St. George where she has been visiting.

Mr, and Mrs Edward McMullin and Mrs Linnie Naegle spent Saturday in St George.

A. S. Anderson and Thomas Stirling were Tuesday visitors in St. George.

Misses Berta Nicholls and Lavern Carlon spent Tuesday in St George

Afton Wade of Cedar City is in own visiting

Robert McMullin returned home Tuesday,

Mamie Beal is in Cedar visiting.

Washington County News
April 26, 1921

Leeds, April 26.—The Parents-Teachers' club met Wednesday evening at the ward hall A goodly number of parents were out Class was conducted by class leader Hazel McMullin and questions were discussed by the members

Mrs Sarah L Porter entertained the other evening in honor, of her birthday, at an old time school party. A jolly good time was reported Refreshments were served by the hostess

A crowd of young people started for the dance at Hurricane Saturday evening but were obliged to turn back when they met the wind storm at Anderson's ranch.

Our schools will close Friday, after a successful school year. We feel that we were indeed fortunate in securing the services of such competent teachers.

A dancing party was given Friday evening at the home of Vera McMullin. All present had a fine time Cake and punch was served during the evening

Our town was visited Saturday evening by terrific wind storm which did some damage to fruit and uprooted several trees.

Mr. and Mrs David Stirling, Ruth Stirling and Mrs Elenor Scott were St George visitors Saturday.

Claus Anderson went to Beaver Monday with a load of bees.

Chas. Hansen is erecting a fine cement store building

Riley C Savage has gone to La Verkin on business.

Work is progressing nicely at Silver Reef

Carl McMullin left Thursday for Nevada.

Marriage licenses have been issued by County Clerk Brooks as follows Mr William Glen Emett of Harrisburg and Miss Alta Harris Sterling of Leeds, April 27; Mr. Jefferson Hunt and Mrs Annie M R Stucki, both of Santa Clara, April 27.

Washington County News
May 10, 1921

Leeds, May 10 —The Sunday school gave an entertainment Monday night which consisted of a three act drama ' Out in the Streets," and two vaudeville sketches, ' Hiram Blows In" given by Ross Angell, and "Vaite a Minute" by Glen Olsen and Chirton Fuller. The characters were all well taken The girls chorus sang several songs All present expressed themselvès as having enjoyed the evening

Mothers day was observed in our Sunday school last Sunday An appropriate program was rendered and each mother present was presented with a white and pink rose and a little book ' Tribute to Mothers," compliments of the Leeds Ward Sunday school.

Mr. and Mrs Milton Moody of St. George spent Saturday and Sunday with Mrs Moody's parents, Mr. and Mrs C Olsen. Milton leaves soon for a mission to the Southern States His many friends in Leeds wish him God speed.

Dr. Hamilton and Bert Johnson of Delta were in town last week on business They started back home, broke the axel of their car and had to stay over two days to get it repaired.

Antone Olsen and Cleo Sullivan have gone to Harmony to shear sheep.

Martin L McAllister and son Ellis of St George are town visitors

Bert Harris left Sunday for Las Vegas to find employment.

Washington County News
May 24, 1921

Leeds, May 24 —Afton the three-year old daughter of Mr and Mrs Antone Oleson was quite badly burned today She attempted to light some matches and her clothes caught fire Mr Olsen s hands were severely burned in putting out the fire

Ben Hopkins of Glendale and his daughters Mrs Lydia Snow and Miss Ann Hopkins were in town Saturday visiting at the home of his daughter, Mrs Edward McMullin

The Bee Hive girls met at the home of Mrs Lizzie McQuaid Sunday night where they perfected a re-organization Ethel McMullin was chosen Bee Keeper

Ethel and Clyde McMullin arrived home Friday They have been attending school at the B A C the past winter

Mr and Mrs Wm Woodbury of St George spent Sunday here the guests of Mr and Mrs Wm Sullivan

Alex Colbath of Silver Reef has gone to Salt Lake on mining business

Mr and Mrs Geo Olsen and Rhea Sullivan leave for Salt Lake Wednesday

Mrs Linnie K Naegle entertained at a rag bee Tuesday afternoon

Lawrence McMullin has gone north to find work

Washington County News
May 31, 1921

Leeds, May 31 —The young people of town took a hay-rack ride Sunday night they spent the evening at the Hansen farm, with the Misses Pearl, Zona Melissa, and Melva Perkins who will leave this week for their home in Arizona

George C Naegle returned from St George Saturday. He brought his son Owen with him, Owen has work at Echo farm for the remainder of the summer

Mrs D O Beal and son Glen returned from a northern trip Sunday While away they visited Cedar City, Ephraim, and Salt Lake City

A dance was given Friday night for the children, under the direction of the parents club A very nice time was reported

A number of the friends of Mrs Ada McMullin spent Sunday evening at her home in honor of her birthday

Alex Colbath, business manager of Silver Reef, returned from Salt Lake City Sunday

Robert P. McMullin left Saturday for the north to find employment

Leeds, June 7 —Mrs Joe Worthen and family of Salt Lake City are here visiting her parents, Mr and Mrs B Y. McMullin She was accompanied by her sister Edith who has been teaching school in Logan

All members of the Parents club are invited to the monthly social at the home of Frank Anderson Wednesday night The club held a dance Friday night

Bishop Edw R Frei and Elder Harmon Hafen of Santa Clara were home missionaries Sunday Their visit was much appreciated

Mr Allen of Clay Springs, Arizona, is in town He came in his car to take the Perkins family home

Miss Billy Wilcox of Silver Reef and Miss Fay Stirling were Hurricane visitors Monday

Miss Evelyn Savage is spending a week at Pintura with Mrs Albert Anderson

Lawrence McMullin returned home Sunday on account of ill health

Mr and Mrs George Olsen returned from Salt Lake City Friday.

Leeds, June 15 —The Parents club were guests of the club president, Frank Anderson, and wife Wednesday night at Echo farm. There were 15 present from Leeds, and Bishop and Mrs Slack, Mr. and Mrs Laurence Kleinman, Mrs. Martin Anderson, Mrs. Ray Naegle and Rex Naegle of Toquerville, Games, dancing and contests between Leeds and Toquerville were part of the entertainment Class leader Mrs Edw. McMullin gave a brief outline of what the Parents club has done for the town of Leeds Refreshments were served by the hostess.

Sisters Miles and Winsor of the Stake Relief society met with the Relief society of this ward Thursday morning and a very good meeting was held. All present enjoyed the remarks of the visiting sisters.

Peaches are ripe We feel fortunate in having quite a nice lot of fruit when we see that some towns in the county are without.

Albert Anderson of Echo farm went to St. George Monday on business connected with the new school house in Toquerville.

Mr. and Mrs Jolley of Washington were Sunday visitors, the guests of Mrs Frank Hartley.

Alex Colbath of Silver Reef was called to Salt Lake last night on mining business.

Evelyn Savage is home from Echo farm where she has been for the past week.

The Boy Scouts have gone for a two days' outing in Bellevue canyon

Glen Olsen is a business visitor in St George today.

Washington County News
June 28, 1921

Leeds, June 28 —Mrs Milton Moody has returned from Salt Lake City and other points She accompanied her husband as far as Salt Lake City on his way to fill a mission He is at present laboring in South Carolina Mrs Moody will spend some time with her parents, Mr. and Mrs E C Olson.

Mrs Joseph Worthen and children have returned to their home in Salt Lake City after spending some time with Mrs Worthen's parents, Mr and Mrs B. Y. McMullin

Our merchant, C. F. Hansen, has moved into his new building The building is nice and plenty of room being a credit to Mr. Hansen and to the town

Dan and Will McMullin have returned after spending some two weeks on a pleasure trip to Richfield, Salt Lake and other interesting places

Miss Fay Stirling and Miss Laverne Carlton have gone to Beaver to visit for two weeks They are the guests of Miss Bonnie Anderson.

Mrs. Fern Howells of Berry Springs has been the guest of Miss Wanda Nicholls the past week.

J M Wicks who has been in poor health for some time has gone to Cedar City to escape the heat

Wm. Hartman left yesterday to work on the Lund-Cedar road.

Iron County Record
July 22, 1921

Alex Colbath of Silver Reef is
in town this week on business and
chatting with friends.

Washington County News
August 8, 1921

Leeds, Aug 2 —The M I A took
an outing to Zion National Park July 25 Fifty eight made the trip,
leaving Leeds at 3 a m and returning in the evening The day in the
canyon was one continual round of
pleasure

Miss Ada Harris has gone to Salt
Lake taking with her the little son of
Mr and Mrs Joe Worthen He has
been spending the summer with his
grandparents, Mr. and Mrs B Y
McMullin

Mr and Mrs Riley C. Savage and
members of their family, accompanied by Veir McMullin have gone to
Salt Lake on a pleasure trip They
intend visiting friends and relatives
enroute.

The Parents club held "Leeds Day"
at the La Verkin hot springs About
75 people enjoyed their bath and
lunch under the trees

The Bee Hive girls put on a play,
"My Aunt's Heiress," which was followed by a dance There was a
crowd in attendance

Mrs Etta Trinkhaus and Mrs
Mame Worthen of St George are the
guests of their aunt here, Mrs Thomas Stirling.

Mr and Mrs Harold Snow of St.
George spent Sunday with the latter s sister, Mrs Edward McMullin

B Y. McMullin has returned from
Beaver where he has been visiting
with his son Clarence.

Willard McMullin and Roy Hartley
left today to work on the Lund-Cedar road.

Born, a son to Mr and Mrs Bert
Harris, July 22, all concerned doing
nicely.

Chas. Wright has gone to Las
Vegas, Nev, where he has employment.

Miss Matilla Langston of Hurricane is here visiting Miss Berta Nicholls.

Mrs Rebecca Angell has gone to
Salt Lake to visit with her daughter.

Leeds, Aug 9 —Antone Olsen, Delbert Stirling, Willard McMullin, Clinton Fuller and Bert Harris left for Las Vegas, Nev , this morning to find employment

We have been visited by some splendid rain storms which have cooled things off and made people feel like new.

Mr. Hyrum Pope and son and daughter from Salt Lake City are here visiting his sister, Mrs Margie Dalton

Mrs Vinie Fuller underwent a serious operation in Hurricane Aug 6. Last report she was doing nicely.

Mrs. Elnore Scott and children returned from Newcastle Monday evening, where they had been visiting

Mrs. Mamie Beal has gone to Hurricane to assist Doctors Middleton and Wilkinsen as nurse,

Born, a daughter to Bp and Mrs. David Stirling, Aug 9, all concerned doing nicely

Mrs Plee Estell is here visiting her parents, Mr. and Mrs Frank Hartley,

Leeds, Aug 23 —Mr, and Mrs Riley C Savage and family and Vera McMullin have returned from Salt Lake City On their return trip they visited friends at Joseph and Richfield

Mrs Mamie Beal is home again after having spent two weeks in Hurricane She was accompanied by Mr and Mrs William Sullivan

Mrs Donald Fuller was able to come home Saturday from Hurricane She underwent a serious operation there some three weeks ago.

Alex Colbath and Dan Doyle have just returned from Salt Lake City where they have been on business connected with Silver Reef.

Frank P. Mcmullin returned Thursday from Salt Lake City where he has been attending school for some time

We were visited today by a fierce downpour of rain which cooled the air off and freshened up things in general

A pleasant surprise was given Friday night in honor of Glen Olsen's birthday, all present had a good time

The Misses Berta and Wanda Nicholls and Mrs Wm Hartman are Hurricane visitors today

Dan and Lynn McMullin and forest ranger Stone were St George visitors Monday.

Leeds, Aug 30 —A farewell party in honor of Mr. and Mrs George E. Porter will be given tonight They are going to take over the management of the La Verkin hot springs We all wish them well in their new undertaking and we realize that Leeds loss will be La Verkin's gain

A fruit festival and social was held Wednesday evening under the directions of the Parents' club A very enjoyable evening was spent in playing games and dancing after which a feast on fruit, Dixie's best, was enjoyed by all present,

We enjoyed very much the remarks of our home missionaries Sunday. Also the sermon of Elder Sorenson of La Verkin

Mrs David Stirling has returned from Hurricane where she has been visiting her parents, Mr and Mrs. Thos. Isom

Funeral services were held this afternoon for the infant son of Mr. and Mrs Bert Harris, who died Sunday evening

Mr. and Mrs H A Jolley and Mr. and Mrs Antone Olsen have gone to Lehi to attend the Jolley family reunion.

Mr. and Mrs. C. E Olsen are visiting their daughter, Mrs. Margaret Haight, in Cedar City.

Leeds, Sept 13 —Alex Colbath, Mamie Beal, Edyth and Ethel McMullin, Hazel Moody and Will Pierce just returned from the Grand canyon They visited Bryce canyon en route home

Miss Reah Sullivan has returned from Weston, Idaho, where she has been visiting the past three months

Mr. and Mrs Jack Brownfield of Milford were the guests of Mr. and Mrs Riley Savage Friday.

Mr, Pace and family of Delta spent several days here visiting his sister, Mrs Maggie Hartley.

Mrs Herbert Haight of Cedar City is here visiting her parents, Mr. and Mrs Olsen

Riley Savage and family spent Sunday afternoon in Toquerville visiting friends

A crowd of young people went to Hurricane to the dance Friday night.

Mrs Ida Tullis of Newcastle is in town visiting relatives.

Bert Harris has returned to Las Vegas, Nev, to work.

Ben Hopkins and son of Glendale were here today.

Stanley Fuller has gone north with a load of fruit

Miss Fay Stirling has been ill for the past week

Dan McMullin was a St George visitor Monday.

Bill Stevens of Cedar spent Sunday here.

DEATH CLAIMS TWO GIRLS
BATHING NEAR HARRISBURG

Miss Hulda Lightner and Miss Dean Talbot met death by drowning in the Dixie canyon near Harrisburg yesterday. The girls had gone out walking through the hills and then went in to bathe in one of the pools in the canyon, below Harrisburg They got into deep water and were drowned in each others arms The long absence of the girls alarmed their relatives who went in search of them, finding them as above stated

Miss Lightner is a niece of Don A Lightner of this city. Her home is in Minersville and she was coming to this city with her grandmother, Mrs Craff, to work in the temple She was about 18 years old Miss Talbot is a daughter of Mr. and Mrs Thomas Talbot of Harrisburg and was about 16 years old.

Pickett Bros of this city have taken out caskets, and it is probable that interment will be made in the Leeds cemetery.

Miss Verne Tullis returned Sunday from Leeds, where she visited with relatives for several weeks.

Donald Forsyth made a trip to Leeds and St. George the first of the week.

Washington County News
September 27, 1921

VICTIMS OF DROWNING BURIED IN LEEDS CEMETERY

Hyrum Leany of Harrisburg, at present residing here, gave The News further particulars of the drowning of Miss Hulda Lightner and Miss Dean Talbot, near Harrisburg on the 21st inst The place where the girls were drowned is about a mile and a-half above Harrisburg in Dick's canyon—named for an old Indian who died there about 60 years ago One of Leany's sons had gone to look for the girls when their long absence had caused anxiety and saw their clothes on the bank—they had partly undressed to take their bath He thought the girls had seen him coming and had hid from him so he returned Later Mr. Leany and his two sons went to the pool The water was riley and they could not see them in the water, which was about eight feet deep The clothes were still on the bank and Mr. Leany said, ' I believe they are in the pool ' The oldest boy, Hyrum, then dived in and brought one of the girls out, the other being brought out just after From their appearance they had become panic stricken and had clutched at each other, they being found in each other's arms

Just before leaving Mrs Talbot had told her girl not to go to Dick's canyon, says Mr. Leany.

Funeral services were held in Leeds and the remains were interred in the Leeds cemetery.

The people of the community were much shocked and grieved at the untimely ending of two bright young lives

Mr Leany is limping around with a cane, his horse having fallen with him while he was out rounding up cattle, smashing the bones in his left foot The accident happened two months ago and he feels that it will be a long time before he recovers the full use of it

Iron County Record
September 27, 1921

Matt Wicks of Leeds is a visitor in Cedar this week. He expects to make a trip to western parts of the county, before returning home.

Leeds, Sept 27 —The town people were terribly shocked over the drowning in Dick's canyon of Miss Dean Talbot of Harrisburg and Miss Hilda Lightner of Minersville Funeral services were held Friday in the ward hall, a number of out of town people being present The speakers were Bishop Ayres of Minersville, Bishop Slack of Toquerville, B Y. McMullin, R C Savage and Bishop David Stirling All spoke words of comfort and consolation to the bereaved families and relatives The Bee-Hive girls of our ward had some cash on hand that they had saved to purchase Bee Hive costumes, and they donated it to the relatives of the girls to buy their burial clothes and paid $10 on each casket.

Walter Slack, Rosilla Spillsbury, Rhea Wakeling, Mattie Naegle and John T. Batty of Toquerville came over to the funeral Friday and rendered several musical selections which was much appreciated.

Mr. and Mrs John A Parker of Joseph and Mr and Mrs R D Young of Richfield spent the past week here putting up fruit and looking over their business interests here

Glen Olsen has gone to Cedar to attend school and Clyde McMullin to Beaver to attend the Murdock

Mrs. Buel and George Cline of Stateline are in town

Matt Wicks has gone to Stateline

Washington County News
October 25, 1921

Leeds Oct 25 —Lynn McMullin arrived home last week from Taylor, Arizona bringing with him his bride Miss Pearl Perkins of that place Their many friends gathered at their home Friday evening to wish them joy and happiness on their journey through life A delicious lunch was served by the hostess Mrs Oscar McMullin who was assisted by her daughter Mrs Geo Olsen

The members of the Parents club enjoyed a chicken fry on the hill back of town Wednesday night, it being the night of election Mrs Minnie Harris was elected president Edith McMullin vice president Lizzie McQuaid secretary and treasurer

Julia Ford of Enterprise was shaking hands with her old time friends and neighbors last week We are all glad to see her in town again

Chas Hansen, Jr and Ross Angell arrived home from Las Vages where they have been working for some months past

Baby boys arrived at the homes of Mr and Mrs Clifford McMullin and Mr and Mrs Charles Angell Oct 19

Miss Kathryne Isom of Hurricane is here visiting her sister, Mrs David Stirling

We have been visited by a generous down pour of rain for the past 24 hours

Robert P McMullin left Saturday for northern points in search of work

Forest Supervisor Mace of Cedar City was in town Friday

Leeds, Nov. 8 —The Parents club gave a Hallowe'en party Friday night Every one present had a good time There were many ghosts, goblins and witches present The gypsy fortune tellers were quite the center of attraction.

Sunday visitors in town were John L Sevey of Salt Lake City, Mr and Mrs Albert Anderson of Toquerville, Mr. and Mrs William Sullivan and Thos Isom and wife of Hurricane.

Riley C Savage, Edward McMullin and Will Sullivan have gone to Lund for freight

Mr. and Mrs Wm Theobald of Toquerville were visiting Mrs R. C Savage Tuesday.

Ex-Bishop B Y. McMullin has been quite ill but is able to be out again

Henry Jolley is laid up with a lame back.

Leeds, Nov 22 —John A Parker and son Harold of Joseph, Sevier Co , were here Sunday looking after their farm Jas P. Gilbert returned with them

Members of the Genelogical Society met with us Sunday afternoon A special meeting was held at 4 p m

The Primary children are out today distributing their Thanksgiving baskets.

Parents club met at the home of Mrs William Hartman Wednesday night

Will McMullin has gone to St. George to attend the D N. C

Glen Emett returned home from Las Vegas, Nev , Sunday.

Born, Nov. 21, a son to Mr. and Mrs Glen E Emett

Claus Anderson of Beaver was in town Monday.

Leeds, Dec 8 —The Parents' club met at the home of Mrs Minnie Harris Wednesday night After meeting refreshments were served by the hostess Club will meet at the home of Mrs Will Carlow, Silver Reef, this coming Wednesday evening

Mrs Will Carlow of Silver Reef entertained at a surprise party for her daughter, Laverne, Thursday night All the young people from town went up and they report having had a most delightful time

Ed. McMullin, Lawrence McMullin, Stanley Fuller and Leland Sullivan have just returned from Modena They went to drive beef cattle

Mamie Olsen, Ethel McMullin, Dan Doyle, Will Carlow and Alex Colbath recently returned from Salt Lake city.

We were visited by a fierce wind storm Saturday and Sunday, and freezing weather was the result.

The Parents' club gave a Leap-year ball Friday night It was a financial as well as a social success,

Riley Savage and Ed. Dalton have gone on the mountain to round-up their pigs

The Primary will give a dance for the little folks Friday evening.

Mrs. Mary Olsen has gone to Hurricane for a visit.

A number of visitors were in town for Thanksgiving.

Leeds, Dec 20 —Margaret Savage had the misfortune to fall Tuesday night and injure her back It was necessary to take her to Hurricane Friday to consult a doctor

The Parents club met at the home of Mr and Mrs George Olsen The lesson 'Strength of Will' was given by Mrs Dallis Hartman and discussed by members after which lunch was served by the hostess.

Forest Ranger Earl Storm of Cedar City and Claus Anderson of Beaver were town visitors Sunday.

Bert Harris and Dan McMullin arrived Friday night from Las Vegas, Nevada

Riley C Savage has gone to northern points for a load of potatoes and flour

Washington County News
January 10, 1922

Leeds Jan 10 — The holidays passed rather quietly due to the very stormy weather which prevailed We had some very nice house parties as well as public dances among these was an oyster supper given by the junior high school at the home of Vere McMullin to which all of the young people in town were invited and a party at Silver Reef which was a decided success everyone in town over 20 years of age was invited dancing and games was the order of the evening and a dainty lunch was served

The road in several places between here and St George have been almost impassable for two weeks due to the recent storms but they are drying out now and a number of cars go through daily

Antone Olsen Will Nicholls Bert Harris and Clifford McMullin have returned to Las Vegas Nev to work after having spent the holidays with their families here

We are pleased to report that ex Bishop B Y McMull n who has been very ill the past few days with pneumonia is reported much better

Clyde McMullin has been unable to return to school at Beaver on account of having a gathered ear which has been very painful

Mrs Caroline McMullin is visiting in Hurricane with her daughter Mrs Frank Sullivan

Parents club will meet at the home of Mr and Mrs Edward McMullin Wednesday night

Mr and Mrs Albert Anderson of Toquerville spent New Year s with friends in Leeds

Edwin Higbee and Lawrence Klein man of Toquerville were in town Wednesday

Mr and Mrs Ed McMullin spent several days in St George during the holidays

Washington County News
January 18, 1922

Leeds Jan 18 — The eighth grade boys and girls were entertained at the home of Mrs Lizzie McQuaid Saturday evening Songs and games were the order of the evening after which ice cream was served

G M Spilsbury and Lawrence Kleinman of Toquerville and B J Jarvis Jr of St George attended the meeting of the Southern Utah Canning Co Monday

Mis Mamie Beal has gone to Salt Lake City to take over the position of nurse in some of the public schools of that place She will remain there until late spring

The people of our town were very sorry to hear of the death of one of our old town residents Miss Julia Ford who died at Enterprise Sunday

We are anxiously looking forward to the visit of the home missionaries who are appointed to labor here

Willard McMullin of this place is filling a home mission at Rockville and Springdale

Matt Wicks is home again after having spent the Xmas holidays at State Line

Ex Bishop B Y McMullin is slowly recovering from an attack of pneumonia

Mrs Minnie Harris entertained a number of her friends Friday evening

Mr and Mrs Riley C Savage and family went to Toquerville Thursday

Alex Colbath of Silver Reef has gone to Salt Lake

J. L. CONNELLY LOSES LIFE AT GRAND GULCH

St Thomas Nev Jan 6 Editor —I wish to submit a brief account of the death of my brother John L Connelly and request that you publish it He was born at Leeds in 1875 and many of the older citizens of Washington Co will remember him

He left the Grand Gulch mine about noon on Dec 21st with a four-horse team loaded with cedar posts The weather was stormy and the roads very bad and he only made about six miles during the afternoon and camped in the canyon after getting down over the worst road

One week later I started from the Grand Gulch to go to St Thomas and found his wagon and two of his horses where he had camped I investigated as best I could and found he had made his bed and slept in it Two of his horses were missing They were horses he had had but a short time They had recently been brought from Utah I decided that these horses had left him during the night and that he had followed them so far before overtaking them that he had decided to go on home and come back later for the balance of his outfit

When I reached St Thomas and found him not there I reported the situation and eight men started immediately to search for him

About 10 o clock a m on Jan 2nd they found the body He had tracked the horses through the mud and rain for about ten miles and evidently could not catch them after overtaking them From the tracks and other evidence he had been chasing the horses and fell striking his head on a rock and died almost without a struggle The body was buried at St Thomas yesterday

He leaves a wife and four small children

Respectfully

Chas Connelly

P S—Will you please publish a few lines relative to his missing horses so any person who perchance may see them may notify his wife Mrs J L Connelly St Thomas Nev by mail I am unable to give brand or accurate description but one is a large sorrel horse about 12 years old and the other is a brown mare about 10 years old and will weigh probably 1050 The horse weighs about 12 or 13 hundred Both were shod

C C

Leeds Jan 31 — Miss Mildred Mc Mullin age 16 and Ward Jolley age 17 were married in St George Monday Jan 30 The bride is the daughter of Mr and Mrs Ira S Mc Mullin the groom is a son of Mr and Mrs H A Jolley of this place

The Parents club met at the home of Mr and Mrs Oscar McMullin Wedneday night The lesson was given by Mrs Donald Fuller and Miss Edyth McMullin read a number of poems from Robert Service Lunch was served by the hostess

We certainly enjoyed the visits an l labors of our home missionaries El ders Whitehead and Woodbury and hope they will keep an eye on the people of Leeds and give us another call some time in the near future

Mrs Thos Sterling Mrs Lizzie McQuaid and Mr and Mrs Liley Savage went to Toquerville Wednesday to attend the funeral of Hans Anderson

Six high priests reported at the St George temple Thursday There are seven in town but ex Bishop McMullin was not able to go down

Will McMullin who is attending school at St George spent Saturday and Sunday with his parents

Grant the infant son of Mr and Mrs Edward McMullin is ill with bronchal pneumonia

Ben Hopkins of Glendale is a guest of his daughter, Mrs Edward McMullin

Robert McMullin spent Sunday and Monday in St George

B Y McMullin is able to be out again

Leeds Feb 14 — Lincoln s birth day was observed by the schools yesterday and an appropriate program was given in each department

There has been quite a bit of sickness in town due we think to the changes in the weather the pneumonia patients are all better

Dan and Carl McMullin went to St George to see the basket ball game between the Dixie and Parowan schools

Frank Hartley has gone out on the Cottonwood bench to do some plowing for Chas Hansen

The Relief Society will entertain at a rag bee at the home of Mrs Mc Quaid this afternoon

Parents club will meet at the home of Mrs Mintie Harris Wednesday night

Dan Doyle of Silver Reef has gone to Salt Lake City

Leeds Feb 21 —Parents club met at the home of Mrs Minnie Harris Wednesday night Lunch was serv ed by the hostess The club will meet at the home of Mrs Frank Hart ey this coming Wednesday night

The Toquerville district school played the Leeds school a game of basket ball Friday and won the game by a score of 24 to 12

Mr and Mrs John Schmutz of St George was in town Saturday visit ing Mrs E C Olsen

Karl and Clyde McMullin went to Hurricane to see the basket ball game Friday night

Born a son to Mr and Mrs An tone Olsen Feb 21 mother and babe doing nicely

Messrs Scott and Mason of Silver Reef made a trip to Cedar City Mon day

Mr and Mrs Cleo Sullivan of Hur ricane spent Sunday here

Leeds March 14 —The people of Leeds were very sorry to learn of the death of Aunt Peggy Hamilton at Cedar City She was formerly a res ident of this place and was loved by all who knew her Her many friends extend their sympathy to the bereav ed family

Alex Colbath has returned from Salt Lake City and everyone is anx iously waiting to know if there is go ing to be anything doing at Silver Reef

The infant son of Mr and Mrs Leland Sullivan has been very ill with pneumonia following flu but is reported to be improving

Lawrence McMullin has returned from Cedar where he has been at tending school this winter

School started this morning after having been closed two weeks on ac count of flu

Two of Geo C Naegles children are reported to be down with the flu

Carl McMullin has gone to Alamo Nev to work

The sympathy of our entire community is extended to Mr. F. S. Hamilton in the death of his mother. Prior to her removal to Cedar City, she was a resident of Leeds, and is considered one of the oldest residents of early Silver Reef. She is held in the highest esteem by all who knew her.

We were very much disappointed in the postponment of Cedar City's Orchestra. We still hope to hear them in the near future. We assure them and their friends a hearty welcome.

LEEDS

After a short close on account of Flu our primary school reopened this morning. The higher grades will commence Wednesday.

The Flu patients are all able to be out again, except the small son of Leland Sullivan; it has a bad case of pneumonia following on attack of flu.

One of our students, Lawrence McMullin, of B. A. C. at Cedar City, returned home on Saturday. Lawrence is certainly well satisfied with his school.

Mr. A. G. Anderson of the Southern Utah Bee and Honey Company, has just finished repainting his place of business. It certainly looks splendid.

The Parents Association pronounced Wednesday as "Leeds Cleaning Day", a general cleaning of streets and ditches, mending ragged bridges. sidewalks, etc., is it's chief aim.

Iron County Record
March 24, 1922

LEEDS

Bert Harris and Wm. Nichols returned on Sunday from Nevada.

Willie McMullin, student of the D. N. C., returned home Saurday.

Mr. Charles Hansen, instructor in Leeds High School, reopened school Monday.

Mr. Scott of Silver Reef was called hurriedly to Montana, his mother being very ill.

We are certainly going in for dramatics, four plays being under prepared for production.

The Parent1Teacher's Assn. met at the home of Mrs. Lizzie McQuaid. A short program was given and refreshments served, after business matters had been attended to.

Messers. Morehouse and Colbath arrived Monday to look after interests of Alvarado Co. located at Silver Reef. The outlook for that camp is very encouraging, a mill will be started in about sixty days, freighting, xecavating, etc., at an earlier date.

Washington County News
April 18, 1922

Leeds Apr 18 —Influenza hit this town Monday a week ago like a thunderbolt from a clear sky Up to the present writing there have been apwards of 90 cases

Mrs Barbara Forsythe of Toquerville spent several days last week here assisting in the home of R C Savage whose family were all down with flu

We would like to see the weather warm up a bit If Jack Frost visits us many more nights he will take all of the fruit

Born baby girls on Mar 30 to Mr and Mrs Geo Olsen and Apr 13 to Mr and Mrs C F Hansen

The infant of Mr and Mrs George Olsen is very ill the after affects of flu

Miss Ethel McMullin has gone to Salt Lake to spend some time

John L Sevey of Salt Lake was here today

Leeds Apr 26 —Most of the people had flu but some are still coming down with it and Edwin Dalton Hazel McMullin and the infants of Mrs C F Hansen and Mrs Geo Olsen are still in a critical condition due to after effects of flu

Grandma Hansen has been very ill for several days following an attack of flu Her daughter Mrs Mortenson of Parowan, is here helping care for her mother

Willie, Clyde and Edyth McMullin went to St George Saturday returning Sunday night

Mrs A G Anderson and son Claus of Beaver arrived Sunday to make their future home in Leeds Mr Anderson has been here for some time having started in the mercantile business

Will Carlow of Silver Reef has just returned from Beaver

Leeds May 1 —We very much enjoyed the visit of our home missionareis Sunday Elders D Jarvis and George Webb They gave us some very timely instructions and we will be glad to have them come again

Antone Olsen came home from Hurricane Friday night He is a victim of the flu being the only case in town at present

Riley C Savage and daughter Margaret and Mrs Hazel Moody are in St George on business

Grandma Hansen is slowly improving We hope to see her out again soon

Clinton Fuller and Ross Angell left for Las Vegas, Nev, this morning

Joe Stirling and Nellie McMullin have gone to Lund with wood

Frank Hartley has gone to his dry farm on Kolob

LEEDS

Charles Wright, Clyde and Vere McMullin motored to St. George for the track meet.

* * *

It is expect the "Rod and Gun Club" of St. George will give a dance here on Thursday.

R. C. Savage and daughter Margaret, and Hazel Moody are visitors in St. George today.

* * *

Charles Hanson has sold his mercantile business to A. G. Anderson of Beaver.

Mrs. A. G. Anderson and son Claus arrived last week from Beaver, they intend making their home here.

* * *

Randall Jones and wife, and Wm. Mace and wife, all of Cedar City, made a short stop at Leeds last week.

* * *

School and all other ward activities began this week. We were once more in the grip of "flu". At one time our cases were between sixty and seventy.

Mrs. Andrea Hanson who has been dangerously ill with "flu", is reported improving. Her daughter, Mrs. S. C. Mortenson of Parowan is here to assist in caring for her.

We are pleased to learn that Silver Reef will soon begin her activities again.

* * *

Alex Colbath, mining promotor, of Silver Reef, is expected from Salt Lake City today.

LEEDS.

Grandma Hanson is still slowly improving.

* * *

We are pleased to learn that Silver Reef will soon begin her activities again.

* * *

Alex Colbath, mining promotor, of Silver Reef, is expected from Salt Lake City today.

* * *

Bert Harris is expected home today to resume his work with the Alvardo Co. at Silver Reef.

* * *

Mrs. Mary Olsen has gone to Hurricane to visit her daughter, Mrs. Wm. Sullivan.

* * *

Mrs. Hazel McMillin is out again after being very ill with Flu. Her sister, Ann Hopkins, is caring for her at present.

* * *

Leeds was visited Tuesday night with quite a fall of snow. Trees and limbs are down all over town as result of excessive weight of snow.

* * *

The Rod and Gun Club dance on Thursday was quite a success. New members joined here. We expect to have some very nice times in connection with the club here this summer.

Washington County News
May 16, 1922

Leeds May 16 —The Silver Reef camp started work again Friday There are several men at work now and a number more are expecting to start work about June 1

The Sunday School held services i honor of Mothers day Sunday A very appropriate program was rend eed consisting of songs stories and recitations after which tributes to the mothers in the form of a collec tion of poems entitled Mother and a boquet of roses were presented to each mother in behalf of the Sunday School superintendency

Miss Ann Hopkins arrived here from Delta where she has been en gaged in school teaching the past winter She will spend a week visit ing her sister Mrs Ed McMullin before she returns to her home at Glendale

Our ninth grade graduates Berta Nicholls Lavern Carlon Leah Nae gle Lucile Harris Evelyn Savage and Glen Stirling attended the grad uating exercises at St George Friday night

Mr and Mrs Sanford Angell of Moapa, Nev , were in town Thursday shaking hands with their old time friends of Leeds They were resi dents of this place forty years ago

Our district school closed Thurs day but the 9th grade will not close until May 30

Alex Colbath of Silver Reef re turned from Salt Lake City a few days ago

Bert Harris came home from Los Vegas, Nev , Wednesday

Iron County Record
May 26, 1922

LEEDS

Charles Hanson was a business visitor at St. George on Wednesday.

* * *

Glenn Olsen returned home Sunday from Cedar City, where he attended the B. A. C.

Earl Storm who has charge of the Dixie Forest Reserve in this locality, is located here for the summer.

* * *

Mother's Day was fittingly observed Sun. Beautiful roses and booklets entitled "Mother" were presented to each mother.

* * *

Among those who attended the cantata at Toquerville unday evening, include, Mr. and Mrs. A. G. Anderson, Mesdames, Minnie Harris, Ada McMullin, Mary Olsen and Hattie Sterling.

Visitors and callers to Leeds last week include, L. N. Marsden, Mrs. Wm. Marsden, Mrs. E. L. Clark, all of Parowan. Bp. Hopkins and daughter Ann, of Glendale. Pearl Mortenson and DeLois Higbee of Cedar. Also F. S. Hamilton of Cedar City.

* * *

We are indeed glad to see Grandma Hansen out again. We consider this esteemed lady has made a wonderful recovery after so severe an illness, since she is eighty years of age. Mr. Hanson has continued in the mercantile business for twenty years. and expresses herself that she will continue soon as strength permits. Great respect was shown her on Mother's Day.

Iron County Record
June 2, 1922

A. G. Anderson, "the honey man", has now launched out in the mercantile business in Leeds, Utah.

While in Cedar the other day he called in the Record office and told a representative that he was doing a good business and that it was steadly increasing. He said that he was catering to the tourist traffic and had opened up free camp grounds at his place in Leeds.

Mr. Anderson is also looking after his bee business, which in addition to his mercantile business, keeps him somewhat busy, but nevertheless he claims to enjoy it.

LEEDS

Mr. and Mrs. Herbert Haight of Cedar City were Leeds callers Tuesday.

* * *

Alex Colbath, Wm. Carlow and Charles Wright motored to Salt Lake City, Monday.

* * *

Peter Delmue of Salt Lake City is a business and social caller today. Mr. Delmue is here buying sheep.

* * *

Mrs. John Joseph, who has been visiting her parents Mr. and Mrs. A. G. Anderson, left for her home in Beaver, Monday.

* * *

Miss Ruth Sterling accompanied by her sister Mrs. Alice Singleton of Eureka, Utah, arrived home last week. She has been at Manila teaching school.

* * *

A well arranged school party was given Thursday by Mr. Hansen's graduating class. Games, ice cream and cake, dancing and a program, were features of the entertainment. Among outside guests who attended, were Mr. Alex Colbath, Mr. and Mrs. Carlin of Silver Reef. Mr. and Mrs. Albert Anderson of Echo Farm. Mrs. Wm. Sullivan of Hurricane, and Mrs. Herbert Haight of Cedar City. The rooms were decorated with a profusion of Leeds most beautiful roses.

* * *

Leeds June 13 —The Stake Primary Board with the officers and teachers from Hurricane Toquerville Washington and Leeds met in Primary conference here June 9 and a most successful time is reported Two meetings were held at 10 a m and 2 p m Lunch was served to the visitors by the local Primary officers and teachers There were 50 out of town visitors present

Sisters Jarvis and Graff of the stake Relief Society board met with our Relief Society June 7 in regular meeting After the lesson was given each one spoke very encouragingly to the sisters

Alex Colbath and Will Carlow returned from Salt Lake City yesterday They were accompanied by Mrs Mamie Beal and son Glen, and Miss Ethel McMullin

Clifford McMullin and Glen Emmett have returned from Las Vegas Nev where they have been employed for several months past

Sunday visitors in town were Mr. and Mrs Albert Anderson of Echo farm and Mr and Mrs Seymore Stapley from Toquerville

Town visitors in St George today are Mr and Mrs Lynn McMullin Mrs Jane Perkins and Miss Fay Stirling

Max McMullin has returned to Las Vegas Nev to work Roy Hartley and Ward Jolly went with him

Frank McMullin has returned from Salt Lake City where he has been attending school the past winter

Miss Leona Savage of Salt Lake City is here visiting with her uncle Riley O Savage and family

Ruth Stirling and her sister Mrs Alice Singleton have arrived here from northern parts

Charles Wright and Wayne Angel have gone to Salt Lake City to find employment

Mrs Oscar McMullin was hostess at a dancing party Friday night at her home

The infant of Mr and Mrs Antone Olsen has been quite ill for several days past

Miss Reah Sullivan has gone to Hurricane to spend two weeks

FISH PLANTED IN ASH, QUAIL AND LEEDS CREEKS

——oo——

A. G. Anderson passed through Cedar Tuesday on his way from Lund to Leeds, Utah, with a 25,000 shipment of fish received from the State fish hatcheries.

The fish arrived in Cedar in splendid condition and were taken Tuesday afternoon to Ash, Quail and Leeds Creeks in Washington county.

In connection with the fish Mr. Anderson had along with him six pairs of Chineese Pheasants which will be turned loose in the neighborhood of the creeks mentioned. These Pheasants are polific breeders and a splendid game fowl, and it is expected that within two or three years this bird will be equally as plentiful as quail now is in Washington county.

LEEDS

——oo——

Alex Colbath and Wm. Carlow of Silver Reef motored from Salt Lake City on Monday.

——oo——

Miss Ethel McMullin and Mrs. Mame Beal arrived home from Salt Lake Monday.

——oo——

Max McMullin returned to his work in Nevada after spending a week in Leeds visiting relatives and friends.

——oo——

Mrs. Ellen Sullivan of Hurricane is the guest of her mother Mrs. David McMullin.

——oo——

Cleo Sullivan left Sunday for Salt Lake where he expects to spend the summer in vocational work.

——oo——

Frank McMullin is home again after spending the winter in Salt Lake, where he has been doing vocational work for return soldiers.

Mr. and Mrs. Sam Leigh of Cedar City, were in Leeds today visiting relatives and former friends and class mates.

—oo—

A splendid Primary Conference was held here last Friday. Towns represented here were, Toquerville, La Verkin, Hurricane, St. George, Washington and Leeds.

Washington County News
June 27, 1922

Leeds June 27 — Grandma Hanson passed peacefully away at 11 30 p m Thursday night June 22 after a lingering illness Funeral services were held in the ward hall Saturday morning at 9 o clock The speakers were Bros David McMullin Andrew Sproul and Riley C Savage They all spoke well of the faithfulness and integrity of the departed The floral offerings were numerous and the hall was beautifully decorated by the young ladies of the town Full obituary next week

Willie and Lawrence McMullin have gone to Salt Lake City They will visit Beaver and Richfield en route

A number of our towns people attended The Vision at Hurricane last Wednesday evening

Reah Sullivan is home from Hurricane where she has spent the past three weeks

Chase Wright is home being summoned by the death of his grand mother

Mrs Hazel Moody is back from Cedar City.

Iron County Record
July 7, 1922

LEEDS

———oo———

Lawrence and Will McMullin left yesterday for Richfield and other points of northern Utah.

———oo———

A crew of men are doing preparatory work prior to installing electric lights in Leeds.

———oo———

Miss Pearl Mortensen left for her home at Parowan, Wednesday after a few days stay in Leeds, the guest of Miss Minnie Harris.

———oo———

The many friends of Mrs. Andrea Hanson will be grieved to hear of her sudden death. Mrs. Hanson was taken ill in April with a serious case of Flu, but rallied nicely and was able to be out some, until last Sunday she suffered a relapse. Everything was done that was possible, but she passed quietly away on Thursday.

Those who are living to mourn her loss, are Mrs. Stina Wardell, of Oregon, Mrs. Sam Mortenson of Parowan, Miss Anne Hanson, Mrs. Minnie Harris and Charles Hanson all of Leeds. All were with her at time of death except Mrs. Wardell.

The floral offerings at the church were exceptionaly beautiful. Her friends here will miss her greatly. She was loved by both old and young as it was said at the services "sister Hanson had not an enemy on earth.

Washington County News
July 25, 1922

Leeds July 25 —The young people who attended the outing at Pine Valley returned Sunday night and report having had a most wonderful time

Most of the people in town have had their houses wired and are now beginning to wonder how they ever got along without the electric lights

Mrs Thos Sterling and children and Mr and Mrs Riley C Savage spent Pioneer day at Toquerville

Charles Wright, Stanley Fuller and Roy Hartley are working on the Pine Valley trail

Will Sullivan and family have gone to Weston, Idaho, to visit with their daughter

Mr and Mrs Edward McMullin have gone for an outing to Bryce canyon

The young folks of town attended the dance at Hurricane last night

Max McMullin was in from Las Vegas, Nev, Sunday

Miss Edyth McMullin is visiting friends in Cedar City

Leeds Aug 1 —Charles Wright Stanley Fuller Wayne Angell Ray Hartley and Rodney Laney have come home They have been working on the Pine Valley trail

Mrs Antone Olsen and children returned from Cedar City where they have been for some time past

Miss Lila McAllister of St George spent the week end here visiting at the home of Riley C Savage

Mrs Jas Wilder of Lovell Wyo is here visiting with her brother Will Nicholls

Edward and Hazel McMullin have returned from Glendale

Tom Stirling was a St George visitor Monday

Andrew Gregerson is reported critically ill at home in St. George. Mr. Gregerson figured prominently in the early days of Silver Reef.

LEEDS
(To late for last week.)

———oo— —·

Mrs. Lizzie Wilder of Lovell, Wyoming is here visiting relatives and friends.

—oo ·

A party of Bee hive girls attended the Mutual convention at Pinevalley on the 24th. Ethel McMullin won first prize for best horse back riding.

—oo—

Andrew Gregerson is reported critically ill at home in St. George. Mr. Gregerson figured prominently in the early days of Silver Reef.

—oo—

Alex Colbath of Salt Lake and Mame Beal of Leeds, were married in Salt Lake City on July 10th. Their many friends here wish them joy and good luck in their married life.

—oo—

Charles Wright, Roy Hartley and Wayne Angel returned home today. They have been employed by the government to make a trail and also to widen former trails. We can now reach the top of Pine Valley Mountain with no difficulty.

Washington County News
August 29, 1922

Leeds Aug 29 —Messrs Dodge and Hamman salesmen for Glen Bros Roberts Piano Co are business visitors in town Mr Dodge is visiting with his sister Mrs Wm Emett at Harrisburg

Mrs Charles Hansen is visiting in Parowan prior to going to Arizona to spend the winter where Mr Hansen will be employed as school teacher

Mrs Maggie Hartley returned yesterday from Washington where she has been visiting her mother Mrs Jolley

Reed Fuller Lawrence McMullin and Charles Wright left today for Las Vegas Nev to find employment

Miss Pearl Mortensen of Parowan has been here the past two weeks visiting her aunt Mrs Minnie Harris

Mr and Mrs Edward McMulin went to St George Sunday evening returning Monday morning

Born Aug 19 a daughter to Mr and Mrs Lynn McMullin mother and babe doing nicely

Leeds Sept 11 —Mr and Mrs Geo L Blesinger and family of Salt Lake City arrived here Tuesday night to visit with Mr and Mrs R O Savage and family Miss Margaret Savage and Lavern Carlow returned with them to attend school this winter.

A number of our townspeople took in the fair and festival at St George

Leeds September 20 —Mrs Bess Reese and family of Salt Lake City formerly of this place spent Saturday and Sunday visiting her parents Mr and Mrs George Angell She was en route to Moccasin, Ariz, to teach school this winter

A goodly number of our townspeople attended conference Saturday and Sunday in St George and report having had an excellent time

Mrs Mary Olsen has returned after having spent the last three months at Cedar City with her daughter, Mrs Herbert Haight

Our public school started Monday with Victor Iverson of Washington as principal and Edith McMullin of Leeds as teacher

Mr and Mrs John A Parker of Joseph Sevier Co, returned to their home today after having spent several days here

Mrs Glen Emett will leave tomorrow for Las Vegas, Nev, to spend the winter with her husband who has work there

Mrs Arthur Woodbury and daughters of La Verkin were visitors at the home of Mrs B Y McMullin yesterday.

Mr and Mrs Victor Iverson have moved to town for the winter from Washington

Riley C Savage attended the Democratic convention held in St George Friday.

Thomas Stirling and sons were business visitors in St George Friday

Mr and Mrs Alex Colbath have gone to Salt Lake on business

Our school house is receiving a much needed coat of paint

MARRIAGES

Marriage licenses were issued by the Co Clerk to the following couples the past week

Herbert Teman Henderson of Kanab and Miss Pearl Heaton of Alton, married in St George temple, Sept 14th

Evan Lazelle Sullivan of Leeds and Miss Ada Workman of Hurricane married by Pres E H Snow, Sept 16th

William Otto Reeve of Kanarra and Miss Wealth Millett of Cedar City Sept 18 married in the St George temple

Washington County News
October 10, 1922

Leeds Oct 10 — A real melon bust was had at the home of Mr and Mrs Edwin Dalton at Silver farm Tuesday night to which all the people of town were invited Their melons are certainly delicious

Mr and Mrs Alex Colbath Hazel Moody and Will Carlow have returned from Salt Lake City and report having had a very pleasant trip

Mrs Caroline McMullin spent the past week in Hurricane the guest of her daughter Mrs Frank Sullivan

Mr and Mrs Will Sullivan of Hurricane spent Sunday here visiting with friends and relatives

Ben Hopkins was here from St George and spent Sunday with his sister, Mrs Ed McMullin

Miss Fay Stirling and Hazel Moody went to St George Saturday and returned Sunday

Mrs Glen Emett has returned from Las Vegas Nevada

Mr and Mrs Iverson spent Sunday in Washington.

Leeds Oct 24—Elders John T Batty and Leo Bringhurst of Toquerville met with us in our Sunday School and Sacrament meeting Sunday We enjoyed their visit very much Elder Bringhurst recently returned from a mission to Ireland and his description of the country and its people was very interesting

Our Mutuals and Primary have started work for the winter The Primary gave an opening party in the form of a children s dance Friday and in the evening the Mutuals gave a party which was followed by a feast on the choice fruits of the land

Lyman Canfield and son of St George and a force of men are making cement blocks for the new house that R C Savage will erect in the near future

Mr and Mrs Clifford McMullin of Echo farm entertained at a straw berry supper Saturday evening a most enjoyable time was reported

Mr and Mrs Scott McClellan of Loa were business visitors in town Saturday

Ira McMullin Delbert Stirling and Mr Beaver are St George visitors today

Millie McMullin has gone to St George to attend the D N C

Lawrence McMullin is home from Las Vegas Nevada.

Bishop and Mrs Stirling went to Hurricane Tuesday

Edward McMullin has gone with a load of fruit

Mrs Hazel Moody is visiting at Silver Reef

Leeds Nov 14—Miss Edyth McMullin and her school children put on the plays Snow Drop and Cinderella Wednesday night It was certainly fine and much credit is due Miss McMullin for her excellent training of the children They anticipate going to Toquerville and Hurricane as soon as the weather warms up a little

Town visitors in St George the past few days were Mrs C E Olsen

J M Wicks Ira McMullin Jack Nicholls Levon McQuaid Tom Stirling and family

Mrs A G Anderson has gone to St George to spend the winter Mrs Wade of Beaver City is here clerking in the A G Anderson store

Election day went off very quietly here The town went Republican with the exception of Senator King getting the majority over Bamberger

Max McMullin has gone to the Jyp camp Nev to work and Willard Mc-Mullin to Newhouse to find employment

Edwin Dalton is moving Joe Stirling's house from its present location to the upper end of town

Miss Zelma Sullivan of St George spent several days here the past week with Miss Fay Stirling

George and Victor Angell have gone to Harrisburg to make sorghum for Tom Talbot

Frank Hartley is home from Cedar City where he has been working for some time

Reed Fuller is home after an absence of several months at Las Vegas Nevada

Iron County Record
November 17, 1922

LEEDS

Mrs. Minnie Harris entertained at a birthday party for her daughter Marjorie.

—oo—

Mrs. Alex Colbath entertained the junior boys and girls at a birthday party for her son Glenn.

—oo—

Dan Doyes, and Dick Mason have gone to Colorado River on a prospecting trip.

—oo—

Mrs. Mary Sullivan returned from St. George last Saturday, bringing home her son Dellas who has been receiving medical attention. Dellas has been in a critical condition.

—oo—

..Our Leeds High school students are attending quite a diversity of schools this year. Margaret Savage, Rhea Sullivan, LaVern Carlow, Ada and Melba Harris are atttnding East and West Highs, at Salt Lake City. Dan McMullin and Clinton Fuller are in Los Angeles at a scholl of mechanics. Bonnie Anderson at D. N. C., St. George. Clyde McMullin, Wanda and Berta Nickolls, at B. A. C., Cedar City, and Virgina Angel at Kanab, Utah.

Leeds Nov 20 —Bishop and Mrs
David Stirling are rejoicing over the
arrival of a fine baby boy   The stork
also visited the home of Mr and
Mrs Wm Lmett and left a baby girl
[Our' correspondent does not give
dates —Ed]

Miss Mabel Jarvis and Ervin Webb
of the Stake Sunday School board
visited our ward and held Sunday
school conference

Martin L McAllister and son John
of St George were week end visitors
here

Mr and Mrs Howard Bringhurst
of Toquerville were Sunday visitors
here

School is closed this week on account of sickness

A good program is being planned
for Thanksgiving

Iron County Record
December 1, 1922

Glen Olsen, brother-in-law of Herbert Haight, went to Leeds Sunday
to spend Thanksgiving with his folks

Leeds Dec 5—Our Primary school under the direction of Miss Edyth McMullin presented the playlets Snow Drop and Cinderella at Hurricane Monday night and at St George Saturday night

Clyde McMullin and Glen Olsen came home from Cedar to spend Thanksgiving and returned Saturday

Mr and Mrs Ed Dalton made a business trip to St George Wednesday and returned with a new car

Mr and Mrs C D Olsen spent Thanksgiving with their daughter, Mrs Alex Colbath at Silver Reef

Mrs Hazel Moody is spending a few days in Hurricane with her sister, Mrs Will Sullivan

Mr and Mrs Victor Iverson spent the week end visiting in Santa Clara and Washington

Willie McMullin came up from St George to spend Thanksgiving with his parents

Matt Wicks and Dan Doyle of Silver Reef have gone to Stateline

Mrs Geo E Porter of La Verkin spent Sunday here

Mrs Ethel Stirling is home from Hurricane.

Delbert Stirling of Leeds was a visitor here Tuesday

Tom and Miss Fay Stirling were visitors here Sunday from Leeds

Mr and Mrs Clifford McMullin were visitors here from Leeds Tuesday

SOMEONE SHOOTS AT HIM.

———oo———

While coming up from St. George yesterday afternoon Joe. Farnsworth, the mail contractor, was fired at on this side of Leeds as hort distance"

He was driving along with a light load when suddenly he heard a shot, and immediately a crosh of glass as a bullet zipped through his windshield, just missing him by a few inches.

Mr. Farnsworth stopped to look ahead to see if he could distinguish who was firing, but saw no one. He was considerably startled, but decided to drive on, which he did and was not further molested.

The time was 5 o'clock and it was too near dark for anyone to be hunting. consequently it seems that a deliberate attempt was made by someone to injure Mr. Farnsworth.

The gentleman has no idea who the person that did the shooting might be and does not have an enemy in the country to his knowledge that would "bump him off" by the gun route.

Mrs. Herbert Haight is now in Leeds visiting with her mother. The lady will remain for a week or so longer before returning.

Washington County News
January 8, 1923

Leeds, Jan 8 —The stork visited the homes of Mr and Mrs Ed McMullin Dec 12, Mr and Mrs A H Stevens Dec 19, leaving a boy at each home, and a girl at the home of Mr and Mrs Max McMullin, Jan 3

Glen Olsen, Clyde and Lawrence McMullin Wanda and Berta Nichols have returned to the B A C and Margaret Savage to L D S, Salt Lake City, after having spent the holidays here in their home town

Donald Schmutz and wife of New Harmony were calling on some of their friends here Tuesday.

William Emett has gone to Delta, having been called to the bedside of his father who is very ill

Mrs Margaret Haight of Cedar City is here visiting with her parents, Mr and Mrs Chris Olsen

Willard McMullin has returned after having spent the holidays in Salt Lake City with friends

Clinton Fuller and Ross Angell returned a few days ago from Los Angeles, California

Lynn and Vier McMullin went to Stateline Thursday on business

Matt Hartley of Hurricane was a business visitor here Monday

A number of our towns people went to St George today.

A G Anderson has built a new store and eating house

Mr and Mrs Clifford McMullin spent Sunday here

Mrs Hazel Moody spent Sunday at Silver Reef.

Washington County News
January 16, 1923

Leeds Jan 16 —Mr and Mrs Alex Colbath of Silver Reef gave a birthday dinner in honor of Mr Newtons 93rd birthday Those present were Mr Newton the honored guest J M Wicks C E Olsen and Mr Buel of Stateline

Elders Hafen and Frei of Santa Clara visited us as home missionaries Sunday Their remarks were very much enjoyed and we hope they much enjoyed and we hope they will call again

Mrs J M Perry, formerly Miss Nina Nicholls returned Sunday from Lovell, Wyoming where she has been the past two years She is visiting her mother, Mrs Wm Nicholls

Dan McMullin returned Sunday from Los Angeles where he has been attending the National Automotive school

Sheridan Ballard and family of Hurricane have moved here Mr Balbusy working on the new road

A G Anderson Willard McMullin and Miss Fay Stirling were St George visitors Saturday and Sunday .

J M Wicks was a business visitor in St George the fore part of the week

Robert McMullin has gone to Bakersfield Calif, to find employment

A number of our town boys are busy working on the New road

LEEDS

Bert and Charles Harris have gone to Nevada.

Robert McMullin has gone to Hollywood, Calif.

Clinton Fuller and Dan McMullin have returned home after spending some months in school at Los Angeles.

Mrs. Margaret Haight of Cedar City is here visiting her mother Mrs. E. C. Olsen. Mr. Haight was here for a short time enroute to St. George.

Miss Minnie Harris gave an interesting book review of Miles Standish in the Relief Society. This lesson is first outlined for literary study of 1923.

Washington County News
January 30, 1923

Leeds Jan 30 — Elders John H Schmutz of St George Hall and Joel Roundy of Hurricane visited our ward the past week as missionaries Their visits were very much appreciated by the people

Grant and the infant son of Mr and Mrs Edward McMullin and also Alice the two year old daughter of Mr and Mrs R C Savage are recovering from an attack of pneumonia

There is a great deal of sickness in town mostly among the children which has developed into pneumonia in a number of cases

Mrs Margaret Haight and children have returned to their home in Cedar City

Mrs Retta McMullin has two children very ill with pneumonia

Born Jan 24 a daughter to Mr and Mrs Victor Angell

Iron County Record
February 2, 1923

LEEDS

—oo—

Alex Colbath left for Salt Lake City today.

—oo—

Mr. and Mrs. Victor Angel are happy over the arrival of a baby girl.

—oo—

Mrs. Margaret Haight and children of Cedar City have returned to their home.

—oo—

David McMullin has returned home from Santa Clara, where he was called as a home missionary.

—oo—

Mina Nicholls Perry of Lovell, Wyo., after an absence of three years, is the guest of her mother, Mrs. Wm. Nicholls.

There is an epidemic of serious colds here, two children of Edward McMullin have pneumonia, also two children of Max McMullin, Clayton Sullivan and little Alice Savage.

—oo—

Elders Smoot of St. George and Hall of Hurricane have returned to their homes. Very splendid cottage meetings have been held and the people have enjoyed their house to house visits.

—oo—

Mr. and Mrs. Porter of LaVerkin Sanatarium were in Leeds one day last week. We are glad to see Mr. Porter looking and feeling so fine, after so serious an accident as he sustained recently.

Iron County Record
February 9, 1923

A. G. Anderson, who now spends most of his time in Leeds, but who occasionally comes to Cedar where he has heavy bee interests, was in town Tuesday. Our reporter in interviewing the gentleman as to his activities in Leeds was informed that he was building bungalows, camp tents, and had enlarged and rearranged his store and hotel, and also has done a large amount of work in making a good road leading into the eastern part of town where his property is located. Mr. Anderson expects to install electric stoves in his tents and bungalows, and also electric washing machines so that the tourists may have every convenience when stopping with him. He also has arranged nice camp grounds, and will add many features of convenience. His place is becoming known from East to West as an ideal place to stop.

Iron County Record
February 16, 1923

A. G. Anderson and W. G. McMullin of Leeds, Utah, have made application to the state Utility Commission for a franchise to operate a burro and saddle horse trail route to carry tourists and citizens to the top of Pine Valley mountain, starting from the Leeds tourist camp.

Washington County News
February 20, 1923

Leeds February 20 —Contractors Fletcher Dixon and Webb of Hurricane are busy here building the home of Riley C Savage

Mrs Adelaide and Mary Savage of Toquerville were visiting at the home of their son Riley Savage Friday

Willard and Robert McMullin are very busy planting their crops at Purgatory flat

Mrs Hazel Moody went to Cedar City last week to attend the Round-up

Mrs Thos Stirling and son Rex were St George visitors Monday

J M Wicks and Sam Pollock re turned from St George yesterday

Mr and Mrs Iverson were week end visitors at Washington

Leeds Feb 27 —A very successful patriotic entertainment was given by the public schools the evening of Washington s birthday The proceeds obtained from it will go to help buy a slippery slide for the school grounds

Mrs Alex Colbath has gone to Salt Lake City to meet her husband who is just returning from New York We hope he will bring good news for Silver Reef

We were visited Sunday by home missionaries Elders Charles Cottam and Walter Cannon of St George We enjoyed their visit very much

Mrs Arthur Webb of La Verkin was the guest of Mrs Riley C Savage Sunday and Monday

Mrs Harold Snow of St George spent Sunday here with her sister Mrs Ed McMullin

David McMullin and Riley C Savage went to La Verkin Sunday as home missionaries

Will McMullin and Duncan McArthur were up from St George Saturday after cattle

Mr and Mrs George E Porter of the La Verkin hot springs were here Saturday

Miss Thelma Workman of Hurricane is spending a few days here

Miss Sabra Naegle of St George spent Sunday at Silver farm

Ed McMullin was in from the bridge camp Sunday

Leeds April 3 —The Clean Town campaign is on and much improvement is being made in straightening up our school grounds streets and sidewalks

Town visitors in St George today are Mrs B Y McMullin Eleanor Scott Ethel and Lawrence McMullin Fay Sterling Minnie Harris and Mr and Mrs Will Carlow of Silver Reef

Miss Bertha Nichols and Afton Wade came down from Cedar Friday to spend the week end visiting with their parents They returned Sunday

Mrs Mary Olsen is home after spending a week visiting with her daughter, Mrs Will Sullivan at Hurricane

The officers and teachers of the Primary entertained the children at an Easter party Friday

Lawrence McMullin came home Monday from Huppton Nevada

The Parents club gave a very successful party Friday night

Born a daughter to Mr and Mrs J A Party, Mar 19.

Iron County Record
April 20, 1923

E. V. Storm, a member of the Forest Service office in Cedar during the past winter, has been transfered to Leeds, Utah, for the next seven months.

Washington County News
April 24, 1923

Leeds Apr 24 —Mrs Victor Iverson and her music pupils entertained the public at a musical recital Sunday evening All parts were very well rendered and much credit is due Mrs Iverson for her efficient work

We are pleased to report that Chris Olsen who has been confined to his bed for some time with a complication of ailments is able to be up and around again

Miss Clara McAllister of St George who is teaching school at Toquerville spent the week end here visiting relatives

Thomas Stirling Jr, met with quite a painful accident Saturday He cut his knee quite badly with an axe

Riley C Savage was called to Toquerville Friday night on account of the illness of his mother and aunt

Earl Storm forest ranger is with us again after having spent most of the winter at Cedar City

Jack Frost visited us Sunday night, resulting in some damage to fruit and early garden

William Nicholls who has been quite ill with flu, is able to be out again

Thomas Talbot is quite ill with flu

Leeds May 14 —Mr and Mrs Chas Hansen have returned from Taylor Arizona where they spent the past winter as Mr Hansen was employed as school teacher at that place

Mothers day was fittingly observed by our Sunday school Special exercises for the occasion were well rendered by members from the various grades

Mrs A G Anderson and daughter Bonnie have returned from St George where the latter has attended school this past year

Mrs Minnie Harris and family are leaving tomorrow for Los Angeles Calif to join her husband who has employment there

Mr and Mrs Thos Blake of Salt Lake City are here visiting with Mrs Blakes brother Chris Olsen and family

Roy Beavers has purchased th farm at Grapevine springs and has moved his family there

Ben Hopkins of Glendale was here visiting with his daughter Mrs Ed McMullin Friday

Antone Olsen has returned from Hurricane where he has been shearing sheep

Quite a number of our men folks have gone to Lund with wool

A hard times party will be held at the ward hall tonight

Leeds, May 29 —Clyde McMullin Glen Olsen and Berta Nichols have returned from Cedar where they have been attending the B A. C

The Primary will give a dancing party Friday night. Ice cream will be on sale.

Miss Catherine Isom of Hurricane is here visiting her sister, Mrs David Stirling.

Tom Stirling and Lawrence McMullin were Hurricane visitors Monday

Mrs Frank Hartley and daughter Thelma have returned from Delta

David and Clifford McMullin have gone north to find employment

A number of the town boys have gone to Lund with cattle

Max McMullin is home from Hupton, Nevada.

Washington County News
July 10, 1923

Leeds July 10 —The Fourth was fittingly observed here   A patriotic meeting in the forenoon with sports and a childrens dance in the after noon and a dance for the adults in the evening

William Nichols and A J Parry came home from the iron mines near Cedar to spend the Fourth

Mr and Mrs B Y McMullin at tended the funeral of Dr Woodbury in St George July 3

Mr and Mrs Milton Moody came up from St George yesterday to spend a few days

Mrs A G Parry has gone to Cedar to spend the summer

For First Class Elberta Peaches, Bartlett Pears and plums call at B. Y. McMullin's orchard, Leeds, Utah. Finest Elbertas for one cent per lb.

Leeds Aug 14—The people of this little town were terribly shocked Sunday noon when the news reached here of the accidental death of Antone Olsen of this place who was instantly killed by a cave in at the iron mine in which he was working near Iron Springs Leland Sullivan was seriously injured about the head by falling rock at the same time and place he is now in the hospital at Cedar City has regained consciousness and the doctors think that he will soon be alright Funeral services for Antone Olsen were held in the ward hall Monday afternoon The speakers were Riley C Savage of Leeds Ex Bishop David Hirschi of Hurricane Bishop Walter Slack of Toquerville and Bishop Stirling of this place all spoke words of praise for the departed brother The Hurricane ward furnished music which was much appreciated Antone leaves a wife and three small children Arlene 6 years Afton 4 years and Bryce 2 years his father mother four sisters and two brothers to mourn his untimely death

John A Parker of Joseph and A G Young of Richfield spent several days here and in Zion park last week looking over the site of the new road which is to be built in the park They are thinking of putting in a bid for the work

A number of people from Hurricane St George Toquerville Cedar City and New Harmony were here to attend the funeral services of Antone Olsen Monday afternoon

Joseph Worthen of Salt Lake City is here visiting his wife s people Mr and Mrs B Y McMullin and family

Mr and Mrs Wm Nichols Mr and Mrs Evan Sullivan and Mr and Mrs A J Perry are home for a few days

Miss Ann Hopkins of Glendale is here visiting her sister Mrs Hazel McMullin

ANTON OLSEN MEETS DEATH IN MINE

Anton Olsen of Leeds was instantly killed at Iron Springs Sunday morning, while working in tunnel No 1 of the Columbia steel company mine

A mass of rock and earth estimated at twenty tons caved in on him and Leland Sullivan also of Leeds, who was working with him crushing Olsen to death and severely injuring Sullivan Two other men were on the same shift but were some distance from them when the cave in occurred They immediately called for help and the debris was hastily removed It was at once seen that Olsen was dead nearly every bone in his body being broken Sullivan while severely injured will appearances indicate recover he is at the Cedar City hospital

They had just gone on shift when the accident occurred The place where the cave in took place was not timbered but the tunnel is timbered to within a short distance of it

ONE MAN KILLED
ONE INJURED

—oo—

ANTONE OLSON OF LEEDS, UTAH, LOSES LIFE BY BEING CRUSHED IN CAVE-IN AT CO-LUMBIA STEEL CAMP NEAR IRON SPRINGS.

—oo—

Antone Olson was crushed to death and Leland Sullivan badly injured when a large amount of earth and rock caved Sunday morning at 3 o'clock in tunnel No. 1 at the Columbia Steel camp near Iron Springs. Screams for help awakened other company employees and fifty men went to the rescue of Olson and Sullivan. Olson was completely covered by the earth and rock, while Sullivan was only partially covered and was able to get out to the mouth of the tunnel before collapsing.

The debris was hastily removed from Olson and it was found that he had been crushed almost to a pulp. Nearly every bone in his body was broken and it was evident that his death was instantaneous. The body was brought to this city and was prepared for burial at the Cedar Lumber Co. undertaking parlors. Monday it was shipped to Leeds, Utah, the home of the dead man, where interment was had that afternoon.

Sullivan was brought to the County Hospital where he is now doing as well as could be expected and has every chance of complete recovery from the injuries he received at the cave-in.

The men were engaged in mucking at the time of the cave-in. Two other men, Glen Olson and Evan Sullivan, were working with them, but one had gone to the mouth of the tunnel with a car of rock and the other was a short distance from the scene of the accident.

The workmen in the tunnel had been on shift for a couple of hours and were removing the muck left by the preceeding shift. The tunnel is heavily timbered to within a few feet of the cave-in.

So far as can be learned no warning of the cave-in was given, the men having no time to step out of reach of falling rock. The slip of rock and earth came like a bolt of lightning from the sky and the men had no chance to escape.

Leeds Aug 21 —Leland Sullivan who was injured at the cave in at Iron Springs mine came home Sunday from the Cedar hospital and is recovering nicely

A crowd of the young people returned Sunday from Pine Valley mountain They report having had a very enjoyable time

Alex Colbath Mrs E C Olsen and Mrs David Stirling were Hurricane visitors Saturday

George and Glen Olsen were business visitors at Cedar City Wednesday

Mr and Mrs Wallace Thornton of Panguitch are here after fruit

Ben Hopkins and son Ben of Glendale were Sunday visitors here

There are lots of peaches being shipped from our little town

Willard McMullin has gone to work on the road at Pintura

THE LOG CABIN INN

LEEDS, UTAH.

Chicken Dinners and Suppers Furnished. Dancing Parties arranged for old, middleaged and young.

SPECIAL PARTIES ARRANGED FOR

Husband—Bring your wife out for a change, even though she is the best cook in the world.

Young Man—Bring your sweetheart and give her an evening's enjoyment at the Log Cabin Inn.

WHERE THE ROSES BLOOM PROFUSELY.

Located on the Arrowhead Trail.   Phone Your Yrders.

Leeds Sept 10 —A number of our town people attended conference in St George Saturday and Sunday and report having had a very enjoyable t me

Riley C Savage and Thomas Talbot were summoned to serve on the jury during this last session of court

Mrs Margaret Haight and children of Cedar City are here visiting with her parents Mr and Mrs C E Olsen

Lawrence McMullin is home after spending some time working on the road at Bryce canyon

Miss Sabra Naegle of St George is here visiting her sister Mrs Marjie Dalton of Silver farm

A son was born to Mr and Mrs Charles Angell Sept 9 mother and babe are doing nicely

Bob and Edward McMullin and Donald Fuller have gone north with loads of fruit

Mr and Mrs Milton Moody are spending the week in St George

Regarding the ad in this issue for recovering of a suit case or traveling bag at Leeds Mr McMullin states the back of the small truck into which it was put by one of the truck party who picked it up, was covered with a wagon cover and bows and the truck appeared to have some furniture in it He thinks the children were coming here to school

Leeds Sept 18—Our district school began yesterday with Milton Moody principal and Miss Porter of Springville as assistant teacher

Mr and Mrs John A Parker of Joseph and Mr and Mrs Robert D Young of Richfield were town visitors last week

Mr and Mrs Clair McMullin and family of Beaver spent last week here visiting with their parents and friends

Mr and Mrs Charles F Hansen are leaving today for Taylor Arizona where Mr Hansen will teach school

Stanley and Reed Fuller have returned from Bryce canyon where they have been working on the road

Margaret and Addie Savage also Phoebe Fuller have gone to St George to attend school

Miss Ethel McMullin went to Lund Monday to work for J David Leigh

Mrs Wm Nicholls and Mrs A H Parry are home from Iron Springs

Alta Emmett came in from the road camp to spend Sunday

Miss Vera Stirling returned from St George Sunday

LEEDS

Leeds Sept 25—Mrs Ida McArthur of Park City spent several days here the past week visiting her sister Mrs Oscar McMullin

Mr and Mrs Donald Fuller were business visitors in St George the latter part of the week

Glen Olsen spent Monday at home with relatives and returned to Cedar this morning

Eugene Harris and Cal Hartley have gone to St George to attend school

Thomas Stirling went to St George with a load of wheat today

A son was born to Mr and Mrs
James A Terry of Rockville and a
son to Mr and Mrs Riley Savage of
Leeds Oct 1   All doing nicely

Mr Karl Alfred McMullin and Miss
Leone Russell were married in the St
George temple Tuesday Oct 16
The bride is a daughter of Mr and
Mrs W T Russell of Hurricane
the bridegroom is a son of Mr and
Mrs Ira L McMullin of Leeds both
are highly respected

Leeds Oct 23 —Mrs Ada McMul
lin and son Lawrence went to Beaver
Saturday to attend the funeral of
Mrs Clair McMullin of that place
Mrs McMullin took a dose of strych
nine in mistake for quinine and died
within thirty minutes   She is surviv
ed by her husband and three small
sons   Clair was born and raised in
Leeds

Karl McMullin of this place and
Leona Russel of Hurricane were mar
ried in the St George temple last
week Their many friends wish
them a long and happy voyage on the
sea of matrimony

Mrs Riley C Savage returned to
her home Friday after having spent
some time in St George She was
accompanied by a brand new baby
boy

Mr and Mrs Albert Anderson and
family and Mrs Mary Ann Savage of
Toquerville spent Sunday here visit
ing friends and relatives

Mr and Mrs Jack Wadsworth and
Willie McMullin spent Sunday after
noon here from St George the guests
of Mrs Oscar McMullin

The Misses Margaret and Addie
Savage spent the week end at home
returning to St George Sunday
evening

Mrs Leland Sullivan has returned
from Cedar City where she has been
for some time past

Mrs Thomas Stirling and son Rex
made a business trip to St George to
day

Iron County Record
November 9, 1923

A. G. Anderson, who is now located at Leeds, Utah, spent Monday in
Cedar on his way from Salt Lake
City where he had been to attend to
some private business matters. Mr
Anderson tells us that it seems that
everybody he met in the metropolis
wanted to know all about the big boom
in this section of the state. He says
it appears to him that the people of
the north are more interested in the
developments here than the people
who live here.

Iron County Record
November 16, 1923

A. G. Anderson of Leeds tells us
that he is going to make some improvements and additions to his
"Log Cabin Inn," by enlarging his
dining room and dance room. He
will also connect every tent camp on
the place with the Inn by telephone
so that patrons can call the office at
any time of the day or night. Mr.
Anderson claims that his patronage
has so increased that he is compelled
to make the improvements mentioned
above.

Washington County News
November 17, 1923

Leeds Nov 17 —While riding a broncho Monday Dan McMullin had the misfortune to have his shoulder bone broken Dr Woodbury of St George was called to attend him

Mrs Oscar McMullin has returned from St George after having spent several days there under the docter s care

We were visited by a gentle rain storm the last of the week The cat tle men especially are rejoicing

A number of our town s people at tended the Armistice day carvinal in St George

Our Dixie College students spent the week end at home visiting rela tives

Mr and Mrs Alex Colbath of Silver Reef are in Salt Lake City on busi ness

Washington County News
November 20, 1923

Leeds Nov 20 —While cutting wood Monday night Veir McMullin accidently struck his foot with the ax cutting it badly He was rushed to the St George hospital where it was found that the second toe was en tirely cut off and the others were badly cut He is getting on nicely

Mr and Mrs Wm Sullivan went to Hurricane yesterday having re ceived word that their grandson had been run over by an automobile

Mrs Wm Hartman who has been suffering from an abscess on her face went to St George for medical treat ment Monday

The new garage being erected by our busy merchant and hotel keeper A G Anderson is nearing comple tion

Robert McMullin went to Para goonah Friday to move Mr Twit chell s family down here

Ward Jolley and Riley Savage went to Cedar last week for loads of hard wall and cement

Miss Porter our primary school teacher is in St George on business

John Tullis of Newcastle was a business visitor here Sunday

Alex Colbath made a business trip to St George Monday

Mr and Mrs C E Olsen are visit ing in Hurricane

J M Wicks went to Cedar City Friday

Leeds Nov 27 —Elders Reid and Gardner home missonaries were welcome visitors at our Sunday service and gave some very timely instructions

Mr and Mrs Milton Moody Reed Fuller and Melba Porter went to Washington Sunday Mr Moody filled a home mission appointment there

Mrs Leroy J Beavers of Grape vine springs has returned to her home after a week s absence at St George caring for a typhoid case

William Nicholls who has been working at Iron Springs spent Saturday and Sunday here

Karl McMullin and Levon Mc Quade were business visitors in St George Monday

Margaret and Addie Savage of the Dixie college spent the week end at home

Mrs Hartman has returned from the county hospital She is improving

A G Anderson made a business trip to St George Sunday

Mr and Mrs C E Olsen have returned from Hurricane

Robert McMullin is leaving tomorrow for California

THE DIXIE CARNIVAL IS A BIG SUCCESS

The best mid winter carnival so far ever held in Dixie commenced yesterday and will continue for three days The weather is delightful the sun shining brightly and warm there are a number of good race horses here and the people are attending the races in large numbers Yesterday the large grandstand which seats 11 000 people was nearly filled and there was a large number seated in autos besides

The first race yesterday a quarter mile free for all was won by Red Bird owner Edwin Higbee of Toquerville time 26 seconds The other horses which ran were Rosco Goose H Mechau of Annabella owner and Dime owned by Higbee

The three eights mile free for all was won by Utah Maid owned by O. W Royce Penny owned by Marion Case taking second place Mackle praug s Cruse was third

The half mile free for all was won by Marion Case s Goldie in 54 seconds Andy Andy owned by Higbee was second and Moonshine Mecham owner took third place

The quarter mile saddle horse race was won by Higbee s Corncutter in 25 seconds Red Cloud owned by Lynn McMullin of Leeds was second, and Watson s Glen Roe was third

Leeds, Mar. 4.—Mrs. Mary C. Olsen is at Hurricane visiting with her daughter, Mrs. Wm. Sullivan.

Lawrence McMullin, Ruth Stirling and Dixie Scott went to St. George Friday.

Mrs. Vier McMullin entertained the ladies H. G. L. club Friday.

Ammon Jolley made a business trip to La Verkin Monday.

John L. Seevey of Salt Lake spent Sunday here on business.

William Twitchell spent Sunday in Cedar City on business.

Mr. and Mrs. Edwin Dalton went to St. George Saturday.

Leeds, June 17.—Edward and Max McMullin have returned from the American Borax Co. mine, near Moapa, Nev., on account of the work having closed down there.

Milton Moody, Karl McMullin and Riley Savage went to Leeds (?) Thursday evening to attend the Elders quorum meeting.

Mrs. Ada Sullivan has returned from St. George, bringing with her a fine baby girl.

Born, June 1, a daughter to Mr. and Mrs. Wallace Thornton of Silver farm.

Miss Hortense Batty of Hurricane is visiting relatives here.

Miss Virginia Angell has gone to Cedar City to work.

Mrs. Elenor Scott was a St. George visitor yesterday.

Mrs. Alta Emett has returned from Salt Lake City.

Max McMullin in on the sick list.

Mr. Rex Stirling and Miss Thelma Workman were married in the St. George temple, June 17.

The bride is a daughter of Mrs. Mary W. Hall of Hurricane and the late Jacob L. Workman, and is an amiable and very highly respected young lady who is well and favorably known in this city, where she attended the Dixie College. The groom is an exemplary young man of Leeds, a son of Mr. and Mrs. Thomas Storling of that place.

Leeds, July 7.—July 4th was celebrated in a very appropriate manner. The day was in charge of the Relief Society. The ward hall was beautifully decorated in the national colors. The following program was rendered with David McMullin as master of ceremonies. Singing, "America;" Prayer by chaplain, Ira McMullin; singing "Battle Hymn of Republic;" Oration, Riley C. Savage; Piano Solo, Fay Stirling; Speech by Goddess of Liberty, Margaret Savage; song, Mrs. Evelyn McMullin and Mildred Jolley; Speech by "Utah," Miss Lavern Carlow; Song, Leola Trumble; Reading Jessie Carlow; Patriotic Sentiments, Mrs. Hazel McMullin; Singing, Star Spangled Banner. Prayer by the Chaplain. There were sports in the afternoon for old and young; children's dance in the early evening and dance for adults at night.

The Ward Primary under the direction of Mrs. Hazel McMullin and her assistants staged an entertainment the night of July 2, to a delighted audience.

Hyrum Pope and family of Salt Lake City and Bill Pope and family of Los Angeles are visiting their sister, Mrs. Edwin Dalton, at Silver farm.

Sunday visitors were Mr. and Mrs. Rex Stirling, Mrs. John Hall of Hurricane and WiWll McMullin and Veril Lund of St. George.

July 4th visitors were Mr. and Mrs. Mark Lamb and daughters of Toquerville, Mr. and Mrs. Frank Sullivan of Hurricane.

Work at Silver Reef has closed down and Mr. and Mrs. Colbath have gone to Salt Lake on business.

Leland and Evan Sullivan, Milton Moody and Max McMullin went to Cedar Sunday, to work.

Mrs. Ada McMullin and son Lawrence went to Beaver Thursday.

Evan Sullivan and Ward Jolley were home for July 4.

Washington County News
August 4, 1924

Leeds, Aug. 4.—Vernon Church of St. George was here today looking up a house to rent for the winter. Mr. Church will be the principal of our school this coming year.

Miss Rhea Sullivan went to St. George Friday to have a boil on her side lanced. It was giving her a great deal of trouble.

Miss Edyth McMullin is home from summer school at Salt Lake, and Miss Ethel came down from Cedar Sunday.

Mr. and Mrs. Victor Iverson of Washington are shaking hands with old friends in Leeds today.

Riley Savage went to St. George last week for a load of finishing lumber for his house.

Mr. and Mrs. Oscar McMullin and son Will left for Salt Lake City today.

Miss Leona Eager of La Verkin is here visiting with Miss Phoebe Fuller.

Willie McMullin and Verl Lund spent Sunday here from St. George.

Mrs. Hazel Moody has gone to Cedar City to visit for a few days.

Washington County News
August 11, 1924

Leeds, Aug. 11.—Mr. and Mrs. Joe Wordren and family of Salt Lake City are visiting Mrs. Wordren's parents, Mr. and Mrs. B. Y. McMullin.

Roy Hartley and Stanley Fuller have gone to work at Zion canyon.

Clyde McMullin and Glen Olsen are down from Cedar City for a visit.

Miss Ruth Stirling is home from summer school at Salt Lake City.

Edward McMullin and Riley Savage have gone north with fruit.

Tons of elberta peaches are being shipped out of here.

Wayne Angell is home from Salt Lake City.

Washington County News
August 18, 1924

Leeds, Aug. 18.—Henry Jolley has returned home from Provo and other northern points where he spent several days.

Mr. and Mrs. Jos Worthen and family have returned to their home in Salt Lake City.

Charles L. Hansen and son Lawrence are here from Clay Springs, Arizona.

Mrs. Jolley of Washington is here visiting her daughter, Mrs. Frank Hartley.

Bishop David Stirling, George and Valla Angell went to Newcastle Friday.

Frank Miller spent several days last week in Cedar City and vicinity.

Miss Fay Stirling has gone to Salt Lake City to spend a week visiting.

Washington County News
September 24, 1924

Leeds, Sept. 24.—Our district schools have started with Vernon Church as principal and Miss Maudeen Prisbrey assistant teacher. With these competent teachers we are looking forward to a most successful school year.

Margaret Savage, LaVern Carlow and Eugene Harris are attending school at St. George. Billy Carlow is in Beaver and Addie Savage is attending 10th grade at Toquerville.

Mr. and Mrs. Bert Harris and family, Mrs. Annie Wright and son Charles have returned from California after an absence of one and one-half years.

Miss Edyth McMullin has gone to Arizona to teach school. Mrs. Lynn McMullin has also gone to Arizona for the winter.

Mr. and Mrs. John A. Parker, of Joseph, are here doing improvement work on their farm.

Mr. and Mrs. Edward McMullin and children have gone to Glendale to visit.

George C. Neagle of Salt Lake City was a business visitor here Monday.

Jack Shurboir has returned to his home in Los Angeles, California.

Dr. C. L. EVENS COMING

Dr. C. L. Evens of the Alexander Optical Company, Salt Lake City, is coming to your town equipped with new instruments for making a real examination of the eyes. It will prove well worth while for any parent to have their children's eyes examined by this method so as to remove all visual handicaps for the work of the school year. The Doctor will be at:

St. George, Arrowhead Hotel, Friday, October 24th, all day.

Leeds, Log Cabin Inn, Saturday, October 25th, from 9 to 11 a. m.

Toquerville, Naegle's Residence, Saturday, October 25th, from 1 to 3 p. m.

Hurricane, Bradshaw's Hotel, Sunday, October 26th, all day.

Springdale, Public School, Monday, October 27th, from 10 a. m. to 1 p. m.

Rockville, DeMill Hotel, Monday, October 27th, from 2 to 3 p. m.

Virgin City, Postoffice, Monday, October 27th, from 4 to 5 p. m.—

Leeds, Oct. 21.—The people of town were shocked to hear of Clinton Fuller's meeting with such a serious accident. He was working on a church building in Salt Lake City when he missed his footing and fell to the ground, breaking his arm and leg and bruising him up badly.

Mrs. Maggie Olsen, Lavern Carlow and Margaret and Addie Savage spent the week end at home from St. George.

The D. C. Sophomore class gave their class party here Saturday night and everyone had a delightful time.

Mr. and Mrs. Henry Jolley will go to Cedar City today to attend the funeral of Mrs. Jolley's brother.

Don Fuller, Glen Stirling and Clyde McQuaide have gone to the hills to drive cattle.

Mr. and Mrs. Edwin Dalton and family have moved to St. George to spend the winter.

Delbert Stirling is building a pickett fence in front of his place.

Miss Ethel McMullin is home from Cedar City to spend some time.

Forest Ranger Earl Storm went to St. George Friday.

Washington County News
November 17, 1924

Leeds, Nov. 17.—Merwin Hartman received serious injury to his left foot at the Iron Mines, Nov. 8. He is still in the Cedar hospital, where he was rushed after the accident. Three toes were amputated. He is doing nicely and will soon be able to return to his home at Leeds.

Mrs. Don Fuller has just returned from Salt Lake City, where she had been to see her son, Clint, who was hurt quite badly. He is doing nicely and will return home as soon as he is able.

Mrs. Dallise Hartman went to Cedar City Tuesday to see her son, Merwin, who is in the hospital there.

Washington County News
November 25, 1924

Leeds, Nov. 25.—Most of our town men and boys are working on the wood road up through the mountains. It will be a great help and improvement when completed.

Misses Ruth Stirling and Valla Angell and Frank Miller have gone to Salt Lake City to visit relatives.

Reed Fuller has returned from St. George, where he has had employment for the past six weeks.

Miss Margaret Savage, who has been very ill for the past week, is slowly improving.

Mr. and Mrs. Joseph Stirling went to Cedar City Saturday to deliver turkeys.

Mr. and Mrs. Edwin Dalton of St. George were visitors here Friday.

O. L. and Ira S. McMullin went to St. George today on business.

Alex Colbath left Wednesday for New York City.

Oscar McMullin of Leeds was a city visitor last Saturday on business.

Max Parker of Circleville and Mrs. Ada McMullin of Leeds arrived here Monday to spend a few days' with their sister, Mrs. Ellen Westover.

Washington County News
December 1, 1924

Leeds, Dec. 1.—The district schoo gave a very interesting Thanksgivin program Wednesday afternoon an the Primary entertained at a dancin, party in the evening.

The Stake Mutual officers came u Sunday night and organized the Mut uals here. We were also visited Sun day afternoon by Prof. Homer of th Dixie college and Elder Nephi Savage our home missionaries.

Mr. and Mrs. Herbert Haight o Cedar City and Mr. and Mrs. William Sullivan of Hurricane spent Thanksgiving day here with their parents, Mr. and Mrs. C. E. Olsen.

Mrs. George Angell intends leaving Wednesday for Salt Lake City, to visit with her children who are living there.

Mervin Hartman came home for Thanksgiving but had to return to Cedar City to have his foot cared for.

Reed Fuller and Charles Wright left Thursday for Los Angeles, where they have employment.

Claus Andrson went to Beaver to spend Thanksgiving with his mother.

Mr. and Mrs. Alex Colbath returned from Salt Lake City Thursday.

Valla Angell returned Sunday from Salt Lake City.

Made in the USA
San Bernardino, CA
30 December 2015